T0294766

NELS ANDERSON'S WORLD WAR I DIARY

NELS ANDERSON'S

WORLD WAR I DIARY

EDITED BY
ALLAN KENT POWELL

Foreword By Charles S. Peterson

THE UNIVERSITY OF UTAH PRESS | *Salt Lake City*

The Defiance House Man colophon is a registered trademark
of the University of Utah Press. It is based on a four-foot-tall
Ancient Puebloan pictograph (late PIII) near Glen Canyon, Utah.

17 16 15 14 13   1 2 3 4 5

Library of Congress Cataloging-in-Publication Data
Anderson, Nels, 1889–1986.
  Nels Anderson's World War I diary / edited by Allan Kent Powell.
    pages cm
  Includes bibliographical references.

ISBN 978-1-60781-255-5 (cloth : alk. paper)
ISBN 978-1-60781-256-2 (ebook)

1. Anderson, Nels, 1889–1986—Diaries. 2. World War, 1914–1918—Personal narratives,
American. 3. World War, 1914–1918—Campaigns—Western Front. 4. World War, 1914–
1918—Participation, Mormon. 5. United States. Army. Engineer Combat Battalion, 314th.
I. Powell, Allan Kent. II. Title.
  D570.9.A67 2013
  940.4ₗ1273092—dc23
  [B]
                    2013005131

Printed and bound by Sheridan Books, Inc., Ann Arbor, Michigan.

CONTENTS

FOREWORD

CHARLES S. PETERSON

A RUNAWAY SON, MULE SKINNER, HOBO DITCHED FROM A DESERT RAIL-road, ranch hand, railway maintenance and mine prop carpenter, Nels Anderson was a graduate of Dixie Academy, Brigham Young University, the University of Chicago, and New York University. He also became a high-ranking labor official in Franklin D. Roosevelt's administration, wrote *Desert Saints: The Mormon Frontier in Utah*, and was also one of the most gifted of what I like to call the "Dixie School" of writers. In addition, he was a longtime State Department and United Nations official and a sometimes expatriate and suspect during Joseph McCarthy's purges of the 1950s.

Anderson's World War I diary came to my attention about ten years ago as the result of a search I asked archivist David Whittaker to make of BYU's holdings with reference to northern Arizona's Snowflake Stake Academy.[1] At the L. Tom Perry Archives the four-hundred-page handwritten account of Anderson's World War I experience had been referred to as the "Nels Anderson Doughboy Diary."

Technically, however, as the diary makes plain, "doughboys" were infantrymen who manned the trenches and "went over the top" as suggested by Ogden-born Guy Empy's *"Over the Top": By An American*.[2] Anderson's interest in engineering gave him a little different take on the war as well as the opportunity to exercise skills gained in his Utah years. His diary had been donated to Brigham Young University in the 1970s by Nels's son Martin, about the same time Marriott Library Curator Everett Cooley was making a drive to bring together the University of Utah's very fine Anderson Collection. As it turned out this war diary also reflected Anderson's attitude during the period he was most closely connected to Mormons and Utah culture.

Although I had never met him, I thought I knew who Anderson was that first day as I leafed through the war diary. I had heard Juanita Brooks tell of his role in getting a records survey project for Dixie of which my own family was a beneficiary when the journals of Levi Savage Jr. and his son Levi

Mathers Savage had been transcribed. Anderson's book on Mormonism, the *Desert Saints*, also became the direct departure point for my doctoral dissertation and my own first book. In time I also read his correspondence with Brooks and Dale Morgan, rejoiced in 1973 when he reviewed my *Take Up Your Mission: Mormon Colonization along the Little Colorado River, 1870–1900*, and was flattered when he sent greetings with mutual Canadian friends in the American Association for State and Local History. I truly knew little about this mythic figure and recall making occasional references that portrayed him as no more than a rootless derelict, rescued by Mormon ranchers and teachers. But I did understand my interest in the Anderson diary and turned to World War I specialist Kent Powell of the Utah State Historical Society. Sharing my interest, Powell transcribed the diary and traced Anderson's course through Europe.

Fortunately, an intense loyalty to his own roots permeates much of his copious writing. His own on-site experience and the legacy of his family are special hallmarks of his scholarly works from which any sketch of his life must draw. Among other things, they show a close family with strong ties. His father, Swedish immigrant Nels Sr., was born of peasant parentage and knew three languages, but was a virtual illiterate. The elder Nels was orphaned by cholera at nine and soon migrated to Germany where he worked for eighteen years. Continuing to America he hoboed through the East and Midwest, working mainly as a mason. At last he married a St. Louis girl of Scottish background and lived first in the late nineteenth-century Hobohemia or skid row district of Chicago where tens of thousands of footloose wage workers congregated during off seasons and hard times. Nels was born there in 1889. Then in a hopeful odyssey that lasted eight or ten years, the family canvassed the West without finding the right kind of land before returning to Chicago where again they lived just off the Loop in the Hobohemia slum. Initially held out of school, Nels and older brother Bill "hawked" newspapers, shined shoes, and became well acquainted with the area's inhabitants and institutions before the family moved to Elk Rapids on the east shore of Lake Michigan.

There Nels Sr. finally acquired a farm and adjacent acreages for his sons. But with domineering ways he drove his children from both the land and the family while his wife's example instructed the younger Nels in a remarkably advanced sense of social justice and patience. Nels Sr. acted out two harsh holdovers from his peasant past: true security exists only in land, and education is not to be trusted.[3] On the latter point he ultimately gave ground in Nels's case, listening to local teacher Henry McNamus's opinion that Nels had intellectual gifts that ought to be exposed to more than the four years of schooling the elder Anderson insisted could be tolerated without leading the child away from the land's security. McNamus also arranged for Nels to live as chore boy for two of his early teenage years in one of the area's upper middle-class homes, enabling him to broaden his social outlook.

Unhappy in high school where he was known as one of the "manure kids" because of Nels Sr.'s practice of collecting fertilizer to restore his farms, Nels ran away from home at fifteen, following his brother into the construction camps that were pushing the last of the railroad systems west. In a youthful display of travel savvy that impressed even seasoned hobos, he located his brother Bill who got him hired with an outfit grading a Santa Fe track southwest from Chicago. Before the summer was over he became a skilled mule skinner and displayed an affinity for the independent self-sufficiency of the hobo workers. When his brother headed home for the winter Nels stayed on, tending the mules with Andy Clark, an old-time "rounder" in whose stories and tutelage he found a continuing interest that when merged with sociology won him national recognition that survives yet. By spring he subscribed fully to the hobo jingle "*Granddad, I want to be a hobo, That's what I want to be, Help it if you can; when I get to be a man, I want to be a hobo too!*"[4]

After participating in this transient work force himself for a few years Anderson began to observe that hobos differed sharply from bums and tramps, that they were actually a necessary type of the genus *Vagrant*; a work force that almost by instinct came together where and when need existed and when the need was filled disappeared again without bidding, protest, or dispute. They were, he argued, not only the product of an essential phase in the process of the moving frontier but also a very sensitive barometer of seasonal change and economic cycles.[5] Indeed, as early as his second year in railroad construction when impending winter shut down a Montana grading job and the hobo work force departed—crowding gondolas and box cars all along the eastbound railroads—Anderson, still a teenager, sensed and saw the onset of the Panic of 1907–8 well before the newspapers began to announce it or the more stable labor marts at home tipped off his folks how threatening the collapse would be. Later, when he wrote about the importance of the hobo as an American labor phenomenon, Anderson also recognized the hobo's role as an essential part of frontier development. Railroad construction, reclamation projects, mining, timber work, and crop and ice harvest, all ran ahead of permanent urban populations demanding a disposable migratory work force that far exceeded the capacity of local populations. The result was a large body of homeless men flowing out from the various transportation centers in the spring and in the fall crowding back into the skid row centers.[6] In good times it was a process that worked well but left hundreds of thousands unemployed in times of collapse.

Following this last winter at home, Nels struck out in the spring of 1908 into the Panic's jobless world. He beat his way on a succession of heavily policed railroads and through hostile cities, visiting the levees and wheat fields of Missouri and Kansas, and looking for mining prospects in Denver and Salt Lake City. Finding no work and convinced by a Wobbly (a member of the Industrial Workers of the World, an international labor union) philosopher in a Salt Lake City park that the Panama Canal was the only sure work prospect, he headed south toward Los Angeles hoping to join a ship's crew there. His luck hopping trains held until somewhere south of Delta where railroad operators pulled him off the same train twice, the first time only to see him thumb his nose at them as he reboarded after the train was moving and the second more permanently, near the Utah-Nevada line. From there he trudged on south along the tracks to Clover Valley, a tiny Nevada oasis where a railroad and a Mormon ranch competed for landscape and use rights as they still do, at what is now called Barclay.

Given a meal and a bed that first night he soon settled into a "bed and board" relationship with the Woods/Terry clan who were devout Mormons but who spent most of their time on the range away from church. They were also committed to education, and at ease with the primitive Mormonism commonly found on the outskirts of Mormon Country.[7] The Terry patriarch practiced polygamy, his Woods counterpart did not, and the younger generations appear to have been leaving plurality as much by natural inclination as by obedience to the Woodruff Manifesto of 1890. Although after a two-year hiatus Anderson rejoined the hobo work force, the Woods and Terry ranches remained his home base for some ten years. And the pioneer Mormonism practiced there in some of the world's roughest and most isolated country— i.e., the Woods/Terry folkways—provided telling evidence of how the Mormon kingdom had first withdrawn and then expanded into utter wilderness. To Anderson, pioneer Lyman Woods—who chewed tobacco and took an occasional drink but stood unflinching at the post Brigham Young had given him—epitomized the best the desert saints, or for that matter any and all frontier America, had to offer. Attractive too was the fact that no one but Tommy Terry, who had just returned from a Mormon mission to England, undertook to convert him. Providing a different opportunity for indoctrination was the fact that at the ranches where he tended stock during that first winter, while families retreated to schools in Enterprise and St. George, were collections of Mormon books. These were primarily history and scripture, which in winter's slack hours he avidly devoured. "Vaguely" troubled by theology that excluded blacks and about the historicity of the *Book of Mormon*, but otherwise profoundly moved by the Mormon story of restoration, persecution, desert flight, and expansion, and thinking that polygamy was solving itself, he was baptized in 1910 by Tommy Terry in a desert spring.[8]

Still regarding the Woods/Terry ranches as home base, Anderson turned for a period of about eight years to a different kind of blue-collar, camp-oriented work that he also associated with the hobo life. This time, however, construction and mining opportunities accommodated his growing interest in school and his military service. In addition to his recognition that the panic was lifting and a sense that his "bed and board" arrangement had to end, his determination to rejoin the "bummery," as he called the hobo work force, was hastened by a series of disastrous floods washing out a hundred miles of Salt Lake, Los Angeles, and San Pedro Railroad track that created a plentitude of jobs on a seven-day-a-week basis as the railroad put its line back in service. The only admitted Mormon in this all-male outfit, Anderson was soon dubbed "The Deacon" and ribbed heavily about multiple wives and schoolboy interests. But in quieter moments he was encouraged to continue his education and not let the hobo life take him permanently.

Among his Mormon friends, people his age were busily pushing on with their schooling and patriarch Lyman Woods confided that he planned to pay for Nels's schooling. Sensing others might resent it, Anderson evaded the prospect. His railroad job required that he shift from mule skinning to the rough carpentry of bridge and building maintenance, which paid better and as the flood repairs ended, opened mining and reclamation jobs to him as well. Like his earlier hoboing, this work kept him in camp but it lessened his need to bum rides on the railroad, although when called by family need he continued to beat his way to Michigan and back unpaid and often wrote proudly of being able to do the one-way trip in as little as four days. His new trade also required him to invest in and carry a hundred pounds or so of tools, pick up new vocabularies, wear white overalls, and loosen his contact with the Woods, Terry, and Hafen families where he lived or worked less often. The impact of this, however, was abated by going to school with their sons and daughters and by contract construction work that he did in the neighboring settlements of Enterprise and Central. Although most of the people with whom he lived were ranchers and "cowboyed" regularly, Anderson never refers to himself as a cowboy and in his scholarly work complained that the romantic myth attached to cowboys contributed to the generally negative view of hobos.[9]

Able to finance himself, Anderson resumed his schooling. By now in his early twenties, he at first found Brigham Young Academy's high school students to be immature and cliquish. To his surprise the Provo school was also little patronized by general authorities, most of whom, he reported, sent their children to Salt Lake City schools and eastern universities. The next two years he continued high school at Dixie Academy in St. George where he fit better and where a student-run discipline system had been set up by Principal Hugh Woodward that seemed to take care of some of the immaturity. Also, pedagogy at Dixie Academy was progressive enough to generate complaints about religious heterodoxy, which in time attracted an investigation by Church Commissioner of Education Horace Cummings. According to Anderson this visit climaxed in a testimony meeting, orchestrated by Professor Joseph K. Nicholes, among students who otherwise might have met Cummings with a protest, thus disarming his suspicions and keeping the popular Woodward out of trouble. Even the most independent students held their peace about Nicholes's image management until the issue passed over.[10] About this time Anderson began to think about going into some professional or white-collar career and without being fully convinced, began to announce he would go into law. His associates at both Dixie Academy and the "Y" tended to have similar goals and were among the most progressive and vocal students.

Plying his work skills summers and during vacations Anderson felt more at home when he later returned to Brigham Young Academy. This time he enrolled in the university division, which numbered about one hundred students, among whom he was more at ease, and he formed friendships with Mormon young people from all over the West. He also brought a brother and sister to Utah for a year or two. During these years Anderson continued to talk about going into law but taught for short periods in Price, Utah, and at St. Johns Stake Academy in northeastern Arizona, which fed idealistic ideas about teaching as a suitable lifetime career. In addition to Nicholes and Woodward at Dixie, Principal Ed Hinckley of Brigham Young High, and especially John Swenson, professor of sociology and economics at Brigham Young University, were highly regarded Mormon teachers who influenced him profoundly. Swenson ultimately convinced him to drop law for sociology and pointed him towards the University of Chicago, whose Sociology Department was rising to national but sharply contested eminence by 1920.[11]

Back from war for the school year of 1920–21, the holding power of Anderson's Mormon connections began to weaken. In the main this was probably a matter of other loyalties claiming him, but events at the "Y" also had a centrifugal effect. In contrast to the later tide of World War II veterans, there appears to have been remarkably little student interest at the "Y" in the immediate post–World War I period. The senior class of 1920, for example, consisted of perhaps sixteen students and certainly no more than twenty.[12] Thirteen are listed in the yearbook as graduates. With a bumper freshman class of eighty-four, the college student body totaled 166. Anderson was elected Senior Class President and became editor of the yearbook, the *Banyon*. His close Dixie associate LeRoy Cox, who was also headed into law, reorganized and renamed the student newspaper.

It was a time of considerable political unrest. Among other things, the powerful Republican apostle, Reed Smoot, was actively working against the League of Nations. Anderson—who to the extent that he understood his political interest was a Democrat—supported the League along with many others at the Y. Anderson got his foot in his mouth trying to make a joke at an illustrated lecture he was giving that attracted Smoot's animus, who publicly admonished the thirty-one-year-old Anderson and other students to remember they were students who should let their parents do the politicking. This stung *Y News* editor LeRoy Cox, who retorted privately, "When we went to War they called us men, but now they treat us like children."[13]

More damaging to Anderson's relationship with the church was the senior class's mismanaged effort to bolster an embarrassingly small cash gift with what was basically an idea about university policy in the way of the legacy it planned to leave its alma mater. With its credits widely discounted at graduate schools and still closely associated with the BYA's lesser functions, the time seemed ripe to offer a progressive idea. As a consequence the seniors called, with what they thought was a conscious effort to be polite, for the university to widen the gulf between itself and the academy's programs, in effect to become a university in fact as well as name. Specifically they advocated more PhDs on the faculty, discontinuation of appointments as compensation for church service, and more books in the "less-than-adequate libraries." Although he worked to distance himself from the movement, Anderson's name was closely "associated with what was soon called the 'demand furor.'" Indeed, he was pinned directly to it by University President George H. Brimhall who, in a parable delivered before the entire student body, likened the class effort to a flea's boast that its bite could move a bull elk. The matter came to the attention of the Church Board of Education and despite the fact that Anderson was able to manage a friendly visit to President of the Church Heber J. Grant about a yearbook mistake, educator apostle and Superintendent of Church Education David O. McKay soon came to put the "demands" issue right. This he did by talking directly to Anderson, advising him sternly to "follow your file leaders." Offended to be left out of the negotiations and agreeing with Anderson that they had "been chastened unfairly," the entire senior class "packed in[to] four cars," along with chaperones, and took off for a spring outing at the head of Provo Canyon. The incident was ignored by the administration but class members became increasingly aware that they had offended the "high[est] authority."

Anderson soon had reason to think that the incident marked him as a "trouble maker" and that it would likely alter his future. A few days after graduation he appeared before Commissioner of Church Schools Adam S. Bennion to apply for a position in one of the church academies. "Under no conditions," he was informed, could Bennion "recommend me for a teaching job. It would have a bad influence on the students."[14]

Feeling that a BA made his blue-collar options less meaningful and that Bennion had closed the door to his best white-collar option, Anderson began to plan seriously to go to the University of Chicago. He and LeRoy Cox spent the summer in an unsuccessful effort to sell Utah Woolen Mills' goods through the upper Midwest. They also took two University of Utah classes to bolster sagging BYU credits, which they were sure would be discounted 25 percent at the University of Chicago. And somehow, Nels conducted a survey of the unemployed in the Utah and Idaho railroad towns of Salt Lake City, Ogden, and Pocatello where he interviewed four hundred migratory workers in a study that became part of *The Hobo: The Sociology of the Homeless Man* in 1923.

The Chicago sociology department quickly recognized Anderson's special preparation for a study of the homeless men that inhabited Hobohemia, his boyhood home. As noted earlier, his hard-pressed parents had cut school entirely from his young life to sell newspapers and hustle the odd nickel running errands for prostitutes, Wobbly philosophers, mission do-gooders, small-time politicos, and saloon keepers until he knew the Hobohemia area and its inhabitants like the back of his hand. He had also visited it now and again during his own "go-about hobo days." Indeed he was so much a man of his past that his scholarly experience in 1921 and later was complicated by class lines, prudish academic standards, and reservations that attached to onsite investigations into what were considered to be marginal if not criminal groups. For Anderson the result was a year of prodigious work in a Chicago slum which culminated with the publication of *The Hobo* under his own name. Countersigned by an unlikely committee of sociological greats, city reformers, and figures who in some quarters were considered to be underworld characters, it became a bestseller before it was signed off as a master's thesis. It made a lasting contribution to the University of Chicago sociology department's famed methodology of "participatory observation."[15]

The Hobo both blessed and blighted Anderson's way for the rest of his life. It made him a still-quoted authority on a group of marginalized homeless men and opened an array of administrative opportunities before him, but frustratingly closed the door of scholarly appointment for which he so longed until he was seventy-five years old. After several years of research, further publication, and reform work in Chicago's underworld he more or less escaped to New York University in the late 1920s. There an administrative potpourri of research projects, adjunct teaching assignments at Columbia, welfare jobs, sticky labor assignments involving Great Lakes sailors and the New York Bonus Army marchers, freelance writing, and research projects brought a PhD at New York University in 1930. More importantly, it also made him indispensable to Harry Hopkins, Franklin D. Roosevelt's right-hand man and certainly one of the nation's foremost figures in opening the "welfare state," first in New York State government and after 1933 in the New Deal's welfare and labor-related programs.[16]

During World War II Anderson went on to wartime work with seamen and shipping that took him to India, the Persian Gulf, and Kuwait. In the latter he supervised the shipment of lend-lease aid to Russia and prepared for postwar and Cold War service in Europe with the US military government of Germany, until mandatory age requirements brought him to retirement. Thereafter he spent an additional decade in Europe as director of a UNESCO office of research before returning to Canada and, at long last, to professorial appointments in the Newfoundland and New Brunswick universities where he remained the last decades of his long life.

It is difficult to know what role Utah's Dixie and Mormonism played in this continuing life. One guesses that by either ordinary Mormon or scholarly standards we have not gone far in understanding its importance. He married twice, both times out of the church. He states several times that in his Utah period he avoided entangling alliances with Mormon girls because schooling came first. However, the World War I diary may be a superior source of information, although some reading between the lines may be needed to make diary entries into statements of romantic interest. Yet there is a suggestive between-the-lines kind of disappointment that one or two of them didn't write often enough nor say exactly what he wished they would. I have heard no oral suggestion of a love affair from St. George people who remember their parents or an older sibling's talking about Nels's affairs, although a romantic interest of his brother Lester is remembered.

There is no question that he took little time for worship in Chicago. During the first year he worked night and day and his time thereafter was filled with all-consuming reform efforts that some judged to be of a questionable nature. After missing church for his first few months in Chicago, two missionaries visited him with soul saving in mind. Thereafter he was visited a time or two by Arthur Beeley, another graduate with an interest in the social sciences and, Anderson suspected, at least tacit authority to shepherd the student flock in Chicago. LeRoy Cox, later a well-known St. George judge, tended to take Anderson's shift from law to sociology personally, especially after Nels failed to look him up during the first months in Chicago. Mormons who did look him up had heard reports of the shady aspect of his research and/or welfare work and to Nels seemed more interested in sensationalism than in him personally.[17]

Finally, his first wife, Hilda, a Jewish immigrant from Russia who worked in the Chicago Public Library, had what seems more a class-related than a religious interest in upgrading Nels from social work to literary writing. In a mid-twenties trip through southern Utah, she was at best disinterested and probably dead set against his reactivating his Mormon relationships. Later, after they moved to New York, her pressure led him to do "articles for good magazines in 1927," which he termed "a successful year for a beginner." About the same time he coauthored the first ever urban sociology text and, trying to move away from *The Hobo*, wrote a parody of it called *The Milk and Honey Route* under the *nom de plume* Dean Stiff. Whatever her position, he attended Mormon Church services more in New York than he had in Chicago but found little need to involve himself in the full package of LDS participation in these years, which in many ways were a secure and happy time as his family got started. Hilda, who later became unhappy in their marriage, seemed at least to be at ease.[18]

While he had an important time-consuming job during his Washington years, Anderson made what were undeniably more than courtesy bows in the direction of his Mormon past when he did the Utah research for *Desert Saints* beginning in 1934, when he also got the Dixie Records Survey started. He found southern Utah in the depths of the Depression. Although word of a more hurried 1970s visit may still be heard among older descendants of the Woods, Terry, and Hafen families, I have heard no remembered comment about the longer research visit of the mid-thirties except Juanita Brooks's Utah State Historical Society speech in 1962 and a *Dialogue* oral history in 1974. Anderson himself recalled that his work, including certain records housed in the basement of the temple, provoked suspicion among some. However, George Whitehead, the temple president, was cordial and coopera- tive, as were the stake president, and the stake relief society president, Juanita Brooks. But one gathers that Thomas Wolfe and Wallace Stegner were correct in their conviction that one can rarely return home. Though not actually met by hostility, it seems likely that Anderson was not met by any larger show of welcome. Much later in his career he renewed cordial relationships with sev- eral classmates and Utah acquaintances and carried on significant correspon- dence with them. Included were Lowry Nelson, Dean Brimhall, Robert Hinckley, George Ballif, and Ernest Wilkinson.[19]

Although in writing *Desert Saints* Anderson abandoned early outlines for a more sympathetic, straightforward presentation of the Mormon expe- rience, the book was not enthusiastically received by representatives of the church, and the compliment he had meant it to be fell flat.[20] Nevertheless he persevered, working on it for eight years. He almost certainly used his Washington savvy to gain access to important Utah/Mormon records, including census data going back to 1854–1900. The book was published first in 1942 with what might be called twelve "History of the Church" chapters with a moderate sociological bent. Anderson also presented four southern Utah–oriented chapters written with a recognizable "Chicago School" sociological spin. These last were entitled: (XIII) "Priesthood Gov- ernment in Zion," (XIV) "Economy of Faith and Plenty," (XV) "Social Implications of Polygamy," and (XVI) "The Mormon Way of Living," in which data and focus are frequently drawn from his Utah experience. A paperback University of Chicago edition appeared in 1966 with a superb preface by Thomas O'Dea that acknowledges Anderson's early recognition of the "near nation" and "native ethnic group" concepts prominent in his own *The Mormons* (1957). While Anderson undertakes an informative postpartum in his own preface, the later edition appears otherwise to be identical to the earlier one.

Desert Saints qualifies Anderson as one of the foremost Utah/Mormon historians of the Depression and early World War II era. Except possibly in closeness of their association and a spirit of protest that illuminated much of their work, he qualifies as a worthy peer to Juanita Brooks, Bernard DeVoto, Dale Morgan, Wallace Stegner, and Fawn Brodie, the five great writers Gary Topping reclaimed for Utah in his book *Utah Historians and the Reconstruction of Western History*.[21] Along with the work of several of those writer's, *Desert Saints* brings what may be called a "Brigham Young as the great Latter Day prophet" thesis into a clear and objective statement. Similarly the book is a classical statement of the Mormon experience as escape, social and economic experiment, desert conquest, and re-entry to national fellowship, this latter as shaped by my friend Leo Lyman and others in similar schools. In it, as in much of Anderson's sociological work, Frederick Jackson Turner's frontier thesis is also put to effective use.

Perhaps most importantly Anderson's 1942 history lays out in limited but specific form several of the great themes that occupied Utah/Mormon writers in the next half century. To name a few, we need to consider carefully the indebtedness of Robert Flanders and Leonard Arrington to his sections on geographic expansion, communalism, and the independent economic commonwealth. In his sophisticated and graceful treatment "of the gathering," William Mulder also followed patterns well understood by Anderson, as do many who have dealt with polygamy. Although he touches on it only briefly, and that deep in a footnote, the census-derived question of how John D. Lee's capital assets could have skyrocketed ten times as fast between 1854 and 1860 as did others in comparable circumstances at the time, suggests a complicity in the Mountain Meadows Massacre on Lee's part that neither writers Juanita Brooks nor Will Bagley really cope with.[22] Similarly, my own interest in Mormon expansion into Arizona and in the Mormon village grew directly from passages of Anderson's calling "Utah's Dixie the inland center of a primitive Mormon" culture from which expansion proceeded to several surrounding states. Set very much apart from the Wasatch Front, which defending the hinterland from invasion fought fire with fire, that primitive culture remained in the memories of most in 1942 and was clearly recognizable in my "Mormon Country" boyhood in the northern Arizona of the 1930s.

Finally, he discusses the Mormon drive to make education and knowledge promote the Kingdom of God into a force not altogether unlike the "opportunity" role played earlier by the frontier and available natural resources. As he points out, there was a time when it was held to "be a sin to 'approximate after the things of the world.'" This was no longer true after 1900, by which time, he avers, Zion both turned "from insularism to identification," and from importing people to the exportation of young people "expensively educated in the knowledge of the world." Between 1900 and 1940 he estimated "as many as 100,000" young people had been exported—and still guessing, but guessing wisely, he calls it a number equal to the emigrant converts who had been imported earlier. Then, calling the decade of the 1860s the time of maximum effort when "every sacrifice was the sacrifice of investment," he points out that by 1940 sacrifices were pursuant to sending young Mormons out and concludes with a question: "Is this . . . the long-predicted expansion of Zion to the world? Is it another kind of missionary movement?"[23]

Aware of the fact that from beginning to end his scholarship and his life were closely related to his own identity, should we join in asking "Is this dilution process thinning out the old distinctiveness? Will Mormonism spread and adapt until it loses its identity?" Let me counter with a concluding question. Does his abiding affinity for Desert Saints (people more than the book) add dimension to the long sojourn of a life spent as a dyed-in-the-wool mendicant and have a vitality that continues? Do the "career public servant" and, at last, the expatriate scholar add to the regional Dixie self-consciousness—in an interest in the "boy hobo," the "sometimes saint?" Is he a continuing advocate of a unique expression of pioneer life? I tend to believe that they do and he is.

PREFACE

THE NELS ANDERSON WORLD WAR I DIARY COVERS A BRIEF BUT critical time period from June 9, 1918 to April 27, 1919. It is important for its rich detailed narrative of the experiences of one private who wrote openly about the destruction and tragedy of war, the day-to-day life of a soldier, and relationships and interactions with civilians—French, Belgian, and German. His day-by-day accounts take us from Camp Mills, New York, across the Atlantic, through southern England, across the English Channel, through France to the training camp at Humberville, and into the fighting of the two major American offensives—St. Mihiel and the Argonne-Meuse—to the Armistice on November 11, 1918. Within a few weeks Anderson marched into Germany as part of the American occupation force in the demilitarized zone west of the Rhine River. He remained there until March 1919, when he returned to France to attend the six-hundred-year-old university in Montpellier in southern France. Nels Anderson was one of approximately 4.8 million Americans who served in the armed forces during World War I. Of these nearly half were sent to France—most in 1918, the final year of the war. At age twenty-nine Nels Anderson was much older than the typical recruit of twenty-one or twenty-two. Volunteers like himself made up approximately 30 percent of the army, the other 70 percent were inducted through the Selective Service Act passed on May 19, 1917, for which the first draft numbers were drawn in July 1917. Anderson, like other American males between the ages of twenty-one and thirty-one, registered for the first draft on June 5, 1917. Subsequent registrations would expand the range from eighteen to forty-five years of age.[1]

Anderson joined the army in March 1918 and was sent to Camp Funston, near Manhattan, Kansas, where he was assigned to the 89th Division.[2] At Funston he applied for assignment to the Engineers and was assigned to Company E of the 314th Engineer Regiment. The regiment left Camp Funston in late May 1918 and traveled by train to Camp Mills on Long Island to await departure for France. Anderson kept a day-by-day diary of his time at Camp Funston and the trip to Camp Mills, then sent the diary home before departing the United States. That diary has not come to light. Fortunately the second and longer part—covering the period from June 9, 1918 to April 27,

1919—did survive and was donated by Martin Anderson, the only child of Nels Anderson, to the Brigham Young University Library.[3]

Nels Anderson had studied at Brigham Young Academy—now Brigham Young University—and maintained ties to the institution and its students during and after the war. He also retained ties to St. George, Utah, where he attended Dixie Academy, and St. John's, Arizona, where he taught the year before joining the army. Anderson joined the Church of Jesus Christ of Latter-day Saints, the Mormon Church, in 1909 and the relationship with the church and fellow members is one of the interesting undercurrents surfacing from time to time in the pages of his diary.

The diary also marks Anderson's latent fascination with people, societies, and cultures that would continue after the war as he became one of America's eminent sociologists. His accounts of fellow soldiers, the French and German peasants, his ongoing correspondence with friends and family back home, are insightful into the social life of the early twentieth century.

ACKNOWLEDGMENTS

Thanks begin with Nels Anderson, who saw the value of a wartime diary and kept it faithfully under difficult wartime conditions. His son, Martin Anderson, offered the diary to Ernest Wilkinson, president of Brigham Young University and longtime friend of his father. Charles Peterson, who penned the foreword to this volume, deserves special recognition. As a mentor and friend, Chas invited me to work with him in editing the diary for publication. Our discussions about the diary and Nels Anderson have continued my education as a historian and a friendship that began nearly a half century ago when, as a freshman at the College of Eastern Utah, I took a western American history class from Chas. Other friends and former colleagues at the Utah State Historical Society, including Craig Fuller, Philip Notarianni, and Melvin Smith have given much appreciated encouragement and support. Thanks to the library staffs at the Utah State Historical Society; Special Collections, J. Willard Marriott Library at the University of Utah; and the U.S. Army War College Library at Carlisle Barracks, Pennsylvania. Staff at the Special Collections and Manuscripts, Harold B. Lee Library, Brigham Young University were most gracious and helpful in providing access to the Nels Anderson Diary and in recognizing the importance of the diary. The readers for the press, Randle Hart in the sociology department and Larry Ping in the history department at Southern Utah University offered helpful suggestions and much-needed encouragement, as did Peter DeLafosse, Reba Rauch, and John Alley at the University of Utah Press. Cathy Ellis shared valuable information on residents of St. Johns, Arizona, and soldiers identified in the Anderson diary. Douglas Alder provided information about Nels Anderson from oral histories conducted in the St. George area and arranged for Charles Peterson to give the 2012 Juanita Brooks Lecture on the life of Nels Anderson, which was the basis for his foreword. Lyman Hafen and his father Kelton Hafen were responsible for an unforgettable trip to still-isolated Clover Valley where Nels spent his first months in Utah. They also provided access to the Dixie College yearbooks for 1915 and 1916 that Nels Anderson left with their family. Finally, my dear wife Brenda deserves many thanks for welcoming Nels into our home for a much longer stay than either of us anticipated, even inviting him to share summer vacations as we followed his diary through the World War I battlefields of St Mihiel and the Meuse-Argonne in France to Kyllburg and surrounding villages in Germany.

NELS ANDERSON'S WORLD WAR I DIARY

INTRODUCTION

WHEN THE TWENTY-EIGHT-YEAR-OLD NELS ANDERSON SET FOOT ON European soil at Cherbourg, France, on June 29, 1918, he carried with him a lifetime of experiences. As a child he had experienced the waning days of the western American frontier, as a youth he learned about the streets of working-class Chicago before moving to rural Michigan. After leaving home at age fifteen he worked as a hobo hitching rides on freight trains moving across the western half of the nation until he became the adopted son of an extended Mormon family in Utah and Nevada. In Zion he worked as a ranch hand before enrolling as a student at Dixie Academy in St. George and Brigham Young Academy in Provo. He taught school in Price, Utah, and St. John's, Arizona, and did seasonal work as a carpenter on railroads, dams, smelters, in the hard-rock mines, and on military posts throughout the American West during his time as a student and teacher.

Somewhat older than most American "doughboys" who crossed the Atlantic to participate in the "War to end all Wars," Nels Anderson carried with him not only a wealth of experience, but also a keen ability to observe and to write about people, places, and events. Following his return from Europe in 1919, he used those same experiences and abilities to write *Desert Saints*, published in 1942 by the University of Chicago Press, and still one of the most important volumes on Utah and Mormon history. Anderson also became one of the twentieth century's most prominent sociologists with his work in the United States, Europe, and Canada.

Nels Anderson's World War I diary is important not only for what it reveals about the war experience for one American, but also about the man himself. A related theme is that of the Mormon experience in World War I. Nels Anderson joined the Church of Jesus Christ of Latter-day Saints in 1910 at age nineteen. Although throughout most of his adult life Nels was not a practicing Mormon as defined by church attendance, abstaining from tobacco and alcohol, and other activities that have come to be seen as a measure of one's faithfulness to the religion, Nels always maintained that he was "a Mormon and that the Mormons were his people."[1] During the war and in the immediate postwar months, Nels did seek out other Mormons with whom he could share his faith and practice their "Mormonism." The diary is the only known extensive day-by-day diary written by a Mormon participant in the Great War. Anderson's later significance as a historian and sociologist adds to the diary's importance.

Nels Anderson was born on July 31, 1889, in Chicago, to Nels and Annie Wilkinson Anderson. Nels was named for his father, who was born about 1850 in rural Sweden. Nels's father became an orphan in early childhood when his parents died during a cholera plague. At the age of fourteen he left Sweden with a relative for Germany, where he lived for eighteen years learning the bricklayer's trade before immigrating to the United States in 1880. Anderson traveled the country working on railroads, in coal mines, on farms, cutting timber in the woods of Minnesota, as a coachman for a German businessman in Chicago, and as a bricklayer in Kansas City and St. Louis. Nels's mother was born in St. Louis to Scottish immigrant parents. She attended school for about five years and was an unskilled factory worker when she met Anderson.[2] Not long after their marriage the Anderson's moved to Chicago where their first child, William, was born in 1888, followed by Nels, the second of twelve children, the next year. As a young man, Nels learned that he, not William, was named for his father because their mother was pregnant by an unidentified man when she and her future husband met.[3]

Nels Anderson Sr. came to the United States in pursuit of a dream. "His ideal was to get an American wife, settle on rich land and have a large family, mostly boys. His boys would all be farmers and have farms near his. His daughters would marry farmers. His children would be stable Americans."[4] If Chicago offered work for an experienced bricklayer, a great fire in Spokane brought the opportunity for the Andersons to move west to help rebuild the city, then more easily acquire the much-anticipated farm.

With Nels carried in the arms of his mother, the small family of four headed west for Spokane in 1889. During the nine years before the Andersons returned east to Chicago in 1898, six children were born. Two—Dorothy and Leslie—died as infants. The others included two girls, Celia and Belle, and two boys, Lester and Frank. Three more children arrived later—Charley, Johnnie, and Irene.

Working as a bricklayer in Spokane during the week and roaming the countryside on weekends, Anderson eventually secured timberland about seventy miles outside of Spokane that he expected to make into a profitable farm. The venture was a disappointment. "Slowly father came to the conclusion that one man's lifetime would not be enough to convert the timber claim to a viable farm."[5] The land was sold for a profit and the Andersons headed east, first to the Nez Perce Reservation where, Nels recalls, "my first memories began," then Lewiston, Idaho, and finally to a ranch on Dude Creek in the Teton Basin of eastern Idaho. Prosperity did not find the Andersons on Dude Creek and after two years they sold their livestock, wagon, and other belongings and boarded an eastbound train for Chicago. Nels never forgot his childhood in the West, his father's efforts to acquire a farm, and his mother's joy in the decision to return to Chicago. As a ten-year-old, Nels adapted easily to life in the big city, making friends among the children of Italian immigrants, demonstrating to teachers at the neighborhood school advanced skills in reading, spelling, writing, and arithmetic, earning money as a newspaper boy on Madison Street, and learning about the city and its people in unanticipated preparation for graduate studies in sociology at the University of Chicago in the early 1920s.

The Andersons remained in Chicago until 1901 when they moved across Lake Michigan to Traverse City on the Michigan side of the lake, and Nels's father became caretaker for a large tourist resort that had closed.[6] The resort was located on one hundred acres of land that could be used for farming. The Andersons remained at Traverse City for two years caring for the resort, planting a few crops on the property, working as sharecroppers on a farm ten miles away, and looking for land to purchase.

Ironically, a murder brought the long-sought opportunity. A man killed his wife and was sentenced to life in prison. He deeded his farm to his defense attorney as payment for legal fees and when the lawyer could not find a buyer for the forty-five-acre farm located on Birch Lake, two miles from Elk Rapids, the Andersons offered $275.00, which the attorney was glad to accept. The purchase included four hundred apple, peach, and cherry trees that Nels reported to be worth ten dollars each.[7]

Nels's father obtained work in an iron smelter two miles from the farm, and Nels and his older brother Bill began caring for the two-year-old fruit trees and planting a vegetable garden for the family's needs.

As the 1903–1904 school year drew near, Nels's former teacher, Henry McManus, made arrangements for him to continue his schooling by taking a job as chore boy for the widow of John Grelich. Aunt Belle, as she liked to be called, provided Nels with room, board, clothes, and six dollars a month in exchange for his caring for the widow's horse and carriage, cleaning the stable, helping with yard and kitchen work, and maintaining the furnace and carbide-burning machine that furnished gaslight to the home. Although Nels missed his family, the two years with the kind-hearted Aunt Belle provided

Nels with the opportunity to complete the eighth grade while enjoying a measure of freedom and privacy. As he wrote, "My two years away from home were akin to a holiday, I was being the favored one in our family. At times I had the guilty feeling that I was escaping my share of family duty. I found myself feeling anxious to go home, yet sad about leaving the only room to myself I had known."[8]

Nels returned home with the hope of continuing on to high school but with the realization that his father considered further education unnecessary and that it was time for his son to focus his energies on acquiring his own farm. However, when his father learned that a high school education was necessary before Nels could enroll in an inexpensive special two-year course for dairy farming, he allowed Nels to attend the nearby Elk Rapids High School where he became known by the nickname "Farmer" among the fifty students in the local school. Nels attended only one year of high school in Elk Rapids. Family tensions in the spring of 1906, brought on by stomach pains for his father and the children's inability to complete all the necessary farm work and continue to attend school, compelled Nels to a spur-of-the-moment decision to run away from home. He would join his older brother Bill, who had left the previous year and was working in Galesburg, Illinois.

Using part of the thirty dollars he took from his father's semimonthly earnings at the foundry, Nels purchased a railroad ticket for Galesburg. It would be the last time that he paid for his rail transportation for many years. He soon learned the ways of the road, jumping aboard trains to travel in boxcars and becoming a part of the army of American hobos—a citizen of Hobohemia. Nels developed an abiding respect for the hobo as an individual with a valuable role in the expanding American economy. He realized, "In spite of all that has been said to the contrary, the hobo is a worker. He is not a steady worker but he earns most of the money he spends."[9] He found that men, like himself, left home to become hobos for a number of reasons—seasonal layoffs, employment opportunities, racial or ethnic discrimination, a life crisis, wanderlust, or "defects of personality."[10] The hobo was not a lazy, shiftless, immoral beggar, but a vital part of the American workforce, comparable to cowboys, seamen, and other temporary, but necessary, laborers.

Nels found his brother Bill driving mules for a grading contractor at Ransom, Illinois, and was hired as a mule skinner at twenty-five dollars a month with board and lodging—a wage much more than the ten dollars a month he could expect working as a farm hand back home. The following summer, in 1907, he earned seventy dollars a month on a grading project in

Montana until cold weather halted work in November. Nels returned home to Elk Ridge to spend the winters of 1906–1907 and 1907–1908 working, during the latter winter as a coal forker at the coke ovens that were part of the smelter operation where his father was employed.

Employment prospects were dismal during the summer of 1908, as the effects of the Panic of 1907 washed through construction and other work at which hobos could usually find temporary employment. Bill, after working the past two summers with Nels, decided to give up the hobo life and seek permanent employment in Detroit. Now on his own, Nels made his way first to Illinois, then Missouri, Kansas, Colorado, and finally Utah in an unsuccessful effort to find work.

Nels arrived in Denver just as the 1908 Democratic National Convention was under way and, desperate for a good meal, he resorted to panhandling. He wrote:

> The men on the streets wearing large white buttons with the name of a state on each were delegates. I saw two men wearing Michigan buttons. On impulse, I asked them for money to get something to eat. I recalled how my voice failed me when I spoke of my want, but also how I resented the sour looks they gave me.... Many other rejections followed but about every fifth person gave something, a dime from one, a nickel from another. Between one and two hours of diligent effort brought in, and I recall that exactly, eighty-five cents. I went into a Mexican restaurant and for the first time ate a big bowl of chili con carne, a full meal, twenty cents.[11]

Nels did not find work in Colorado and decided to continue west to Utah in search of employment. He climbed inside a truck on the brake beam of a Denver and Rio Grande passenger train and hung on for the long ride across the Colorado Rockies and the eastern Utah desert to the Price railroad station. Grateful that he had not fallen from the train during the twenty-four hour ordeal, Anderson found provisions in Price and directions to continue on north four miles to Helper where he could easily catch a freight train to the smelters in Murray. From there it was a short six-mile streetcar ride into Salt Lake City.

Anderson found no work in the smelters or on railroad construction projects in the region and little encouragement that things would turn around soon. One recruiter for the Industrial Workers of the World that he met in a

Salt Lake City park believed that conditions would only worsen until people became so desperate that they would rise up in a mass revolution. The red-haired recruiter did suggest that if Nels was serious about finding work he should make his way to Panama, where there would be a high demand for workers for the next several years in constructing the Panama Canal. Passage to Panama could be obtained on just about any of the many ships leaving West Coast ports for the region. Nels boarded a passenger train for Los Angeles, again riding beneath a passenger car on the brake beam. After traveling more than three hundred miles south from Salt Lake City, however, Nels was "ditched" at Crestline, just across the Nevada border. He continued walking along the railroad line in search of a place where he might board a freight train to continue his journey to the coast. However, Los Angeles and Panama vanished for Nels after he followed the railroad line into the north end of Clover Valley and accepted an invitation to supper from a man mowing hay in a nearby field.

That man, Lamond Woods, was part of an extended Mormon family whose patriarch (and Lamond's father), Lyman L. Woods, had come west in 1848 as a fifteen-year-old youth. Following his marriage to Maribah Ann Bird in 1856, the couple established a home in Provo where four children, including Lamond Cresson Woods, were born. Called as part of the Muddy Mission to southern Nevada, Lyman established a homestead in Clover Valley in 1869. Lamond's wife, Elizabeth, was the daughter of Thomas Terry, another early Mormon pioneer who established the Terry Ranch at the head of Shoal Creek, twelve miles west of the town of Enterprise and about twenty-five miles northeast of Clover Valley. Both the Woods and Terry families would be central in Nels's life for the next several years as he became something of an unofficial member of both families, a relationship that he cherished the rest of his life.

Lamond Woods noted that his brothers-in-law, Thomas, Lou, and Joe Terry, needed help on their ranch and Nels accepted the offer of work under a different arrangement that more approximated his own family life than the daily wage he had earned as a mule skinner. As he recalled: "Nor was there any discussion between Tommy and me about pay at any time. Tommy suggested that I needed additional clothes and he brought them, nor did he put the cost down on any account. Talking about wages in that situation had no place. I felt myself accepted by the three Terry families, not as someone hired. I wasn't working for any of the brothers in particular."[12]

Jacob Buchar, a young Austrian immigrant who had worked several years in the coal mines of Pennsylvania before losing his job during the Panic of 1907 and who landed in Modena in search of employment, had also been taken in by the Terry family and worked under a similar informal arrangement. The two were entrusted with the day-to-day care of the ranch as the three Terry brothers and their families were not full-time residents of the ranch. "We occupied one of the houses, did our own cooking and washing, did the daily chores respecting the animals, and put in five or six hours a day on long-neglected work. Jake's background was village and farm life in Austria. Work was as much a way of life with him as for me. Above all, he was not lazy. If the Terry brothers came, they had no need to inspect what had been done or to 'lay out' what they wanted done."[13]

In their spare time, Nels and Jake began studying Mormonism utilizing a substantial collection of church books at the ranch. Because Jake could not read English, Nels would read selections from the books and summarize other sections so that both young men became acquainted with Mormon theology and doctrine.[14]

Nels's interest in Mormonism had been stimulated by reports of Thomas Terry's recent proselytizing mission to Texas and attendance by Nels and Jake at the July 24th Pioneer Day celebration in Enterprise in the summer of 1908, not long after Nels landed in Clover Valley. The highlight of the celebration was Grandfather Woods talk about his experience as a Mormon— becoming a member of Brigham Young's household at age fourteen after his parents died, coming to Utah in 1848, serving as a guide and scout, and his call to settle Clover Valley. Years later Nels wrote of the event that Grandfather Woods had "a manner of speaking that invited conviction. I was never more carried away."[15]

In the spring of 1909, Thomas Terry suggested that Nels return to Clover Valley, where he could do chores for Grandfather Woods and assist with other work on the ranch. Nels welcomed the opportunity to become better acquainted with the pioneer who refused to leave the home and ranch he had built as a calling from Brigham Young. Lyman Woods was Nels Anderson's model of a Mormon. Dedicated and loyal, proud of his Mormon heritage, willing to accept the *Book of Mormon* and basic doctrines on faith but not worry about the mysteries and intricacies of a complex theology, Lyman Woods still made his own choices. He avoided Mormon polygamy, claiming to be unworthy but more likely motivated by a devotion to his first and only wife. He saw merit in the young men and women following the Mormon dietary code of forgoing coffee, tea, alcohol, and tobacco, yet chewed tobacco all his life, and during a trip with Nels enjoyed several glasses of whiskey at a Salt Lake City saloon.

In January 1910, Nels Anderson was baptized a member of the Church of Jesus Christ of Latter-day Saints. Thomas Terry performed the baptism and Lyman Woods confirmed him a member of the Mormon faith. Nels did not undergo a miraculous conversion nor express a conviction of being "born again." His reasons for becoming a Mormon, as he admitted, "were mixed, probably being more social than religious....My reading of Mormon literature certainly had some influence, not so much the theological material as the Mormon story."[16] Becoming a Mormon meant something more than joining a new faith. The decision to accept baptism as a Mormon also represented, at least in the view of most of the members of the Wood and Terry families, a conscious choice by Nels to bind himself for this life and the next to the two families. He would not be like other travelers who were the recipients of their hospitality and good will before wandering on, their names and stories soon forgotten.

Grandpa Woods urged Nels to think about going to school "before it is too late," and offered to pay the cost. Nels accepted the suggestion, but not the offer of money. Instead he went to work as a carpenter replacing bridges and repairing tunnels on the railroad south of Clover Valley that had washed out in a recent flood. After fourteen months of work, Nels enrolled at Brigham Young Academy in Provo. Grandfather Woods made arrangements for Nels to stay at the home of his oldest son Jimmy, although Nels left soon after his arrival to find his own accommodations because of a conflict with Jimmy's wife, Clara.[17] Nels attended the Provo school for two years, working as a carpenter for the railroad during Christmas and summer vacations. At school he lived frugally, having sent part of his vacation earnings home to his family in Michigan. He attended some dances, sporting, and social events, joined the debating society and track team, and was part of the Dixie Club—a group of students from southwestern Utah and southeastern Nevada. Academically, Professor John C. Swenson, who comprised the economics and sociology department, introduced Nels to the field of sociology. Swenson allowed Anderson to enroll in an upper-level course in social problems and was impressed by his critical review of Josiah Flynt's 1899 book, *Tramping with Tramps*, for its omission of the go-about workers of the Middle West and West whose story Anderson knew so well from personal experience.[18]

Nels interrupted his education for the 1913–1914 school year to help his brother Lester come west and find a job working on the railroad maintenance crew. Later in the year, the brothers combined their earnings to purchase a machine for making building blocks and a small cement mixer. They contracted to build a school and meeting house in Central, twenty miles from Enterprise, as well as houses in the area. The partnership was successful but temporary and after a time Lester returned to the railroad maintenance crew for a few months before quitting to go home to Michigan.

In 1911, the year that Nels first enrolled at the Brigham Young Academy in Provo, the LDS Church established Dixie Academy in St. George. Thomas Terry built a home in St. George and the Terry's offered Nels a place to stay in what was to have been Grandfather Woods's room. Nels stayed with the Terrys for the 1914–1915 and 1915–1916 school years, paying a nominal amount for meals and a room, and handling chores when Thomas was away at the Terry Ranch. With an eye toward becoming a lawyer, Nels joined the academy's debating team. With the Great War raging in Europe the debate topic was whether or not the United States should increase its standing armaments. The 1916 Dixie yearbook shows Nels as a serious and intense scholar with rimless glasses. His ambition and debating prowess is noted in the inscription, "His highest desire is to be President of the United States. His debates will perhaps win him this place in the White House, but never a wife."[19] The author of one of the jokes included in the yearbook was undoubtedly familiar with Nels's goal to become a lawyer and the recent partnership with his brother Lester. In an attempt to alter the name, ever so slightly, or perhaps to reference a nickname never disclosed by Nels, the joke reads:

> After Nels had attained great fame as a lawyer, he and his brother went to a certain town in Colorado and opened a law office under the name of "Nelse Anderson and Bro." Later the partnership was dissolved. Nelse packed his few belongings, including the sign board that he had outside the office, on a donkey and started for a mining town. Upon his arrival one miner walked up to him, looked at the sign, then at Nelse, and finally at the donkey, then said: "Say, Stranger, which of us is Nelse"?[20]

Nels enjoyed a wide circle of friends at Dixie Academy and some friendships would continue for many years. Ione Terry, the daughter of his hosts Thomas and Roxa Jane Woods Terry, was a year behind Nels at the academy and they enjoyed something of a big brother–little sister relationship.[21]

After his first year at Dixie Academy, Nels found his way to the silver-mining town of Eureka, thirty miles southwest of Provo. During the summer of 1915 he worked the night shift as a timber man twenty-two hundred feet underground, earning ninety dollars a month after learning how to set timbers from a patient and helpful middle-aged Italian immigrant. Nels apparently returned to Eureka the next summer before enrolling at Brigham Young Academy in the fall of 1916 with two of his fellow Dixie students, Sam Brooks and LeRoy Cox. He took a class from John C. Swenson, his favorite teacher, and joined the debate team. At the end of the fall term, Nels returned to his parents' home in Michigan after an absence of eight years. The homecoming was cordial. His father reported that he had purchased forty acres of land for Nels to become a farmer. Nels revealed his plans to become a lawyer, and his father joked that was fine with him because "the lawyer always gets the land and the money too."[22]

After the brief visit, Nels returned to Utah. Without sufficient funds to continue at Brigham Young Academy, he took a four-month job in Price teaching the eighth grade. It was his first white-collar job, but he found "teaching was work for which I was illy qualified."[23] He roomed with two unnamed University of Utah law students, who were out of school for the year to earn money to continue their education. They supported Nels's initial attempt at teaching and with "the guidance they gave helped me get through the four months without feeling myself a failure."[24] He earned less as a teacher than he had working on the railroad or in the Eureka mines. During the summer of 1916 he went to Bingham Canyon, where the pay was higher than at Eureka, although the mining reported to be more dangerous. The Bingham Canyon work proved unsatisfactory; lead poisoning was common in one mine and in the other excessive water made for miserable working conditions. Construction work building forms for the cement poured to construct the Mountain Dell Reservoir dam in Parley's Canyon east of Salt Lake City offered an alternative that Nels readily accepted.

In the fall of 1916, Nels encouraged his sister Belle to come to Utah to attend Brigham Young Academy with him. Without enough money to see them both through the school year, Nels borrowed money from Thomas Terry and worked again at Eureka during the Christmas break. When war was declared on April 6, 1917, many students arranged to take their exams early so they could enlist in the army.

Rumor held that college students who enlisted would have priority to become officers. Nels considered enlisting but, still in debt for both his and

Belle's school expenses, he opted to seek work. With America now at war, jobs were plentiful and, according to Nels, "It was like deciding which ripe apple to pick off a tree."[25]

He decided to go to Garfield, fourteen miles west of Salt Lake City. Nels started out building trestles but soon became a millwright helping to prepare a processing mill for the heavy equipment to be installed. Although Nels registered for the draft at Garfield, he felt guilty about not being in the army and was reluctant to discuss the war with his fellow workers.

While working at Garfield, Nels received a telegram from his mother that his father was dead. He had died by drowning while fishing when his boat capsized. His sister Belle received a similar telegram and that night they spent the evening "remembering and laughing about his ways of thinking and doing, all in respectful tribute," before Nels began the three-day journey to Michigan.[26]

Although he did not arrive in time for the funeral, the time with family was important. The brothers talked about enlisting soon. Nels returned to Utah to finish his work at Garfield before moving on to Oregon where he worked eight weeks at Fort Stevens constructing barracks and other buildings for the army. While in Oregon, Nels received word that Howard Blazzard, a fellow student at BYU and now principal of the church academy at St. Johns, wanted Nels to take a teaching job at the Arizona school. He accepted and reported to the St. Johns draft board, which arranged for his draft registration records to be transferred from Garfield to St. Johns. Nels informed the draft board that he preferred to enlist in the army as soon as the school year was over, rather than be drafted, and the board agreed.

The St. Johns experience proved to be much more enjoyable than had been the teaching assignment in Price. Nels was well-liked by the students, enjoyed the social climate of the Mormon community, found a new home with Grandma Lytle, and good companionship with her twenty-five-year-old daughter Nell. The 1917–1918 school year passed quickly and a few days after school ended, Nels enlisted and departed for Camp Funston, Kansas.

Nels Anderson served in the United States Army from April 27, 1918, until his discharge at Fort D. A. Russell, Wyoming, on August 2, 1919. His military service took him to Camp Funston, Kansas, for assignment to Company E of the 314th Engineers Regiment, 89th Division, and a few weeks of training before traveling by railroad to Camp Mills, New York, an embarkation camp for those going across the Atlantic. The twelve-day voyage on the ship *Carpathia* brought the 314th Regiment to Liverpool and a five-day stay in

England before crossing the English Channel to France on June 29, 1918. Nels participated in the St. Mihiel offensive in September, the Meuse-Argonne offensive in October, and was on the banks of the Meuse River outside the city of Stenay when the Armistice was signed on November 11, 1918. He marched into Germany on December 4, where he spent three months as part of the American occupation west of the Rhine River. He then returned to France to attend the University of Montpellier for three months before his departure on July 1, 1919, for home and discharge two days after his thirtieth birthday. The fifteen months of military service, the subject of this volume, was a small part of the ninety-seven years that Nels Anderson lived. Nevertheless, it was a time of transition and transformation. Although he would continue to write about hobos and workers the rest of his life, he left the ranks of the laboring hobo and never picked up a hammer or saw as a hired worker after his return. If his travels around the west as a free-spirited hard-working youth had given him some advantage in the classrooms of Dixie and Brigham Young Academies, his return from the battlefields of France, the villages of Germany, and the lecture halls at the University of Montpellier, brought an even greater measure of maturity, independence, and sophistication as he took up his studies at Brigham Young University (BYU) and continued on to graduate studies at the University of Chicago.

Upon returning to BYU for his final year, Nels was elected president of the class of 1920, a senior class that numbered sixteen and included his old Dixie friends, Sam Brooks and LeRoy Cox. With Cox as editor of the student paper, the *White and Blue*, and Anderson class president and responsible for the student annual, the *Banyan*, the 1919–1920 school year promised to be a memorable one. It was also a controversial one, as the returning veterans came into conflict with the school administration and LDS Church authorities on several points.

The first point of contention came when Anderson and others voiced their support for Woodrow Wilson's League of Nations, in opposition to the position of U.S. Senator and LDS Church apostle Reed Smoot and other Mormon leaders who saw the League as a threat. As events reached their climax, Anderson earned the wrath of Reed Smoot and was forced to write a formal letter of apology. In an effort to promote student interest in the BYU yearbook, he and W. P. Cottam, the yearbook photographer and future distinguished professor of botany at the University of Utah, doctored photographs from the university photo collection to "entertain" their fellow students at an assembly. When the photograph of two monkeys appeared on the screen, Anderson commented, "Smoot and Lodge are not the only ones talking about the League of Nations." Two of Reed Smoot's daughters were in the audience and informed their father that "Nels compared you to a monkey!" Smoot was incensed, resigning from the university's Board of Governors and demanding an apology from Anderson, "declaring that he would not tolerate any such ridicule that Anderson's motives were 'base,' and that his conduct had irrevocably sullied his, Smoot's reputation."[27]

This was not the last time Anderson challenged Reed Smoot and his politics. A far more sophisticated and wide-ranging criticism of Smoot as a United Sates senator came in 1926 with the publication of an essay by Anderson in the *American Mercury*, edited by H. L. Mencken. The essay was entitled "Pontifex Babbitt." Later, in 1958, when Alfred A. Knopf published excerpts of the essay in the anthology *Among the Mormons: Historic Accounts By Contemporary Observers*, edited by William Mulder and A. Russell Mortensen, Anderson recalled, "Some Mormons did not like this article. [The] last time Smoot stood for re-election, (to be defeated) his [opponent's] campaign workers asked permission to quote the article and they did."[28] Smoot, who had served five terms in the senate and who was known as "Dean of the Senate" because of his longevity, was defeated by Elbert Thomas, a Mormon and supporter of Franklin D. Roosevelt.

The second point of contention came when the class of 1920 was unsuccessful in raising sufficient funds to finance a suitable gift for the school. The class, undoubtedly influenced by Anderson and LeRoy Cox, hit on leaving as a legacy an idea—that BYU should become a real university, a "university in long-pants," with a genuine university atmosphere, higher standards, and recognition for BYU graduates equal to that for other university graduates.[29] University President George H. Brimhall saw the movement as subversive and a critical threat to his administration by campus "radicals." He passed his concerns on to LDS Church authorities and they sent David O. McKay, at that time one of the Twelve Apostles and later president of the church from 1951 to 1970, to meet with the alleged ringleader. According to Anderson's account, he was called out of class to meet with McKay:

He was sitting alone and did not shake hands or ask me to sit. He asked about "these demands" the senior students were making. I was not aware that we had made demands. I told what we were doing and gave

---

the several reasons why. After my two or three minutes of explanation about which he asked no questions, he spoke. "All I can say to you, young man, is follow your file leaders. Good day."[30]

Anderson reported the interview to the other class members who responded with anger and defiance. LeRoy Cox seethed, "When we went to war they called us men, now they treat us like children."[31] He proposed that the entire class disappear for a night and day, which they did, staying at a lodge in Provo Canyon with a married couple as chaperones. The administration and faculty did not respond openly and awarded their degrees, glad to be rid of Cox and Anderson, who headed off to the Dakotas to sell Utah knitted sweaters and underwear door to door.

During his senior year, Nels Anderson had been encouraged by Professor Swenson to give up the idea of becoming a lawyer and instead study sociology at the University of Chicago. The four months of peddling woolen goods earned the two graduates only two hundred dollars each—not enough to begin graduate school—so they opted to work the winter at a sugar factory near Salt Lake City and attend summer school at the University of Utah; the extra credits earned there would be accepted at the University of Chicago. Selling his treasured carpentry tools and making his farewell "ride on the rails" from Utah to Chicago, Nels Anderson entered a new phase of his life, one that took him from both the Mormon community and the life he had lived as a hobo and itinerant worker, and set him on the road to becoming one of America's most respected sociologists.

A week before registration for the fall term, Nels Anderson arrived in Chicago to look for lodging, a roommate, and work. He found part-time work at the Chicago Home for Incurables near the University of Chicago. His roommate, Guy Johnson, a graduate of Baylor University and a student of sociology, told Nels that as a veteran he could get his tuition paid by the Laura Spellman Rockefeller Fund. He introduced Anderson to Professor Albion W. Small, the dean of sociology professors at Chicago, who signed him up for classes, and Ernest W. Burgess, three years older than Nels, a modest, self-effacing professor who was easy to talk to and who became the chairman of Nels's thesis committee.

Reflecting on his acceptance into the University of Chicago sociology department, Nels remembered, "I had nothing in academic knowledge to offer when I applied for admission to the department. That I was accepted at all surprised me. In the interview with Albion W. Small...I seemed more unpromising with each of my answers, causing little frowns. His interest picked up when he began asking personal questions, how I reached Chicago on freight trains with less than twenty dollars and my seeming lack of anxiety about getting by, supporting myself as a student. I wondered since how he would have justified accepting me."[32]

Nels began his studies knowing little about theories and the literature of sociology. Guy Johnson helped to fill the voids and explained that Nels would need to identify a special interest in sociology on which to focus his study. About six months after arriving at the University of Chicago, Nels attended a lecture for social workers by Ben L. Reitman, a physician who specialized in venereal diseases.[33] During the discussion period Nels objected to the doctor's lumping working hobos with the tramps and bums who did not work. Reitman encouraged Nels to undertake a study of the "homeless man," and secured funding from the United Charities, a leading private welfare agency, that provided Nels with ninety-five dollars a month for a stipend and expenses for a year to study homeless men in Chicago. The funding allowed Nels to quit his part-time job at the Chicago Home for Incurables and to spend more time interacting with fellow students in discussing methods and theories of sociology. Yet his fellow students had, in Nels's estimation, little interest or understanding of the homeless. As Nels reflected, "If I spoke of the hobo or other men in my sector of Chicago, their ways of life and work, it was all remote from their understanding. They would respond with some sort of weary willie humor, which reminded me over and over of a sort of culture gap between my colleagues and me. It seemed wise to talk as little as possible about my study among my middle-class fellows; their values and outlook were so different from mine."[34]

The study was to focus on the homeless men and the area around Madison Street that they occupied. Nels had a clear understanding of what was needed and how to proceed.

I knew that such a study should identify the different types of homeless men in Chicago, who they were, from whence they came, where they had been over the years, what sort of work they had done and where. I knew one would have to talk to many men, talk to some several times and one would need a system for gathering and recording the information.

Belatedly the thought came that a study of the men would not be complete without much information about Madison Street, why men gathered there and not elsewhere, and about what kept them there, or in any other Main Stem. There would have to be descriptions of typical restaurants, saloons, flophouses, missions and other establishments.[35]

Throwing himself wholeheartedly into the research, and working long hours every day, he collected material for a thousand-page study of the homeless. He painfully condensed this to a volume of 302 pages published in 1923 as *The Hobo: The Sociology of the Homeless Man*, the first in a series of studies of the urban community and city life from the University of Chicago Press. In addition to its vivid portrayal of life for the working hobo, the book called attention to the economic importance of the itinerant workers as they fulfilled a vital role in railroad construction, mining, timber, and agriculture comparable to that of the merchant seaman, the oil-field workers, and the free-roaming cowboy.

The Hobo fulfilled the requirement for a master's degree, which was awarded in 1925, but the study did not land a much-desired permanent teaching position. Professor Burgess did arrange for him to gain teaching experience as an instructor for a class in sociology in Elkhart, Indiana. Burgess also recommended Nels for a teaching position at Rockford College for Women. He did not get the position and learned indirectly that it was because "some professors objected to me because of my identifying with hobos. They thought it meant equal familiarity with 'other underworld characters.'"[36] Finally, with Burgess's help he secured a temporary six-month appointment for two quarters of the 1925–1926 school year at the University of Washington in Seattle as a replacement for R. D. McKenzie, who was on leave.

The University of Washington experience convinced Nels even more that a professorship would be the preferred occupation, but with no opportunity to land a teaching position on the West Coast, Nels returned east where a former professor, William I. Thomas, recommended him for a part-time teaching position at the New School for Social Research in New York City. During the next four years, 1926 to 1930, Nels cobbled out a life as a teacher, researcher, writer, and student. He taught extension classes and worked on studies of the YMCA in New York and other related topics. In 1928 his *Urban Sociology*, one of the first textbooks on the subject, was published by Alfred A. Knopf. He earned money as a freelance writer, publishing articles in the *American Mercury*, the *New Republic*, *Century*, and *Outlook*. He also took classes at New York University and, at the age of forty, completed his doctoral dissertation, "The Social Antecedents of a Slum: A Developmental Study of the East

Harlem Area of Manhattan Island, New York City," in 1930. In 1931 he wrote *Milk and Honey Route: A Handbook for Hobos* published under the pseudonym Dean Stiff.

With the Great Depression just beginning, the early 1930s was not an ideal time to land a teaching job in the social sciences, as the prospects of a university professorship were slim to nonexistent. The challenges of the Depression did offer employment possibilities to individuals with the training and experience to work in state and federal government bureaucracies seeking to ease the Depression-related human suffering.

During his work in New York City, Nels became acquainted with Harry Hopkins, who directed the newly established New York Emergency Relief Administration under Governor Franklin D. Roosevelt. Nels's first assignment was to work with veterans and participants in the Bonus March on Washington DC. President Herbert Hoover refused to meet with the marchers and requested the governors of the states to ask the veterans to return home. In a spirit of cooperation Governor Roosevelt agreed, assigning Harry Hopkins responsibility for the task. Hopkins, in turn, hired Nels to do the frontline work of contacting participants and arranging transportation home for those in emergency situations. The project ended when Hoover ordered the military under Douglas MacArthur to drive the Bonus Army out of Washington.

Hopkins then sent Anderson west to Buffalo, where the port city on Lake Erie was being overwhelmed by increasing numbers of idle merchant seamen. He established a center for the unemployed seamen that Hopkins found to be successful. After the election of Franklin D. Roosevelt in 1932 and Hopkins's appointment to head the Federal Emergency Relief Administration (FERA), Hopkins asked Anderson in 1934 to move to Washington DC as the labor relations officer for FERA. Of the work, Anderson wrote:

> My office was there to handle complaints and demands. Trade unions complained that jobs were for "reliefers," too few for the union members. Industrialists complained continually, holding that work relief was preventing recovery, standing in the way of private enterprise. All work projects, they argued, took business from the private sector. Minority groups in hundreds of communities claimed they were discriminated against in getting work relief jobs. Often they were.
>
> Most demands came from unions of the unemployed, mainly in cities. Understandably, they wanted higher payments or they wanted higher classifications. The allowances were too low and the number of

jobs available, around three million, was far too few. Funds provided by the Congress were never ample. We had to meet the delegations and in our office, as in the state offices there were sit-in strikes.[37]

Anderson worked effectively in the environment that existed under Harry Hopkins, but for other New Dealers, such as Rexford G. Tugwell, considered the most left-wing member of Roosevelt's "Brain Trust" and known in inner circles as "The Bolshevik," Anderson had nothing but contempt. Tugwell earned a PhD in economics from the University of Pennsylvania and helped draft the Agricultural Adjustment Act and the National Industrial Recovery Act before his appointment to head the Resettlement Administration. Anderson admitted, "I never liked him. He was a half-assed politician and a half-assed liberal, and you didn't know which half to look at."[38]

Although he was invited to the White House on at least two occasions, Anderson never wrote about his relations with or feelings for the president and first lady. He did, however, in conversation note that "Mrs. Roosevelt was taken in by all the liberal groups…[and was] always putting pressure on her poor husband to do things." As for the president, Anderson's only comment was that he "had a technique for pushing your hand away as he shook it."[39]

In addition to his full-time job with the Roosevelt administration, Nels Anderson carried out the research and writing of his important history, *Desert Saints: The Mormon Frontier in Utah*, published by the University of Chicago Press in 1942. The book took six years to write and according to Anderson, "The writing of *Desert Saints* was slow work; it was done in Washington as my regular job allowed. As the fact-gathering continued, my 'project' became my hobby, taking every hour I could spare over six years. As is usual with hobbies, it became a work of love. The book served as a link between my real occupation and the one I had dreamed of."[40] In 1933 Nels obtained a Social Science Research Council grant-in-aid and a grant from the Social Science Council of Columbia University to study Mormon communities and families. He used the grant to spend four months during the summer of 1934 in St. George researching *Desert Saints.*

Anderson remained at his post in the New Deal relief work until the outbreak of World War II, when he moved to the War Shipping Administration, the agency responsible for training new seamen and operating centers for seamen around the world in a coordinated effort to meet the tremendous wartime demand for thousands of seamen. When no one could be found to accept the assignment for the Persian Gulf area, Nels "volunteered for the job, the feeling I had during World War I, to be in action."[41]

A key responsibility was to facilitate the shipment of food and matériel sent from the United States to assist the Russians in their fight against Nazi Germany. Anderson also sought to meet the needs of seamen and to serve as a labor relations broker between the ship owners and the laborers. He walked a fine line between the seamen and the military, to whose discipline both he and the civilian merchantmen were subject, but who had no appreciation for the dangerous work that the "hobos of the sea" performed. His work took him throughout the Persian Gulf and to Egypt, India, and after the war was over, to London.

In 1946 Anderson returned to the United States and worked for a short time for the Federal Housing Administration trying to increase apprentice training in the construction trades before taking a job with the United States Military Government (OMGUS) in Germany. He crossed the Atlantic once again in 1947 and traveled to Berlin where he found the once-proud city in ruins.[42]

His initial assignment was to interview Germans about anti-Semitism to understand the past persecution of Jews and to assess whether the anti-Semitism that had resulted in the death of more than six million Jews had diminished and would possibly disappear in postwar Germany. He also taught an English class for Berliners before his relocation first to Frankfurt, then to Bonn.

He was soon moved into the labor relations section of the military government with the assignment of helping reestablish trade unions and specifically unions free of communist influence. Two labor academies were established to train leaders, some of whom were brought to the United States to see American labor relations first hand. One of Anderson's assignments was to secure funding for several research projects to study socioeconomic problems relevant to German workers.[43] One series of studies was carried out with research grants to ten German graduate students who examined the question of how the heavily bombed city of Darmstadt went through the recovery process to become economically and socially viable once again. Anderson took pride in the fact that the students used their studies to meet the dissertation requirements for PhD degrees from the University of Frankfurt.

After seven years of employment with the High Commission and then the United States State Department, Anderson was "retired" from his civil service position six months before the mandatory retirement age of sixty-five. With some bitterness, Anderson considered the premature retirement as a way for State Department officials to avoid terminating him. The State Department was considered to be politically conservative, antilabor, and fearful of the McCarthy-era probe for communists and socialists in government agencies. Anderson, whose pro-union sympathies and work in the Federal Emergency Relief Administration and the Works Progress Administration during the New Deal were well known, had been investigated at least three times while with the High Commission in an unsuccessful search for communist connections and disloyal activities. The State Department saw Anderson as a liability and, without consulting him, initiated his retirement and directed him to return to the United States.

The government pension fell far short of Anderson's needs, and he knew he would need to continue to work to meet his obligations. During his years with the High Commission, Anderson had worked with a considerable number of German and European academics. They recommended him for the position of director of research at the UNESCO Institute for Social Science in Cologne. As no suitable European scholar was willing to take the position because of its uncertain future, Anderson was offered the job. Having given up hope of ever becoming a professor and with personal ties to Germany, he welcomed the offer and served as director for nine years until the office closed in 1963 and its programs and projects transferred to Cologne University.

At age seventy-five and once again looking for employment, the offer of a one-year visiting professorship at Memorial University in St. John's, Newfoundland, was a godsend. In Canada Anderson at last found a home and an academic position that had long eluded him. He taught at Memorial University for two years—1963 to 1965. During the summers he taught at the University of New Brunswick in Fredericton. The second summer UNB offered him a professorship. Because he was over the age of sixty-five he was not eligible for a tenured position, but it was understood that he would be a "visiting professor" for as long as he could or wanted to teach.[44] During his time at UNB, he served as head of the Sociology and Anthropology Department and saw the establishment of a separate Department of Sociology with a PhD program. As if making up for lost time, Anderson excelled as a teacher while continuing a full schedule of research and writing. Before he stopped teaching in 1977 at the age of eighty-eight, the university students had honored him by dedicating their 1972 yearbook to him, and the university undergraduate sociology students by naming their club the Nels Anderson Society.

Graduate students attend classes in the Nels Anderson Seminar Room graced by a portrait of the venerated professor painted by Stephen Scott. The University of New Brunswick awarded Anderson an honorary doctor's degree in 1972, and his sociology colleagues with an honorary life membership in the Canadian Sociology and Anthropology Association in 1977. Nels Anderson continued to live in Fredericton and remained academically active until a month before his death on October 8, 1986, at the age of ninety-seven.

1

CAMP MILLS, NEW YORK, JUNE 1918

APPLIED FOR ENLISTMENT TO LOCAL BOARD SALT LAKE COUNTY SOME time in March 1918 got my exam in Arizona passed and as soon as my school got out reported to draft board 8 St. Johns.[1] Got sent to Funston applied to get into Engineers. Did some training at Funston but the Division began moving shortly after I was assigned.[2]

We entrained for the coast about May 28 and went via Chicago, Buffalo, and Hoboken thence to Long Island.

Stayed at Camp Mills several days stocking up and checking up.[3] I was dreading the sea voyage more and more as the days passed and we got reports of our ships being torpedoed by U boats.[4]

I kept a diary all the while till we departed but I feared to take it across so sent what I had written back to friends. I thought that I might get it later if I were permitted return. Since I have returned I find I had no desire to get it for the life of a soldier is so well known and that it would be very common place.[5] I have copied my overseas diary. I figured I may as well keep it. It is a very common place record but is a true one and may be of interest to someone sometime. At least it will keep me from getting my experiences mixed with the other fellows.

JUNE 9, SUNDAY I cut my diary in half today and sent the first half home. It looks very much like we will be gone tomorrow and I might lose what I have written. In this business one can never tell what the morrow will bring and the record of the few weeks I have been in the army might interest some one.

I loafed today, the first time since I have been in the uniform. I allowed myself to be too lazy to write letters. It is one of those dreamy warm days one reads about in "Their Yesterdays."[6] My wants today could have been easily satisfied—a visit to a cool milk celler [sic] after that lay on the grass in the shade and sleep. If I get out of the army I am going to take a week and relax. I feel like one who has been driven.

We didn't do much today but eat and police up. I spent most of my time at the Y.M.C.A. mincing through the books and magazines.[7] We are under orders now to be packed up so that has delayed somewhat my getting to a service. I will be late but I think I shall go down perhaps I will hear something good. I need a little religion to buck me up. Several "Y" Huts here most of them are holding forth, like the soldiers, in tents. This evening there are several religious services going on.

JUNE 10 Monday, a day of uncertainty. Last night they kept us so agitated with contradictory orders that I didn't get to go to the "Y" service. We packed our barracks bags. We packed them three times and packed them four times. Each time we put in what they said and each time we kept out what they said but there is such a confusion of things here that no one seems to know yet what goes in the bags or what stays on our packs. As it is we have all our equipment that we usually carry besides overcoat, rain coat, shoes, and a lot of personal stuff we hate to part with, in and on the pack. Mine is as big and as heavy as a shock of wheat. In the barracks bags go all the stuff we don't need to use on the trip. These bags are sacks made out of overalls goods they hold about a bushel.

I used to think it took courage to be a soldier but I have decided that I have had more call for patience.

I was late to reveille this morning but no one saw me slip into the line. We had a good breakfast but not half enough. Eggs, spuds, mush and bread. After breakfast we started packing our barracks bags again. We also rolled our packs. Then we had venereal inspection.[8] This is probably the last inspection we have before we go on the water. Several fellows were culled out of the company. Some were glad and others had to fight back the tears. There are a few fellows in the company who don't want to go across. One fellow was as blue that when word was brought that his mother had come clear from Missouri to see him, he didn't have spunk enough to go down to the information bureau to hunt her up. The fellows hooted him so that he had to go.

Just before dinner we carried our barrack bags over to another part of the camp and loaded them in boxcars, good riddance.

Nothing to do this afternoon but stay around. I'd feel better if I could work. I get nervous when left alone with my thoughts. I notice most of the fellows are but they keep their minds occupied hanging around the canteen trying to buy something. I want to be there too for I have of late an unexplainable craving for sweets but I have so little money that I think I better hold it in reserve.

I sent for some books to New York. A letter came this afternoon saying they had been sent chances are we will leave and I will have neither books or money.

Orders tonight that we leave 3 o'clock in the morning. I will not go to bed as it's too much trouble rolling and unrolling the pack. I imagine we will learn a lot in the next two weeks but I don't think I would go back now if I could.

JUNE 11, TUESDAY   I slept in my overcoat and slicker last night. Got along nicely but for my knees. These new overcoats are too short for blankets on a cold night. It rained all night; that with the cold helped us to rise without a bugle at 3:30. We found the camp flooded, in the tents and out. Plenty of mud. Breakfast of potatoes (we ate them skins and all) corn beef and coffee. The only virtue any of it had was that it was warm. After breakfast we cleaned the place up and lined up for departure.

They march us about a mile to the station. There must have been a lot of red tape to it for we had our packs on nearly two hours before they got us to a place where we could rest while they brought our cars up.

On the way to Brooklin [Brooklyn] we had strict orders not to raise windows to talk or write or in any way communicate with anyone. Lest the[y] find out we are coming. We thought we would go somewhere else to embark than the place we are (Hoboken)[9] We are not allowed to tell where we are, where we went or how we went. It is best not to mention names or numbers or facts so I propose to keep such stuff out of my diary. (all the forbidden things I am putting in from memory as I copy my diary from notes.)

We crossed from Brooklin on a big car ferry came down the East River under those big bridges and across the mouth of the Hudson past those great skyscrapers. It made me think of the pictures in the geography.

After a great deal of roll calling and checking to see if we were still under our packs they marched us on the ship then led us four floors down into the hull of the vessel. They gave me a very isolated bunk in a very obscure corner. Fortunately there is a porthole by my bunk. It is big enough to put ones head through which is very convenient in case I find it necessary to feed the fishes.[10] It is worse than a steerage bunk but I care not as long as it lands me safe.

The most popular subject is submarines. It is only a few days since they sank ships not far from here off the Jersey coast. Of course we must be willing to take the chance so will the subs.

We can see the effect of war already on foreign countries. This is an English boat manned by Englishmen many of them Tommies who have done their bit the rest are men and boys too old or too young for service. I notice that all the ocean going vessels are painted like crazy quilts. It is to deceive subs. The sandwiches went fine. They gave us a feed after we got on the boat but the mess hall is so greasy and stinking I dared not eat till I was hungrier. I have too little money to pay 5 cents each for apples, so it looks like my stomach is doomed to suffer.

2

CROSSING THE ATLANTIC, JUNE 1918

THE TWELVE-DAY VOYAGE ACROSS THE ATLANTIC WAS AN ORDEAL FOR Nels Anderson, as it was for nearly every other American soldier transported on the fleets of ships that took them to France. Fortunately for Nels Anderson, the crossing was made during the more pleasant days at the end of spring in good weather when the harsh turbulent winter storms did not add to the danger and misery.

The German submarine or U-boat remained a threat to Allied transports and Nels Anderson recounts the rumors and fears of his traveling companions without discounting them. Cautious and aware of the dangers that the frigid waters of the Atlantic held for survivors of a torpedoed ship, the passengers on board the *Carpathia* in June 1918 were relatively secure from the threat of enemy submarines. This was not because of a shortage of German submarines, which at their peak in October 1917 numbered 127. In the fourteen months since the United States declared war on Germany, US Navy Admiral William S. Sims had implemented the convoy system with groups of ships sailing under the protection of fast moving destroyers armed with newly developed depth charges loaded with three hundred pounds of TNT. In addition, a listening device had been perfected which could detect and determine the direction of submarines up to twenty miles away. Other weapons in the arsenal against the submarines were 110-foot-long submarine chasers, modeled on New England fishing boats, reconnaissance aircraft, and a North Sea mine barrage that stretched from Scapa Flow at the extreme northern end of the British Isles eastward to near the west coast of Sweden.[1] Despite these measures, German U-boats did sink three transports on the eastbound voyage—the *Tuscania* with the loss of 13 members of the 32nd Division, the *Moldavia* with 56 men from the Fourth Division, and the *Ticonderoga* with the loss of 215 soldiers and sailors.[2] In addition German submarines sank four westbound transports including the *Carpathia*, the ship which Nels Anderson boarded on June 11, 1918, which went down on July 17, 1918, 120 miles west of Fastnet, Ireland, while traveling in a convoy bound for Boston. Five crew were killed and the remaining crew and fifty-seven passengers were picked up by H.M.S. *Snowdrop* and returned to Liverpool.

The *Carpathia* was launched from Wallsend-on-Tyne on August 6, 1902. The twin screw Cunard steamship was 558 feet in length and 64 feet 3 inches wide with a depth of 40 feet and gross tonnage of 13,603 tons. The *Carpathia* made its initial voyage leaving Liverpool on May 5, 1903, for New York City. The vessel was used by wealthy Americans for summer cruises between the United States and Europe with stops at Liverpool, Gibraltar, Genoa, Naples, and, at times Messina, and Palermo. The ship also carried immigrants, mostly Hungarian, from Triest and Fiume to the United States. In 1912 the *Carpathia* was the first vessel to reach the survivors of the *Titanic*. It was modified for service as a troopship after the United States entered the war.[3]

In the twelve entries that cover the trip from New York to Liverpool, Nels Anderson offers an insightful description of life for the American soldiers on board the ship. It is clear that the trip was no vacation cruise. Men were assigned a small bunk where they spent most of their time when not allowed on deck. Food was horrible—made worse, Anderson suggests—because the crew of the *Carpathia* was British, not American. Seasickness and stench accompanied most of the men from the beginning of the trip to the end. Good water was scarce. The trip was as Anderson writes, "a good test of patriotism," and he vowed that "if I live through this trip and through the war, I'll never leave the U.S. again for pleasure or profit."

JUNE 12, WEDNESDAY   Our first day at sea. I have been looking forward to and, in a way, dreading this day for a long time. Now that we are at sea I suppose that it would be no offense to write about the ship we are on at least. Surely this is a bit of information that the Germans won't profit by. This is the "Carpathia."[4] An old freighter with place above for a few passengers. She has been fitted out to carry about three thousand soldiers in the places where she used to carry beef and pig iron. She travels about 15 miles an hour and her tonnage is about 300 car loads. She was the first ship to arrive on the scene to rescue the survivors of the "Titanic" in 1913.[5] We laid at the dock all night but pulled away at breakfast time. A tug towed us part of the way out but now we are traveling on our own power. Going out of the harbor we passed hundreds of ships riding at anchor. I had no idea that there were so many ships. Many of them were small tramp schooners that I imagine engaged in coast trade though many of them had the oversea paint on.

I saw my first sub-chasers today. They are a speedy snappy little boat but I'll see more of them. I wanted most to see the statue of liberty. She is the only girl some of us will have for the next few months. At least the one we are to fight for. I did not get to though for she was on the other side of the vessel. All of the world I could see was from my little port hole on the starboard. They kept all of us out of sight going out of the harbor for reasons that are very evident whether necessary or not. It was not long till an order came to close all port holes so we are left in the dark but for a feeble electric light here and there.

Some more orders—never go on deck without your life preserver. Always have on your belt (cartridge [*sic*] belt) with your first aid packet and your canteen full of water. Failure means court martial.

Towards evening they permitted us to go out on the deck. No land in sight. We were one ship in a group of twelve. There wasn't a sub-chaser or a battleship in sight. They are what we are most interested in but I suppose the powers that be are providing ample protection. They put us through our first fire drill. I am assigned to a raft. It is 4 x 5 feet and 8 inches thick. 15 men are assigned to each raft. I don't know how many are in a boat.

There is a great deal of sea sickness. Fellows are vomiting everywhere so besides all the horrible smells that were here we have added the smell of vomit. No ventilation. Every one who knows how is cursing unless he is too sick. There are two canteens on the ship at which the men buy oranges and apples. They throw the paper and peelings on the floor all of which makes more slop and stink. If the British came to America under worse conditions in worse boats to fight us then we owe a great deal of thanks to the ocean for fighting our battle.

JUNE 13, THURSDAY   About 11:00 o'clock last night we were routed out for fire drill. I didn't get out of bed till orders were changed. It was just an alarm to see if we were on the alert. We were instructed not to undress and never to get away from our life preservers. From now on we go to bed by merely laying down with our shoes on.

I didn't eat any breakfast. I could[n't] muster the courage. I wasn't exactly sick. I haven't been but I have a very juggy feeling from the bad air. I spent some time oiling my gun but most of the forenoon I spent out on deck in the fresh air. The air was cold. There was nothing to see or talk about. Not even a sea gull. Some of the fellows claim they saw some fish. I wasn't that lucky. Even the ships that were with us yesterday have left us and are out of sight. It seems that we are as helpless as the ship is slow.

Many of the boys are still sick. Few showed up for dinner. We had a pretty fair feed too. Meat, beans and rice. The Y.M.C.A. has opened up a little library. I read a copy of Kiplings short stories. They didn't appeal to me so I drew another book out "Lions of the Lord."[6] It turned out to be a story about the Mormons. It tells of their sufferings in the East and their hard journey west. The author is partly sympathetic and still prejudiced, especially in his interpretation of doctrines.

If I could eat the chow they feed us I would be all right. I have no sea sickness, just hunger and my stomach still revolts at the menu.

JUNE 14, FRIDAY   This promises to be anything but a pleasure trip. My fond wish is that time would pass faster. We learned this morning why it is a good thing to keep port holes closed in day time. Today Henricks, my corporal, had his head out the hole, enjoying the scenery as well as the air when a huge wave slapped the side of the vessel. It not only wet him all through but it filled his bunk with salt water till he had to dip it out with his cup. He got salt water on everything he had that would rust so he spent the rest of the day cleaning.

I didn't have any appetite so didn't go to breakfast. I did try to eat some of the dinner but didn't go to supper.[7] I have resolved that if I live through this trip and through the war I'll never leave the U.S. again for either pleasure or profit.[8] I wonder if all the soldiers who cross have to ride under such wretched conditions. It's too bad but if it is the best Uncle Sam can do and if it will win the war we ought to be willing to stand it. A trip like this is a good test for patriotism. I wish some of the folks at home who hate to do without sugar and white flour had to take it.[9]

At 9:00 o'clock we had inspection, at 10:00 o'clock boat drill and a lecture on getting over board by men as green as ourselves who received their lecture from green men over them. We would have little system in case of need. Each crew is supposed to throw their raft over and then jump in after it. It's about 30 feet to the water. Men are apt to jump on one another but that is a chance we have to take.

The sun beat down all day. There was little breeze so nearly everyone who could get on deck was out lying in the sun. The boat was rocking a great deal from the swells and it was hard to walk around on the deck without stepping on fellows as the vessel reeled. Many of the men would spend their time hanging over the rail watching the water. There is nothing to see in the water except swells and blue but still one likes to watch that. The very immensity of the sea is an awe to us land lubbers.

We are not allowed to throw anything over board (we have been told too, that if anyone falls overboard he must stay. The ship will not stop to pick anyone up). One man was given K.P. for the rest of the trip for throwing an orange peel overboard. Most of the slops are "officially" thrown out at night lest the subs see that ships have passed this way. Such orders are made by our army officers. The crew of the ship make mock at the idea and throw stuff out at will.

I am still reading the book I started yesterday. The author does not hit the bulls eye of truth. The story is cast and staged in Southern Utah around the Mountain Meadows. I don't think the author has been in Dixie and he certainly never looked into the history of the people of Southern Utah much less study their religion that he misinterprets so.[10]

JUNE 15, SATURDAY I am out on the deck writing this. There is a lively breeze and the sky is cloudy but I feel fine. I had a good nights sleep. I ate no breakfast and I shaved and changed under clothes, all of which has helped produce the desirable effect.

Well we have either caught up to the transports that ran away from us the other day or else they have waited for us. At least we are plodding long at the tail of the convoy of 12 ships. Way out ahead of us sometimes we can only see its smoke, is the battleship acting as our escort. I am thinking as I look at this convoy of troop ships plowing their way eastward—what a fine picture to send the Kaiser. This is what the Lusitania is bringing as democracy's answer to the war lords of Germany.

I spent the day learning the semaphore. The semaphore is a system of signaling used by the boy scouts. I don't know whether the boy scouts originated it or not but we are expected to learn to send messages by the semaphore system.[11]

Last evening the 330th Infantry band entertained us after that the chaplin [chaplain] preached but I did not attend. I wasn't in tune.

I neglected to mention that I saw some big fish yesterday. They would weigh about 200# [pounds] each. I have learned since that they were dolphins (whatever they are). Some of the men claim that they have seen sea lions and flying fish which, of course is possible.

Evening—all in all a pleasant day. We had a knot tying class this afternoon. I watched the ships signaling to each other by the semaphore system and I was sorry I could not catch what they were saying.

We had to go out on the deck for exercise this afternoon. The ship rocked so that it was hard to stand. Most of us are beginning to feel good again only we are hungry for something good to eat. If I could get at someone's milk celler it would please me as well.

They gave us fish and prunes for supper. Fish were wretched though the prunes were good. After supper they herded us all below with orders to stay there till we had been inspected. A bed inspection this time. In the army they seem to fall over each other trying to invent new kinds of inspections. After that we remained below "in the 'atch" as the Tommies say singing and yelling and cracking jokes about the fish that some of the fellows had to vomit up. I wish I had a good drink of water. I can't drink the junk they have in these barrels it is worse than alkali.

JUNE 16, SUNDAY   Next Sunday I hope we are not rocking in the cradle of the deep. We ought to be in merry England. They came around this morning to count us. It was rumored that a man fell over board last night. If he did he has my sympathy for a man over on this trip is S.O.L.[12]

He wouldn't be missed much in a ship load but a fire side somewhere would be saddened by his absence.

I didn't like the sound of the menu so I didn't go up to breakfast. The cooks are so sloppy and dirty that they should be court martialed. They are all English men and seem to think that anything is good enough for the "bloody Yankees".[13] It is criminal to ask men to wash their dishes as we do. 950 men eat in the same mess hall I do and they all wash their kits in two tubs of water. Before half of them are through it is worse than swill.

I took a shower bath with salt water this morning. It is so hard that it is useless to use soap. Even when one takes a bath he must hang his life preserver up near. It may be necessary to have it and then some one may steal it. 2 men serving K.P. now for losing their life preservers.

A Tommy tried to sell me some raisin rolls. They were about as big as the graham muffins Nell used to make.[14] They sold at a very moderate price, 3 for 25 cents. He stole them from their mess. These Tommies don't eat the same stuff they feed us.

10:00 o'clock fire drill. Crew from raft 15 (mine) fell from grace because two men failed to appear at roll call. After drill venereal and lice inspection.

This afternoon I was unlucky. The O.D. [Officer of the Day] found some orange peel in the aisle where my bunk is. 40 men sleep in the aisle but he only found three of us. He made us clean up the whole deck. That is the worst kind of injustice but one has to take it and say nothing. I wouldn't mind so much if I had not been so particular not to throw stuff on the floor. Such treatment will make the best of men sour.

I blowed myself this afternoon for a couple of bottles of ginger ale. I couldn't drink the stuff so I gave it to a fellow in "F" company. I learned of a job that is open in the boiler room think I will apply. A great many soldiers are working down there they get 25 cents an hour.[15]

I got in an argument with a fellow this afternoon over the American press. I held that most of the news we got in the U.S. was colored and that anything in the line of opinion was apt to be colored with what we wanted to be true. Even official reports in war time were tempered with the spirit of the times.

At a time like this we are always listening for as much bad as we can about the enemy. We shut our ears to good things. Certainly all the bad in the world isn't in Germany. Well this fellow called me pro German which made me mad and [I] retaliated by telling him that I volunteered for the service where as he was drafted, which after all is no test of ones patriotism.

I wrote, or rather started, a long letter to Nell this evening. I can find plenty to write about.

JUNE 17, MONDAY   They say a fast ocean liner passed us last night. One thing certain, it wouldn't have to be very fast to pass us. This vessel is so slow that all the others have to zig zag back and forth to give us a chance to keep up. This is a beautiful day and the world looks brighter than anytime on the trip. We are getting the boat cleaned up so it does not stink as it used to. There are only a few foul smells remaining and they seem to be native with the vessel. Dinner was good but the breakfast was abominable—liver and bacon and bread. Dinner beans, beef and bread. I have had a hard time drinking either the water or the coffee of late so I have tried a new stunt cheap too—one lemon three drinks, three lemons ten cents.

Before I came to the war I did think I was humble but never so much as now. It looks like there is a lot more of it coming before the thing is over.

I hope that when we get to the end of this trip they stop a few days near some big city. I want to get a chance to do some studying. I want to study something about military engineering even if it doesn't help me to get along better in the army it will be of value when I get out—if I get out. Very often I feel like I am not going to cross this ocean again. I feel little and insignificant as a lamb must feel that goes to the slaughter. I wouldn't get out of it if I could and knew that death was ahead. It would be worse than death to turn back on some petty excuse and for the next 40 years make apologies for myself. Now if I come out all together I can be proud of the little part I played and my friends won't have to help me find excuses. No young man's future is worth much if he has shirked his duty in this war. The men who rule in the U.S. for a long time to come are going to be those who have played their part in overthrowing autocracy. I expect to go to congress some day and I can't afford to have a slacker record against me.[16]

My time has been spent in studying the semaphore and in writing letters that I will mail later. I make myself ridiculous sometimes waving my arms about trying to make the letters of the alphabet. I am progressing nicely. I am getting so I can spell words.

JUNE 18, TUESDAY   I went down into the engine room this morning. It is great to watch those big engines work. They look like they are big enough to pump water enough to irrigate a county. I went down to get a job firing but all they could do was to take my name in case they needed someone later. There were about 40 names ahead of me, of other yanks who were broke, so I gave it up as a bad job. Posters have been pasted up all over the ship warning us to write nothing home about the morale location or number of troops. Nothing must be said or written in any form or manner that would give information to the enemy. Soldiers are to cease talking about the war or the army among themselves and last but not least soldiers must cease criticizing among themselves. The army is not a place for opinions but for effort. This is but one form of discipline and we must have discipline to win.

I think it is a good thing even if it does go against the grain. But the funny part of it is that cussing and grumbling has increased. Men who were generally quiet are saying harsh things against militarism. I propose to conform. I think it is for the best that we submit for a while to a certain amount of bondage for the sake of victory. Herewith I resolve to keep a stiff upper lip and in all cases whether I am treated fair or not to keep the corners of my mouth screwed up and my tongue still.

Some of the fellows tried to tell me that diary's were forbidden but I am going to keep on writing mine until they stop me.[17] I think I am safe as long as I don't put anything down that would not pass in a letter. There is a certain amount of comfort in a diary. It is a sort of companion but a war diary must not be a confidential companion.

It seems that more than two thirds of these fellows smoke cigarettes. I mention it because their supply is getting low and some of them are, for that reason, very miserable.

I wrote a letter to Grandma Lytle and am just finishing one to Mr. Prescott.[18]

Before going to bed someone treated us with some apples. The money came from some fund I know not where. I know I got two pretty good apples and went to bed with a good taste in my mouth.

JUNE 19, WEDNESDAY   We must be getting near to the other side. There is so much fog around us that we can't see more than a mile away. We are probably striking the Gulf Stream.

Early this morning or late last night I can't say, I know I was dreaming of being in Salt Lake City when I was awakened from my reverie by the whistle to fallout for life boat drill we no more than got started than they told us to go to sleep again. It was very thoughtful of them to wake us at that hour. It was to get us in the habit of starting quick and keeping our stuff together in case we are hit. A very good hint. I sleep with my stuff tied to my leg so no one can grab it before I wake up.

Gee! I'd hate to be torpedoed at night. More men would be killed by jumping in the dark than would drown. If a man jumps 30 feet and lands with hobnail shoes on another fellows head someone will go down with out drowning. I figure it is safer to get off last than first so if we are hit I am going to take my time. This afternoon at fire drill it took 5 minutes for all the men to get on the deck and in their places. In case of danger there would be a lot of confusion and many would be hurt.

I wrote a letter today to a girl in Nebraska who wrote to me just before we left Camp Mills.[19] While I was writing the chaplin came into the room and started a meeting. He preached a good sermon in which he told us "ye are the salt of the earth."

We had a pretty good super but for some fish. The fish were good but they were cooked so very few of the fellows ate them. Mike Hart said that those fish never were caught. They got tired of living and just "gave up."

JUNE 20, THURSDAY   We had a regular hoe down dance last night. A poor place to dance, only a mouth organ to step to and a dearth of girls but we danced just the same. Following the dance we had a squaw wrestle and then our captain brought a couple of cases of oranges down out of which we got two a piece.

Not a ship in sight. They are probably near but there is a drizzly fog that obscures the vision. I had to help clean up quarters today then we had to stand out on the deck in the rain for an hour till we were inspected.

All of the fellows who have money are not eating at the mess but are eating out of the canteen. It is costing them in some $3 and $4.00 a day. I prefer not to do that because I only have five dollars and I might need it worse before the end of the trip. Many of the fellows are going broke. There is a great deal of gambling going on which is breaking some of them. Four of the fellows were arrested today for gambling. But there is a lot of it in the army especially crap shooting.

Well we had a big "Sing" this afternoon led by a real live "Y" man. I sang "Throw out The Lifeline", "Let the Lower Lights be Burning" and a lot others till I was hoarse.[20] Then the chaplin talked to us a while. I believe I am going to like our chaplin.

We spent about an hour this afternoon knot tying then I wrote a long crazy letter to Eva Overson.[21] This evening I went to a bible class. Imagine being in a bible class with a life preserver tied around your neck. I am to be on duty tomorrow so it will be necessary that I stick around close.

JUNE 21, FRIDAY   Today we are in the real original danger zone with the emphasis on the "danger." Our ship is a long ways behind the rest of the group most of the time and that has a tendency to make most of us a little nervous. They are even more serious than usual. I want to laugh when I hear men arguing religion and I have heard more today than anytime on the trip. Several of the fellows are reading the Bible. It seems that men will swing over when they are in danger. They are humbler and more prayerful once they are face to face with the stern reality. This isn't general but it is true of many of the fellows. It is good to turn ones thoughts to God in case of danger but it is better to have done that before. A fellow has no time to pray when a ship is sinking; he must act then. His praying should have been done before.

I have been on the sweeping detail today. It isn't hard now that most of the fellows have gotten into the habit of keeping things clean. One thing about this job it never wears out. As soon as we get our section swept once they start us over again.

Everyone is watching the water and looking for submarines. I have been up two or three times. None of us could tell a sub from an oil barrel but its good pastime. The sun is shining but there is a cold wind blowing so it seems more like November than the first of Summer. Waves are rolling very high. One fellow says "the country around here is getting hilly." Some of the boys are getting sea sick but that is probably due to the English chow.

I spent the afternoon in signaling and knot tying. They tell me that one must know all these things in order to be a first class private. That's my aim. Nothing like having ambitions, especially in a military way. I am already dreaming of Napoleonic achievements.

JUNE 22   This or tomorrow will be the year's longest day. They are the longest days I have ever seen. We are taking the "Northern route" which brings us a thousand miles north of where I have ever been.

It is a clear, cold, windy day. The sea looks as chilly as blue. Every time I think of subs, I shudder at the thought of having to go down in that cold water. It would be much more comfortable to be torpedoed farther South. A fellow would die of cramps in this water. But here it is where ships have been torpedoed and here begins the real danger zone.

All Americans have been forbidden to fire the boilers from here in. The boilers are way down in the ship and in the middle. Most ships are hit near the boilers and even if not the boilers usually blow up and men who work in the marine engine room have small chance to escape.

The Battleship that escorted us over turned back this morning and we are now being escorted by a number of submarine chasers. We all feel safer too. Perhaps there never was much danger. These are British chasers. Not half as high as some of the waves in fact they are out of sight half the time except for a lone man who is fastened in a little observation tower. I imagine that it takes a good seaman to ride those little ships. They are the "broncos" of the sea and a man must be on the alert always.

I had quite a talk with some fellows this morning on Mormonism. It is surprising how little some fellows know about us. He told me that he heard the Mormons believed in free love. He was surprised when I told him that marriage was the most sacred ordinance in our church.

Afternoon: I am on guard this afternoon. My company is "toilet guard." So many men use the toilets and so many miss use them that guards are placed over them to avoid rushes and to keep the places clean. My squad was given the toilet at the rear of the boat. When I would have time I would go out on the rear deck and watch the water boil up in the wake of the ship.

Gee! What mountains of waves. The ship rolled so that one was forced to hold to something most of the time. There is a 6 inch gun and a couple of gunners stationed at the rear of the vessel to be used in case of subs. I don't imagine they could do much in such rough weather.

Some how or other a rumor has got on board that Austria and Turkey have quit. Most of the fellows are highly elated but I don't think there is any reason to be. No one wants peace more than a soldier and that is why they believe all rumors they desire to be true. I don't think peace will come until we have a lot of parleys before and these countries won't quit without Germany's consent. I am sticking pretty close to my belt and life preserver. So are the rest of the fellows.

Just think I haven't undressed to sleep since I have been on the ship.

JUNE 23, SUNDAY   Guarding is a joke in some respects. Think of eight men being placed on guard in one toilet. They have nothing else for us to do so they must figure that it is better to be poorly occupied than not at all. A guard shift is 24 hours and is worked in two hour relays a man is on two and off four.

It was a funny job I had last night. There are many funny jobs in the army. My job was to stand on a soap box and watch the latrine over a screen wall between it and the wash room. My work consisted in being on the alert that no one dirtied the place and when there was room for 1 or 2 or 3 persons yell it out to the guard at the door who kept the crowd back. Such precausions [precautions] are very necessary.

Day light found us in sight of land. It is on our right (Ireland). Later we saw hills on our left (Scotland). As we moved on during the day the channel we were in narrowed and then widened and we passed islands and ships.

This was England that great headquarters for the British Empire and that is Ireland. Poor oppressed long suffering but now turbulent Ireland. Maybe I'd better say no more England is our Ally. And there is Scotland the home of so many great men who have risen to fame in other lands. I have a warm feeling for Scotland for I fancy I have some distant kin there.

These light houses along the shore make me think of Sam Brooks.[22] His dad was born in a lighthouse somewhere along this coast.

Fellows are feeling good. There is more laughing and joking on board this morning than any time since we have been on the trip. There is still danger and the destroyers are darting here and there among the ships like hungry birds looking for crumbs.

We had our last venereal inspection today. They have been almost daily since onboard to make sure all the fellows are free from disease. Hereafter it is court martial to contract venereal disease whether prophalaxis treatment has been taken or not. To contract willfully any disease that renders one physically unfit to do his duty is an offense.

This has been a great day. Most of the time we have been on deck watching the shore. There is not much to see but it is good to look at. We have all rolled our packs. I don't know why but it is a good thing to get things together. Everyone has lost something. I lost my razor and was growling about people who couldn't keep their hands off other fellows things when I found my razor under the bunk. It looks like we land tonight.

Nels Anderson in his army uniform. The photograph was taken in 1918 before his departure for France. *Special Collections Department, J. Willard Marriott Library, University of Utah.*

On his first day at sea aboard the *Carpathia*, June 12, 1918, Nels Anderson indicates that the vessel "has been fitted out to carry about three thousand [soldiers]." He recognizes the *Carpathia* as the ship that rescued the 810 survivors of the 2224 passengers on board the *Titanic*. Photo shows the *Carpathia* at Pier 54 in New York after the rescue of *Titanic* survivors. *Brown Brothers.*

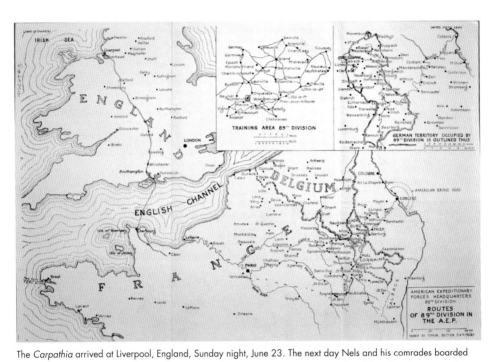

The *Carpathia* arrived at Liverpool, England, Sunday night, June 23. The next day Nels and his comrades boarded a train for Winchester in southern England. Nels wrote of the trip, "I enjoyed every bit of the ride today. Many things of interest came to our notice as Merry England passed in review for us." On this map from the Nels Anderson diary collection, Nels traced the route from Liverpool to Southampton, the debarkation port for crossing the English Channel to Cherbourg, France. The first map in the upper right corner shows the locations in France of towns where units of the 89th Division trained before going to the front. Anderson has circled Humberville, where his company trained. The second map shows the western area of Germany occupied by the 89th Division after the armistice in November 1918. *Nels Anderson's World War I Diary (MSS 1299), Perry Special Collections, Lee Library, Brigham Young University, Provo, Utah.*

Company E arrived in Humberville on July 2, 1918. The following day Nels climbed a hill just outside the village to write in his diary. "I have a splendid view of the surrounding country. On the slope to my left some children are herding some cows.... In front of me is the town (Humberville) and our barracks and on the right another gentle slope covered with little patches of planted pine forests. In the midst of such a quite peaceful scene, one wonders why there should be strife and disorder." *Allan Kent Powell Photograph.*

On the green in front of this chateau, the soldiers were reviewed on the American holiday—the Fourth of July—and on the French national holiday—Bastille Day, July 14th. Anderson recorded "we honored the day by a battalion parade on the chateau green. It was one of the best drills we have put on." *Allan Kent Powell Photograph.*

> ...of aight then we proceeds to dig a
> connect up with his comrades. Naturally
> ditches would not be in a straight line.
> make a sketch of a finished trench
> ...t of hardwork ... pump ... 8 ft
> ...but I ... firing base ... walk
> ...ts the best
> learn. We are told that the soft earth
> ...est kind of fortification so we really
> ...th to know how to dig in.
> ...clerks have started a little newspaper
> "Latrine Gazette" It is printed on the

During their training, Anderson's company was instructed in how to dig trenches, of which, Anderson wrote, "In peacetime we would simply call it ditch digging." This excerpt from his entry for July 20, 1918, shows a sketch of a trench while the diary entry explains how to dig a trench. *Nels Anderson's World War I Diary (MSS 1299), Perry Special Collections, Lee Library, Brigham Young University, Provo, Utah.*

On August 8, Nels received word that his beloved younger sister, Belle, was killed in an accident. He concluded his diary entry for that day, "She was the only one in the family that believed in me. May God help me to be the man she believed me to be for she was more than a sister." *Special Collections Department, J. Willard Marriott Library, University of Utah.*

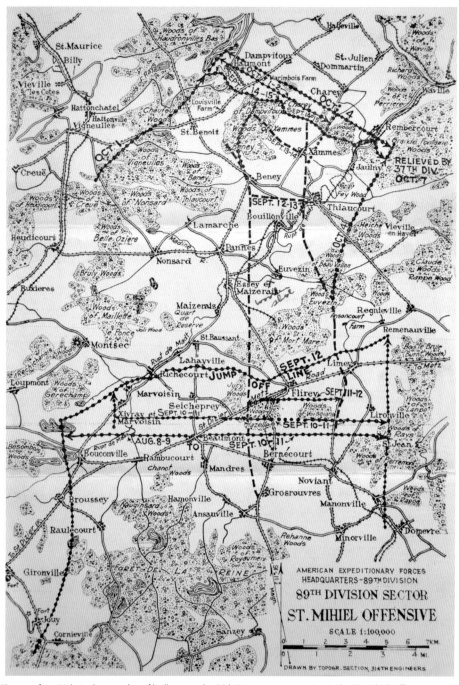

This map from Nels Anderson's diary file illustrates the 89th Division's participation in the St. Mihiel Offensive in September 1918. Note the penned addition, "wooden shoe," in the center of the map near Euvezin. Nels records in his diary entry for September 29, 1918, "Today I wandered around over the hills. I visited a lot of dugouts but didn't see anything I liked worth bringing back except a big wooden shoe. . . . So far the shoe is my first souvenir."

Nels Anderson's World War I Diary (MSS 1299), Perry Special Collections, Lee Library, Brigham Young University, Provo, Utah.

Company E occupied this village of Bouillonville, which was protected from German artillery by the steep hill behind these houses. *Allan Kent Powell Photograph.*

Nels Anderson visited this German cemetery in Bouillonville on September 18 and recorded "It was a beautiful well ordered place the plants and flowers were well trimmed and arranged. . . . In the graveyard were graves where 8 and 9 names were on the wooden crosses. . . . I suppose it is right it is the only place where a soldier hears the command "Rest in Peace." *Allan Kent Powell Photograph.*

The St. Mihiel Cemetery, located on the western edge of Thiaucourt, contains the graves of 4,153 American soldiers, including members of the 89th Division. *Allan Kent Powell Photograph.*

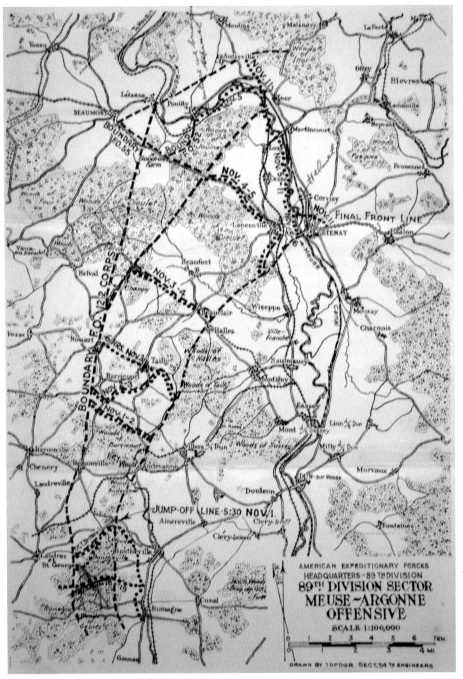

The 89th Division Sector for the Meuse-Argonne Offensive which led to the Armistice on November 11, 1918. Note the penned reference to "Helmet" near the town of Laneuville. It was here that Nels gave a helmet he had picked up to a Red Cross lady, as he records in his dairy entry for November 6, 1918. *Nels Anderson's World War I Diary (MSS 1299), Perry Special Collections, Lee Library, Brigham Young University, Provo, Utah.*

This photo of American soldiers in the Argonne Forest shows the stumps of trees still standing after the vicious battles. Nels Anderson entered the forest on October 14th and recorded, "I shall never forget that woods. Not a tree in it three inches through that has not been pierced all the big trees are torn with shrapnel and their limbs and tops have in many cases been blown off." *Courtesy Harry S. Truman Library.*

The ruins of a church near Romagne. Nels Anderson was near the church on October 21 and recorded "The place was in a little cut and the infantry dug in there throwing the mud or dirt out with the road. We had to widen the road for 2 way traffic the road bed was good. It is a big open place and many of our boys were killed taking it. I saw one grave with 20 little crosses. Many Germans still lie unburied." *Allan Kent Powell Photograph.*

knew it was too late. We were up against
as bad a proposition as going over. For after
about 8 o'clock the Dutch started shelling the
roads to prevent supplies coming up. It seems
that their guns were mostly centered on
the high ways. They had already started to
shell R— when we went through. As we passed
by the Red Cross in Ro— they gave each of us a bar
of chocolate and box of cigarettes. Philips and
I were walking together I tried to trade my box
of cigs for his chocolate. He wouldn't but started
to eat it he said perhaps it would be his last.
It was too. An hour or so after he was killed.
The shells were coming over pretty fast and
they caught us on an open slope. They were only
small ones some gas. Another lad and I were
together we noted that they were coming over in
two and threes about 10 seconds apart so we took
advantage of those intervals to run from one
shell hole to another and flop. Philips was
not taking that precaution, I saw him and another
fellow get it. They were in the open. A shell came.
They fell to their knees and before they could
flatten out another hit 25 feet from them and
perhaps 100 feet from us. It got them both. Two
other fellows were killed and several wounded in
our company on the same hill while several trucks
had been hit and were burning on the road.

I mention Philips because we were intimate.
He was homesteading in New Mexico, was engaged
to a girl from there who was living with his
mother in Kansas waiting his return. So perish
our fondest hopes. Every boy that is out down
over here had been building castles in the air

This diary entry for November 1 recounts the death of Nels's comrade and friend named Philips and three other soldiers by enemy artillery fire. *Nels Anderson's World War I Diary (MSS 1299), Perry Special Collections, Lee Library, Brigham Young University, Provo, Utah.*

(above) On November 4, a detail that included Nels Anderson was sent to the village of Taille [Tailly] to search for booby traps and "to inspect a fine chateau over there that was to be a hospital. While we were there orders came for the doctors to hunt another place as the General wanted the Chateau for headquarters. The doctor in charge did not take the orders very gracefully. . . . That Chateau would have accommodated 300 patients." *Allan Kent Powell Photograph.*

(left) The end of the war was bittersweet for Nels Anderson. That day he learned that a good friend from St. Johns, Lehi Smith, had been killed. In his diary entry Nels recorded, "He was a good conscientious soldier. Came in when I did left a 2 weeks bride behind. Last time I saw him he spoke of her and how happy he would be when they could settle on their little farm." Lehi Smith is one of 14,246 American soldiers buried in the Meuse-Argonne Cemetery, near Romagne, France. The cemetery contains the largest number of American military graves in Europe. *Allan Kent Powell Photograph.*

(December 9, 1918) Headquarters for the 89th Division were located in this Kyllburg Hotel. As a runner for the Regiment, Nels made frequent trips to the division headquarters. *Allan Kent Powell Photograph.*

Nels Anderson was stranded overnight in the village of Densborn, where he and a fellow soldier spent a long and hungry night sleeping in this train station. Nels recorded in his diary for December 10, "Sgt. Major gave us the wrong dope on trains and we lose three hours because of missing a train. We are now in Densborn where we'll have to spend the night in the station. I am awful hungry. The lieutenant we brought a message to offered to get us something to eat but Agey the lad I am with tried to be heroic and said we were not hungry. I had to be heroic to and keep still." *Allan Kent Powell Photograph.*

Nels Anderson spent Christmas 1918 in the village of Nattenheim, where he celebrated the holiday in the home of a local family and attended services in this church. He recorded, "Go to the church here very crowded. I can't understand but it was to do with Xmas. Drop a mark in the hat to make up for my ignorance." *Allan Kent Powell Photograph.*

Nels Anderson left from the Kyllburg railroad station for the university in Montpellier, France. He recorded, "I found I had made attachments in the outfit that were hard to break. I parted with my helmet and gas mask and guns as though they were living friends. All the fellows wished me good luck and the major had the Ford bring me [from Oberkail] to Kyl[l]burg." *Allan Kent Powell Photograph.*

This house in Oberkail was the residence of the seventy-five-year-old Mother Bauer, who became Nels's landlady and friend while staying in the town. Nels found the house most interesting and wrote in his diary for January 5, 1919, "I go up into the attic of this house today. It is a regular curiosity shop. . . . This home is full of antiques. Nearly every piece of furniture is old some pieces 200 or 400 years old." *Allan Kent Powell Photograph.*

The Eifler Hof in Oberkail was headquarters for the 314th Engineers Regiment for most of their time in Germany. The building, now a private residence, is located across the street from the home of Mother Bauer. *Allan Kent Powell Photograph*.

3

ENGLAND, JUNE 1918

IF NELS ANDERSON WAS DISAPPOINTED THAT THE *CARPATHIA* DID NOT
sail directly to France, he made no mention of it in his diary. Other members of the 89th Division landed at Saint-Nazaire a port on the western
coast of France at the mouth of the Loire River where the first American
combat units had arrived in June 1917. Given that the *Carpathia* was an English ship with an English crew, it is understandable why the vessel landed at
Liverpool. The 314th Regiment spent only five days in England, but Nels
Anderson was an enthusiastic visitor writing of the trip from Liverpool
through Manchester, Sheffield, and Oxford to the rest camp near Winchester, "I enjoyed every bit of the ride." Moreover, Anderson expressed
interest in England, its people, and his desire to understand them better. "I
would like to be turned loose in England for a while. I would like to visit
so many of the places of charm and interest, better still I would like to mix
with and study the people. People and their ways are more interesting, if
one wants to study, than things or places."

The time in England helped Anderson understand better the magnitude
of the war and its impact on the civilian population. The English people
impressed him with their character, their patriotism, and their resolve. While
waiting to entrain for the Port of Southampton, Anderson chatted with some
English ladies and was moved. "They were in the war with all their heart; one
had a husband and son and the other two sons at the front while they are
back here starving it out."

JUNE 24, MONDAY   Well we are here but it is forbidden to say where "here"
is. I will leave names of places blank and fill in later. We tied to the dock last
night before bed time. This morning early we rolled our packs and went
ashore. From the time we hit the dock till we left the ship this was the noisiest
bunch of men ever heard. Last night some one suggested that they give three
cheers for the mess hall. They did phew! phew!! phew!!! They gave us a hasty

breakfast this morning. Those on the end of the line didn't get any for want of time. They passed around two big sandwiches each to carry with us.

We left (Liverpool) in the oddest little passenger cars I ever saw. They are more like play cars. Divided in sections large enough to hold 8 men each with little room to spare when we got our packs in. Cars over here look more like wagons. I believe they call them wagons. I was surprised however at the speed.

I enjoyed every bit of the ride today. Many things of interest came to our notice as Merry England passed in review for us. It is not hard to see that this country is at war. I saw pretty girls shoveling coal and working on the section. All the children we saw were working and the only men we saw in civilian clothes were bent and gray. Every able man, it seemed, was in the uniform. We saw many women in black. Many men in blue uniforms which we learned are wounded. We passed an aviation field. A big prison camp with a high barb wire fence around. Saw a lot of men working putting up buildings and clearing land. They were within the barb wire and I think were prisoners. We passed a college town famous in educational history but only got a pass-ing glance at the place. I could see that the buildings were of gray stone and vine covered.

There seems to be a lot of waste country in England. It may be used as pasture but I think that all the tillable soil was worked. I never saw so many gardens in all my life. I can see already that Americans are not a gardening people.

We thought we were going to London but 50 miles was as near as we came then we turned South and went to (Winchester) where we de trained and were marched 8 miles out to a "rest camp" where we are "resting."[1] We were so tired we could not have gone much farther. I saw so much to interest me coming from the station here that I did not mind the trip so much. It seemed that all the little children in town came out to meet us. They would walk along the column holding our hands or perhaps beg pennies. Most of them seem well and strong and, as a rule, they are clean.

Well we are lodged in tents and sleeping on the ground. There is room for about 16 or 18 men in a tent but 22 men have been crowded in. While I was down to the "Y" the men in my tent made their beds. When I came back there was no room inside for me and my stuff was scattered so I could not find half of it. I cussed and growled but it doesn't do any good to get mad in the army. The last man must take what's left. I made bed outside.

I attended a good service this evening. After service the chaplin urged the fellows to join some church before crossing the channel. He said if they didn't have the provisions at hand they would make arrangement to have a man admitted to any denomination he wished to belong to several fellows went up. He was a very liberal preacher.

JUNE 25   I am reminded, as I look at things from this new point of view, that I have new reasons for being thankful that I am an American. I am thankful that my father left Germany to enjoy the freedom we are going to fight for. I am glad that I can wear the uniform with the conviction that it stands for the principles of justice and equality. We may not always enjoy that justice and equality in the army but it is necessary that we go through this in order that we might have the right to enjoy it later. I am thankful too that I don't use tobacco.[2] Those who do are having their troubles here. There is little to be had and that at high prices too high for so many of the fellows who spent all they had for something to eat on the boat.

This morning they moved us into barracks and the rest of the day I have been on a detail with 3 others mowing weeds with a British scythe. A British captain was directing the work. He was very willing to talk. He told us that England has put 4,000,000 acres more of land in cultivation than before the war. Before the war she raised 1/5 of her food and now she raises 4/5.

He is a bombing officer (whatever that is) and is back on account of wounds. Many wounded men here, but they are men who are recovering and on light duty.

Now regarding the food. We have good clean food but not half enough.[3] We are not allowed to buy any nor are the people allowed to sell. I don't imagine they have any to sell.

I think that they have it figured out how much it takes to sustain a soldier and so dish it out accordingly. We Americans are used to eating all we want perhaps we over eat. Uncle Sam pays for this food we eat or rather the meals we eat and it may be that England is governing herself accordingly. I don't imagine that our mother country would give us two slices if one was sufficient. As it is nothing goes into the slop bucket.

There was nothing doing at the "Y's" this evening so I wandered around the camp. I came upon a drunken Tommy who was entertaining a group of Yanks with accounts of his adventures. He may have been a little boastful but there is no doubt that he was, at least part gold, for he had a distinguished

service medal presented by the king. He seemed to regard us green yanks as
if he was aware of all the greenness we felt was in us. We may get ripe later.
We *may* get picked.

I am lonesome this evening. There is not a soldier among the thousand of
yanks that I know so I just walk around alone.

I heard some English talking this evening and it seems that the Italians
are making a great drive.

JUNE 26, WEDNESDAY   After breakfast the captain called us together and
gave us some instructions on the giving of information and on our conduct.
He reminded us that we were in a foreign land and our conduct would be
the basis upon which America would be judged. I like the way Captain
Rader puts things up to the men. He told us in a general way what information we would be allowed to give. It is not necessary to warn us against saying where we are going and what to do. None of us know. If we are good
soldiers we won't ask or even care.

I would like to be turned loose in England for a while. I would like to
visit so many of the places of charm and interest, better still I would like to
mix with and study the people. People and their ways are more interesting, if
one wants to study, than things or places.

This town is like most [of] the English cities. Beautiful and peaceful
viewed from without. We were permitted to visit the place today. We had to
go in company formation, however, and chaperoned by officers.[4] (Winchester) pleased me from within. Most of the streets were clean and the
homes neat and tidy. All the buildings of red brick and about the same shape
and size with the same kind of chimneys and the same kind of roofs. There
were no street cars, and few automobiles but many bicycles. Women were
doing all kinds of work. The children I saw playing were very quiet and serious about it and all the old men were quietly and patiently doing something
or going somewhere.

We visited in company formation, the great castle of the place also the
cathedral of historic importance in which were many interesting things in
the line of memorials and monuments. The walls were covered with tablets
on which the names of military men were carved. Soldiers and sailors who
gave their lives in foreign lands for the glory of the crown. That makes me
think of the letter, personal letter (?) each one of us received from the king
when we landed in Liverpool. It was a welcome to the yanks. I sent mine to
Grandma Lytle.[5]

The walls and floors and windows of this place are spotted with tablets placed in memory of great spirits of the past. I walked over many a stone in the floor on which it was carved "Here lyes"…Most of them are in Latin.

Before we left they played the Star Spangled Banner on the big organ. It was very impressive and majestic.

There were many things in the stores and streets of interest. One sign read "Mourning clothes a Speciality." Business will create specialists even who make capital of sorrow. Another sign named the price of potatoes but added "Bring your Bags." Paper is scarce here. The average American daily is 10 times the size of an English daily which are no larger than the school paper at home called "Current Events."

With all this inconvenience we see the British have high hopes of early victory. I believe just from the looks of things that the morale of the country is good.

I read much between the lines of the speech of Von Kuhlmann's.[6] It is evidence of a division or a coming division in upper circles in Berlin. So I am going to make a prediction (the last one) I look for peace in 9 months.[7]

JUNE 27, THURSDAY   Two months ago today, I left St. Johns for the army. I ate dinner at Hamblins. We had a street meeting. I was very nervous as I was on the programme. At 2 o'clock we left for the R.R. in a big Cadilac. I believe I have learned a lot of things since then at least I know more about the army which I had always looked upon as a very undesirable institution but nonetheless necessary. I used to sympathize with soldiers because I had always thought the army more hard than it is. It could be less so perhaps.

I went to a picture show tonight where I saw some good moving pictures taken on the Italian Front also saw Charley Chaplin perform.

The show was closed by a prayer from the "Y" man, a very eloquent prayer for victory and fervent thanks for the recent Italian gains on the Piave.[8] Imagine the Lord has His hands full dealing with the conflicting prayers of humanity.

I had a very good talk at the show with a Tommy. He was very anxious for peace and just as confident of victory. He was home on furlough from the front. I like to see the British and Americans fraternizing. They agree like brothers, many hot arguments. The Americans seem to think that they had to come because these other countries couldn't lick Germany and are foolish enough to say so.

I bought a piece of cake(?) from a gypsy shopkeeper this evening. He was charging such prices that a pound of cake would net about $2.00. I ate about half of it when I found a big fly. My stomach threatened to revolt but I managed to check it. I ate the rest of the cake too because I was hungry.

There is a good deal of what yanks call "beefing" about the food. They tell us that we are getting all we need. Perhaps we are. We have been used to measuring our needs by our wants. We are just learning what the word "rations" means.

We went on another sightseeing trip. Yesterday our trip was all of 8 miles today it was longer. We climbed up on a hill that was Caesar's camp when he took this country. The old site was surrounded by a deep moat and other defenses that are disappearing. We had a beautiful view of the country. I can't describe it but everything looked fresh and green and beautiful. We could get a beautiful survey of (Winchester) whence came so many of our pilgrim fathers and the name of our (Winchester) in New England.[9] This was where the great angler Isaac Walton lived and a lot of literary characters I can't name now.[10] (Alfred the great) belonged here. His statue is in the town square. I said everything was green but I failed to mention the great patches of yellow and red one can see every[where]. England has two pests that are better to behold than to contend with they are the poppy (red) and mustard.

This afternoon was full of expectations. We expected drill and inspection and a lot of things that failed to materialize. After supper however we had to fill out a paper giving our age, name, educational qualifications and a few things.

This evening Heinricke and I went out to [no location given]. Heinricke is my corporal.[11] He is a fine fellow clean cut and clean living. He is good company and, I believe, a good soldier. I don't know many of the fellows. I have done very little mixing but I like Ed Heinricke better than most of them so far. We went down to a great open air concert where Harry Lauder the great Scotch singer was giving a concert and making talks to 2000 or 3000 yanks and Tommies. He is a "dyed in the wool" German hater and preached total extermination.[12]

JUNE 28　　We leave here for somewhere else. We roll packs early. At breakfast 3 sandwiches were issued to each of us also a little corn beef. March to the railroad where we came in the other day. While we were waiting for the train I had a chance to talk to some English ladies. They were in the war with all their heart: one had a husband and son and the other two sons at the front while they are back here starving it out.

It was a short ride to the port (South Hampton) where we were to ship across the channel. I didn't see much of the place as we were unloaded in a great warehouse where we spent most of the day. The boats were there to take us but we could not leave till night. We saw a great many English soldiers waiting to ship across. Most of them wore wound stripes and were on their way to the lines for another try. They were a jolly noisy bunch of fellows.

This day was very uninteresting. Nothing to see but the docks and ships. We watched the tide come and go but that is a very common thing. Tides will come and go long after this war is forgotten. A few big ships came in some went out. A lot of small ones were going and coming all the while. There is an aviation station way across the mud flats (water when the tide is in) and a plane flies in or out once in a while. We naturally think most of the journey and submarines and of where we are going. No one [knows] anything about anything as rumors are very popular and presumptions are very numerous.

4

ARRIVAL IN FRANCE, JUNE 1918

WHILE ENGLAND HAD BEEN AN INTERESTING AND, FOR THE MOST PART, enlightening experience, France was quite a shock for Nels Anderson. Landing at Cherbourg, Anderson found "this place the opposite to the last place we stopped streets are dirty and so are the people."

Nearly twenty-nine years of age and a veteran of hobo life and riding the rails in America, Anderson was far better prepared for the strange world of France than the average eighteen- or nineteen-year-old soldier just leaving home for the first time. Nevertheless, even for Anderson, the first "three days seemed like months." An astute observer, Anderson offers interesting comments on the French, army life, and the trip from Cherbourg past Paris and on to the company training site at Humberville, in the heart of the Champagne-Ardenne region of France, approximately forty miles northwest of the American Expeditionary Force headquarters at Chaumont.

JUNE 29, SATURDAY   A year ago today I was building aircastles. I had it all planned how I was going to work 3½ months more and save $150.00 a month out of that. I was going to pay my debts and have enough left to go to school another year and finish. I thought of the war but could not see how the war would last longer as the English were about to take Lens and I figured that the moral support of America was enough to win the allied cause.[1] Next day I learned of daddy's death and had to go home where I spent the summer.[2] I have been on both oceans since then and across 20 states and how, what I least expected I am in France in the uniform. So much for the uncertainty of things.

We scooted across the channel in a hurry last night. We were packed in like sardines but the ride was not long. We were well escorted by chasers and an observation balloon that was tied to a chaser. I shall not speak of the cold uncomfortable night. The big thing is that we are here on the continent.

It would not be possible to describe my feelings as I stepped on French soil where is the theatre of the world's greatest struggle. It is only paralleled by the feelings that came to me as we sailed out of sight of American soil and were on the high seas.

I don't know what part of France we are in other than that this is a coast town (Cherberg) [Cherbourg] and about 3 miles out is the "rest" camp where we are. On the way out we about gave out being weak from hunger and the journey. The sun was very hot and many men fell exhausted.

This place seems the opposite to the last place we stopped streets are dirty and so are the people. Like England all the men wear uniforms (some have red pants) I saw a woman pushing a great cart with wheels 6 feet high and many of them carry big packs on their heads. The children line up along the road and beg "sous", whatever they are. Some of them could say "Give me penny." I gave all the big English pennys I had and so did the other fellows around me.

We are up against another exchange problem. They used to beat us in England because we couldn't count their money. They may do the same here. I think cheating is general. An American soldier when he buys holds out his money and lets them take what is due and takes the change without knowing what he gave or what he got.

JUNE 30   Have been on K.P. all day. They called us at 5 o'clock and we went to work at six. With the exception of an hour or two we have been on all day. Not hard work but we have had to be on the job. I took some time to go to the Y.M.C.A. to send away for a book. I wanted a book on Engineering so I sent through the Y to London where the Y.M.C.A. will get me my book, perhaps. I sent a $2.00 bill to them to make my case good or "more binding" as the soldiers say.

This has been quite an interesting day. I got to study hungry men. We seat 16 to a table and are allowed a certain ration to the table which is to be divided as equally as possible. There is not any more than 8 or 9 men can eat. So many of the fellows try to cheat and there is a great deal of dissatisfaction and growling from those who think they have come away with less than their share. A man who is reserved is going to come out of the shuffle with less than his share, later such a man is going to sour on the army. A man with faith in all men is going to have his faith shattered when he gets in a food grabbing contest where some of the men think only of themselves.

The English soldiers have charge of things here. It is British hospitality we are sharing. We K.P.'s work under the direction of Tommies today, most of them pleasant fellows.

Last night some of the fellows stole away and went down to this town where they had access to French boose [sic] and French women though I believe their reports were somewhat exaggerated. There seems to be a few loose women around the camp. There were many trafficing around the camp in England. An English soldier told me that there was more prostitution around the camps in France than elsewhere, which was a natural thing for him to say. But there is a great deal of immorality here whether it is due to poverty or loose moral teaching or patriotism I can't say. At least the moral standards seem low here. There does not seem to be the modesty we have in the states. Men and women use the same public toilets. We saw that as we passed through the streets yesterday. We had no sooner landed yesterday than a French woman came around with assortments of lewd pictures to sell the fellows. Such pictures as one would carry at his peril in America. This woman knew that such things being new for most Americans would find ready sale.

JULY 1   The last three days seem like months. 8 days ago we left England. The last 3 nights I slept with clothes on and nearly froze.

Last night we entrained from somewhere in France to somewhere else. We entrained if these French go ahead wagons can be called trains. We are packed 40 men in a car.[3] It would be bad enough to put 40 men in an American boxcar but it is worse in these being half as large. 40 men with packs does not leave any room to sit down with comfort. But it's war and probably this is the best transportation the government can provide.

We spent a very miserable night and the day so far has been very tiresome. We are not making very good time and there are many long stops. I wish they would let us get off and stretch ourselves at the station but that is not allowed even though we stop a half hour. The road bed is good and the rolling stock seems to be in good shape. I don't see why they can't go faster.

I have no idea where we are going or where we are. Whether we go to Paris or not I can't say. Probably not. It wouldn't do to take us through Paris. So far we have missed all the big towns except Liverpool. We saw a great iron structure once today we thought it looked like pictures of the Eifell [sic] Tower. We did not go near to it at least there [is] a great town near it. We could see no one to talk to except French who we couldn't understand. A Canadian

Frenchman in my squad tried to talk to these Frenchmen but he could get little information out of them. I don't suppose they understand his French.

We see a great many trainloads of material and trainloads of French troops both going and coming. It is hard to say where or from. The front must be near. We pass tent cities now and then and great stores of supplies. We see guns on cars and part of aeroplanes on cars. We saw two broken planes on cars. I just begin to feel that I am getting into the midst of things.

The other fellows think it funny that I should keep a diary. They ask me many questions about my purposes. One fellow borrowed it the other day to copy parts for a letter to his girl. He soon gave it up as a bad job. He was trying to write a serial letter.

This trip has been a very noisy one. I fancy the French think we are wild. At least when we yell and wave our arms at them they look askance in return but say nothing. The children all recognize us. They all beg. I can't tell the girls from the boys. They all wear little black aprons. There is a way to tell them, the girls don't smoke cigarettes and the boys put their hands in their pockets.

I have not fared well today. I am both hungry and thirsty now. Lost out on dinner because I held back when the chow was passed thinking a fair share would be left. I got the wrong canteen and didn't drink because I didn't want to rob the other fellow. Later found my canteen and it was empty.

TRAINING IN HUMBERVILLE, JULY 1918

THE VILLAGE OF HUMBERVILLE, WITH FEWER THAN A HUNDRED INHABitants, remains today much the same as when soldiers of Company E of the 314th Engineers Battalion arrived on July 2, 1918, to set up camp as Nels Anderson recorded "outside a very quaint little French village such as one reads about in stories." The village church stands with a monument to the French soldiers from the village who served in the Great War. The public washhouse, mentioned by Anderson, remains but is no longer in use. The washing area is adjacent to the small stream that runs through the center of the village and the charming stone bridge that spans the stream. Undoubtedly Anderson and his comrades crossed the bridge many times en route to the chateau where company headquarters were located and on whose green formations and parades were held. Behind the village and chateau rises a steep hill—the site of strenuous training exercises for the American soldiers and also a place of refuge for Nels Anderson to make entries in his diary, write letters to loved ones at home, and to observe the village life of their French hosts. Nearby are other small villages that housed other American companies and were visited by Nels Anderson as he sought out friends and acquaintances from Utah and Arizona.

During the month Company E spent in Humberville the men drilled, stood guard duty, served on K.P., dug trenches, and listened to lectures on a variety of subjects including range finding, gas attacks and defense, proper conduct if taken prisoner, and cleanliness. After a few weeks Anderson was assigned to a reconnaissance school to learn more about map making, triangulation, scouting, and reconnoitering.

While in Humberville the company was issued steel helmets, overseas caps—"handy little caps but they are no good in sunshine"—to replace the broad-brimmed campaign hats, and legging wraps that caused the troops considerable trouble to put on and wear. During July the number of American soldiers in France reached one million.

In retrospect the month spent at Humberville was a peaceful, if not pleasant period of waiting, anticipating, and preparing to move forward to the front lines. At the same time, elsewhere in France American soldiers were quickly earning reputations as aggressive courageous fighters participating in engagements such as the Second Battle of the Marne which began on July 15th as German forces struck westward along the Marne River near Soissons and Château-Thierry. The United States suffered twelve thousand casualties during the nearly three weeks of fighting that marked the last major German offensive of the war, which ended with the Germans retreating back to their previous lines. Meanwhile, as the fighting raged along the Marne River, Anderson and his comrades in Humberville, along with thousands of other American soldiers scattered throughout the villages and countryside of northeastern France, prepared for the first American offensive to be launched in September.

JULY 2   We had one worry all forenoon. Where we were and when going. Someone started the rumor that we were going to Italy.[1] I was in hopes it were true yet I was not as interested in my destination as I was desirous of getting off the train for I put in a miserable night.

Well we are in camp again. Where it is I can't say but it is not Italy. No one knows what part of France we are in unless it be the officers who may have maps.

It was a tiresome march out here from the station. But we are here and happier than we have been since we left Mills. We have got away from the stomach robbing British. It is hard for a man's heart to warm towards a people if they send him away hungry.

We are not very far from the firing line no doubt we will start edging our way toward the front soon. This is a beautiful country all the land is in grain or pasture. Everything is quiet and picturesque. It is hard to conceive of war almost within hearing.

Our barracks bags came this afternoon. We have not seen them since we left the states. At least I haven't but they came along on the same ship. I couldn't help but reflect as I unpacked mine of the thoughts and misgivings I had when I packed it at Mills. I must have had an exaggerated idea of the submarine danger. I still think the worse part of the journey was on the water. On land, if a fellow must die, at least he can fight back, on the sea he is helpless and that's humiliating.

We are camped outside of a very quaint little French village such as one reads about in stories. It is much better to read about than to smell or behold.[2] It is a very rural place and the people live simple lives. They received us almost affectionately. One woman ran along shaking hands with the fellows. She kept repeating "Goodbye goodbye." She probably meant good day. She made a great impression at least.

The Captain congratulated the company on its deportment throughout the trip. Then he made a little talk asking the fellows to be careful of their conduct while here. He said that no rulings had been made against drinking wine, of which there seems to be plenty. But in the absence of orders he asked the company not to make orders necessary because orders generally curtail freedom and impose hardship on all the men whereas they are meant for only a few.[3]

We had a poor supper tonight so most of us are going to bed hungry. One man stole a hunk of cheese the Lieutenant and mess sergeant are looking for it now. I fared better on the journey than most of the boys. Our squad stole some bread and jam before we left the British camp besides we had a can of peaches and a tin of Argentina beef.

I wrote a letter to Nell this evening.

JULY 3, WEDNESDAY   This is a fine day. I have been occupied cleaning up the barracks and shining my rifle which was in pretty bad shape. The captain took us around this morning and told us where to go and where not to go. He cautioned us against abused privileges for abused privileges are taken away. I can see that before long we will be hedged in with a lot of rules. There is always someone ready to override the privileges he has. He also told us we were in the war zone and war zone discipline would go from now on. We will be allowed to visit about here in town but could go no farther away without pass.

I am writing this on a high hillside. I have a splendid view of the surrounding country. On the slope to the left some children are herding some cows. There are several grain fields around (no fences in France) and the children are to watch the cows from getting in the little fields. One cow is in the middle of a patch of wheat and the children are trying to chase her out. While they are doing that another cow is taking advantage of the chance and is lining out towards another field not more than 50 yards away. It reminds me of the time I used to watch cows under similar conditions. I thought life was a trial too so I can't help but sympathize with the boy and girl over there.

In front of me is the town (Humberville) and our barracks and on the right another gentle slope covered with little patches of planted pine forests. In the midst of such a quiet peaceful scene one wonders why there should be strife and disorder abroad.

One of the men on guard last night, Gillette (fellows call him "safety razor") was found walking his post with his rifle hanging on a post and bottle of wine in his hand. More inside of him. He is in the guardhouse today. A serious charge over here. Men have been shot for less.

Well I came up here to write letters so I had better tend to my duty.

JULY 4TH, THURSDAY   Independence day. We were told this morning we would be given our liberty for the day. There is no place to go so I thought I would celebrate so I went around town to try to buy a cup of milk. I did not even know the word for milk so I had to go through the motions of milking with my cup between my knees. She understood and led me into the house. I was sorry I asked her because she had less than a half gallon on hand and she insisted on my taking some. She wouldn't take any money so all there was for me to do was to go. I went to the barracks and partook of my little feast, hardtack and milk then I took a can of that bitter marmalade I hooked in England and presented it to the old lady. She seemed pleased but I wonder if they like that stuff.

Well we had the best feed since we left the states. Boiled meat, gravy and bread. It sure hit the spot. After dinner they marched us down to the big flat place to the left of the town where we "enjoyed" a ball game between a couple of picked teams. I didn't care to go down but after the game started I was interested. The men who knew the teams made a lot of noise but I am still a stranger. Imagine these French people, who looked on at a distance, thought we were wild.

At 4 o'clock we had a Battalion review on the chateau green. It was a beautiful ceremony and very impressive. A few French spectators. Buglers played both the French and American National Airs.

JULY 5, FRIDAY   Mail came in last night. I was one of the few who got none. I may have a letter next time. This mail left the states too soon after we did.

We drilled this morning. We have a good lieutenant but I don't care much for the sergeant who leads our platoon. He never misses an opportunity to bawl men out. It is not right that such men should be put in charge. He is very good when the officers are around but other times he never fails to remind us he is boss. He never said anything to me but it hurts me to see other men abused when they have to stand there and take it. One dare not look his feelings.

I am on guard this afternoon, so at different times during the night I will be walking "my post in a military manner"—mild, indifferent manner. I am guarding the kitchen. There is nothing in the kitchen to guard but we just play there is and guard it anyway. I just about starved today. One of the K.P.s threw a biscuit (hard bread) out to a dog. I threw a rock at the dog and when no one was looking I got the biscuit which helped some. Under ordinary conditions I would have too much pride to do such a thing but I am in the army now.

JULY 6, SATURDAY   Now regarding guard. It was a hard night. I had no idea a person could get so tired just from walking post. I had a dark lonesome post and I got sort of nervous so I put the bayonet on my gun. It had a marked effect on my nerves. Later, I got ashamed of myself and took it off.

We had a nut for the Sergeant of the guard. He has been drunk all the while. He has caused us a great deal of unnecessary work and inconvenience. This afternoon he called out the guard for the Officer of the day. Three men got their rifles mixed and there was some confusion. The officer said nothing but after he left the sergeant called us out and lectured us on efficiency and discipline. He smoked two cigarettes during the lecture and now he would stop talking to bum a match from one of us to light his cigarette which would go out during his most eloquent moments. Later he recommended to the top sergeant Beauchamp—that we be punished. Beauchamp told him that tomorrow was Sunday and the men must rest so some other time we will be called out after supper and drilled for I don't know what offense unless the top Sergeant takes cognizance of the fact that the fellow was drunk. Gray, the Sergeant of the Guard, is very popular with the officers so he won't be penalized.

JULY 7, SUNDAY   This morning I cleaned up, washed some clothes and took a bath.

This afternoon Ed Heinricke and I got a pass and took a stroll over to another little town. We visited two towns; they were, or are, small quaint towns. We visited an old church in one of the places. It was more than 300 years old. It smelled stale and musty within like an old celler. I thought as I surveyed it within and without how long would it stand if the Huns came along. They don't seem to have a very high regard for old landmarks.

I note by the paper that the Germans are losing ground. I am very glad of that for it is time the tide was turning.

There is a Y.M.C.A. at one of the other towns but it didn't do us any good for both I and the corporal were broke. We came back as empty as we went but for what we saw.

I must note about the modesty of these people, or rather the lack of it. They have toilets or latrines on the streets right where most of the people pass. Those who use those places are scarcely concealed from view and it seems that they are not much concerned whether they are or not.

This evening I wrote a letter to Mr. Prescott and another to Mother. I wrote home for a pair of field glasses but later I learned we would not be allowed to have field glasses so I crossed out the order.

The Chaplin came over this evening and we held services out on the grass. We had some rather violent singing and then listened to the chaplin unravel his text. With both hands earnestly. I wish some one would write to me. I feel deserted. Probably I am.

JULY 8　　I can't find my pen. I must have loaned it to someone. I am in the habit of doing such things. I must not lose it for it would be hard to get another over here. Especially without money.

Time is full of events. We drilled all the day. I am not a star driller. I don't like it but I am doing my best because I need a little of that stuff to be a good soldier. I want to get just as little as I need. The sun beat down unmercifully. We worked very intensively and many of the men gave out with heat. I didn't because I couldn't concentrate hard enough to get tired.

My corporal has been made a sergeant and I am in a new squad. I am like a horse working on the wrong side of the tung [tongue] but then what's the difference. If I am not dead I will be out of the army in a year and all this will be forgotten. All I want is to get out with a good record and a whole skin if possible.

They issued us our helmets today. They are made by the Ford Motor Company and are as heavy as a Ford radiator. Made of very durable steel with greater qualities of service than comfort. I suppose there are many household purposes to which they could be put. A lot of the boys may have sore blistered heads especially those who had their heads shaved recently. Shaved heads are the fad now.

We got orders tonight to send no more picture post cards home. Lest the Germans learn we are here. I wonder who thinks of all these things.

JULY 9   They are driving us pretty hard now. I don't mind it because I need the training. While we are resting they give us lectures. Today the lecture was on "demolition" or the art of demolishing things in war time that is a special duty of the engineers in a retreat. They also lectured on the rifle and its parts.

It rained a little this morning but it didn't stop us. It made our guns a little rusty is all. It was good to have a rain to cool the air and lay the dust.

Today I subscribed for the A.E.F. paper The Stars and Stripes.[4] It comes weekly. I didn't have the money 8 francs so it was charged.

This evening we had Battalion parade on the hill. It is quite a climb up there and back for a little ceremony. When the colors passed by I don't think Old Glory ever looked better to me.

All the fellows with cameras had to turn them in today. No more pictures. We can't even draw pictures without permission. They also told us not to send home for parcels because none would be brought without an [e]ndorcement [sic] from the colonel. I wanted a few things too. I wrote to Nell for a handy kit.

My corporal Heinricke was made sergeant. I am glad for he deserves it. A sergeant was reduced to private (not private life). His name is Silcott an odd fellow. He didn't want to come over then when he had to he tried to be transferred and then asked to be "busted"—made a private.

A lot of the fellows say they don't want promotions but there are a lot of them breaking their necks for consideration.

JULY 10, WEDNESDAY   Many picture postcards were returned today. They had been sent by the boys from places in England.

More drill and more lectures on military courtesy and other things both good and bad. We had bayonet work today. I don't like the bayonet. I hope I never have to use a bayonet or have to meet it. I would rather be shot than cut with a bayonet.

The captain gave us a good sound talk today. He said that we must get the idea out of our heads that we are fighting for France or England. That is quite right too. We are really fighting our own fight. No nation is in this war for the others sake but to secure its peace and safety in the future.[5]

We heard that we would get some mail today but it must be only a rumor as no mail has showed up.

There is no day in the army without its funny things. There is humor in most things over here. Even serious things produce laughs. The lectures some of these sergeants give for instance. This afternoon we had a lecture on the wind in relation to range finding. The Sergeant didn't have his subject well in hand but he put on a bold front, and proceeded. He told us in a vague way how to tell the speed of wind. He asked me how fast the wind was blowing. I looked at the leaves and judged four miles an hour. He asked me how I knew. I told him I didn't. I asked him how I could tell he evaded the question and very uncomfortably proceeded looking at his watch every few moments as if he was very anxious for the time to pass. After the lecture, I asked Staff what he learned. He said that he found that an East wind blows West except when it comes from the North and then it blows South.

Tonight at retreat they taught us who our regimental and division commanders are. I have forgotten most of them and their order already. I remember that a fellow by the name of Wright is in command of our division and if he dies or is killed or removed the next in command is Mr. Winn, whoever he is.[6] Colonel Johnson commands this regiment and I have forgotten who is next in command but I think it is the oldest major. I am not much interested in that sort of knowledge. All I want to remember is that I belong to Co. E 314 Engineers and I fancy the generals and other commanders will get there whether I know of their existence or not.

JULY 11, THURSDAY   We left Camp Mills a month ago today.

More drilling and lectures and a sort of examination by the Major. He had each platoon in each company drill for him. He told our platoon we were the best in the company and he told our company it was the best in the batallion [*sic*] but he told something to each of the other companies that made them think they were the best.

This evening we had Batallion review again. These Batallion reviews are getting to be monotonous. The hill we climb is about 250 feet high that is too much to ask a fellow to make three times a day in such hot weather. If it made better soldiers out of us I wouldn't mind but parading in company front with an empty belly won't help win this war. It looks like they would dispence [*sic*] with such stuff.

Mail came in today and I was remembered for a wonder. A letter from Nell in which she sends love. Speaks of heat in Arizona and says she will not run for office. Eve Overson wrote a very interesting letter also a page from the St. Johns paper in which was a letter from G. W. Berry stating big things the 89th would do especially his regiment the 342 F.A.[7] I note also that Edna Butler and Smith Gibbons also Agnes Brown and one of the Hamblins are

married. Agnes was one of my students. Edna was one of my hopes.[8] A good
letter from Mother also one from Belle and Charley in which they speak of
sending a box of candy. The Nebraska Girl wrote saying she sent a box of
candy neither of them can come so I have cause for the blues. I got two letters
from girls whose addresses I got on the way from Funston to Hoboken.

They issued tobacco tonight I drew mine and sold it. We are promised
tobacco every 6 days.

JULY 12, FRIDAY   Things ran very smooth today. We are getting to be very
efficient. We can do squads right or left with our eyes shut.

Lieutenant Howbert, he is the lieutenant of my platoon, gave us a lecture
on gas attacks and gas defence. All the lecture consisted merely in reading
some pamphlets put out by the A.E.F. and marked "Confidential."

Just a word about Lieutenant Howbert. He is a Colorado School of Mines
man, and a prince of a fellow. The only officer I have met outside of our captain who had the qualities of a leader. He tries to avoid saying things that hurt
the men's feelings whereas many of the others and most of the non-coms are
ever on the alert for opportunities to "ride" the men.

I sent a letter and some money to Appleton to have the books I ordered
in Camp Mills forwarded. I need something to study.

I am writing a letter to Nell this evening. I expect two from her next
mail. Since it takes a month for a letter to reach home, I had better start some
on the road.

Sergeant Cohn stopped by my bunk to chat for a moment. I like Sergeant. He is a real human sort of fellow. Very considerate and always cheery.

There is a great deal of noise out here tonight; too much red wine. It
makes the best of them talk though it is not very strong, so I am told. It looks
very much like rain tonight. I wish we would get a small shower.

JULY 13, SATURDAY   We stood a genuine army Saturday inspection. It took
all day to get ready and to do the job. I never stood a real field inspection
according to the I.D.R. [Infantry Drill Regulations] before so naturally I was
much interested as well as bored. I am pleased to say that I pass all right.

By the way we did drill some this morning. One of our new officers, a
second lieutenant otherwise known as a "Shave tail," made us a speech.[9] It
was calculated to stir us up to aspire to military greatness. During his talk he
used the following expression several times, "Up on your toes men. Remember the private of today is the General of tomorrow." It is forbidden fruit to

laugh in ranks, but there were many suppressed groans that were prophecies of laughs that came later. It put the soldiers in humor for a great deal of joking after supper. There are a couple of fellows in the company who are not very bright. Each one thinks the other doesn't know anything. They hate to be mistaken for each other so the fellows take advantage of that and call Fields, Cooper and Cooper, Fields. Someone must be the goat.

They made a talk this evening on how to conduct ourselves in case we are taken prisoners what to tell and what not to.

There is an old lady up on the hillside trying to catch her cow. She is very feeble and the cow keeps running away from her. It's a shame I must go help her. War is Hell, such things bring it home. I hope our old women will never have to work as these do.

JULY 14, SUNDAY   I was walking about town today and saw a home made American flag. The red stripes were not the right red, the white stripes were too narrow and the stars were all sizes [on] it. There were not enough stripes and the stars were too few but the flag like the one Betty Ross made told a volume about the attitude of that little French home and the spirit of the hearts within it. The little home made flag hung side by side with the tricolor of France as perhaps Betty Ross's first flag hung beside the red white and blue of it when we were in our national infancy.

Today is a big day in France. If my dates are not mixed it was on July 14 that the Bastile fell.[10] I thought I would spend the day studying but I had a chance to go on a pass so I spent the time visiting among the neighboring towns in which are quartered different units of our division.

I was fortunate in finding the 353 Inf as I hunted up some of the Arizona boys who were with me at the detention camp. I found Guy Rencher he was cooking and he gave us a good feed. I went down to the creek and found Johnny Slaughter washing his clothes.[11] I found Lehi Smith from Snow Flake and he got me another feed which took all the wrinkles out of my stomach.[12] It was the first time I have had all I could eat since I left Camp Funston. I got to see the two Mexican boys from Springerville Salazar and Padilla.[13] Smith says they are good soldiers.

Smith and I walked about town. I broke my last $1.00 to buy a book for a diary.

I rode a French freight train part of the way back home. It seemed good to get on in good American style though some Frenchmen looked askance at me.[14]

We honored the day by a batallion parade on the chateau green. It was one of the best drills we have put on.

A French officer just came into the barracks he wanted the fellows to get him some sugar. It seems that they can't get sugar or bread or tobacco without cards and he had none. One of the boys went to the kitchen and stole him some sugar.

Got a newspaper today the first since we left England. I have very little faith in these papers printed under the auspices of the A.E.F. the news is too well sifted. I feel that I spent July 14, 1918, very well.

JULY 15, MONDAY   It is a hot day. We almost smothered climbing the hill this morning. We hit it hard all forenoon. Bayonet drill sure brought out the juice. The lieutenant who gave us the lecture about the private of today being the general of tomorrow is a brute or an idiot. He says "let 'em sweat it will bring the wine out of them." He assumes that all of us have been swilling down the wine. I am glad I don't because I have a better chance of doing my bit when such a creature drills us. I am glad, too, that they didn't make us wear our tin hats today as they make one's head ache in this heat.

This afternoon we had a battle in the woods. I don't know yet what was done or how it was done. I think that each opposing side was fearful of casualties so they avoided each other. I spent most of the time lying in the shade while the scouts were out trying to get scent of the "enemy." I was a "reserve." I think there was a few prisoners taken and one of our men was marked "dead" so our side lost.

I have decided that I am not cut out for a soldier. I am neither patient or aggressive. It seems that one must have no regard for anyone's feelings or wishes to make headway in the army. I have resolved my course in the future will be this. I am going to do whatever they tell me as best I can. I will always do what I think is right. Always there when I am wanted and out of the way when not needed. All I am going to be at the office is a name on the roster. I am not going to have a mark against me or my record. I take this stand because there is nothing about the army that attracts me and all that interests me is my duty to give full measure each day.

I am very lonesome here in this outfit there is no one with whom I have anything in common. Most of them are more interested in wine and loose women both of which there is a limited quantity here. So most of them go in that direction and I am left in a little world by myself. Outside of Sergeant Heinricke I have few friends here.

JULY 16, TUESDAY   I was drafted into the kitchen today K.P. is no snap here with so many pots to wash at each meal. It has its advantages but they are few. One gets out of drill on that day but he has to carry several barrels of water which is worse. The best thing about Kitchen Police is that a fellow gets plenty to eat which is quite an item in these lean days.

K.P.'s must help serve the chow. It is not a bad job where one serves something that can be measured or counted to each man but to serve meat or potatoes or beans where one has to measure it out by guess and sight it is hard to treat them all alike. When there is not enough to satisfy them each man imagines he is being short changed. There is only a certain amount for the company and it takes good managing to distribute it out among 250 men without having any left or over feeding some and cheating others. There is no one else to growl so they cuss the cooks and K.P.'s.

One fellow tried to tell me I was picking my friends. I should have held my temper but I failed. I thought he would come and get me but I guess I bluffed him.

There seems to be conflict in political circles in Germany. I wish there were more. There seems to be [a] general advance on.[15] One of the fellows was to the railroad today and saw two train loads of wounded. They are having a blanket tossing outside believe I'll go take part.

JULY 17, WEDNESDAY   I am starting my diary in a new note book. I hope this book lasts till the war is over. To do that the war must be over soon or I must write very little and to the point. Such notes as I may write I can rewrite later. Pershing has said "Hell, Heaven or Hoboken by Christmas." Lets hope so at least.

I am drinking out of a tomato can today. Someone got away with my cup while I was on K.P. yesterday. It may have been taken by mistake when we served the prisoners. I must go inquire at the Guard House.

I entered a new world this forenoon. I am in the reconnaissance school. That sounds big but is deceiving. It is that branch of engineer service that has to do with map making, scouting and reconnoitering for information. I am pleased too for I like work where a fellow can be out of the regular cogwheel formations. If I can make good in this line I will be pleased. At least I can get interested and that will speed the time. Hereafter in the forenoons I go to school and drill only in the afternoon.

Well we spent the morning measuring our average stride on different kinds of roads and grades. I have an average step on the level of 34½ inches.

Sergeant Cohn has charge of the work. Sergeant Miller is helping him he is another first class fellow.

Bayonet work this afternoon. I will never be a shining success in that line. I can't growl like an animal. One must snarl and yell till he is horse [hoarse]. Very hot on the hill no water all afternoon.

JULY 18   I have been pretty sick today. I could eat very little dinner and no supper. I had a hard time to stay in the ranks this afternoon. At retreat I think I disgraced myself. I stood about half through the formation when my knees got weak and I knew I had better drop out so I wobbled a few feet behind the lines and lay down. After I vomited I felt better. While the men were at supper I went down and took a roll in the creek so I feel quite myself again. I will be all right in the morning.

We got orders today to send home our serial numbers so that the folks could write to the war department in case letters ceased to come. I wrote a letter to Dolly and sent mother my number which is 2845704.

This forenoon the recon. school had a short hike to pick points for map making then we measured by instruments the heights of hills. Heinricke and I were paired off together. I am glad for we work together pretty well. I made a little tripod and he has a compass which at present is all the tools we have but for a homemade rule.

I notice by the bulletin board that I have been made first class private. That means I get $3.00 a month more and that is about all there is to it.[16]

One hears now and then a rumbling in the distance. Some say it is guns but I think it is thunder. We are not that close to the front. If it isn't guns we hear now it won't be long till we do hear them.

JULY 19   I spent the forenoon running a traverse. A traverse is [a] course that one travels or wishes to travel drawn to a scale on paper. One starts with a point on a piece of paper. He must always keep his paper square with the world that is North must always be north and when he moves along his traverse he draws the line of movement that means the direction and distance according to his compass and paces. The problem is to make the paper or map picture the true course so that when the traverse is finished the man won't be one place but according to his map somewhere else. I took a course through woods and around a hill. My work or pacing was not accurate so I ended up on my starting point in fact but 500 paces away in theory.

I don't know whether it's good or bad news but I received a letter from C.R.[17] There wasn't much in it to enthuse a fellow unless he chose to read between the lines which is a dangerous thing since a person usually reads what he desires to be true.

We went for a practice hike this afternoon. It took about 3 or 4 hours and we about spent ourselves as the sun was hot and the roads were dusty and we had no water. We passed by a lot of signal corpsmen at work they were sending different kinds of messages I didn't understand. We saw the machine gun teams going through their practice shooting imaginary shells at imaginary huns. So we are not the only ones who are intensely preparing for the grim game we will soon be playing.

I tried to find out where Bushman's regiment was but failed. No one knows where anyone else is so its useless to ask. No one has time to know.

I made some observations today as we plodded along. These fields my but how small they are. I have seen many potato patches with not more than 200 or 300 plants in and most [of] the grain fields are less than an acre. Most of these farmers can carry their bean crop home on their backs.

They are very thrifty and hard working people but their methods of farming are very antiquated. For example I saw a family plowing they had two horses on the plow they were hitched single file. The mother led the first horse the daughter the other and the father held the plow. It takes two men to drive a wagon—one to lead or drive the team and another to walk behind and wind the brake.

In a town was a public wash house where the women were kneeling around a concrete pool and washing clothes. They beat the dirt out here with a paddle.

We had Battallion parade again tonight but it was a fizzle.

JULY 20 This morning they gave us a lesson in trenching. In peace time we would simply call it ditch digging. The ground is very hard and rocky. I sweat and raised blisters from a broken pick handle. It is a big job to dig a standard trench and before it is finalized much dirt is moved. Of course it is done by degrees. One starts a trench by laying on his belly and throwing enough dirt ahead of him to form a protection then he keeps making the hole bigger and the pile higher till he can stand up and be out of sight then he proceeds to dig a ditch to connect up with his comrades. Naturally those trenches would not be in a straight line. I will make a sketch of a finished trench.[18] It is a lot of hard work to do this but I suppose it is the best way to learn. We are told that the soft earth is the best kind of fortification so we really [realize] it is worth to know how to dig in.

The clerks have started a little newspaper called the "Latrine Gazette." It is printed on the typewriter and published on the bulletin board every evening. It contains all the local gossip and many jokes, stale and otherwise. Some of the humor is crude and sometimes but the paper is a good way to get a little seasoning in camplife.

JULY 21, SUNDAY When oh when will pay day come. There is hardly a cent in camp and our money is nearly a month past due. I don't need money for any personal wants for I have gotten so I am not wanting things anymore. I have a few little obligations I need to meet and for that reason I wish they would pay me my $1.00 per.

It rained all forenoon. Some of the boys are growling because it couldn't rain any other time but Sunday. I enjoyed the time. I wrote a letter to C. Rogers and another to Nell and her mother. War news is very encouraging lately. I told Nell she would see peace before snow fell in Arizona. Although that sounds good I wouldn't bet money on it. I can't conceive of this war lasting much longer. Surely God will not permit all these peoples to suffer through another winter when it is so evident that the Central powers can't win. It looks like He has some way in His power to make them see it.

This afternoon the sun came out so I went out to resurvey the traverse I failed on the other day. I had better luck this time but the map today is far from perfect. I made it on a scale of 1/10,000 to 1. I became so absorbed that the afternoon passed before I was aware I was setting up my tripod on the hill behind camp when I saw the fellows falling out for retreat. I had to make a run for it. Got there just in time.

My first number of the Stars and Stripes came today. It is a paper published by some of the leading soldier newspaper men over here. It is full of pretty good stuff, jokes humor and write-ups. It is an effort I suppose to express the spirit of the A.E.F. I am sending my number (paper) to Grandma Lytle.

JULY 22, MONDAY I took my first lesson in landscape sketching this morning. It is very interesting. I learned how to make a map of a whole country from two points. It is called triangulation. All one has to know is the distance between his points of observation. I am liking my reconnaissance work better every day. In it one can work towards an end. There is a fascination in working for results.

This afternoon I dug trenches with the rest of the company. It seems funny that I have to come to the army to learn to use the shovel and pick. I'd rather have some work in timbering and making dug outs. We are not learning anything this way. All we do is throw dirt and the sergeant's argue how it should be done. They have one sergeant for every 10 or 12 men and one man could run the whole works. One sergeant reprimanded me severely for going after a drink of water. My canteen was a hundred feet from where I was working, he asked me who gave me orders to get a drink.

We have had pretty good food of late with the exception of bread which is often moldy. All the moldy bread is thrown away but they don't give any credit for moldy bread. It is counted the same as good bread. It is the men who lose. The doctors condemn the bread but they don't try to get an addition to make up for it. The doctors are very interested in us. They take this spring water that the people have been drinking for 200 years and chlorinate it so that no one can drink it. It is to kill germs. I would rather risk the disease than drink the water.[19] We also come in contact with the doctors in venereal inspections. We just stood one. The medical department does a good thing by insisting on sanitation we are expected to keep our clothes clean and take a bath as often as possible. We clean up the quarters every day. They lecture us now and then on cleanliness. I don't know whether habits of cleaning up that are forced on a man are a good thing or not but certainly some of these men are washing and mending clothes for the first time. Each of us got a can of grease to shine up our old hobnail shoes with.

The wheat is getting ripe and the people are making ready to bring in the sheaves.

JULY 23, TUESDAY   It has been a very pleasant day for me even if it did rain the afternoon. This forenoon we had a very pressing job we ran a traverse through a triangle of towns about two miles a part. I had pretty good luck connecting up my points but I got in late for dinner.

France has very good roads but the outfits they drive over the roads are very amusing. One sees a horse hitched in the shafts and another hitched in front to the shafts. One very seldom sees a span of horses hooked abreast. I did see a horse and a bull marching on opposite sides of the tung. These people prefer single file to column of twos formation.

I saw some Austrian prisoners today they were working on the roads and were chaperoned by French men with long bayonets.

On account of the rain we spent the afternoon listening to lectures. Some of the time I was in a class on direction finding and map reading. Later we had a lecture in demolition and gas masks. Gas masks were issued and we had practice in putting them off and on.

The principle of the gas mask is simple—a hood is placed over the face so that the person can only breathe air that has been strained through gas neutralizing chemicals. A clamp is put on the nose and all air is breathed through a rubber tube the end of which one holds in his mouth. The glasses often get cloudy they get so faster if one breathes in his mask.

Besides our gas masks they issued a hundred rounds of ammunition each. It is a heavy load but it is part of our burden from now on.

They gave us special orders on keeping our hair short and shaving every day.

No Batallion parade today on account of the rain. Several men volunteered to go over to the railroad to unload wood they would rather do that than parade so would I but they got the job first. Imagine how they will feel when they learn there was no parade.

JULY 24, WEDNESDAY If I were back home I would have a big time today. They may be having a celebration as it is but I am satisfied they are not having the good time they would have if the boys were home. 10 year's ago today I went to my first pioneer programme at Enterprise. I heard Grandpa Woods speak of his journey across the plains and the entrance of the pioneers into Salt Lake Valley, July 24, 1847. I was impressed with the talk. It was not a sermon as much as a plain talk of experiences. I found myself in love with the old man and in sympathy with the people who suffered such hardships that they might build homes out there in the desert where the howling mobs would not molest them.

We worked on "Fortifications" this morning. Trenches are fortifications and it was hard digging too. After one digs down a foot then he strikes a semidecayed limestone and progress is difficult. I don't mind working at this but I do mind being interrupted by the dozen or more N.C.O.'s who have nothing to do but supervise. They all try to be official and first one will come in and measure the work and then another. Then they will give orders to have the impression that they are "on the job." I'll never succeed in the army because all this shamming bores me too much. During work gas masks were kept close and every now and then some "loot" would yell gas. We are expected to get our masks on in 6 seconds. All who were slower than that are called "dead." Jim Hughes was "dead" two times.

After dinner we had some very strenuous rifle and bayonet drill. Then we practiced throwing grenades. It was the first time we have thrown live grenades and some of the fellows were a little nervous. Some threw them without pulling the pins and others didn't throw them far enough to land to get them in a gravel pit where they would explode. These grenades explode in 5 seconds. I watched the doughboys yesterday. They have the edge on us when it comes to throwing grenades or in bayonet practice either.

Several of the fellows we culled out in Camp Mills on account of venereal disease joined us today. They were the happiest looking fellows I ever saw. Also we had about 50 new men come as replacements to fill up our company to war strength.

Orders came today to turn in all the equipment we don't need. I think that means personal stuff too see later.

JULY 25, THURSDAY   I am tired tonight. This forenoon I went out on reconnaissance between here and a couple of other villages. I was late for dinner but I got a good map of the country we covered. This afternoon we dug trenches again. I found some nice shell fossils in the lime rock I would like to send some of them to Professor Busse if it were possible, but there is no system here where by anyone can send anything home he is lucky to get letters off.

Meals are getting worse. We are eating these new French potatoes. I eat 20 for dinner skins and all, yet I was hungry enough to eat 40 more. For supper we had hot tomatoes, which I don't like, and cold salmon. I don't care much for "goldfish" either, but a fellow will eat anything here just so it fills up.

Mail came this evening but none for me. I feel like I used to feel when Santa Claus used to pass me up.

Lieutenant Howbert offered to lend me some books on engineering. I think I shall go get them first opportunity.

We had batallion parade this afternoon wore our tin hats. I don't know why we wore them unless someone wanted to see how we looked in them.

We are going up front soon. Fellows talk about that more than anything else now.

JULY 26, FRIDAY   Three months ago today I left the classroom for the army. I wonder how long before I can leave the army for the classroom.

Before we went out this morning they had us sort our equipment and took all that we will not carry. We made them into rolls it includes some extra clothes our overcoat and one blanket. After that the forenoon was spent in sizing and reorganizing the company. There are 28 squads in the company now they start with the big fellows in squad one and run down to the "boy scouts" I am in the 19th squad. That takes me out of the 4th platoon to the 3rd. I am glad of the change because there is a good bunch of sergeants in the 3rd whereas they have a little bully in charge of the 4th platoon. I hate to lose my old lieutenant, though we have a pretty good fellow in charge of the 3rd platoon.

Not much drilling today just enough for the new squads to get used to each other.

Some more mail came today but I find myself still in the lurch. I expect a letter or two from Nell next time. At least she is honor bound, if her promise is worth anything, to write to me.

They issued wrapped leggings last night and we wore them today for the first time. We had a lot of trouble getting them on too nearly everyone was late for reveille on their account. When we climbed the hill this morning many men had to fall out because their leggings were wrapped so tight the blood could not circulate properly. They also issued oversea caps to replace our campaign hats. These are handy little caps but they are no good in sunshine.

Our reserve rations came in tonight. Reserve rations are rations we carry on our backs instead of in our stomachs.[20]

Looks like rain. Hope it doesn't. I hate to dig trenches in the mud.

JULY 27, SATURDAY   This has been a nasty rainy sloppy day. The boys who went on the hill got wet. I was to reconnaissance school. We found inside occupation but the roof leaked so that it was not even dry there.

We spent the morning class trying to discuss the value in civil life of the things we learned in the army. We decided that the reconnaissance section offered a great deal of training that would be of value in civil life. Sergeant's Cohn & Miller spoke on some of the important things we must learn. Cohn spoke of a probable need of a great deal of stick-to-it-ive-ness in actual practice. Our work is not as important in this kind of warfare as in the old kind of campaigning. A man only means a yard or so of trench line in this war. Every foot of the country is pretty well mapped already so all one needs to know is the location of things on existing maps.

We had inspection again today. Our "mobile equipment" That means everything a soldier carries. The mud prevented our going on the hill so we held inspection on the green. One of the loots gave us a lecture on how to roll an ideal pack if there is such a thing. Our packs get heavier every day. They are always giving us something new to carry.

It is quite amusing in a barracks when soldiers are preparing for inspection. Some singing, some cursing some arguing and some merely talking. Everyone is at it. Shaving, brushing, packing. Or perhaps looking for something and accusing everyone of stealing it.

No retreat tonight account of rain. So we had inspection in barracks with full packs on and our faces towards the wall. The little Lieutenant who told us the private of today is the Gen. Of tomorrow inspected my pack he asked me if I was a fish peddler in private life. I didn't say anything because I don't know yet whether it was meant for a compliment or not, but I think he was trying to bawl me out in an original way. Someone giggled and he yelled out to a fellow to my right to wipe his smile off.

I got mail tonight. A letter from Belle.[21] It was written on May 24 and has been better than two months on the way.

She says that Will is in the Canadian army so there are three of us in the service. Another interesting letter from my Nebraska girl, Miss Theressa.

Everybody is rejoicing tonight because the inspection to be held tomorrow by the division commander is called off.

JULY 28, SUNDAY   A beautiful day. I started a letter to Miss Nebraska this morning but didn't have the heart to finish it till tonight.

I put in for a pass this morning no sooner had I got the pass till I was put on a detail to carry powder. I carried my share quickly and beat it. I started off toward a place called Neuf Chateau to get trace of the 342 machine gun outfit. There is where Bushman is. I ran upon his outfit quite accidently. He has been less than 3 miles from here all the while.

I ate dinner with him and then the two of us started for (Rimaucourt) We were lucky to get a truck and the result was Bush and L.L. Smith and I were together all afternoon. We couldn't stay long as I had 4 miles and he had 6 to get back to our outfits for retreat. Bush and Smith both come from Snow Flake so they had quite a reunion. Smith is very homesick. He was married only a week before he came to the army. It is just 3 months ago today since the three of us met at Holbrook to entrain for Funston. It did me good to meet those fellows today. We agreed that we could get more joy from living our religion than any other source especially at this time of uncertainties.

Everyone I talked to expects to go up to the front soon. I wish we would.

JULY 29   We had our rifles, our feet and our equipment inspected today. Yes we even had another venereal inspection.

In the field inspection we pitched our dog tents. It was a new experience for me. I spread out my 60 or more articles not mentioning ammunition and made a good showing. Everything in good shape but I was short one shoestring for which they took my name.

That is the second time my name has been taken today. At formation this morning when the company was called to attention I was caught wrapping my leggings. The lieutenant told me that that was no place to dress. In civil life I would have thanked him for the information but one must not show his appreciation in the army.

It was 2:30 when we got in for dinner. Our appetites were twice the size of the portion given to satisfy them. There was a great deal of growling and cursing. It seems that at inspection the colonel asked Cooper how he was satisfied with the feed. Now Cooper isn't very bright and he was some what frightened that the colonel would speak to him so he said that he had plenty and it was good feed. Poor Cooper, they have hooted him all day. There is an ideal example of the way men are held under the thumb. It may be all right to do it. But it is evident that if men are put in a position where they dare not speak their mind then they have no confidence in themselves when they are spoken to by those over them.

We throwed grenades again this afternoon under the direction of the little lieutenant who asked me if I peddled fish in civil life. He is afraid of a grenade. I learned what his name was today. He is Lieutenant Fickle, very properly so.

JULY 30, TUESDAY   First time I have got out of work since I have been in the army. We drew a map of the trenches we have been sweating over for so many days. The rest of the company worked but the reconnaissance section. We did some pretty accurate work by means of triangles. Fuelle and Nelson and I worked together. They are both very agreeable fellows to work with. The second half of the afternoon we took a lesson in barb wire entanglements under Lieut. Fickle.

I am afraid Lt. Fickle is getting to be very unpopular with the men. He did something this afternoon that was an outrage and it will be a long time before he will have the confidence of these men. It was my platoon too although I was working near on my trench map and wasn't included.

They had been called out of the trenches for a 5 minutes rest. During the rest some of them did something he didn't like so he fell the whole platoon in "the guilty and the just." He made them do "on your belly on your back" for nearly 5 minutes. A strenuous exercise too. A man flops on his belly— jumps up—falls on his back then up and then down on his belly again.

Later on during his lecture on barb wire entanglements, Jake Pallock went to sleep. To punish him he made him run to a woods and back, about ½ mile.

Food is still low. I am just as hungry when I have finished my meal as before. One of the lieutenants made a speech to us about the food. He didn't say anything about more to eat just told us not to call the cooks "bellyrobbers." I don't blame the cooks but I do blame the somebody somewhere who is short changing us on rations. I know the infantry and machine gunners get worse than we do.

JULY 31, WEDNESDAY   On Wednesday July 31, 1889 I was born. I have never been able to find out what kind of star shone over me. Enough that my father must have been thoroughly impressed by my initial appearance for he named me after himself. I wonder if he would have believed then that his namesake would in 30 years be bearing arms against the country he grew up in. If he were alive today, I believe, he would be proud it is so.

Had enough to eat for breakfast and dinner today so I worked with a real good will. We made elevation levels or contour lines on a map during the forenoon. This afternoon we had close order drill and some bridging. While we were resting in the shade we tied knots. Didn't drill very hard today.

Today is payday. We had just about given up the idea. In the army they pay according to rank sergeants according to their grade, corporals, first class privates, and bucks. I got 142 francs or somewhere about $25. or $30.00. It is worth about 1000 figs at the present price the French tax us for fruit.

I don't like these over sea caps especially at retreat. When they call us to attention I must look right into the sun.

It just occurred to me that I am getting out of guard and K.P. pretty regular lately. Why?

AUGUST 1   This morning our reconnaissance outfits came. They will be given to us later. Palmer and I ran a traverse with the aid of a box compass. We kept notes of our paces and directions and later we sat down in the shade and drew our map. Some system. We had good luck too for greenhorns.

They took our barracks bags away from us today. I put most of the stuff I didn't care to lose in the bag. Some pictures and books and letters. I kept the sweater Grandma Lytle made me and a little sewing kit she gave me. I hate to part with some of the stuff I have been carrying so long. I came to Funston with more than a suitcase full of stuff. It was the least I could bring. Now all the personal stuff I have I can hold in one hand.

The war is 4 years old today. I don't see how it can last another year. I got a paper today but everything seems to be at a standstill. I note though that Henry Ford is running for Senator. I hope he wins.[22]

A lot of men are in the guard house today. They have been dry so long that pay day was too much for them. They are spending freely. There are a few loose women here and it seems that they are collecting a pretty good toll. I am glad that these women are not a temptation to me. I don't think the wine ever would be. A fellow can be a better soldier without that stuff.

We had a very good supper tonight. They gave us sliced tomatoes.

Well we have been thinking about the front so long that Imagine we would be disappointed if we couldn't go.

AUGUST 2   Not much excitement but much expectation. Some of the teams started ahead today they don't even know where they are going.

We [had] a lot of noise and riot here last night. A fellow by the name of Powers came in drunk he was quarrelsome and wanted to fight anything from a corporal up. Some of the fellows joshed him and that made him worse. It ended by Beauchamp, the top sergeant coming in. He tried to persuade Powers to go to bed then had to threaten him with a beating. I don't think they will do anything with him. He is inside of the circle. There is many a poor fellow here would be in the guardhouse for doing less.

We didn't do much drilling today on account of rain. I took advantage of the opportunity and wrote some letters.

This evening they distributed our reserve rations. It consisted of a little sugar, some coffee and salt. Three, no four, packages of hard tack and a can of corn beef. That is called two days rations. It is not to be eaten unless in case of emergency and then not without orders.

AUGUST 3, SATURDAY   We waited around all day for orders. I don't even know what the nature of the orders might be, or if there were to be any.

This forenoon Heinricke and I put in the time very pleasantly filling in details on a map. All we did this afternoon was stand inspection and have gas drill. In the inspection we stood at rigid attention for more than an hour. It was a rigid inspection too. 55 men failed to pass. I must be lucky to pass these inspections and get out of K.P. and guard. All the 55 men did not have their names taken because of dirty guns some were put on the delinquency list for dirty shoes, being unshaved one man struck at a big fly that was biting his face. A little spider was busy running around over my face some of the time. Wherever he went he left a web that itched terribly. An itch that can't be scratched is always the worst.

Strange I don't get any mail. I hate to write letters in good faith and then get no response. I sent Nell my Stars and Stripes. There was a big write up in it trying to start a movement to adopt a war orphan. I thought it would interest her now that all her hopes have gone to war. She has been crazy to adopt a little girl. She can get all she wants over here for 500 francs each.

The 4th platoon went somewhere today when they left they gave us the laugh because they would get out of drilling. Later it developed they were sent to clean up a camp left by other batallion and we did very little drilling in their absence so the laugh turned. It seems that Block a little jew [*sic*] and Shornhauser a little German got in difficulties and the rest of the men wouldn't let them fight till this evening. They are going out on the green now to settle it.

AUGUST 4, SUNDAY   Now regarding the fight last night. I had no time to stop to see it. The crowd was too big anyway so I went down to the creek to wash some clothes. When I got back it was over, even the yelling. One man was spread out on the ground some friends were taking off his gloves and rubbing his bruises. Others were trying to patch up his bruised feelings. It was the little Jew. Some friends were escorting the victor away the biggest crowd went with the victor (as usual) That is the good old American way to settle differences but it doesn't always decide the right.

Two of our sergeants supply sergeant Harvel and Sergeant Miller went away to O.T.E. I look for Miller to get a commission he deserves it. The C.O. clerk was made supply sergeant. He is another Jew, Stroheim. There is an opening for a company clerk. Cohn tried to get me to apply but I don't want that kind of a job.

A word about the feed. Somewhat better we had beefsteak for breakfast, think of it! I am getting so I can eat anything even cooked tomatoes. I have to smile as I think of how the fellows rush the officers table after they have finished to get the stuff they leave. When our captain was here he wouldn't permit the officers to eat any better than the men. He is off to school now and the loots get all they want. I am afraid we will lose our old captain. This is the first day that stuff hasn't been picked off the officers table. We had plenty for supper tonight.

I think we pull out tomorrow. They must have expected orders today for no man was permitted to be more than three hours away from camp. I didn't try to get a pass but went up on the hillside and did some landscape sketching. It was my first efforts in that line and looked it.

6

UP TO THE FRONT, AUGUST 1918

ARRIVAL AT THE FRONT WAS A PROCESS OF INITIATION THAT BEGAN WITH the sound of canons firing in the distance, and moved past farmers still working in their fields to previous battlefields marked by barbed wire entanglements, shell holes, abandoned trenches, and recently dug graves. As the soldiers moved forward what had been the distant rumble of artillery became punctuated with the screams of shells passing overhead and enemy aircraft brought new dangers. Food was often scarce and uncertain and poison gas was a serious threat. Nels encountered the first live Germans—prisoners of war captured during recent fighting. Sleep was snatched whenever it could be in cramped, stuffy, rat-infested dugouts or the small two-man tents—much inferior accommodations compared to the comfortable homes and barns available to soldiers in the rear. In return, inspections and formations temporarily ceased as the odyssey to the front ended with soldiers crouching in trenches straining to see across no man's land and waiting for orders to sneak out at night to lay wire or to go "over the top" during the day to engage the enemy the Americans had come more than three thousand miles to fight. The sector into which Company E moved—still in the Champagne Ardenne Region—was about fifty miles northeast of Humberville and included the villages of Minorville, Novient, and Flirey. August was a particularly difficult time for Nels Anderson because he learned of the accidental death of his younger sister, Belle, in June 1918. Anderson blamed himself and the Germans for her death.

AUGUST 5   Yesterday was August 5 but I was too busy to write. When we were not moving or working we were on the alert waiting for orders.

The forenoon we rolled packs and policed up the camps. We put all the barracks in order and left the place and the town much cleaner than we left [found] it. All the stuff we didn't burn we gave to the natives, that is personal stuff. Many of the men had stuff they brought from home but could take no farther such as wash basins clothing pillows and blankets.

Many of the boys spent their spare moments stocking up on red wine which they seemed to think was more conveniently carried inside. So when we left at 12:30 some of them were so drunk we had to lift them in the trucks. I had to lead one fellow in my squad to prevent his pack over balancing him.

I don't know where we are today.[1] I could find the name of the town if I would go hunt it up but that would help very little. The big thing is we can hear guns and there is no doubt about it this time but back to yesterday.

We had some ride. We were crowded in trucks (27 in our truck) and transported about 50 miles. It took us 18 hours to make it. The ride was a bore. We made many stops for reasons of their own. I am told it was to prevent enemy planes from making observations. I do know however that it rained on us a great deal especially during the night. Everyone got wet and cold and ill humored. Our truck and one other got lost from the train in the dark and we were stranded for several hours which didn't help our feelings much.

While the day light lasted yesterday we had a hilarious time especially in these French towns. We yelled at everyone through we know nothing to say but "Oui, oui." It seemed that we came up hill most of the way and too, the land seemed to be getting poorer. Some places the crops were pitifully poor. But the peasants were patiently gathering all the soil would yield.

While we stood by the road hundreds of automobiles passed us. All traveling without lights and all loaded with soldiers.

One of our lieutenants came back and found us. We got to this place about 4 o'clock at daylight we got to bed in barns and some places worse. I almost forgot to say that many of the trucks are driven by Negroes. When we came within hearing of the guns our driver said, "I doan wanna come up hier I aint lost nothing hier."

AUGUST 6, TUESDAY   We are living in billets. Billets, as I understand it means get in somewhere as best you can and if you get a stall or a perch with the stock or chickens you are lucky provided it is dry. I am lucky. Have a wooden bunk in a big rock barn. It is on a hay floor over a stable. It would take a poet to describe the place. Enough that the roofs are tile and the walls rock. It goes against the grain for some of the boys to sleep in barns but I've done it before.

The street is very sloppy and smells sour. So do all French towns I have seen after a rain. This town is different than most others in several respects. The church is practically new, being built in 1845. Yet they have not departed from the latin for over the door is written "Dominus Dei." [House of God].[2]

Scenery here is pretty. One feature of art and craft that makes this town different is the canal. It is a navigable canal the big flat boats are pulled by cables. I don't know where it comes from or where it goes but it goes out of sight into a tunnel that is long and straight judging from the row of lights within it. It is not possible to see the other end. There must be fish in the canal too for I saw several Frenchmen angling along the banks. None of them had any fish, however.

I cleaned up my gun and equipment today everything rusty and dirty.

Lieut. Fickle the fellow who told us we had a chance to be generals made a speech today. He is in command of the company and has that privilege. He told us if any of us got drunk the whole company would take a 15 mile hike tomorrow. I don't know who told him but it may be so, it could be.

Today is a day of rest he told us so I have shaved up and I sit me down to write a letter to Luther W. Terry.[3]

Later—Just got started on that letter when they ordered us out for gas instruction. S.O.S. It bores me if they taught us something it would be different but all they did was run us up and down the road with our masks on. After that we were told to get pack rolled for inspection at retreat. At retreat we loaded packs on a wagon, or two wagons. It dawned upon me we were going to move. It was a 5 km hike without packs to another town I don't know which direction we came as there has been no sun all day. When we got here the packs were all in a pile in a barn. It took me till 4:00 o'clock to get mine but now I go to lay the body.

AUGUST 7, WEDNESDAY   I feel fine this morning. A fine day. Nothing has happened so far except a breakfast of boiled potatoes and corn and hard tack. The doctors started the day with venereal inspection. Now I am in my billet and alone with my thoughts all the other fellows are out hunting vin rouge while the officers are trying to close up the shops. I think I shall try to find a dry place in the sunshine and try to write to Clara.

Later[.] Beaucoup drinking today when it came time to leave town no less than fifty men were drunk there were two fights and much loud talk (wars and rumors of wars) none of the fellows were helplessly drunk just talkative. Ward, a fellow spent most of his time when my old platoon sergeant wasn't looking yelling curses at him. Staff knocked down the rifle stack, Gilette came late (drunk) and Lt. Fickle made him run up and down the street with full pack he fell down two or three times, then the loot ordered him dipped in the water trough. It was done. Perhaps I have said enough. I might express an opinion about abused authority. I only hope we can keep away from liquor hereafter.

Well we marched into (Toul) and I have got myself placed somewhat.[4] It was a three mile hike and fellows who were rearing so to go got pretty tired, they were bawling for rest at the top of their voice. It really wasn't a bad march for those who started sober.

They loaded us on a small narrow gauge flat cars that we labeled U.S.A. and in less than an hour after we hit the place we were being jerked out of town by a little dinky Engine. It was a Yank crew and they pulled the whistle just like back home. We shot over French fields, through woods, down lanes and along shady roads till at the end of an hour or two we got here. We passed a lot of barb wire entanglements and old trenches manned with fake canons. I suppose they were fortifications to protect the city of (Toul). Arrive in the dark.

Up here the guns are shooting, many of them.[5] I don't know much about directions or gun sounds but I fancy the lines are not over 3 miles. We see flares go up in the air every now and then, probably signals.

It is funny how elated everyone is. I feel like tomorrow was the 4th of July. I am wondering tonight how the tiles would scatter if this barn I am sleeping in got hit.

AUGUST 8, THURSDAY   Didn't spend as much time thinking of the guns last night as I did trying to get the maximum warmth out of 2 blankets and a rain coat. Then in my half sleep I was trying to figure out if trench lice could be over come with chlorine or tear gas.

Well Germany is nearer today than ever before. The trenches are right here but the thing that impresses me is how unconcerned the people seem to be of that fact. They are still sowing and reaping as quietly as if they were 50 miles back. There are a few French soldiers here also.

I went out and found a Y.M.C.A. this morning. It was a welcome sight. There was a lady there serving out cocoa. She made the place seem homelike. I got some paper and wrote a letter to Nell also sent 20 francs to Charley and 20 to the bank.

Now that I am this close I am worrying about my diary. I don't want to lose it and I want to keep it up. If I go up to the trenches I must not take it so all I can do is trust to luck. I propose to learn nothing of military value and if it is necessary to learn anything learn it but write it not.

Evening The mail tonight brought a cloud of gloom for me. Belle was killed in an accident. It happened last June sometime. I got a letter from Mr. Prescott. He thought I knew all about it but sent a newspaper clipping by the local paper to inform me in case I had not heard.

It is harder on me because I know I will have most of the blame for I persuaded her to come out West to go to school with me. When Father died I came home and had to leave her alone in Salt Lake. During the summer she got a dose of ptomaine poisoning. It left her very weak she was not strong it seems when she got killed. She was hauling a stove on the wagon. The stove fell and crushed her skull.[6] Mother blames the fall to her weak condition and in a letter to Mr. Prescott, which he forwarded she blamed the Mormons and indirectly me because Belle went out west where she seems to think she was deliberately poisoned. That is how far people can go when ruled by prejudice.

There is no consolation for me except in my work. I am going to soldier hard so that if my folks are ashamed of me because of my religion they won't need to blush for me as a soldier. I am a different man tonight than ever before. I blame the Prussian system for it all for had the boys been home Belle would not have had to do a man's work. She was the only one in the family that believed in me. May God help me to be the man she believed me to be for she was more than a sister.

AUGUST 9, FRIDAY   I spent a miserable night. I dreamed of Belle while I was asleep and when I was awake I couldn't get her off my mind. I thought of a time when she was a tiny chubby babe and I was a little boy and we were playing in the woods. How I loved her then. We played house. I remember how I thought of how I would kill a bear or a giant or something that might come to get her. Then I thought how I sneaked away to the coast because I could make more money and left her alone in Salt Lake. It would have been the right thing to have stayed with her for it broke her heart to see me go. She wrote me afterward about it. Now the memory of my selfishness breaks mine.

All night long we could hear the boom of big guns and now and then the rattle of machine guns. Once in a while we could hear the hum of airplanes. I used to think I would tremble in the presence of such sounds but on the contrary I sort of regard them as a refuge where I can keep my mind of my lost pet.

This morning I feel like I am deserted. All the other reconnaissance men have gone out to do something. I wasn't even called to go dig in the trenches. I am told they went out to dig trenches. I went down to the creek to bathe and wash my clothes. I had a hard time to get out of the sight of women who were working in the fields. They didn't seem to notice me as much as I did them. They have different standards of modesty here and it is hard for us to get used to them.

I also wrote letters this morning to Sam Brooks and Mrs. Nelson.[7] I wrote to Appleton to have books I ordered in the states, but failed to receive, sent to Nelsons.

I see and hear many interesting things here. One thing is gas masks we must carry ours wherever we go. Everyone here women, children and priests carry gas masks. It seems odd to see a group of women gossiping with gas masks hung on their sides. Even the horses carry gas masks here.

I passed the church yard today and saw a yank using a tipped over tombstone for a barber chair, proving that Americans can cope with any situation.

The Y.M.C.A. is doing a good work here. They have a good hut and are giving us all the attention they can. A little hot chocolate every day some reading matter and a place to loaf and tell yarns. The division we are relieving still have a lot of soldiers here.[8] They have seen a little action it seems and those who talk much have many of men from our division as listeners.

I feel like I am good for nothing. I wish they would put me to work. Perhaps they will tomorrow.

Got a letter from Theressa my Nebraska girl. It was written July 4th.

AUGUST 10, SATURDAY   I have just been watching an air battle. A German plane came across and was attacked by 4 of our flyers and a lot of anti-aircraft guns on the ground that, as a rule missed him wide. The planes fired on him from all angles but he went right on through. It is sure thrilling and makes me wish I were flying.

Last night one of our men was robbed while he slept that makes the second pocket book taken in two weeks. So even here a fellow has to hide his stuff of value.

Most of the forenoon I was writing a letter to Mr. Prescott and reading the newspaper. I note that the British are making advances as well as having great losses. Imagine that there will be a big drive on this front soon. We will have to if we make "Hell Heaven or Hoboken."

I wish the Camp Lewis division would get stationed near here perhaps I could get to hunt up some of my friends. Most of the Utah boys went to Camp Lewis and most of my friends are Utah boys. I know no one here.

I enjoyed myself this afternoon. I was making forms for a "pill box" whatever that is. I was making forms to be taken out and set up on the work. It is funny that they haven't noticed I am idle. I have done more construction work than most of these fellows not barring sergeants of my age.

Everything is quiet this evening. Once in a while we hear guns and see puffs of smoke in the air that denotes they are shooting at aircraft. I am lying on the grass taking life easy. All around me are yanks and French soldiers writing letters or laughing and joking. I find myself wondering if the dutch are doing the same over there beyond the horizon.[9] And I am thinking what will I be doing a month from now, six months from now, a year from now. Isn't it a good thing that a soldier can't see into the future.

AUGUST 11   One thing I don't like since we have come up here and that is the petty aristocracy the sergeants have created. I don't think captain Rader would have permitted it but these officers in charge and the sergeants have sort of drawn themselves off into a class by themselves. They eat by themselves, and have assumed a monopoly on all the choice quarters. It may be military but it's not American.

Our town suffered an air raid last night, so I hear. I was asleep so don't know where the shells fell or the nature of the damage.

I went up to Lt. Fickle and told him that I was tired of lying around, so he took my name and detailed me to go out with the second relief. So I go out with a shovel in the morning. So I can feel better on that point.

We haven't had an inspection since we came up here nor have we heard a bugle the buglers are on K.P. We haven't stood any formations so the front lines are not without virtues. May it continue for I hate drills and formations.

I watched an observation balloon go up today. There are several of them within sight of hear [here]. They have them fastened to an automobile at times and lead them along the road. They are the silent sentinels of the air.

I wrote a letter to mother today. It was the hardest letter I ever tried to write.[10]

AUGUST 12, MONDAY (WRITTEN AUGUST 20)   I fell out with the boys at 4 a.m. to go to work. I was glad of the chance. Before we went out the sergeant called several men out of the line. I was one of them. We were to go out to the front lines to do some carpenter work.

At 8:30 we started with full packs and what tools there were for our new field of action. I had strange feelings for now I was to see the trenches that I had read about so much. As we marched along the road it seemed that we were sneaking upon a dreadful thing. Lt. Howbert had charge of the detail and he had us march in single file along the side of the road about 30 paces apart. Every time a plane flew over we would squat down and remain quiet till he discerned with his glasses whether it was a friend or enemy. After we had left (Minorville) about 3 miles we came to the last tilled ground then the barb wire entanglements began. In the open spaces the grass had not even been grazed on for at least two years. I saw my first shell hole but there was grass growing in it. I picked up a piece of broken shell. We passed a mound at one end of which was a little wooden cross. On the cross was crudely painted "Soldat Francais." An old rusty rifle was lying on the mound. A little farther I saw another grave but the cross was fallen. On the mound some pink flowers were blooming. We saw several graves as we proceeded on most of them the markers had fallen or were missing. Nature was covering the mounds with grass and soon all traces would disappear crops will grow where their bones are mouldering and those remains will only hold sacred places in the hearts of those who mourn for them and perhaps in the mourning won't last long.

As nature camouflages the graves and the shell holes the French have camouflaged their works. We passed some gun positions manned by the French. They were so disguised that at a distance they were hard to see. The French are masters at camouflage and the Yanks are faithfully imitating them. When we got to a woods held by our infantry our lieutenant led us to a clump of bushes that turned out to be a shelter and place where we could leave our equipment. Later we ate dinner at a kitchen I never could have found. It was so cleverly hid by the yank cooks and K.P.'s. I expect to learn more of camouflage.

We came out here to put gas proof doors on dugouts. There are a lot of dugouts here and deep ones too. These gas doors are really heavy felt curtains we make out of blankets. Two doors are made to an entry.

I am happy to be here it is good work though we haven't much at present to work with. We have tacks but not enough hammers so I use my bayonet.

We had a saw that wouldn't cut because of big patches of rust and no set. We had no tools to fix it so I contrived a saw set out of my gun bolt.

We found a dugout to sleep in. It is about 20 feet deep and contains 4 small rooms and place for 12 men to sleep. It has two entrances.

There are 14 men out here 10 of them and the Lieutenant slept below and the rest outside because they didn't like the damp air in the dugout. We have to have a gas guard so I volunteered to watch the first half of the night or till 2:00 A.M. The gas guard must merely stay awake and smell for cloud gas if a light wind comes from the enemy or watch for gas shells. I didn't have any idea what gas smelt like and can't tell the sound of a gas shell from another. Gas alarms were given by means of horns and gongs, anything to make noise.

Several times enemy planes flew over. They flew very low, and as soon as they would get far in land a score of searchlights would be seeking them out. I heard for the first time the whistle of shells. They were coming from Fritz too. They come towards one with a horrible blood curdling sound. I thought everyone was coming right over where I was but they burst before they got that far. I got mighty nervous too till I heard some shells from the French guns going towards the German lines. Several of the shells burst what I thought was close. In all, three gas alarms were turned in but they were only alarms.

Kaiser, is a fellow who would rather sleep outside and get hit than be smothered by bad air in the dugout; he said he had only once to die so what matter when it came. He changed his mind when he heard those shells whistle and slept in the dugout. I wanted to but had to stick till 2:00 A.M.

All night long wagons with water and food and supplies were coming up. All supplies are brought in the night with no lights. Those skinners who bring the stuff up are Heroes.

AUGUST 13, TUESDAY   I didn't sleep well the second half of the night. These dugouts are damp and cold. I have had a cold for several days but it is worse today. We had no breakfast this morning. Some of the boys had a little food they brought out with them but it was so little that I hid out while they were dividing it for what little there was would stimulate more than appease ones hunger.

On our way out to work today we passed a very interesting spot in the road called "Dead Man's Curve" I don't know why it is so called unless because of a grave yard on each side of the track or road for French soldiers.

On one side of the road opposite the graveyard is a dugout city built on the side hill but no one was in it. On the curve the road ducked down into a hollow and since a low place is a gas trap a guard was stationed there to make everyone wear masks till they got across. It seems that a lot of our men were gassed there a few days ago and the gas is not all gone. It is far from a cheerful looking place. The tops of many of the trees are shot off and many others are dead from gas, I suppose.

I worked today with a fellow by the name of Kaiser. He is all yank through but likes to talk. He is a good worker and we get along well we put a door on this morning as quick as five fellows put up another. I am glad that I am at it and perhaps have a little too much zeal.

I found a can of corn Willie and resolved to have it for supper.[11] I did. I ate a lot of it none of the other fellows had come in yet. When they came they looked at it but said it was spoiled. I spent the next few hours expecting evidence of poison but none came. I am sorry now I threw it away.

Water is scare up here. It is hard to get any to wash or shave with so we just wet our faces and let the towel do the rest.

We are learning two new orders up here they are "Spread out" and "Under Cover." Men are not supposed to bunch up. Under all conditions keep spread apart and when planes are in the air keep under cover or stand still till the plane is placed as a friendly one or not. Allied planes have the red white and blue circles painted on the wings. Hun planes have the black cross. Some say they can tell an allied from a boche plane by the hum of the engine. I can't.

AUGUST 14   I met a fellow this morning over in the second line infantry who was with me in the detention camp. He is from Arizona but I can't think of his name. He told of two German prisoners being taken at that place a few days before. They came over and gave up. They were very clever to get by the first lines. They were Alsatians and tired of the struggle.[12] All they had on was shirt and pants one of them had a small piece of soap in his pocket.

They say that all these trenches were once held by the Germans. And the Dutch made many of these dugouts. It may be right for the firing bases are all on the wrong side. It was in one of those dugouts that we ate breakfast about 10:30.

Near where we ate dinner was a large steel truss that had been blowed off of one of its abutments by the French to halt communication for it was a

R.R. bridge. On the other side was the remains of a town (Flieury)[13] Only the parts of walls stood and the church tower even was half shot away.

Today I noticed a lot of unexploded German shells. Learned that they were called "duds" and also that many German shells don't explode that many times they are tampered with by allied prisoners. This afternoon I saw a dud that had been shot into a tree about a third of its length. There was a French wine bottle sitting on it. I hoped it was a prophecy of future conciliation.

This afternoon we worked at a different place and about a mile from our camp. We got supper there too and all that we could eat.

After supper while I was washing my mess kit out with green leaves, a doughboy captain passed and asked me why I didn't go to the kitchen and wash the kit in hot water. I told him I didn't know there was any hot water. I was squatted on my haunches while he was addressing me and I got a severe reprimand for not rising to attention. Perhaps he is right I am getting a little sloppy and there is a tendency out here in the woods to forget to pay our military compliments.

Lieutenant Howbert is such a good human sort of a fellow so like one of us that I find myself neglecting my duties.

AUGUST 15, THURSDAY   Went around Dead Man's Curve again today to gas proof a red cross station. We had a very light breakfast and no promise of dinner so our sergeant, who is a good rustler got the medics to fry us some pancakes.

Our Lieutenant went into the outfit today and came out this evening with a bar of chocolate each. Chocolate is quite a treat in France. Twenty cents a bar. He said he would allow three men to go in a day to stay in camp a day to rest and clean up. We don't need the rest as bad as the clean up for some of the fellows haven't had their shoes off since we have been out.[14] It has been too cold to undress and then it is too much trouble dressing and undressing. We are not supposed to sleep two together in the army but all those rules are being disregarded out here. They are good to worry a fellow in the barracks but here a fellow must do the best he can do.

I saw a German shell land in a lot of grenades and other stuff today. I don't know what was in the pile but it made a lot of smoke and racket. Lieutenant brought a paper and I saw where Allies have brought down a total of 404 Hun planes.

ore long. The yanks didn't come over to hunt quiet sectors. They came into
the thing for some scrap.

Went clear up to the front trench today. I used to think that one went to
the front lines as a lamb to the slaughter but our boys have picked plums in
No Mans land and our raiding parties have gone clear over to the German
second lines and found no one. But then this is a quiet sector. Some say a
German rest camp.

I am glad I am over here. I won't have to take another fellows word for it.
A man's future is going to depend largely on how well he played his part in
this war. Though the part I am playing is of little consequence. These gas
doors may never be used.

AUGUST 17   Every day something comes to my attention that causes me to
reflect how wasteful war is. I see so much needless waste on the part of soldiers. They throw away so many things and since we are not charged with
things lost up here the waste is worse. Rifle cartridges lie everywhere as well
as equipment. This is a brief mention of waste on a small scale. Probably
before we get out of it we shall see waste on a large plan.

I see the value of training. The training a soldier gets is of itself no value
because many of the things he performs in training are never used in active
service, but as a means to an end the training puts a soldier in tune and in
trim so that he can be handled better in a place like this.

Our boys are having a hard time up here to get tobacco. Most of them
are out of humor today because of no smoking.

I saw a sentiment written in a dugout where I worked today. It read,
"The good old U.S.A. is all rite but Franch is a hell of a place, bleve me"
Robert Caine, Beaukiss Tx.

This evening Sergeants Russell and Goff came out with the Lieutenant
to inspect the dugouts. Engineers are to supervise the trenches and dugouts
the doughboys are going to dig.

The Dutch guns, about 4 of them, and some of our guns carried on a
conversation this morning. None of the shells landed near. Last night some
gas shells landed in (Novient) I can tell the sound of a gas shell now they had
a wobbly whistling sound when traveling.

AUGUST 18, SUNDAY   I met a fellow today in the infantry who had religious
scruples against war. I felt sorry for him he was a conscientious objector who

didn't make his claims for exception because he was afraid they would be interpreted as cowardice. He seemed a fine fellow and we had quite a chat. He got confidential and told me what his prospects were if he got out alive. He showed me a picture of his prospects. I congratulated him and told him I wished I had such a girl waiting for me to come home. I told him I believed this was a righteous cause we were fighting and God would judge us more by the attitude we took toward things than the things we did. We should not spill blood unnecessary but if we shed it otherwise it should not gall our consciences. He left feeling pretty good. He and I agreed that it was better for a few Germans to die than that the government and education they fight for continue to curse the world.

Passed a shell hole today. In the shell hole was the grave of a French Lieutenant on the little cross was carved his name and the appreciation, "An Ideal Soldier."

Most of the Frenchmen we meet up here sport medals. I tried to talk to one today, he had a war cross and told me, with his hands that he got it for connecting up a telephone wire under shell fire.

I picked a few berries today. Kaiser called them French Briar Berries but I ate them for blackberries and they tasted pretty good. They are just beginning to ripen.

I should mention canes. Everyone has canes up here. Some of us fellows don't carry them because we are usually loaded with lumber and tools as we go about. We also have to carry our rifles wherever we go. I have learned that canes are a necessity and not a fad. One must not make lights up here. Not even smoke a cigarette in the open and canes are used as feelers at night.

AUGUST 19, MONDAY   We built a charcoal fire in our dugout last night to dry the place out. Went to bed with a slight headache but gave it no thought. Next thing I was aware of was that I was making a great struggle to get out of there but made no headway. I know someone was calling my name and trying to help me. Next thing I knew I was in the trench outside and a doctor was administering smelling salts or something. I have vomited all over myself and was made aware that charcoal like cascarets "Works while you sleep."[15] I was laughing and crying by turns as one coming out of chloroform.

The cause was that the stove had used up all the air and we were gassed by the bad air. If one of the fellows down there had not realized our situation in time and given the alarm I would have been out of the race today. The boys who carried us out nearly got gassed in the attempt.

No sooner had that excitement settled till Fritz starting sending over his compliments. The barrage lasted for about 30 minutes. We got into the entrance of the dugout and were practically safe though several shells scattered dirt all around us. Today we asked a medic if anyone got hurt and he had heard of no one. That is the Kaiser's hard luck.

This afternoon I walked into the company or rather back to the company for my day off and to get cleaned up. I found a box of candy waiting for me from Miss Theressa. It was in pretty good shape but somewhat melted together. I will take it back with me and divide it with the boys.

AUGUST 20   I feel fine today, good sleep. Cleaned up washed clothes, am not [now] at the Y.M.C.A. writing I sent short notes to Nell, Clara, Charley, Prescott, Theressa, Blozzard, and Grandma. So they will have a line on me if they are interested. Strange that no one writes. I don't get half the letters I feel are due me.

All my time today has been spent copying notes into my diary. I kept these notes on a few scraps of paper while out on the front. I go pack up to go out again.

Evening—I walked out alone. Two other fellows started with me but they stopped at (Novient) to try to get some vin blanc. I had my package of candy and was anxious to get out here to eat it. Well it is consumed now all feel better. We were concealed under a big beech tree while we ate it. Five boche planes were circling over head the while and all the machine guns around were trying to get a bead on them. Several pieces of schrapnel from anti aircraft shells that burst over us fell near. One must keep under cover when those shells break or at least keep his helmet on.

AUGUST 21   We are about out of work here. I hate to see the job run out because it is the most pleasant one I have had in the army. I can get interested on a job like this and times goes fast. It is so much better than being with the company where a score of non coms are barking at us.

Our sergeant went in today for orders. In the mean while we have been dodging around on the old jobs where we stuffed cracks and killed time. When work ran out I went out scouting for berries and fruit of which I found some. Flowers and fruit come and go in their season as if they were quite unconscious of the woes of man.

I stand gas guard again. Beautiful night. Big round mellow moon. Same moon that used to shine on me in better days. I thought of the other nights such as this. I wondered if they would ever come again. My musings were not long for some shells came over to disturb things and I spent the major part of my watch under cover. A lot of planes flew about us and the machine guns were shooting at them or where they sounded to be.

AUGUST 22, THURSDAY   There is an unlimited supply of rats and mice out here. Last night a rat ran over my face twice. They have eaten into every package of hard tack we had out here. So most of [us] are out that part of our reserve rations. They can't get into our corn willie but they did chew the stock of my rifle because it was oily I suppose. We have a very good alabi [alibi] now if we wish to eat our hard tack. We can say the rats got it. There is no use of giving orders to the rats for they know no law especially out here.

I wish pay day would come. I need money to send home. I get $3.00 more this month being first class private. I ought to get 170 francs this month. I am getting more familiar with this French money. I used to go into a store point out what I wanted and hold out all my money and let them take what they desired. One French woman told me not to hold out all my money to her she might take too much. Meaning not to tempt her. It was good advice. I must have been tempting someone judging from the way my money has been slipping away.

We tried to wind up the job today but didn't and so some of us are to stay over and come in tomorrow. The rest have gone. I stood gas guard till 11:00 o'clock then crawled in with shoes and all on. Germans sent a lot of gas over some where but none got to us.

AUGUST 23   Another fellow and I had an argument about dodging when one heard a shell coming. He and I were going up to the second trench to finish some work we left yesterday. As we were going through the woods we heard some pieces of schrapnal sing by. They came from shells shot at an airplane. He jumped behind a tree and in doing so dropped his stuff in the path so I could not get by without difficulty. I told him there was no use dodging when he heard the thing it was too late to dodge and lets go. Well that started an argument. He said he could tell if a shell was coming by the sound. I held the shell had to get there before it could make the sound. We have no way to settle it so we both think we are right. His name is Sillinder and the laziest man and greatest bragger out here on this detail. He is the only man in the group that goes around with his gun loaded. No need of it.

We finished up this morning and walked in this afternoon got here about 3 o'clock and have loafed the rest of the time.

New orders are rifle inspection three times a week, gas instruction and gas drill every day and wear tin hats always. Most of the soldiers have taken to the fad of covering their hats with cloth of different somber hues and they draw all kinds of things on their hat covers. I have a piece of green canvass [sic] over mine on which I have sketched with a pen all the things I know how to make from a cannon to a girls head.

NO MAIL YET !!*?

AUGUST 24   Got up this morning with the idea that I would go out with the company to work but we gas curtain experts (?) were kept in to put doors on a big dugout here in town that is used as a telegraph and telephone center. It was a small job and we finished early this afternoon.

I went down to the Y.M.C.A. to write a letter while there I got in the line to get some tobacco for a fellow and some candy for myself. The line was half a block long. It took me an hour to get to the counter then I ate too much of the candy. The "Y" only sells a limited amount to each soldier and everyone buys all of each article he can get and other fellows will take it especially tobacco.

Some new soldiers came in today. They are the last draft just landed for labor. It seems that they area pretty raw and have been marched hard with harsh treatment. I talked with some of them. They told me of one of their number committing suicide. This is the story whether it is true or not. The men were exhausted this fellow's feet were all in. The officer in charge abused him for not having guts and told him he hadn't gone through half of what it would be necessary to. The fellow shot himself.

The army isn't to blame for such things it is the men who misuse the authority given them. I hope I am spared from such. No mail.

AUGUST 25, SUNDAY   I neglected to mention the good bath I had yesterday. The A.E.F. is establishing bath houses at different points. We have one. The soldiers call them "Louse dips." A fellow can get a good bath and a change of clothes. Almost too good to be true we don't even have to wash dirty clothes.

Last night I went to a picture show at the Y.M.C.A. John Bunny, who has been dead several years, starred in one reel. It wasn't a bad show. There was music by some of the pioneer infantry who came in yesterday. Singing good piano out of tune.

Went to church at the "Y" this morning. The "Y" secretary gave a good talk from Jonah about paying the price for whatever course we take in life— if we so [sow] wild oats we must reap wild oats—and so on. He is right it is as hard to avoid good consequences as bad ones.

The chaplin of the ([illegible]) inf. gave a very sane talk this evening. He cautioned against forming habits here we wouldn't want when we got home. He advised to make our stay here a period of study. That is right too but I don't want to study some of the things they try to make me learn. It is of no advantage to me to remember the number of my gas mask or the name of every screw in my gun.

I want to think about things that will make me useful as a soldier and later, if I make it out OK, as a citizen. A very quiet day.

AUGUST 26   My name was on the proning list today that is a list of men who are allowed to rest and clean up for a day. A man's turn comes every 7 or 8 days. I have been idle so much of late that I didn't care to be idle. Well I went out to work. Some of the fellows said I was crazy but I felt that I knew my own likes and dislikes best. I was somewhat curious to see what the rest of the company was working at also.

They put me to work on a concrete job. Perhaps I had better not say what we were building. Enough that it was not a milk celler nor a summer kitchen. I was on the second shift. The first shift went out from 4 A.M. till 2 P.M. We went on from 2 to 10 P.M. We started in at 9:00 o'clock.

Whoever had charge of the concrete work on the other shift either didn't know much about concrete work or he didn't care. They had poured concrete all the shift it seems, without tamping it. We spent our time digging the rocks away from the forms and tamping grout in. They do some odd things in the army they will put a charcoal artist in charge of a concrete job and a blacksmith at the head of a camouflage detail.

Weather has been ideal of late but it looks that rain is due pretty soon. In fact it rained some while we were eating. Had peach pie tonight. It was great. They bring our chow out to us in a cart.

AUGUST 27, TUESDAY   I spent the forenoon cleaning up a bit. I also wrote a letter to the Dixie paper.[16] Yes, I sluffed a gas lecture this morning. Gas lectures are jokes anyway they tell us the same thing over and over that we have been hearing a hundred times. We have a gas N.C.O. He has one lecture and he has said it so many times that I can almost tell the subjects in their order and can repeat many sentences verbatim.

We went out to work at 1:00 o'clock and from then till 10:00 P.M. I plied the pick and shovel in a little 6' x 6' shell proof shelter in the reserve trenches that the dough boys had been digging. There were 4 of us together. Aven, a fellow from Salt Lake whose dad owns a store in Bingham Canyon, 2 others from Missouri and myself from nowhere.[17] Two of us worked hard but we don't get anymore consideration than if we hadn't.

Coming home it was very dark. Not a star even. Once in a while a star shell went up over the trenches and we got a light from it. We traveled indian fashion but one could not see the man ahead of him. I dropped out of line to pick up what looked like an illuminated watch dial but couldn't find it as I had to wait till everyone passed and it got kicked or stepped on. I could not strike a match to find it. I got lost from the platoon and could hardly find my way back to town. I need a letter badly mail would be more welcome than payday.

AUGUST 28   I didn't go out to work this afternoon for the reason that we go out to the front again. I speak of the front as though we were not there. We are and several shells came over near where we were yesterday. The last day or so big shells have gone over us and lit two or three miles farther in.

Near where we were yesterday a shell hit a French gun and hurt several men, killing one or two Frenchmen and a yank. I saw the dead Frenchman this morning also some of the wounded ones. I did not find myself awed as one might suppose. I found myself looking upon their mangled bodies with less feeling than ordinary.

A German airman came over and shot down a big observation balloon near here. I got out in time to see it coming down in flames with a huge cloud of black smoke trailing it to the ground. The two observers were floating gently down with parachutes and a mile or so away the German plane was hastening home flying low as if unconscious of the machine guns that were chattering at it.

Carl Anderson and I visited a French plum orchard today. There were two kinds of plums. Little blue ones and smaller yellow ones. There were many blue ones but they were very wormy. The yellow ones were very scarce but we managed to get a few to eat and some to bring home. The trees and fruit seemed to be the victims of every plague and pest plums are subject to.

I can't say that I have a very high regard for the Frenchman as a fruit grower. I have not seen a well trimmed or cared for tree in France.

I got two letters today. One from Charley, he is the bravest Roman of us all. He has the courage to stay home and do the plain every day duty. I enjoyed his letter but was amused at his attempt to cheer me up. He seems to think I am in grave danger. The other letter was from Mr. Prescott. He spoke of the joy at home over recent victorys. He said the people are behind us. He is right some of them are a long ways behind us and intend to stay there.

Attended a very good prayer meeting tonight.

AUGUST 29, THURSDAY   Walked out to point in the 2nd line trenches about 6 miles from here. 12 men went out. We had two jobs to do. One big dugout to gas proof by the demolished bridge near (Flieury). The other place was a buzzer station on the opposite side of (Flieury). This town is almost wholly destroyed by shell fire and trenches are dug through the place. There is scarcely a whole roof or chimney in the town.

Every home in the town stood for a broken heart. The families were perhaps scattered like fragments of the hearthstones they had to flee from. The beautiful shade trees that graced the lanes and roadsides had been blasted by shell fire or blighted by gas for Dead Man's curve was not far away. I was reminded of Longfellow's Evangeline and Goldsmith's Deserted Village, but those are scars on England's record and should be forgotten.[18]

This is only one of a thousand such towns that have been torn to the ground by the war lord lusting for power even though he has to wade through rivers of innocent blood to accomplish his purposes.

I was working on the Buzzer stations we got through early and went back to the bridge where we found the other boys would have about three hours work. I had to go back to the other job after my bayonet which I forgot while I was over there the Germans started shelling the place. I got rather nervous but there was no need as no shells came near. On my way back through the town I stopped to pick some plums as there were several trees that had the small yellow plums on. I picked my steel hat full and all I could eat.

As I sat there among the blighted trees and gardens grown to noxious weeds and observed how the fields everywhere were spoiled by wire entanglements and shell holes it occurred to me that here is a land that is even cursed for mans wickedness.

We walked home that making about a 13 mile hike with light packs besides our work. I was very tired. Bed at 11:00 o'clock.

AUGUST 30, FRIDAY   We came in very sweaty and consequently I nearly froze last night trying to sleep. I put on everything I had and covered with all I had but that didn't help much. Being awake a great deal of the time I had a chance to hear a great deal of shelling. Some landed near but I think most of them were meant to prevent men from working on a railroad that is being built near here. I wouldn't be surprised to hear of someone getting bumped off.

I saw a French man drinking Vin today. He had it in a leather bag and by pressing the sides of the bag squirted the Vin through a small hole in the cork into his mouth. He offered me the sac and I tried it. Some of the wine hit my mouth but I can't say I like it.

This morning was spent as usual—rifle inspection, gas instruction and venereal inspection. When will these wonders cease. When we get in gas the instructor is apt to be the first man gassed.

I went out with the company this afternoon and put in the time laying narrow gauge track.

A very interesting bombardment took place this afternoon. Hans and Fritz shelled some place about 3 miles from here in a line so that shells had to pass over us to get there. He had been sending those big shells over for several days in the same direction. Well the third shell today hit. He didn't send anymore it wasn't necessary. He must have hit a pile of ammunition that set fire to other piles. For five hours the explosions continued. After dark it lit the country up for miles around and I am afraid even to guess the amount of money that went up in smoke.

We were told today that [we] would take our places along side of the doughboys in the near future. I expect a drive is due soon.

AUGUST 31   Another month gone, soon it will be fall and soon it will be winter. I dread the winter. If we have to go through it I wish they would start soon and get it over before the bad weather begins.

Some Negro labor troops came in last night. A lot of the fellows are kicking because they are using the Y.M.C.A. I can't agree.[19] As far as I am concerned they are welcome to use the Y they stand shoulder to shoulder with us in this fight and they do their bit at home to support the Y.M.C.A.

This morning's paper brings news that the French have taken Nojon and the British have captured Bafaume. They will soon be to the old Hindenburg line and then I expect the Huns will make a stand. This is the Hindenburg Line we have here. It is 4 years old and may be hard to break.

This afternoon I worked in a tunnel to drain a dugout. It was a dirty wet job.

I got a letter from Ruby Potter.[20] She is in California and seems to be enjoying life. Another letter from the Book Company I sent to for some books while at Camp Mills. They couldn't send the books so sent a check for $3.00 which is worse than no money here.

SEPTEMBER 1, SUNDAY   Changed shifts today. We go out in the morning instead of at 1 o'clock. I worked this forenoon in the same muddy hole. It is hard digging and our tools are not good. It will take us a long time to get this tunnel through if they don't work any faster from the other end than we do. If we had plenty of powder we could make headway. I got mad today because they sent in another fellow down to shoot a hole I drilled. If it had been in civil life I would have walked off the job. If I had never handled any powder it would not have been so bad but I know I've shot as many holes as the man he sent down to do the work for me only I didn't recommend myself here after I drill no more holes. I will not know how.

It is better I believe to have the afternoon off only I'd like to get out of these foolish street cleaning details. Since the yanks came here I'll venture that the town is cleaner than it has been in a hundred years.

We have to spend some of our spare time every day cleaning up the town.

I have been itching a great deal of late. I can't find anything on me so it must be a skin disease. Down at the bathhouse today I notice other fellows covered with little red bumps such as I have got. They said they were fleas and would jump off when a fellow took a bath or changed clothes and then jump back on him.

I went to a testimonial meeting at the Y. A good service. I took part and feel the better for it.

SEPTEMBER 2, MONDAY   Today is labor day in the U.S. Here it is just Sept. 2nd. I can imagine many a poor kids dreamy summer has been interrupted by the stern reality of study to commence today or tomorrow. This will be a great day for prize fights picnics in the parks and many speeches both great and small will be made by men both great and small in honor of the day or for the sake of a programme. Over here we are merely working and waiting.

Batallion moved last night. It was expected but orders did not come till 11:30, after we had settled down nicely to sleep. Say wasn't there some cursing. Everyone from Gen. Pershing to the lowest man that rules us, both wisely and otherwise, got cursed. We had to roll our packs in the dark. We had to load all the equipment out of the storehouse and office and kitchen in the dark. I got put on a detail to finish up the cleaning in the morning but those other poor birds didn't get much sleep. Neither did we for that matter. No one objected to moving after dark but at least we could have got ready in the daylight instead of loafing around.

It was only a 3 Km. Move and we are here probably none the worse for it. This town (Noviant) is as near the front as we can get.

Saw a funeral this afternoon. An American soldier who got killed yesterday some how. Perhaps he died I don't know anyhow he was brought to the "Y" but in a rough wooden box that was draped with the flag. His hearse was a two wheeled cart and they shoved the coffin into the hut through the window, due to the narrow hall. It was a very tearless matter of fact funeral. Though I believe it left its impression. I find men up here don't say as much to each other about their softer feelings. A man is a different man here yet I can't say why.

SEPTEMBER 3, TUESDAY   Most of the company stayed in today to clean up the town. It is the first job yanks have in these French towns. Most of the people here are poor and can't afford a horse so they pile their cow manure in the street in front of the house. Some of these accumulations are very huge and far from fragrant, and when an American soldier must clean up and haul away such messes it wouldn't be safe for some one to tell him not to call a Frenchman a Frog.[21] I expect the manure is the cause of so many flies and yellow jackets here. Someone gets stung every meal.

I mentioned horses being scarce. The war has taken most of them for that reason many of the people hitch their cows up.

I was on a gas curtain detail again today. We gas proofed dugouts for a yank battery near here. They are National guard artillery men and use French guns. The guns are very complex and they say that Americans are not allowed to take the guns apart as the recoil is a French military secret.

SEPTEMBER 4, WEDNESDAY   Gas curtains again. Nothing unusual happened. We didn't even work hard. As usual a very ordinary day, no mail or money. Not too much heat or too little. We did sign the pay roll for august but that is not very exciting since July's centimes are still due.

There was a very stupid air battle today. A boche came over and got a balloon. Two or three planes chased him but he got away and they went home. He went his way rejoicing. The yank flyer probably was some rich man's son who couldn't stop to bother with one boche.

All the fellows are sitting out in the street singing to the tune of "Glory Glory hallaj--- "All we do is sign the payroll—But we never get a ----- ----- cent,:

Carl Anderson and I went out stealing plums today. A Frenchman tried to get us to leave he waved his arms and said "partee partee" or go away. We agreed that we were having a good *party*. We joshed with him a while and he got real chummy. He filled our pockets with plums and told us that the wormy ones were saved to make wine out of.

I wish they would start this drive soon we need excitement. I have just about come to the conclusion that if I am to die let it be now. Let us get this job over with we want peace but the only way to get it is to go right on through.

SEPTEMBER 5, THURSDAY   The experiences I am getting here are quietly but surely leaving their impression on me. I can't see the processes work but I know I can perceive the results as I look back. I can't say whether the change is a desirable one or not but I hope it is. This war is a great silent creator of men or rather a recreator of men. One of the soldiers said it made men out of boys and monkeys out of men. But I hope it let us return home as monkeys.

About daylight this morning a very heavy barrage started. I couldn't tell whether it was coming or going so I went out to see. It was going so I felt better. It lasted nearly an hour. I really hated to have it stop.

In the barn across the street (as I write) are two rough boxes, coffins for a sergeant and corporal who got killed last night. The chaplin is standing by waiting to make the burial and go through the ceremony. They are bring[ing] one of the men up the street wrapped in a blanket. A chill runs up and down my spine. We will be going up against that same thing in a few days. And before we get out of it will see worse sights than that.

Nothing much to do today as I walked about two miles down the road and took a bath washed my clothes got back about noon. This afternoon I cleaned up for inspection. I am sleeping on the floor in a hay loft very dark so that they inspected us with a lantern the major checked me up and complimented me on the shape my equipment was in.

SEPTEMBER 6   Last night I went out to work with my platoon we came in at daylight. All we went out for was to be occupied. We were digging camouflage trenches. That is we dug the trenches shallow and wide so that the dutch would think we were figuring on falling back.

It was a very disagreeable night rained enough to make it muddy and a little chill so we had to work some all the while to keep warm. It was not a rush job and about all most of the fellows did was dig a dry place and lay down, two and three together, and sleep in spite of the chill night.

Having no work today I took a tour out through the country in the direction where I thought Bushman was I visited three towns and found some men from his batallion but I failed to locate him. I think he is out on the lines.

I missed my dinner but got a few plums to fill in till suppertime. A meal lost won't hurt me since we have been over eating of late. A lot of the men are out on detail and the cooks don't seem to be aware of it for they cook about the same amount. So we just drop in the line for seconds and divide the spoils.

Rained hard this afternoon. Good thing for it flushed out the streets. Sleep tonight.

SEPTEMBER 7, SATURDAY   Got on a torpedo squad today and spent the time learning to make a contrivance to blow up barb wire entanglements in front of the doughboys. We are told that it is dangerous business and that it took 10 squads of men before they got the torpedo under the wire some where in the Chateau Thierry drive.

There is a torpedo squad from each platoon and all the men are volunteers more men volunteered than was needed. Strange that no one but privates stepped out in my platoon. I crave a little excitement.[22] I want to do something to get it back on the Huns. Belle might be alive today where it not for them.

Three German prisoners came through here today. All of them were ragged and dirty and two of them had an empty beaten look in their faces. The other, a sergeant, held his head high and walked with a haughty mien.

I spent the evening arguing and talking Mormonism with a friend. He said there were three religious groups he had no use for they were the Mormons, the Catholics and the Christian Scientists. I talked to him a while and found that he knew nothing about any of them.

AUGUST [SEPTEMBER] 8, SUNDAY   This afternoon I saw a beautiful rainbow in the sky. One end rested on our side and it arched No Man's land, the other end beyond the enemy lines. I wondered at which end was the pot of gold. It occurred to me, too, that the rainbow, at least was neutral. The elements are not taking sides in this affair. I wonder if God is as ready to bless or punish either side as it gives expression to what is right.

I went to a very impressive song and sacramental service this evening. In fact it just broke up and I am in the "Y" writing. In the prayer over the bread the chaplin prayed that if it was necessary in this war for our bodies to be broken for humanity as Christ's was broken for us that we would have the courage and the faith to hold out. If we establish the principles we fight for even if we fall the coming generations will bless us and the Christ who gave us faith.

They brought in two dead Germans today to be buried. They were dressed in very shabby shoddy clothes and both died with their boots on. Big heavy Prussian boots.

I got permission today to stay on the torpedo squad. I see pictures of ourselves snaking across no man's land in the mud with that long torpedo. That would be exciting and I don't imagine any more dangerous than any other work around the front. Then, it is a job that has to be done by someone.

Got a letter from Grandma Lytle today also two Grand Rapids papers I sent some papers Stars and Stripes to Grandma and a note to Nell.

SEPTEMBER 9   I haven't done a thing today for myself or my country. Oh yes, I ate three meals wrote a letter to Clara and spent some time reading a book by a French author Pere Late. The K.C. [Knights of Columbus] has a small but good library here.

I thought I would get a novel of the lighter vein but am some what disappointed in this one as it is neither light or heavy. A cold chilly day.

Rumor has it that a lot of dutch were killed in a raid last night but then rumor is always killing someone up here.

7

THE ST. MIHIEL OFFENSIVE, SEPTEMBER 1918

THE ST. MIHIEL OFFENSIVE WAS THE FIRST MAJOR ACTION OF THE AMERican Expeditionary Force of the war and served as a proving ground for the American soldiers and, for General John J. Pershing, a vindication of his insistence that the American soldiers fight as an independent force with specific objectives and responsibilities. From the entry of the United States into the war, the French and English had expected and insisted that American forces be used as replacements for the staggering losses they had suffered for nearly four years and continued to suffer in light of the German spring offensive. Until the American success at St. Mihiel in September 1918, American companies, regiments, and divisions had fought as individual units with the Allies. After St. Mihiel, opposition to the independent American army working in concert with but separate from the other Allied armies vanished.

The St. Mihiel offensive was named for the town of St. Mihiel located on the Meuse River and at the westernmost point of the German line south of Verdun. The St. Mihiel salient itself, an area of approximately two hundred square miles, resembled a large triangle with the easternmost point at Pont-a-Mousson on the Moselle River, the western point at St. Mihiel, and the northern point located near Verdun. Six American divisions launched the attack on September 12, pushing northward along a twenty-mile front that stretched from Seicheprey on the west to Pont-a-Mousson on the east. Anderson's 89th Division was given a center location with the lst and 42nd Divisions to the left (west) and the 2nd, 5th, 90th, and 82nd Divisions to the right (east). French troops were located to the west of the 2nd Division around the village of St. Mihiel and further north along the western side of the salient between St. Mihiel and Haudiomont.

Meeting little resistance, the 2nd and 89th Divisions captured the key towns of Thiacourt and Bouillonville the first day of the offensive.[1]

E Company was given two assignments during the offensive, "to cut the way thru the German wire for the 353th Infantry and clear the road for advancing units, supporting artillery, ammunition trains, and supplies."[2] However, the day before the offensive began, Nels Anderson was assigned to the regimental headquarters as a runner, where he served for five days during the offensive. Initially disappointed that the assignment was "a sort of candy job," that kept him from going "over the top" with his company, Anderson took solace when he learned that when his company went over the top with the doughboys at 5:20 a.m. on September 12, they met little opposition and the company was soon assigned to road construction work. During his ten days at the regimental headquarters, Anderson was able to observe the course of battle and the tide of German wounded and prisoners of war that swept back across the American lines.

Returning to his company at Bouillonville on September 16, Anderson resumed the duties of making pickets, laying wire, and digging trenches while under fire from the Germans. Anderson pitied the doughboys who were also assigned to nighttime trench digging. "Some of those fellows are sick enough to be in the hospital. They don't get enough water to drink much less wash. All day they have to stand to and keep out of sight and then dig at night besides." He was also moved by a German military cemetery that he visited just outside Bouillonville. "It was a beautiful well ordered place the plants and flowers were well trimmed and arranged it is the only place where a soldier hears the command 'Rest in Peace.'"

Americans suffered approximately seven thousand casualties among the six hundred thousand men who participated in the offensive while the Germans lost about seventeen thousand men—twenty-three hundred killed or wounded and the rest surrendered to become prisoners of war. Given the tremendous losses in other World War I battles, the St. Mihiel casualties were considered light. By September 16, when Anderson returned to his company, the battle was over and soldiers were already beginning to move northward to the next and final push by the Americans, the Meuse–Argonne offensive.

SEPTEMBER 10, TUESDAY   Atmosphere is getting pretty tense around here of late. We had our last gun inspection today. They didn't say whether it was the last for some of us or all of us. I feel the yellow creeping up my spine or is it that I am a little nervous. I am not sure whether I am a coward or not but I feel just like one feels before he goes into a contest, a debate or a race.

Last night a bosh [Boche] plane dropped a lot of propaganda stuff. They said they were ready for us and asked when we were coming over. That said we could take (Metz), but it would cost us 100,000 men. How do they know we want (Metz).

We received a lecture today on German traps. The experience of the allies in other drives is that [they] leave all kinds of traps where a person can blow himself up or poison himself or fall "in the pitfall digged for him."

The French love story is not very interesting.

We practiced on our torpedo squad today. Put on an exhibition for the company today. Blowed an opening through an entanglement so that 4 squads could go through abreast. They call us the suicide squads.

Pay day today. I scarce thought of it. I drew 155 francs sent $10.00 to the bank and $10.00 to Charley. It took me 3 hours to get to the y man who sends money. Everyone was sending money home. Some of the boys drew 3 & 4 months pay. Crap games are in abundance.

SEPTEMBER 11, WEDNESDAY   I am tired of this inactivity especially at such a time. There is nothing to think about except what one does not want to think about. One gets so he would charge or slay or do something rather than set around idle.

The last few nights there has been a steady stream of wagons and guns and trucks moving toward the front. I can't imagine where they hide them all. Last night I went out to watch the procession. I never saw a busier street in an American city. Mostly big guns and shells.

Afternoon. We got orders to roll light packs and leave all our extra stuff in a bundle with our name on it.

It will be impossible to take my diary with me. Hate to leave it as it has been my best friend. Heinricke and I agreed that in case one got bumped off and the other didn't the live soldier would care for the others personnel effects. I don't feel so nervous as I did this morning. Am quite myself again.

The captain detailed me to go report to the colonel as regamental [regimental] runner whatever that is. I asked some of the other fellows and they say that a runner is a messenger. So so long.

SEPTEMBER 12 TO 21 SAT   It has been ten long days since I have written in this little book. I have done a few things, experienced some and seen many more during that time. Many an isolated man in a lifetime has not experienced a greater variety of things.

I have noted partially the happening or some of the things I observed and I am re writing those notes which mean nothing to anyone but me.

They sent me to Regimental headquarters as a runner. I hated it at first because I thought a runner had a sort of candy job. I didn't want that later I learned that it wasn't necessary to use the torpedoes and I got more variety as a runner than with the company. They went over with the doughboys but there was little opposition so the engineers dropped back to make roads whereas I got to visit around some.

The night of the 11th and 12th I stayed in a dugout. It was a safe dugout. I know because I helped gas proof it and then the General had selected it for headquarters.

I spent a miserable night as well as a cold wet one. It was raining hard outside and I pitied the poor fellows who were waiting out in the trenches for the day.

About 1:00 A.M. the barrage started. I never had any idea of what a barrage was before. There were a thousand guns within hearing and they were all shooting as if they were trying to burn their insides out. I went out on the hill. It was dark and the rain was pouring. I saw cannons all around spitting fire and the noise was deafening.[3] I thought of the line "The night has a thousand eyes the day but one."

Well the barrage lasted till about day light when the small guns stopped but the 6 inch ones kept it up. The small ones we learned stopped because the fellows had gone over and had advanced as far as their range so they had to move closer which they proceeded to do. The small guns are called 75's they shoot a shell from a cartridge. They shoot fast and well. A French gun, mechanism is a secret.

About 7 o'clock this morning of the 12th we learned that our boys had advanced 4 miles that they were going ahead as fast as they could walk and were gathering prisoners as fast as they came to them.[4] An hour later several German prisoners were brought in to be questioned by the intelligence department. I listened to the officer question them. I could not understand the language but from the dictation the officer made to the stenographer I could glean the nature and amount of information he was getting. It wasn't much, they told all they knew but it was evident that they were never allowed to know a great deal one could learn more if he took into consideration the items of interest about their appearance. Their rags and their brow-beaten demeanor, especially.

At 10 o'clock we moved up to the old second lines and headquarters were stationed in the big dug out we gas proofed near the wrecked bridge.

Though hdq. advanced about 3 or 4 miles we were still about 3 miles behind the boys. More than that in some places. We met our first prisoners about that time. There was a dressing station by headquarters and the wounded yanks and Germans were coming in in great numbers. Few yanks as compared to boche. It was raining and chilly most of the while and I pitied the poor fellows who had to have their wounds dressed out in the open. One poor Dutch kid had a bullet hole through the fleshy part of the right chest. He had his shirt off and was trying to clean the wound. It was not bleeding. Many Germans came in with big ugly schrapnel wounds (I suppose) in their heads. Some came hobbling in. Some with leg and other flesh wounds. Two Huns came in leading a yank he was in great pain.[5] They were unattended. Some German red cross men and doctors were helping with the wounded. An M.P. came in with 4 wounded prisoners. It was hard for them as 2 of them had to be assisted. He was cursing them and poking them along with his pistol. It was a splendid chance for the brute in him to express itself for here he was his own law. That is a good time to see the stuff a man is made of.

Afternoon of the 12th I went out with Colonel Johnson.[6] He went out on an inspection trip with a French Captain. We crossed the open stretch of a quarter mile between the opposing trenches known as No man's land. It had been practically unvisited for 4 years. Our Engineers and a lot of others were making a road across this stretch across the German trenches beyond and connecting up with the good road behind the German lines. It was a difficult problem as the ground was muddy and the more it was worked the muddier it got. There was an endless string of traffic trying to get over and no material at hand to make roads of. So over the stretch of about 2 miles of new road was scattered about 1,000 men all doing the best they could to get the traffic by. When a train or a truck got stuck the whole line stopped. It was raining and cold. Everyone was cold and hungry and wet and tired. Everyone was out of humor some were even discouraged. The Colonel went along pleading with them to keep up so that the guns and food could get through to support the boys.[7]

Horses everywhere were laying down because they had given all the strength. The poor horses and mules they are the silent sufferers that have to share in all of man's misfortunes and few of his joys. I saw several fine animals that had to be dragged to the side of the road and shot.

All day long strings of prisoners were coming in. Most of the well ones were carrying wounded men mostly Germans. I acted as the colonels special runner all day there was nothing to do but follow him around. I made two trips back to headquarters once with a note and once with some papers we got out of a German officer's headquarters in a dugout. I was fortunate to get all I cared to eat but I had no place to sleep so spend the night tramping around on the dry side of the bridge abutment. When I got warm I dozed a bit and in time morning came.

Morning Friday 13th. An unlucky number for me for I was idle all day.[8] The only order I had was to stick around in case I was needed. So it was a day of idleness. I don't like idleness at such a time though there were a great many men around division headquarters who seemed to take it well. The guns were quiet last night and all day. It is because the small guns are moving up though the big guns still shoot. Roads still bad and the chain of traffic still moves but very slow. I haven't heard shell from the enemy all night. Prisoners still come in. They have built a bullpen here for them where the[y] hold them till a thousand or so accumulate then they journey back. It seems that most of them have been told that we would starve them so they have brought loaves of black bread with them. It is the color of mahogany and about as hard. Many prisoners come back unguarded because there are not escorts enough.

If it takes as many wagons and trucks to supply the Germans as it does to supply our army they did well to get it out of the way so quickly. I know if we had to retreat as quickly there would be a great deal we couldn't take. So far I haven't [seen] any deserted trucks and few wagons though a great deal of material was left. I sleep a little the second night. Find a pile of blankets and get some more from the salvage dump. Salvage dump is a pile where stuff is thrown taken from the wounded and other sources.

SEPTEMBER 14   Move about 4 miles near the front though the front is more than 4 miles away. This little town is beautifully located but it is pretty well shot up by our barrage.[9] It must have been a headquarters but there's a great deal of evidence that there was a hurried departure.

I did not come in town with the hdq. Bunch. Another fellow and I came in a round about way. I got to visit a lot of other places along the front (Old front). Came over another road in. Met a fellow from my company who was lost learned that my company had been directly behind the doughboys all the while and had only two men killed. Silcott who used to be a sergeant and tried to get out of coming across. He got killed by our own shell. He went too fast. I don't know the other man. I saw several dead Germans on my way up here also one dead yank.

There is a big chateau in this town. It was elegantly furnished but somewhat dirty. It had escaped shell fire and after being cleaned up was used for divisional headquarters. I spent the day cleaning it up.

Judging from what I see around here the German officers must live pretty well. At least the[y] eat better than the men. With most of them war is an opportunity but all I have seen in the line of soldier food is black bread and potatoes. Oh, yes they raised a little vegetables such as cabbage there was a big cabbage patch in this town before the yanks came but they ate some of the best heads and pulled up many of the others to throw at each other. Vandalism will out in the yanks. I my self cut a fine cabbage and could only eat a third.

Evening several of us yanks quartered ourselves in some German officers place he had it pretty well furnished with French made furniture he had pillaged somewhere. It was on the safe side of the hill where the Dutch held it but not now that is the reason perhaps some yank officer didn't rank us out of it. We found a lot of fancy stationary and each of us wrote a letter or two to be mailed at some future date. After that we played we were generals and spread a lot of maps out and planned the next days battle.

On Sept 15 I had a good nights sleep last night. Glad we were on the hillside out of town for the Germans dropped some shells over we knew there would be some one coming up soon so we wrote a sign and fastened it on the door "Reserved for Officers" Sure enough two sergeants came up and we made the bluff work they hunted another shack.

I was released and sent to my company which was stationed at (Bouillonville) about 3 miles behind the lines.[10] I was glad to get back. I asked Lt. Howbert not to put me on such a detail again. I'd rather take my chance with the rest of the boys.

When I left I never told Sgt. Falk my platoon leader of it and he never missed me till the drive was over and I was marked as missing. It seems that no record was made of my leaving.

The afternoon I was on a detail with Sergeant Russell making pickets for entanglements. From Russell I got all the details of the drive in which he played a very important part. Russell has two prisoners to his credit, a team of horses.

On Sept 17 Forenoon I spent time making pickets it seems that we are going to put up a lot of wire. This town is a sort of center for the little dutch military railroad that the yanks hold there are two or three engines here and some cars. Most of the day I observed yanks getting the engines in running order. They painted big U.S.A. on the sides and used the whistles fully. Most of the track has been blown up by the dutch but can be readily mended.

Evening I go out with a squad of men to dig trenches with the dough boys. The dough boys know as much as we do about the game but engineers are supposed to oversee the work.[11]

On Sept 17, I got two letters. One very dry matter of fact one from Clara. She hoped that I was well. Thanks, awfully. Another letter from Alberta Cram.[12] It was forwarded from Arizona. She wanted to learn Fred Pearce's address so would I. I like Fred and wonder where he is. Alberta's address (lest I forget) is 1535 Major St. S.L.C.

I took time to write short letters to Clara and to Nell.

I must not forget. I had a good visit last evening with L. L. Smith from Snowflake. I also found Johnny Slaughter in the same company both boys came through the drive without a scratch. Johnnie and I sat in a hole and talked quite a while. Johnnie is from Springerville Arizona.

Evening I go out to work with the trenches and I dig. We are not supposed to work but I haven't got the nerve to stand by and watch tired men dig themselves in when I am able to work. Some of those fellows are sick enough to be in the hospital. They don't get enough water to drink much less wash. All day they have to stand to and keep out of sight and then dig at night besides. Of course the more they dig the more comfort they will leave and hence the work. There is scarcely an hour when the first and second line trenches are not subject to a harassing fire.[13]

Sept 18. Came in before day light very tired. It is about 3 miles to the place we worked. We go and come across the fields as it is safer than the roads. Sleep the forenoon but afternoon I write a letter to Clara. Seeing Smith sort of revived the old interests. She is a prize worthwhile but I dare not even think such thoughts for the war is not yet over.

Outside of this place is a German military cemetery. I visited it. It was a beautiful well ordered place the plants and flowers were well trimmed and arranged. A contrast to the French cemetery at dead man curve. In this grave-yard were graves where 8 and 9 names were on the wooden crosses. On many of the crosses is written (Rhuen (or ruehn) in Frieden." I was told it means "rest in peace." I suppose it is right it is the only place where a soldier hears the command "Rest in Peace."

In the evening I was put on a detail to go out and put up wire in front of the first trenches. Some details last night found they got shelled pretty bad.

Captain bawled the whole company out and said it *would* be done if it took every man. Well we went out and put up the wire. We got shelled pretty heavy. Lieut Fickel had charge. He was a lot more humble than the day he made some of those same men do "on their belly on their back." He did "on your belly" pretty quick himself and spent most of the time in a trench. I didn't run back to the trenches for the dough boys had only small holes dug and it wasn't right for a lot of engineers to crowd in on them. I found a big stone and laid behind it. I must have been safe for nothing hit me. Jake Pollock was in the trench and got hit—not bad.[14] I didn't get hit but I had all kinds of dirt sprinkled on me. I felt a tense feeling as one in a game but it wasn't fear. I had fear before this drive started but it was because of apprehension. I don't believe one ever hears the shell that hits him because it has to hit him before it makes a noise and I noticed that I could see the flash of the explosions before I heard it and whenever I hear a shell hissing or whistling I know it is not going to hit me.

SEPTEMBER 19 Slept the forenoon but the afternoon I ran onto H. Gibbons from St. Johns. His mother asked me to be his guardian angel but I have not even known where he was till I chanced to find him today.[15] I gave him very newsy letter I got from Eva Overson the other day. It interested him more than me for she lives in his town. I got a good letter from Mr. Prescott today so there is one man who is loyall.

Huns dropped a few shells in this town last night and today but they have had the bad luck to miss us.

SEPTEMBER 20 My day off. I spent it running over the hills trying to locate the 342 F. artillery. I find every Batallion in the Army but the right one. Get dead tired and bout to give up when I locate Gerald W. Berry's battery. He was a B.Y. student with me. I never knew him very well but he knows people I do and we have something in common so I enjoyed the visit. I learned where Grover Brown's battery was later but had no time to hunt him up.[16] He is located on the hill in front of (Thiercourt). A place that is shelled a great deal.

The Funston artillery is just coming in they did not get in the drive but were in training someplace. Their horses are in very bad shape.

SEPTEMBER 21, SATURDAY It seems an age since I have had a bath or a change of clothes. Either some skin disease is bothering me or it is fleas but I have scratched holes all over my hide. If it is fleas they are too quick to stand inspection.

This morning sergeant Falk called for a detail. I volunteered, but never again do I volunteer unless I know what I am to do. The men have been defecating all around these buildings until things were in pretty bad shape. Well, we were cleaning that up today and building a latrine. The reward for being willing to work. Some of the other fellows didn't fare any better they were cleaning out buildings for officers quarters and cleaning the streets. Some have been on burying details. The Germans left a lot of dead behind that had to be cared for. There is a lot of Pioneer infantry burying dead but they have had too much work as it takes a long time to cover all the ground. The most unpleasant part of a drive is this, the cleaning and policing up. Also hunt for traps.

SEPTEMBER 22, SUNDAY   Last night I went out on a wiring party. We went out with some infantry men to help us. Another fellow and I were with a squad of doughboys they had had no experience in barbwire but we got along O.k. The worst part of putting up barb wire is to carry the wire and stakes up. It is considered a shift work to put up 100 yards of double apron that is two sections and can be done very quickly but it was our bad luck to get shelled two or three times though no one got hurt. The dutch missed us all the way from 100 to 200 yards. The dough boys they sent us must have been men they wanted to get rid of at least some of them were. One man in our party played sick and two others growled a lot about having to do the Engineers work.

When we come in off the night details the Red Cross is always open and serves hot cocoa. The Y.M.C.A. the K.C. and the Salvation army are all here to give what material and service they can. The trouble is they seem to have trouble to get stuff in. There is also a commissary here but enlisted men can't buy anything from them without an order from the commanding officer.

The M.P.s just moved in on us they are taking possession of the town. There is much wrath and gnashing of teeth because of it nearly every man that passes an M.P. is stopped and told to take off that German belt or boots or puttees, or button that blouse or wind your leggings the other way or why didn't you salute that officer. One soldier came down the street with one German legging one yank legging his jacket on his arm and his shirt unbuttoned. This was his answer to the M.P. "Say guy we captured this town a few days ago and we can take it again if the M.P.'s get too fresh." The M.P.s are not to blame but the orders are foolish. This is no dress parade but the front lines. They got my name today for wearing my knit sweater outside of my shirt.

I met L. L. Smith again today. His company is back for to get equipped. We had a little time so together we went over to visit Gerald Berry had a reunion.

Yesterday our extra packs caught up with us so today I had a chance to bath and change clothes. Didn't work today because we go out to put up wire tonight.

SEPTEMBER 23   It occurs to me that days and nights are about equal again. From now on the days will be getting colder as well as shorter. I hope we deal the final blow before the weather gets too bad. There has been a lot of rain and mud of late and I fear it will become more disagreeable as the summer wanes. We are going to suffer but the poorly clad under fed enemy will fare worse.

I spent a miserable night in the rain and wet and this morning my headaches and so do my bones. We put up wire again. We fared very well. Very little shelling while on the job around (Xammes) where we have been working the last few evenings.

When we got back here after work, we stopped, as usual, in the Red Cross for a cup of cocoa. While we were gossiping with the man jerry sent a few shells over. My stop at the Red Cross delayed me just long enough to avoid the shells for three of them hit Billets No. 27 and 29 killed one man and wounded four. I sleep in 27 and came in to find my bed covered with rocks and pieces of tile. Most of the fellows went into the dugouts but I went with my blankets on the hill as the dugouts were crowded. I met a doughboy there and together we dug a shelter in a big shell hole. We spent the rest of the night there though we got very wet and cold as it rained most of the time. I don't know who the fellow was we didn't try to get acquainted. While we were lying there the Germans continued to send over their compliments. The doughboy said he would rather be at the front. We both felt better about 4 o'clock when our guns opened up an answering barrage that silenced Jerry.

When we got back into town that morning we found the streets pretty well littered with stones from the buildings. Some brigadier general who had his H.D.Q. across from my billet moved out today. He probably moved for "strategic reasons." I wish all the rulers and generals in the world had to spend a few nights in shell holes with the rain beating on them. A lasting peace would not be hard to obtain.

I have been sick all day can't eat and have a high fever. Every muscle is lame. I think I shall go see the doctor.

SEPTEMBER 24, WEDNESDAY   The doctor marked me quarters so I did not have to go out last night. It was an awful night. I don't see why some fellows like to ride the sick book up here. I would rather be well and take my chances. All the consideration one gets from the doctor is the benefit of a doubt that you are sick and some salts and A.D. Pills.

I went out with Sgt. Askew to show him some pickets and material I located the other day on my tour looking for friends. I didn't have any nip to work. There was a lot of those barb wire barricades for roads and gaps in wire entanglements they have a French name that sounds thus (shivvie de freeze) we came upon a lot of wire entanglements that were wired for electricity. An experiment probably.

On our way out to work the Dutch shelled the town but their range was a bit high. One shell hit in the supply (QM) dump. It got two men and some horses. We had to pass the place a few moments later and saw the horses all torn apart, two yet struggling, and an auto burning. The shelling continued all day though it is only a big one now and then.

This evening Most of the fellows went to the dugouts. I shall try to stay in my bed. It is dry and warm there and I can't afford to spend another night in the wet. I have made my choice of two chances. I'll do my best to get well and if the Lord wants me to live through He will look after me.

I write a note to Clara and to Prescott.

SEPTEMBER 25, THURSDAY   A night's sleep did me well. I am not really sick but am dreadfully weak in the knees.

I went out to (x) on a detail with Sgt. Kemp. I don't know yet what we were supposed to do. About all I did was fill a few sacks of sand. The work didn't bother me but the trip out and back almost exhausted me.

On our way out the Germans shelled the road. Small caliber projectiles and none of them came near. Kemp was lying near me in the ditch a little piece of rock or something came singing toward us. Kemp tried to pull the hero stuff he picked up a little piece of shrapnel lying near. I crawled over and looked at it. He hadn't noticed the rust on it. It wasn't hot either. Many a soldier is going to carry home pieces of shrapnel that "almost hit" them.

I dodged between the shots from one shell hole to another till I got into an evacuated trench where I found an old copy of Colliers weekly. It was wet and dirty but I got an hours good reading. When the fire ceased we went on into (Xam) and worked, or pretended to. It was a dugout for officers and no one was much interested. There were not many soldiers in the place but the Germans dropped a big H.E. [Heavy Explosive] over now and then. They made one direct hit on our building but everyone was under cover.

Papers are full of news of victory on the Bulgarian and Palestine fronts. It seems that they are having a walk away over there.

I found a dutch bayonet today with saw teeth on one side. There are two reasons for saw teeth.

SEPTEMBER 26   Nothing eventful has happened today. I am glad for I want to prone. I have been weak and ailing all day. No appetite no pep.

Last evening a barrage was expected so everyone was assigned to dug-outs. I decided I'd rather take my chances in the open than in a wet crowded dugout so I took my bed and sought out a place to spend the night. I found a place behind a big concrete arch near town. It stood between me and the enemy and was in line with the German cemetery I mentioned the other day. The cemetery seems to have a charmed existence not a shell from either side has struck there yet. The Kaiser seems to have a great deal more of respect for his dead than for his living.

Along in the nights our 75's opened up a splendid bombardment that lasted about 5 hours but in spite of that I had a good night.[17]

About 7 o'clock 6 hun planes came over to size things up. They took a lot of chances. More than I have seen any of our aviators take. Perhaps they take them but most of their chances are taken in the papers. One plane came so near that we could read the numbers. I didn't have my gun but all the sol-diers who did shot at it with either rifles or revolvers. He go[t] away. I have heard rumors since that one of the planes has been brought down.

We moved back three kilometers today. We are at, or near, the town where division hdg. is (Euvezin). I made the hike all right though my pack just about got the best of me on the way. If I were home I would go to bed for a week.

SEPTEMBER 27   Yesterday I was as badly discouraged as a fellow could be.[18] I couldn't find a place to sleep. So Sergeant Cohn and Askew made room for me in their quarters that warmed me up a little bit. This morning I sat around with nothing to occupy my mind but a sore belly and a general empty dead feeling so I got the blues again. I thought I would try working this afternoon and this afternoon the worm turned. Sergeant Falk took my shovel away from me. "Man you are not fit to go to work come in here to the doctor." The doctor gave me some A.D. pills and told me to rest a day or so. Perhaps tomorrow I can eat a bit and go out next day. That is the first bit of consideration I have had in the army.

On top of the foresaid I had my joy added upon by the receipt of a real letter from Clara one from Charley and another from Mother. Clara sent her picture. I had almost forgotten what she looked like. Mother sent the picture of Johnny in the uniform. He looks more of a soldier than I do. Those letters were the best medicine yet. Just think right now as I write it is shining high noon out there in the golden west where all my hopes are centered.

SEPTEMBER 28   This month's slipping away fast.

I feel better today. Tried to eat a little this morning and at noon but each time cramps was the result. I expect though to live them down in a day or so.

Everyone here is interested in the paper a yank will give his last centime for a paper. No one is more interested in the march of events as is the soldier. He has reasons—perhaps. Today's paper brings [news] of many prisoners being taken by the British in Bulgaria. It tells of airplanes dropping bombs on Berlin and the Kaiser hiding in a celler. How do they know he hid in a celler? Foch says we have the Germans on the down hill move. I hope they are wise enough to realize it and quit soon.

Today I got some elephant iron and built myself a little shelter in the open. I felt that I ought to move out of the Sergeants quarters. Some of them didn't mind my being there but I can't impose on the good natured ones. So I sleep in the open tonight. The only other choice I have is a dugout which is safer but cold and damp. There is not much danger back here.

On the whole I am enjoying the day and in my good humor am writing a letter to Clara.

SEPTEMBER 29, SUNDAY   I have lost track of the day somehow but it must be Sunday as the Stars and Stripes came yesterday and it is generally on Saturday. I got a good comfortable letter from Grandma Lytle today. I thought it was a letter from Nell since it was addressed in her writing. Nell has placed me on the extra list it seems but then I have Clara's picture here to fall back on. There is always a substitute. Perhaps I have something to hope for there.

Since I was told to stay on the sick book again today, I wrote letters and fixed up my quarters. Wrote to Mother Charley and Grandma.

I have found a lot of German overcoats and bed sacks [with] which I draped my little shelter so it will be more comfortable. I found a mattress full of straw in a dugout on the hill. It may be lousy but am risking it.

I still am not able to eat without suffering from terrible cramps so I don't eat. I did go down after appel [appell—roll call] to town where is a small Y.M.C.A. and succeeded in getting a small can of apricots but I could only eat a few so I gave them to another sick man.

Today I wandered around over the hills. I visited a lot of dugouts but didn't see anything I liked worth bringing back except a big wooden shoe. I am going to keep it for a souvenir. There is quite a passion for souvenirs here. Every dead German I have seen had been robbed of everything, rings, watches, buttons, and all pockets turned inside out. So far the shoe is my first souvenir.[19]

This afternoon I went down to the creek to wash up and I found Booker taking a bath in a big dutch coffee pot and Cohn fishing with a safety pin on a string. I followed Booker in the "tub." One sees things every day that makes him wish he had a camera. Cameras are forbidden up at the front and for that reason the papers print so many camouflage pictures of the front and one can detect the fraud very easily.

SEPTEMBER 30, MONDAY   Well I mustered up courage enough to go out to work today. I didn't do as much as I might have under more favorable circumstances but the work was of no consequence and I am content with the thought that I was occupied.

The water they give us is not good. They get it from the creek and it is very stale and brackish as it has a chance to stand in so many ponds and holes. I have not eaten much for fear of cramps. The very thoughts of corn beef kills my appetite so I am not eating till hunger comes back. One fellow said today that it took more courage to face the chow line than the enemy. I am not the only one who can't eat and there are many others sick.

Today's paper shows allies pushing on all fronts and Bulgaria is quitting. I hope they keep knocking.

They paid us today. I got 167 francs but it is no good to me as there is no place to spend it. I can't even send it home.

Saw H. Gibbons today. He was doing K.P. We exchanged some letters and passed on. His outfit is camped near here. Big guns not very lively the last few days.

OCTOBER 1, TUESDAY   Last night Parmer got me to move out of my little shelter into the shack where he is located. I am comfortable here.

I went out again on the same detail I was on yesterday. We were scraping mud off the road. Perhaps we are doing some good I can't see it though. This afternoon Sergeant Falk put me on a timbering job. I reported with Corp Parmer to the master Eng. He asked me if I had ever done any timbering. I told him I had. He asked me if I was an expert I told him I wasn't and he was in doubt because this was a very particular job. I asked to be permitted to look the work over. I had to smile when I saw it very simple square sets with logging all around. I could see that the M.E. had an exaggerated opinion of a stiff job. I told him so and he let me stay. Palmer [Parmer] is in charge and we look forward to a few days of pleasant work timbering a dugout for the General Hdq. To hide in from "Buffen Whiffles" [apparently Anderson's translation of the name for a type of artillery shell].

The Company issued at a very low price a lot of candy to each squad. My new corporal, a red headed fellow, that I bawled out one time when I was on K.P. He tried to tell me I wasn't dealing the bread out fair. He remembers me for he didn't count me in on the candy so I am S.O.L. I didn't say anything. No use we are in the army.

OCTOBER 2, WEDNESDAY   I note that Bulgaria is out of it and the British have rounded up 10,000 Turks.[20] The German Chancellor and Foreign Secretary resigned. All signs of an early peace.[21] I sent 80 francs home and 80 to the bank today was very fortunate to get the chance. Worked again on the timbering. It is a pleasant job as well as being a bomb proof one. The days are getting to be so short that one has very little daylight left after his work is finished.

I feel good today but this grub they give us, dried carrots and other dried stuff is awful. We hear of so much praise for yank genius, "dry the food so as to save shipping space." I wish some of those contractors had to eat some of the dried stuff they send us. It is delicious if one reads the papers.

Last night I undressed to sleep and this morning I have a bad cough so much for trying to start a fad.

OCTOBER 3   It seems that there are a lot of idle officers around division headquarters Generals and colonels and majors. They stand around in groups all the day. One would think if he did not know better that it was an officers rest camp.

Two of our boys were sent off to an officers training school. One of them has an uncle in the division who is a colonel and a major for a brother in law. The other fellow went because he was a good man and deserved it. Ah yes the first lad's father is a congressman another point in his favor. They are both good boys and I congratulated them. I told them that I hoped the war would end before they got their commissions.

I expect it to end soon now if one can judge from rumor. Rumor has it that Austria has given Germany notice that she is going to quit. Local rumor says that a French major bet with a yank major that the war would not last 8 days more the bet is said to be 20,000 francs. I hope the yank loses. I would help pay the bill.

Yesterday I received a letter that I had sent to Mr. Prescott last July. I sent it to Rockford Ill. Instead of Mich. I sent it to the right address also sent one to Charley.

OCTOBER 4   I had a real bath today. I got into that big dutch coffee pot I mentioned the other day. It holds a half barrel of water. I put a fire under it and got inside. I took a good half hours soak. I forgot there was a war for 30 minutes. We don't have to wash clothes lately. The supply sergeant issues new ones for our dirty ones.

Paper bears news that [no location given] has fallen and the British are still herding in the Turks. So it looks very much like Germany's sick man will be on the allies hands soon.

I am getting mail hungry again. One fellow got 19 letters today. He is only a 19 year old boy too. A big lazy hulk of a boy. He joined the national guard for adventure. Now he is in the national army getting labor.[22]

He is a good work dodger, however, and can get by pretty well. The reason I mention this fellow is because he is the only soldier I have ever seen that is immune to a bawling out. He gets neither hot or cold.

This evening the enemy dropped a few shells close enough to make us hunt our holes. We are not out of range yet by any means it is only 5 km straight across to the front. I don't think they were after us but the road crossing near here.

I like my timbering job. Parmer is a good partner. It is just like working in civil life. I would rather stay here than go back for a rest. I know that a rest means a lot of drilling.

OCTOBER 5, SATURDAY   I got a good letter from Mr. Prescott in answer to one I wrote on Aug. 9th when I was in a different mood. I appreciate his endeavor to console me on Belle's death though his consolation is a poor comfort or substitute for the faith I have to draw from. He is a man who does not believe in religion his religion is philosophy and centers in the head more than the heart. He also said he expected an early peace and that I'd get back home safe.

They put Parmer on another job so I got a new partner a fine chap too his name is Rogers. I picked him because (I told him) I have a partiality for the name.[23] Today's paper tells of the fall of Lens and advance to Lille. I am anxious to learn who the new chancellor will be and what will be his policy if a German Chancellor can have a policy.

I got a good cheery letter from Theressa Mac of Nebraska today. Doesn't hit the spot.

Fleas are still assailing me. I know they are fleas now for I saw one the other day. I hope to get used to them in time.

OCTOBER 6, SUNDAY   This morning we went out to work but they told us all to come home. The general's bombproof is abandoned. I don't know why. I don't care. All I know is that I have spent the day reading and writing as follows. I read a good letter from Mrs. N. L. Nelson the first real human letter I have received over here. N. L. Nelson wrote in a good fatherly manner both wrote on Belle's death. I also got a letter from mother and with it the Elk Rapids Progress. There was nothing in the progress of interest to me because there is no one about home that I know.

Well I wrote a letter to Clara and one to Prescott. I don't know why I wrote the first. We all do foolish things when we have nothing else to occupy our minds.

The air is full of wild rumors. The central powers are suing for peace on the allies terms. I hope they mean business. The best way to show it is to stop shooting their guns.

There does not seem to be any work scheduled for tomorrow and judging from the general rumor we are scheduled for a move back for a "rest." Tomorrow will be two months we have been up here.

OCTOBER 7, MONDAY   This has been a gala day for me. We have been waiting for orders to move so far the orders have not come. In the meanwhile we have occupied ourselves as best we could. We rolled our packs early. Gee what a pack I have hope I don't have to carry it far.

I was idle in one sense of the word today but busy in another. I gave my undivided all the day to my stomach. This morning I took my bread and butter and made toast by the fire in the stove in our shack. This afternoon I rustled some potatoes in a German kitchen cleaned them up got some lard out of the same kitchen, about a quart, and I french fried some potatoes. I had a whole mess kit full of nice brown crisp potatoes. I have been craving something like that a long time.

After dinner another lad and I took a German rifle and a lot of ammunition of which there is plenty lying about and we went up on the hill and had a shooting contest. We shot a hundred shots each. I think I got the best hits. After that the gun was so hot we couldn't touch it so we left it and came back with an armful of Hun "Potato masher" grenades that we gathered. Some other fellows got some more grenades and we went fishing in the creek in a manner that Ike Walton (or whatever that great fisherman's name was) would condemn as unsportsmanlike. We would throw those grenades into the deep places along the creek and if there were any fish there they were not long in showing their white bellies. We would get them before they had a chance to change their minds, and in that manner got about 10 pounds of pretty fair fish. We cleaned them and fried them in dutch greese. They were a good feed for about 12 of us.

An early supper and it seems that we are scheduled now to move someplace so I must get under my pack.

8

THE MEUSE-ARGONNE OFFENSIVE, OCTOBER 1918

THE MEUSE-ARGONNE OFFENSIVE WAS THE CLIMAX OF THE WAR FOR THE American Expeditionary Force.[1] As part of the final offensive that stretched along a nearly four hundred-mile front from near Verdun on the south to Ypres and beyond in Belgium, the American force was responsible for the extreme southeastern zone. Though much smaller than those of the French, British, and Belgians to the west and north, the Meuse-Argonne region was of extreme importance to the Germans as it protected the railroad line that supplied the southern half of Germany's frontline troops. More than a million Americans participated in the offensive—26,277 died and 95,786 were wounded.[2]

Pershing and his army faced several difficult obstacles. All troops, equipment, and supplies could only be transported on three muddy, poorly maintained roads. The terrain was extremely difficult. To the east, across the Meuse River, the Germans still held the heights of the Meuse. To the west, German positions in the Argonne Forest offered ideal artillery locations so that from the east and west the enemy's long-range canons could reach almost any sector in the American zone. In addition, American forces had to cross at least three ridge lines also fortified with German artillery as they advanced northward—the high ground of Montfaucon, a long rise near the town of Romagne, and the Barricourt Ridge. It is not surprising that most of the death's noted by Anderson in his company were the result of artillery rounds fired from these positions while the engineers worked to maintain and repair the all-important roads.

The offensive began on September 26, 1918, with nine divisions launching the attack along a twenty-mile front from the Meuse River on the east to deep into the Argonne Forest on the west. Some German strategists were not convinced this was the major offensive, holding out that the Americans, with their most experienced divisions including the 89th still in the St. Mihiel region, were really looking east to the city of Metz on the Moselle River. Pershing's initial plans had called for a thrust toward Metz, but with the fall of Montfaucon and the movement of experienced divisions from St. Mihiel to the Meuse-Argonne the American general set his sights on the city of Sedan. In this city French troops had surrendered in 1870 during the Franco-Prussian War—a defeat that saddled France with a German-imposed one billion dollar reparation and the loss of the border provinces of Alsace and Lorraine to a newly unified Germany. For the Allies, the capture of Sedan meant they could concentrate artillery fire on the double-track German railroad that passed just outside the city and served to supply German troops all along the Western Front as far north as the English Channel.

For Anderson and his company, the move from St. Mihiel to the Meuse-Argonne offensive on October 8–10 involved a twenty-mile hike with full packs at night, which was a real test for the 314th. As Anderson wrote, "last night was the hardest one I ever put in. I never so nearly exhausted myself. I did not know it was possible for me to do what we did last night."

After the arduous hike, Anderson climbed onto a French truck for a thirty-mile ride to the edge of the Argonne Forest. The two-day march through the Argonne left a deep impression on Anderson: "I shall never forget that woods. Not a tree in it three inches through that has not been pierced all the big trees are torn with shrapnel and their limbs and tops have in may cases been blown off. Shell holes are so numerous that they touch each other in places."

The march took them to the west of Montfaucon, the first major objective in the American offensive, and carried them forward to the Hindenburg/Kriemhilde Line south of their second major objective, the town of Romagne.

In the final days of the war, as he moved forward to the west bank of the Meuse River, Anderson saw friends wounded and killed by artillery barrages, experienced gas attacks, and lamented the fate of French refugees forced from their homes. The last night of the war found him at work helping to build a bridge across the Meuse to the town of Stenay.

OCTOBER 8, TUESDAY   Last night was the hardest one I ever put in.[3] I never so nearly exhausted myself. I did not know it was possible for me to do what we did last night. We did 20 miles, or better, with full packs. I had more than a full pack. I had a can of salmon a big can of lard and a large wooden shoe besides some personal effects I should not be carrying.

When we started out about five o'clock we thought the hike would not be more than 6 or 8 miles in length and so we set our heads on that distance. After that every town we came to we thought was the place if not surely the next. We were thus disappointed several times. I am satisfied I could have made the hike better if they had said that it would be as long as it was. Instead they lied to us as if that would help us over the road. They thought I suppose that if butter will fool bread down a misconception of distance will fool us over the road.

It was a miserable night too. Rain all the while. So dark we could not see the ground. The first 6 or 8 miles were over bad roads many shell holes and rocks, we had to walk by faith.

They marched us in the good old I.D.R. fashion, 50 minute hikes and 10 minutes rests. Not more, not less than 50 minutes for the I.D.R. says 50 minute hikes and 10 minute rests. We were wet through from rain and sweat the ground was wet and as were our packs and during a 10 minute rest we would get so cold and stiff we could scarce start. The marches seemed miles long and my shoulders would be as dead from my pack before the 50 minutes would come due. They were always prompt to stop on a 50 minute period. If it was in a mud hole then you would stop because so say the orders.

Before the march was half over men began to drop out. Some of them dropped out because their feet gave out. Marching with full pack at night is hard on ankles. Some of the fellows dropped out because they were more discouraged than tired. Before the trip was half over they told us it was 2 km more at the end of 5 km the fellows started grumbling and cursing. Every officer in the army got cursed in general and a few in particular, within their hearing too in some cases but they said not a word.

A lot of the fellows threw stuff away. Three men big fellows too fell in the road and had to be left with some one to look after them.

We got in [in] the morning with about ½ a company. All day long men have been dragging in. Everyone is so lame that walking is difficult. We are billeted in barns though we had a hard time to get the people aroused enough to let us in at so early an hour. They seemed sulky and displeased. It is probably a good thing they could not understand English for things were said to them that no censor would pass.

Everything we have is wet, all that will rust is rusty. I have been cleaning all day.

This is a nice little town (Euville) away out of gun shot of the enemy. It seems to be a wine center. There are a few small stores where high prices are made a speciality.

"Red," a man in my squad bought a box of chocolate, about a pound and it cost him even 30 francs. I go to Y and write letter to Nelson.

OCTOBER 9   I saw a French funeral this morning three little boys in white walked ahead of the procession carrying a cross. A white bearded priest followed. Then came the hearse pulled by a sleepy horse. The horse was draped with a gown or covering with only two holes to see through. It made me think of the covering the knights used to have on their chargers. Most of the mourners were women and they walked around the hearse holding on ribbons that were tied to the coffin. So much for that.

I talked to the chaplin and he told me that even Colonel Johnson didn't know where we were going or when or why so that problem is settled. I tried to get the chaplin to send my wooden shoe away but I couldn't get paper to wrap it.

There are a lot of pretty girls in this town but most I have seen are begging for cigarettes. One young lady whose husband just returned was a prisoner and escaped very charming but she smokes.

I stole some potatoes from the kitchen and went out of town where I got my greese and had a fry.

As I said this is a wine town all the wine is not in barrels. A lot of our boys tried to lay in a supply but they have over stocked and the result is they are doing some very foolish and some very disgraceful things here.

OCTOBER 10, THURSDAY   We moved again last night. We did not walk this time however. A French truck train brought us. It was about 50 KM ride we came through Commercy and to the rear of Verdun but where we are now I can't say.[4] It was a cold ride but a cold ride is better than a hike. They carried us about 3 km past our town and that didn't set very well. There was no room in the town so they took us out of the town about 3 more km. I suppose they were looking for a place to put us to bed. The[y] found it. In a woods the mud ankle deep in most places. Some of us got shelters but none of us got dry places. We curled in as best we could and napped till 7:30 when they rounded us up and brought us to where we are now. This is an old French barracks.

I think the whole division has come over for I saw hundreds of French trucks. Most of them driven by Chinese under French command. They all had soldiers from the 89th. I saw a French officer kick a chinaman this morning. French also have a colonial discipline.

We area resting today the sun is shining and we can lie on the grass. Philips and I have just had a potato fry with the dutch greese. After that we lay on the turf and listen to the guns shoot. They seem to be out 10 miles away. The captain says that this is a hot front though he did not say where we are but I think we are behind the Argonne.

OCTOBER 11, FRIDAY　　Yesterday I slept in tall grass for my bed. The result is I had a good night's sleep. No work in sight so I sneaked away. Went and hunted up Bushman's outfit. We had a good visit for we had both been through the drive since we met. He had a B.Y. yearbook and we enjoyed that the major part of the time. We saw in there the names of friends we liked. I learned that B. Glen Smith was to be principal at St. Johns and "Billie" Coleman as well. Bush walked back with me. It did me good to meet him. Tomorrow I'm to go over and we will have a potato fry provided I can steal or beg the potatoes somewhere. There is a French war garden here but it is guarded.

There seems to be a great deal of cannonading on this front. Many wild rumors are afloat about the Germans dropping back 35 miles and thousands of prisoners being taken.

Captain preached a sermon on throwing stuff away. I am guilty. I threw a pair of shoes away.

I found out where I could get some potatoes from a Frenchman so I dunned a fellow for three francs he owed me for many days and went and bought some for tomorrow.

Am going down to the creek for a shave and to wash towels.

OCTOBER 12, SATURDAY　　Squads right—left—as you were—Right shoulder arms—silent manual without numbers—on left into line—Right front into line—right turn—We put on an exhibition drill for our new loot. He made a speech to us when he took possession of the platoon. It was as follows "Well I hope we get along all right." That can mean anything. He is probably a man of deed and not words.

They are giving us new and clean clothes to replace dirty or worn out. Gen. Woods says go into battle clean and well dressed. The Captain says that the other drive was a picnic as compared with the next one. But then he is a windjammer.

Jim Hughes and I slipped away this evening and went to the machine gun outfit where he found his friend and Bush and I had our potato fry.

Well they are going to let us send for Christmas packages. Every man received a slip to send home today. It is compulsory to send it to someone. I sent mine to Mrs. Nelson. Should have liked to send it to Clara, but I am afraid.

I saw a paper today. Wilson has declared that Germans must get out of occupied territory before we will talk peace. I am anxious to move up and get it over with before the nasty weather starts weather is fairly good now except for the rains and mud.

OCTOBER 13, SUNDAY   We had Batallion review last night and the major told us that we would have services on the hillside by the chaplin at 9:30 but this morning lo and behold they routed us out at a very early hour and when 8:30 came we were well on our way along a very muddy road through the Argonne Forest. There were thousands of other soldiers laboring along the same road and other roads but all going in the same direction with burdens on their back as great as ours.

We have had a hard days march through mud all the way through a forest that was fairly riddled with machine gun fire and everywhere trees were torn up or their tops and branches wrenched off by shell fire.

I believe there was a battle in this forest in another war but those old warriors would stand agast if they saw how the place looks after its last battle.

We are camped in the woods tonight our kitchen has not caught us and we have no water. Some of the fellows have reserve rations that they are eating. Some of the same fellows shared my rations the other evening. Here after not a son of a gun eats out of my rations till I feed myself first. The fellow who pitches tent with me had brought nothing but rations in his pack he throwed away his over coat and blanket. He never offered to share his hard-tack though he will share my blankets tonight.

OCTOBER 14, MONDAY   We rolled packs early and spent the day waiting. I don't know what we were waiting for no[r] did anyone know how long we would wait. Had a good feed today it consisted of cabbage and a loaf of bread that I stole from "C" company. They gave us a lot of stew for dinner so with my bread and some bacon that Smoot got somewhere my squad fared well.

Towards evening we walk out of the woods to where we are. I shall never forget that woods. Not a tree in it three inches through that has not been pierced all the big trees are torn with shrapnel and their limbs and tops have in many cases been blown off. Shell holes are so numerous that the[y] touch each other in places. Holes are full of water and the ground is mirey from so much rain. The only way to get a wagon along is over the old plank road that is so slippery a horse can scarce stand much less pull. So we have to help get the wagons through the wood to the clearing beyond where the mud starts again.

On the way up here we saw many dead horses some deserted ones. Some dutch cannon aimed west but silent. Much ammunition we won't have to dodge, two planes, a yank and a hun that had fallen.

We are camped in our pup tents on a muddy hillside. I don't know how far the front is but Montfaucon is on our right and guns are all along this road—that is 6 inchers. I sleep pretty good tonight.

OCTOBER 15   It has been a very dull day. They had us roll our packs this morning. We could not leave lest orders came to move, but none came. We have nothing to occupy our minds except wild rumor about the war and arguments about the rumors. There are thousands of soldiers (our division) scattered around over these hills they all have their pack rolled to go somewhere. None of them have anything to do but set on their packs. Just now a rabbit started up some soldiers started after him. Everywhere he went there were soldiers and all yelling and running after him. Everyone yelled even us though the rabbit was a half mile away. A fellow in the 383 finally grabbed him though hundreds missed him.

I would be very pleased on a day like this if I had some material to write letters. I didn't carry it because I thought I would get more and envelopes get wet and stick.

Evidently we are not going to move for they are having us pitch our tents again. I am with Provaznik.[5]

OCTOBER 16, WEDNESDAY   It rained all night. I was damp and cold all the while. Provaznik's shelter half leaked and so we both crowded to my side.

I have had awful cramps along with other fellows. It must be the stew we had for breakfast. I could eat no dinner.

Wood is the big problem here. There is so little that they are tearing down the fruit trees. There is a little German graveyard near. All or nearly all the wooden crosses have been stolen for fires. One fellow got us in trouble by tearing some lumber off the side of the building Batallion hdq. is in. So even in the yanks an element of the vandalism we condemn in our enemies.

I went over to a great meeting of doughboy non-coms. The general was telling them how necessary it was for them to be on the job.

I have been hearing a lot of bull about my being made a sergeant. I got the straight of it today. I had been recommended by Falk for corporal and the captain turned me down he did not know me all I was to him was a name on the muster roll. I don't want to be anything more to him either. The men loved our old captain but this fellow is a snob.

The rain keeps pouring down and the mud gets deeper and deeper. We have dug ditches around our tents which help some still we can't keep dry within. Cramps. Cramps.

OCTOBER 17   We worked today on the roads. Traffic is heavy here and with so much rain the roads soon break through. Our job has been to make drains and shovel the slop off. In some places we broke rocks if we could find any to fill in the ruts.

I worked faithfully too. Came in this evening all wet and mud be-splattered from passing automobiles.

A great big observation balloon moved in here by our camp today it is as big as a circus tent. A balloon is a bad thing they draw the enemy fire.

The paper says the Kaiser bunch have failed in their attempt to make peace. It seems that the allies see fraud in the move so the thing must go on. I wish they would hurry up this mud and rain night and day without shelter or decent food is getting me. Many men are riding the sick book already some are lazy but most of them are sick.

OCTOBER 18, FRIDAY   I am very tired tonight. It is about five miles out to work that hike on top of a day's work seems to exhaust a person. During the day ones patience becomes exhausted trying to shovel that sticky mud. One spends most of his time cleaning his shovel.

Last night I slipped away and hunted up L. L. Smith. He had a little shelter near here, we had good visit. He told of seeing Silas Decker of Arizona who is in the 107th Aum. Train Co. "B." He is working on a Nash quad truck and passes over this road every day. I watched for him all day but did not see him so one in the army may come that close to dear friends and they pass and repass as ships in the night and never know each other.

This balloon was up making observation today and got fired on. Shells landed all around but no one got hurt. They were air bombs or rather shrapnel exploded in the air. They are the big reason for helmets.

It has been an ideal day to work. The sun is drying the mud. I hope it keeps up. I believe I will get over my out-of-orderness.

Got a letter from Theressa Mack today.

Must go to supper. They say it is good. Has not been of late. I wish the officers had to eat some of the stuff they have been feeding us or permitting us to be fed with.

OCTOBER 19   Looks very much like we are going to move pretty soon doughboys are going up now to relieve the (32nd) division infantry.

Rain continues today and our tents continue to leak our rain coats won't hold out rain. During the last few days we have had to flatten our tents when we went out to work. They say it is to prevent airplanes from seeing us. There are dozens of things that would tell an airplane we are here. Ours not to reason why—ours to realize that with the pup tents flat on the ground during a rainy day everything under is wet. I have given up the idea of keeping my gun from rusting.

I spent the day making torpedoes for barb wire in case we need them up here later on. If the Germans don't quit before then. British are advancing on a 20 mile front. Ostend & Lille fell so I expect to see our friend, the enemy, go belly up soon. I would like to go over the top once with the doughboys. It is a chance I missed last time and is a sensation I must experience.

Today I got a nice letter from one of my S. [Sunday] School girls. She and some of her friends remembered me very kindly and told me not to get killed in the war. It sort of pleased the boys when I told how interested my friends were in me. They who do write seem to think I am a good soldier. I am glad I am as far away they can't find out. I know that I can hold my own in civil life where I expect to rise above the rank of private.

OCTOBER 20, SUNDAY   I never was so nearly discouraged. Wet to the hide. Everything in our pup tent is wet. We have worked all day on the sloppy roads in the rain. There is no prospect of either the rain stopping or our getting dry. More than a third of the men are sick and they don't get any consideration outside of pills from the doctor.

The division we relieve has been trailing out all day. Their artillery will not move just the infantry etc.

A lot of us got arrested today. We were carrying rocks for the road when some doughboys who were policing the sector for stragglers from the relieved division picked us up they held us an hour or so till an officer came to see whether we were ourselves or not.

The Allies are advancing very fast in the North and the outlook for an early peace is bright. I am feeling pretty well and I hope the Lord will bless me with enough strength and courage to hold out. It is not worse than the Germans have to put up with and I don't believe they are as able now to endure what we can.

OCTOBER 21   A very pleasant day to work. Not much mud and sunshine most of the while. We were working on the road to a place called (Ivoiry) to the left of (Romaigne————— can't spell it).[6] The place was in a little cut and the infantry dug in there throwing the mud or dirt out with the road. We had to widen the road for 2 way traffic the road bed was good. It is in a big open place and many of our boys were killed taking it. I saw one grave with 20 little crosses. Many Germans still lie unburied. In the distance 3 miles we could see our shells exploding behind the enemy lines. They sent a few in our direction but no one was hurt. I notice a great many of the German shells are duds. Last night I counted 8 out of 10 that failed. They were aimed at the big guns that are near this place where we sleep.

I dread these big guns near the camp more than I do the shell[s] that come. They only stand a small chance of getting a fellow but these big guns raise me clear off the ground, especially if I am sleeping with one ear down.

I sent my wooden shoe home today through the chaplin cost me 5 francs.

I wish the weather would get cold. I am tired of slop and mud.

OCTOBER 22, TUESDAY   Time is still dragging and so is the war. This is a day for our company to rest and clean up. Write letters if we wished and could get material. I was very fortunate to get several envelopes and a few extra sheets of paper. There is a fellow here who is in the company office he is dog robber or orderly for the officers. He is a Canadian Frenchman, Michand. He has a girl in S. Dakota and I write his love letters since he does not write English. That entitles me to some special favors and since he has access to more paper supply than I do I get the benefit. I also write a few letters for myself—Clara—Theressa—Prescott—Mother—Grandma.

I am lucky to have a good buddy. His name [is] Provaznik. He is an Austrian but yank born, a taylor [sic] by trade from St. Louis. He is also the batallion taylor and being such does not have to go out to work with the rest of us. They have him for gas guard nights and as such he has free access to the kitchen. He brings in every morning little hunks of bacon and flour or butter and we cook a little on the side in front of our pup tent. I found a fry pan the other day and we made pancakes today. All we had was water, flour, sugar & salt but we fried them well and they were good.

I feel very well but many of the men are sick. Several have gone to the hospital in bad shape. We need sunshine to dry us out. A little sunshine and letters will keep me well.

OCTOBER 23, WEDNESDAY   Am dead tired tonight. We worked today at a point by the front lines. It is about 7 miles out so we did good 14 miles besides our days shift. We were making a new road through the woods to get supplies over when the drive starts. The roads out there are pretty well shot up and the Germans still have shells to throw over at us. They dropped several in the woods today that were too close for comfort.

There were several horses that had been killed by shell fire, lying along the road. They were not there when we passed the other evening. One place a caisson had been hit by a projectile. The horses were terribly torn up so the drivers must be killed. There are many of the German horses lying around yet some of them were stinking. I hope I don't get on a burying detail. It is a nasty job.

Dutch airplanes were active today. We saw two of our balloons go up in smoke. Some of these dutch fliers are certainly plucky. The men who go up in the observation balloons are no less so. Imagine it takes guts to leap out of those baskets and fall a couple of hundred feet before the parachute opens. They say it is cowardly to jump without reason or if there is a chance of the danger passing. They also must not jump too late. I saw several of them jump the last few days.

In the shells that came over today was a very irritating gas. It was not strong enough for masks but made us sneeze and burned the throat and nose. I hope our gas does the same.

OCTOBER 24, THURSDAY   4 months of foreign service today. I hope there is not that much left. I have had enough of this to satisfy my curiosity. I have no desire to be a hero. When the Germans are willing to come to our terms I will be pleased to quit.

They routed us out at 5 o'clock this morn but after breakfast were advised that two platoons would go out to work the other two the 3rd and the 2nd to go out tonight. I am in the third so I spent the major part of my

time trying to find the 355 Supp. where Greg Rencher is. I found them and
we had a little reunion. He showed me some of his letters from his girl, some
pictures and we parted to go back on the same ship. I also hunted up the
Y.M.C.A. They didn't have a thing except a few envelopes so I took my
allowance (5). Went or rather came back to write a letter to Lester in which I
told him to rest easy that he was not missing anything. He is a sergeant at
Camp Custer and was retained when his division came over (85th).

It is hard to get the newspaper here so we get no reports except from our
guns that are beating a tattoo on the Hindenburg line.

I neglected to say that yesterday I got letters from Charley, Lester, and My
Nebraska girl. Charley is entertaining high hopes of going to school some
day. He has been faithful and I intend to see him through if I get out of this
alive; if not my insurance will give him a lift. God help me to help him for he
has the courage to stay home and do the plain duty.

OCTOBER 25   We worked last night till twelve o'clock the whole regiment
is busy trying to finish the road across the bog to get up supplies and get the
guns over when the drive starts. We are working in three shifts making the
roads out of the buildings that have been shot down in (Romagne). It was a
muddy nasty job in dark and nothing but big spoonlike German shovels to
work with. We were shelled some but only the gas from the shells bothered.
It was sneezing gas and some of the boys put on masks. Later on I wished I
had for I was sick from it.

On our way in we got a few farewell shots that scattered dirt around us
but hurt no one. I did not run. I was tired and I have got my self to believe
that it is foolish to run for to run feeds fear and if the shells are going to get
one they will get him any way. It is probably not the truth but such a fatalist
philosophy is very convenient at such times.

Last night Provaznik made a raise of some more syrup and flour so today
we spent most of the time frying pancakes. He got some of the scraps and
ends of some doughnut dough and we fried that also. It is a good pastime and
feeds the fancy if not the stomach. Besides that we got two doughnuts each
for dinner.

I went to the Y this morning but could not even get a paper. Fellows are
getting sour on the Y.

OCTOBER 26   Worked almost down last night on the same road job. Got in
at two o'clock. We go out at noon. I expect the drive will start soon guns are

crowding up close to the front. And they are stacking the ammunition high—many gas shells going over and many in reserve. I hope it starts soon and gets finished up. If I am to be bumped off why delay. If I am to go home let it be soon. I am not feeling well inside nor looking well outside.

OCTOBER 27   I wish I could write down just how it feels to be under fire for four or five hours. Last evening my platoon went out to make roads we took axes and were going to make a corduroy road across a bog. While we were crossing an open field at a point where we could easily see our shells breaking behind the hun lines a boche plane flew over we all flopped and remained quiet he circled low for a while or till the machine guns got to[o] hot for him then he beat it we went on our way we hadn't gone far till a couple of buffen whiffles came over but we proceeded to a point in the road where we were to work about that time the shells came over pretty regular. We figured they had our number so we scattered and stayed scattered for about 4 hours. I sat down behind the foot of a big beech tree and not a shell came near enough to hurt but every once in a while I could here [hear] our fellows at different places yelling "first aid." Many of the shells were gas and I could see the air being laden other places through openings. I came out in the open to see if the fellows were gathering but they were all scattered about in shell holes so I rested behind the tree and ate my sandwiches lest they would become gassed and I go hungry.

The firing ceased after a while and we gathered ourselves together. We had one killed, four hurt and several gassed which is quite a loss for being under cover.[7] By that time the gas had soaked through the whole place and it was necessary for us to wear masks. I stopped to help carry wounded. It is hard work trying to carry a wounded man over a bad road at night with a gas mask on. We made a stretcher out of two sticks and a blanket that made the work more difficult for the sticks bent so. We left the dead man. He had several other dead men there to keep him company. I saw four of the 32nd division boys who have been lying there since the last drive. I shall never forget [one] who was evidently killed by the concussion. He was lying on his back, knees bent up. Arms outstretched fingers spread out and tense. Head thrown back, mouth open, eyes staring, face very blue. It seems hard to leave the boys unburied but its war.

This morning I went out with four or five other fellows to get our man. It was a beautiful quiet forenoon even up there at [the] front. I won't have to go out tonight so am going to write a letter or so. I got letters from Charley, Mother, & Prescott also a couple of Grand Rapids Papers.

I went to see Beauchamp about making an allotment to Mother but it seems that the red tape is too great. She needs the money too. I can send money but the Gov will not add to it.

OCTOBER 28, MONDAY   I got a pretty good nights sleep last night and but for the cramps I feel all right.

This forenoon Provaznik and I dug a hole in the ground for our bed that gives us more room in our pup tent. We made a little stove in the ground in front of the tent so now when we want to cook things that Prov can manage for we can do so without leaving the tent. We had pancakes again today.

Am going out to work again after dinner. Weather is good, roads bad. Last night the boys say it was very quiet at the front with the exception of a barage [barrage] our guns put over. The tables may turn this evening. At this game a fellow never knows when he puts on his shoes whether they will ever be taken off again.

OCTOBER 29, TUESDAY   We put in a long shift last night. We went out at noon and got in at 3 o'clock this morning. We were digging about 2 miles of camouflage trenches along the hill side behind (Romagne)[8] They had a regiment of the 354th Infantry to dig and an engineer was placed here and there along the trench to look after it.

I was made a runner along with three corporals and we carried reports every hour down to the Batallion P.C. (Post Command) in (Romagne). Richardson and I worked together. It took just about 2 hours to go to P.C. and return then we had to start back so we were walking all night long. We spent 3 hours before the dough boys came out staking out trenches through the brush.

Rich & I got to go home 2 hours early. We had next to the last try to make and Falk told us that we needn't come back unless the major sent a message. We were lucky to catch a ride all the way. Of course riding is prohibited up here but auto drivers never pretend to see. It is court martial for a skinner to permit men to ride with him. It is to save horse flesh. The other poor devils didn't get started till we were in bed and they had a 7 mile hike to make. Sherman was right. ["War is hell."]

(Romagne) was badly shelled last night every time we went in the gas would smart our throats and noses but not enough except once for our masks.

During the day several men and horses had been killed in front of the major's hdq.[9] It is on a main road.

Going along a trail last evening I fell over a dead man. He was a 32nd div. lad and had been lying there for days. I couldn't help but think how I would have shuddered at such an experience a year ago.

Got up this morning to learn that our balloon had been set afire by a Boche air plane yesterday afternoon the observers escaped.

I am a full fledged soldier. I found a grayback (cootie) on me. Don't know where from.

OCTOBER 30   I was a runner again last night. Corp Philips and I were together. I like to be with Philips he is not yellow. We only made two trips to P.C. the rest of the time we sat around freezing and trying to keep awake. The Huns did not shell much but the allies sent over an eye opener for the boys across the way.[10] During a quiet spell we were greatly amused by some French who were moving cannon into position. They were stuck in the mud and they were yelling and beating their horses like their lives depended on it. They did more yelling to get a couple of guns under way than the yanks would do to move a regiment.

We have a new Lieutenant he is an odd duck. He walked in with Philips and I. Or I should say we walked in with him. I wished all the while he would do something to get away from us. We walked all the way in and though truck after truck passed us he never suggested that we grab one. I was very tired.

I got up about dinner time but I did not dare eat on account of the cramps. I learned that I don't go out tonight. I am glad for perhaps I can rest away the bellyache.

Germans are scattering peace propaganda over our lines with airships. They have done that a great deal of late. It is calculated to demoralize our troops. In the pamphlet that I read today was a plea that the "new" German government be recognized and peace hastened.

K.C. sent over a little tobacco for the boys today.

OCTOBER 31, THURSDAY   Today is Halloween. Being so I wrote a rather saucy letter to Clara hoping to provoke a response. I also wrote last night and this morning to two of my schoolgirls, to Theressa and Mr. Prescott. I had a good sleep last night but had to change my position once in a while to wear out a cramp inside of me. They have been with me all day but I am fairing better than some of the other fellows. Some of them are suffering from a sort of bloody flux. Patterson went up to the Captain yesterday and told him that the doctors were not helping him any and he was so weak he could not make it out to work without endangering his health. Perhaps Pat had an exaggerated opinion of his case but he went to the wrong man for sympathy, the captain told him to go out and if he fell down it was time to take care of him that is an average illustration of the concern that fellow has for his men.

I don't think the doctors care much either. I hope they do. Of course good doctors get imposed on by men who want to ride the sick book but that is no reason they should look upon all the men as fakers. I never will go to an army doctor till I am sure it is the last resort then I will have to doubt his interest.

"The command is forward" or will be in the morning. There is a general uneasiness in camp. This time tomorrow we will perhaps be trailing through the mud with a gun in one hand and a shovel in the other. I expect it to be raining like every thing though tonight is going to be clear and cold. If it stays cold I will be pleased for it will be easier to keep roads in shape and the guns can keep up with the infantry.

We had doughnuts for supper, very heavy and greasy. I ate one but no more for I want to keep the cramps down. I would do anything rather than go on the sick book now. No matter no one can get on the sick book so I hear so that means the drive starts in the morning. Most of the boys enjoyed the doughnuts. I am afraid they will be the last some of them will enjoy.

Provaznik and I will have our stuff in one bundle to be left with the rest of extra stuff. All we will take is a light (very for me) pack. We have agreed that if one does not get back the other will take care of the personal property. I keep my notes on paper, leave this diary.

Nov 9th I write for the last nine days of the drive as I have noted briefly the events.

NOVEMBER L   My belly was in turmoil all night but the cramps had subsided some about 2:30 this morning when they routed us out. I did not eat any breakfast. We roll light packs store other stuff and start on brisk hike. Barrage was nicely started far and near the guns were booming. I thought we were going up to go over with the infantry but they dilly dallied around outside of (Romagne) till about day light then I knew it was too late. We were up against as bad a proposition as going over for after about 8:00 o'clock the

Dutch started shelling the roads to prevent supplies coming up. It seems that their guns were mostly centered on the highways. They had already started to shell R[omagne] when we went through. As we passed by the Red Cross in Ro[magne] they gave each of us a bar of chocolate and box of cigarettes. Philips and I were walking together. I tried to trade my box of cigs for his chocolate. He wouldn't but started to eat it said perhaps it would be his last. It was too. An hour or so after he was killed. The shells were coming over pretty fast and they caught us on an open slope. They were only small ones some gas. Another lad and I were together we noted that they were coming over in two and threes about 10 seconds apart so we took advantage of those intervals to run from one shell hole to another and flop. Philips was not taking that precaution. I saw him and another fellow get it. They were in the open. A shell came. They fell to their knees and before they could flatten out another hit 25 feet from them and perhaps 100 feet from us. It got them both.[11] Two other fellows were killed and several wounded in our company on the same hill while several trucks had been hit and were burning on the road.

I mention Philips because we were intimate. He was homesteading in New Mexico, was engaged to a girl from there who was living with his mother in Kansas waiting his return. So perish our fondest hopes. Every boy that is cut down over here had been building castles in the air.

After we got out of that mess we did not get much fire till evening. We spent the day filling up shell holes along the roads and patching up a road over the dutch lines. Many prisoners came in but not as compared to the other front most of them were wounded but all the well ones were utilized to carry wounded yanks on their own. Provaznik and I were together all day he speaks German and talked to some of them. Some of them seemed pleased to be alive but the older ones were pretty sullen. They were poorly dressed and poor in spirits. Most of them were very young. After about noon very few wounded came in. It seems that after the first shock the dutch put their attention on the retreat at least there were few wounded. They took us back to (Romagne) to spend the night it was about 3 miles. We had to go to bed without supper. Prov & I went to bed without a bed. We each had a blanket and our over coats and we dug a hole to shield us from the wind. Thus we shivered the night away.

NOVEMBER 2   We woke up this morning to find that we were lost from the rest of the company. We went our way and they went theirs in seeking a place to sleep and so it was up to us to find them. We got out our reserve rations and cooked some breakfast. I had some bacon we hooked a half loaf of bread and we made coffee.

We decided that our outfit had got up early and started towards the front so we started out. Found one of our sergeants who was also lost but he did not seem to worry much about it for he dallied away so much time that Prov. and I went on ahead. We left him talking with a doughboy of the 90th Div in (Bantheville) Bantheville was as near to my idea of the land "desolation" as could be. It looks as bad as the best pictures and the artists go as far as the brush will let them.

Prov. and I plugged along for about 10 km's and caught the outfit at (Remonville). Along the roads were scattered the bodies of many dutch and yanks. My gun was very rusty so I traded with one of the dead yanks. One German lying in the gutter had his head blown off below the level of his shoulders he had been run over by vehicles that had to turn out. 3 yanks with wound tags on had evidently started back to be dressed but a shell got them. All along the roads were our six in. and smaller guns that were taking new positions. One big one fired as we passed. It nearly broke my ear drums. One must stand on his toes and hold both ears when they speak. We were passing a traffic jam in the road. It was nearer to cut off across a field so we did it. A German plane flew low and shot at the string of autos and teams. I don't think he got anyone but I saw a woman in a red cross station near us and was impressed by the calmness she showed. Perhaps our crossing the field saved us from the plane.

We cooked our dinner out of our reserve rations. The rest of the day we shoveled mud and carried rocks on the road. It started to rain and it rained all afternoon.

Tonight I go out to patrol the roads to keep the traffic moving. Falk called for volunteers. I said I'd go because I had missed out in the morning. I think one other man volunteered the [officer] had to detail several others. I am to do nothing all night except be on the job and see that no trucks get stalled on my section of road. It is going to be wet and cold but I am wet and cold already.

NOVEMBER 3   Spent a long uncomfortable night managed to get some hot coffee about 2:00 that helped some. Dutch shelled some but all of them went by me. One hit an ambulance a little ways back. Killed wounded and all. We are relieved at 7:30 this morning and I don't have to go to work till noon. I go up behind town and build fire for to dry myself out go to sleep and scorch shoes burn rain coat.

After dinner men who work[ed] last night go up to join company. We go over a very gummy muddy road to (Barricourt). Pass by a woods where the Germans killed many of our men with machine gun fire. I am always going to give the great share of glory of this war to the dough boys. They are the ones who go up against the real thing. We endure more shell fire perhaps but they go up against the machine gun as well as shell fire. We have hardship and hard work but they usually have t[w]o casual[tie]s to our one.

This afternoon we went way up near the front to help put in a bridge and this evening we came back to the muddy woods mentioned above. We had no way to mend things so we got a long rope and when the trucks got stuck we would tie on and pull them out. We kept that up till 8:30 when we hiked on to (Barricourt) I was lucky to get a little straw to curl up on. It has been a quiet day. The doughboys are still advancing but without much artillery support a few wounded are coming back and once in a while a prisoner. The dutch must be running ahead to make a stand. Our guns are coming up as fast as possible.

NOVEMBER 4, MONDAY   Dutch must have held these positions very light as there are very few dead. I see where machine guns have been scattered about 400 yards apart on the important points to hold the yanks back some. The machine gunners are all dead.

Sergeant Askew took a detail over to (Taille) [Tailly] to inspect the town for German traps. I didn't find any but one of the other fellows did, or said he did. We were to inspect a fine chateau over there that was to be a hospital. While we were there orders came for the doctors to hunt another place as the General wanted the Chateau for headquarters. The doctor in charge did not take the orders very gracefully but there was nothing to do but move. He had us inspect some billets on a muddy street in town. That Chateau would have accommodated 300 patients and they could have been made comfortable. But the General's comfort had to receive first consideration. No one can tell me that that man has the interests of the soldiers at heart. German war lords can't be any less considerate.

This afternoon I carry rock for roads and push mud off the streets here in (Barri[court]). I got away long enough to make a tour over the hill. Came back with two German blankets that had been thrown away. I saw a German soldier (dead) with finger cut off. Some one robbed him of his ring. I figure on a good night's sleep.[12]

NOVEMBER 5   They wake us at 3:00 to go some where to do something. We line out over the muddy road. I don't know the direction except that it was toward the front. We marched for several kilometers before I learned that the captain didn't know where we were. I am not surprised at that. We had taken the wrong road so we cut across the sloppy fields for a mile and a half to the right one. We found the right road a good 4 way boulevard which pleased us very much, being engineers. The retreat here does not seem to have been as orderly as it might have been. They left guns and wagons every-where and all along the road was great heaps of shells some as large as two men could lift. Many horses and men were lying along the road and the thing I noticed that I never saw elsewhere was out of some of the horses great hunks of flesh had been cut.

We came upon "D" Company building a bridge the Dutch had blown out. Captain Coy was working as hard as the men. The road went into a woods and for a mile and a half large trees had been fallen across the road.

I was sent out with a party to inspect the road. We found that the road was in good shape but for the trees which were soon removed though it was a lot of work. Beyond the woods the road crossed a big open place of a mile beyond which was a river. We learned the river to be the Meuse. The big town on the other side was Stenay. All the bridges had been destroyed. There is a little town on this side of the river that according to the natives the Ger-mans just left during the night they told the French to get out for they were going to shell the town. I'll never forget those poor people leaving. We met the first ones at the bridge "D" Co was building and we continued to meet them all the forenoon. They were mostly old men and women and children. Many of them tottering and feeble. They were carrying heavy bundles and wheeling barrows or pulling wagons loaded with their treasures. Some of them left a lot of their stuff because of the trees in the road. Some of the chil-dren were crying and the babes would not be soothed by us, they were afraid of soldiers. The enemy sent a few shells over and some lit near but the people didn't seem to mind.

I saw an airplane come down today. It fell on the other side of the river. It was blazing fearfully. I don't know whose it was but no doubt he was killed if not he is a prisoner for he fell on the wrong side. No man's land runs right down the river.

We are stopping in a town about 3 miles from the river. Our kitchen is here. As we passed through this town this morning I noticed a nice gold ring on a dead German lying in the street. I thought it would make an excellent souvenir so I went around after supper to get it but when I took hold of his cold stiff hand I got ashamed of myself. It was a wedding ring I think and I am glad now I didn't take it. I know that it would have been a reproach to me forever. I don't need souvenirs that bad. I don't know what my friends will think of me for even desiring to rob the dead.

NOVEMBER 6, WEDNESDAY   They put me on a detail this morning to search for mines and traps in the town this side of the river. I cannot write all here about them.[13] In fact I know very little myself about them but it is enough that the Germans left live mines behind them that could be exploded by various means both mechanical and chemical. I liked the job because besides being interesting it gave us first access to every building in town. Finding the things was not difficult as nearly all of them had some wire or string tied to them so that by opening a door or moving something one would touch off the lighter.

We found a lot of nice souvenirs belts and helmets and such but did not pick it up since there was no way to carry them except on our backs and we will have enough stuff we have to carry. We have no way to send them home. I saw the Red Cross lady I saw the other day when the plane fired on us and I gave her a helmet and some aprons and things to be used in her work. The aprons of course were French but she needed them. The town was right on the river bank and within range of Hun machine guns on the other side of the Meuse. We could hear machine gun bullets splat up against the buildings any time during the day is [if] anyone would expose himself in a street that faced the river. We had to cross that street on the run. The red cross lady had a field glass and wanted to get a look at a German. She had so much curiosity that she knew no danger. She gave me some cookies and chocolate for my trouble and left in an ambulance in which was a wounded yank and a German. One of "F" company officers got picked off by the river near here. He was a good chap too got his commission since he came over here.

One good thing about this job is that we are eating well. We have access to all the good things to eat that have been left behind. We have collected about 30 gallons of jam a lot of potatoes and flour that we sent back to the outfit. We have taken possession of a French home where are all the utensils and dishes we need. We are as much at home as little golden locks in the bears house. The people left and took nothing with them. In some of the houses the clocks were running yet. We found rabbits in cages and a she goat tied in one place. We milked her and Carl Anderson & I drank the milk.[14] It was good coming from such an ugly source. I have seen stocks of linen in some of the wealthier homes that many American wives would be proud to own. All the people have not left I am told but I have not seen any. Some of the boys saw a couple of old ladies who are trying to stay.

The Germans shelled the town all day but we have not been in a shelled place at the time. This afternoon I spent some of the time guarding our stuff and getting supper.

NOVEMBER 7   This has been a rather boresome day. Powers and I have been bring[ing] in the sheaves and watching our stuff. We have been bringing together all the eatable stuff we could find to send back to the Company. We cabbaged a jar of jelly each for ourselves. There was not much of that and we knew that if we sent it all back that the cooks and officers and sergeants would gobble it all. At least that is the way all good things have been divided in the past provided there was only a little.

I found an American penny in a French home today also found a change of underclothes some clean towels and handkerchiefs. We found milk cans and flour bags that came from America. Learned that the Red Cross distributed stuff to these people through Switzerland. So the Germans did not stop all the food. Of course they stopped much. A lot of the good things that are supposed to come up to us at the front never get here also.

This afternoon we go home. Trip here has been a success as well as a good experience. We found in the neighborhood of 90 mines, very few of them cleverly laid. They laid them in a hurry on leaving.

Left a couple of men to guard the food and we go back to the outfit in the hope that now with plenty of flour the cooks will make us pancakes.

The town was shelled all day. Building across the street hit. We were glad to leave.[15]

NOVEMBER 8, FRIDAY   Still plenty of mud but frost nights. A shell hit in the street in front of our billet killed two.[16] I did not know till this morning.

I did not go out to work today but I think I shall go out tonight. I write two letters but they are returned because I say too much about a possible crossing of the river in a night or two. Our guns are getting pretty well set in.

Our Old Lieutenant Howbert is back. He has been away to school. We are all pleased because he is a prince of a fellow. Lieut. Fickle has been sent back to S.O.S [Services of Supply].[17] He showed the yellow feather. I wonder if he still thinks that "the private of today is the general of tomorrow."

I have resolved that as soon as peace comes to try for the officers training school. I hate to ask now because it would look like I was trying to get out of something. Sergeant Falk leaves for the training school today or tomorrow. Two of our sergeants have been busted Cohn and Grenuwal they were both good men. Cohn shot at an aeroplane and then they were both guilty of some other offence or at least they got the blame.

NOVEMBER 9, SATURDAY   I slept last night and worked this morning. We were shoveling mud off the road and putting rocks in ruts. Tore the buildings in this town down to get the rocks. Cohn and I worked side by side all day we had a lot of sport over his fall from grace. He used to be my teacher in the reconnaissance school. There was a French anti aircraft gun located near us. I got to talk to one of the Frenchmen who spoke English he said that some German delegates had come through the lines to talk peace and that they had 48 hours from noon today to come to the Allied terms as stated by Foch.

About noon a plane flew over and got the lay of things a few moments later they started to drop shells so close that the French had to move their gun. They dropped some shells into a little town off in that direction where the q.m. dump is. I learned this evening they got 42 yanks. One of our wagoners Tithers was over there.[18] His team got killed and he never got a scratch, he was on his wagon too.

I talked with the French man about all the dead horses that there are along the roads with big strips of meat cut out of them. He says that the Germans ate it. I thought so all the while. Some of the horses look like c[o]yotes have been there. I believe I would rather eat horse than the canned meat they have. It stinks so.

Got two letters today. One from Charley and one from Nell. Nell seems to have given up her claims in Bro. Slack.

NOVEMBER 10, SUNDAY   How I would like to spend a Sunday at home go to Sunday School, read, rest meet friends and indulge in some of those old common place pass times that are after all the most substantial.

Tomorrow noon is when peace is promised. I have put faith in it. If it fails I will never expect it till it comes. Most of the fellows have no faith at all and will be surprised if the guns stop tomorrow noon.

I am a busy body these days. I tried to prone the body as much as possible and at such times write up notes in this diary.

It is quite a job copying in my notebook the back notes but am about caught up.

Our beds came yesterday and so Provaznik and I have made our bunk on a pile of rubbish in a little loft so we can rest when we can.

Lieutenant Howbert is in charge of the detail tonight. We go out to put a bridge over the river. I was left out but got in with Sgt Goff.[19] There will probably be some excitement and if it is the last night I want to be in it. There can be little more danger up there than here. Along the road from here to the river men are getting killed every day. Indeed there is more shelling a mile back from the river where our guns are hid in the woods.

It seems that the yanks are going on with the drive up to the last hour whether the Germans give or not. It seems too that there is a lot of needless slaughter. A lot of men will be killed before this time tomorrow and it looks like they might just stand fast till then.[20] But as I said before "Ours not to reason why" War is war and "orders is orders" as the fellows say.

9

WAR'S END, NOVEMBER 1918

THE AMERICAN SUCCESS DURING THE MEUSE-ARGONNE CAMPAIGN AND the prospect of Germany entering its fifth winter at war gave the Allies hope that a German surrender would be offered or, if not surrender, an armistice could be agreed upon in the late fall of 1918. Several events foreshadowed the armistice. In late September Erich von Ludendorff and Paul von Hindenburg, Germany's top ranking military officers, concluded that Germany must seek an armistice. A month later, on October 26th, Ludendorff submitted his resignation. Rumors of a threatened Bolshevik revolution at home, mutiny in the German navy, and a march of thousands of army deserters through the streets of Berlin circulated. Austria, Germany's wartime ally for more than four years, signed a separate treaty with Italy on November 4, leaving Germany to fight on alone. Hoping to negotiate an armistice based on President Woodrow Wilson's Fourteen Points, German leaders responded positively to a November 5 message from President Wilson through Secretary of State Robert Lansing declaring that Marshal Foch had been authorized by the United States government and the other allies to communicate the terms of an armistice to properly accredited representatives of the German government.

The German armistice delegation crossed through the French lines the night of November 7, an event that Anderson recorded in his diary entry for November 9. The Armistice was signed by the German delegation at 5:10 a.m., November 11 in Field Marshal Ferdinand Foch's railroad car in the woods near Compiegne, a French city about fifty miles northeast of Paris.

The immediate peace called for Nels Anderson to reflect on his past, his good fortune, and his future. Thankful that he had not been killed in the last days of the war, as was his friend Lehi L. Smith from Snowflake, Arizona, or wounded in the last minutes of the war—though an enemy shell came close, dazing him with its flare and peppering him with pieces of dirt—Anderson wrote in amazement on November 11, "So this is peace and I am alive. I am so surprised. I don't know how to act so I just sit and think. I don't feel like yelling no one is yelling around here. How good it is to be alive. I had set aside all hopes and now they assert themselves one by one. I have a future again. It is the greatest thing to live for. I was glad to get in this fight that my future would not be an apology."

With the war over, the question on everyone's mind was "where do we go from here?" Most hoped for a quick return trip home, though the pragmatists knew there was much cleanup work to be done in France and that an occupation force would be sent to Germany. Anderson favored unknown Germany to the well-known France. His only regret when orders came that they would leave the next day for Germany was his weak physical condition after several days with an illness that robbed him of his appetite and his strength. Nevertheless, on November 24, Anderson began the march to Germany with the rest of the 89th Division.

NOVEMBER 11   On the 11th hour of the 11th day of the 11th month; 5 months to the hour almost from the time we marched on the good ship *Carpathia* (which was torpedoed on its way back) we heard the last guns shoot. I didn't hear it because I was asleep.[1] I didn't wake till straight up noon. The first thing I asked was have the guns stopped. "Hell yes an hour ago." Now about last night.

It was a bigger job to get out there than to put up the bridge. We went a round about road through the woods. The mud was very deep and sticky. I never saw worse mud. I marvel that they ever got a caisson over it. The Dutch who went that way left a lot of their stuff. One carriage and many horses were stuck at different places. I was reminded again that war is hell—for horses. There were many who gave up the ghost through that woods. We went to a saw mill where I was unlucky enough to be put on the squad to stay there and load material on trucks or wagons to be hauled to the river where the bridge was being built. Putting the bridge over was the least of the job the material had to be carried. I got up to the bridge a time or two. They had a little shell fire. I shared in that and we also shared in some they did not get at the bridge. One shell hit so close to me that the flare dazed me but I only got hit with some pieces of dirt. I didn't even know we were being shelled back there for the guns were making such a noise about that time that one could not hear shells come.

We got the bridge over and the doughboys started across the river at 10:30. About 12:00 o'clock we started home. We got in this morn about 4 o'clock. Before 11 o'clock the yanks had advanced 4 miles in places (11:00 this morn). They were creeping up all night and many of them got knocked off as late as 20 minutes before the zero hour.

On our way in last night I passed the 3rd Battalion of the 353 Inf. I took time to look for Co "I" found Company "I" but learned that the fellow I looked for L. L. Smith had been killed just before the drive. A shell hit him in his dugout. He was a good conscientious soldier. Came in when I did left a 2 weeks bride behind. Last time I saw him he spoke of her and how happy he would be when they could settle on their little farm.[2]

So this is peace and I am alive. I am so surprised. I don't know how to act so I just sit and think. I don't feel like yelling no one is yelling around here.[3] How good it is to be alive. I had set aside all hopes and now they assert themselves one by one. I have a future again. It is the greatest thing to live for. I was glad to get in this fight that my future would not be an apology.

Now it is over I am going to try to get to the Officers Training School or some school where I can spend my time well.

NOVEMBER 12   We got up this morning to find all the outside quiet and serene. It is hard to describe the majesty of the morning as I felt it. No minnie wurfers to hiss and bust.[4] No dodging from one building to the other or sneaking along the side of the road. No ban on lights or fires. A man can light his cigarette without hiding and he can smoke it in the open. Automobiles carry lights but they can use them now. There is no fear and nothing to excite fear.

We went out and scraped mud off the streets in (Laneuville) the place where we inspected 2 days for mines. There were no snipers to shoot at us as we crossed streets that opened to the river. I walked around and found a nice dress helmet (dutch) Now that the war is over perhaps I can carry it. The great danger now is that someone will steal it. The Germans say that the yanks are fighting not for land or power or money but for souvenirs.

Wagon trains trucks and guns have been crossing the river at this point all day. They are hot on the trail of "ze enemy."

Stole some potatoes today and had a potato fry this evening. Cooks need to ginney up, all they give us is sour bread and skins they have plenty of flour but don't make a thing with it but good things for the officers. Our captain likes good things.

I tremble for the future I am afraid they will have us on burying details there are so many men and horses lying about.

NOVEMBER 13, WEDNESDAY   We were in the midst of a potato fry last night when Stein came up with orders to get into bed and get some sleep as they would rout us out at 1:30. I've got to tell about Stein he is a jew and being so has a good job. Most jews get good jobs. I don't know why unless it is because they are the Lord's chosen people. He has a rather checkered army career. He was in the British army and wanted to get out. It cost his dad, who is a rich merchant in St. Louis, $5,000 to get him out. He was drafted got along ok but went a.w.o.l. at N. York got busted from corporal made again over here and was corporal in this drive or at the beginning. Turned scared in the shelling where Philips got killed got an officer's horse and nearly rode the animal down or till he got back out of range. Well he was just brought back. They will bust him again. He is a good kid but gets scared and nothing feeds fear like running. If I had run back I would be in jail yet.

Well we just go in bed when orders came to roll packs. We did (we always do) and sat around till 2:00 a.m. When they hauled us to where we are now wherever that is.[5] It is both on the railroad and on the river. We have been busy most of the day loading on cars and then carrying steel rails to be used in making a bridge over the Meuse.

The 2nd Engineers are also here they are sporting two service stripes and sort of look down on us new birds. We are new but we went some after we did come.

We are sleeping in pup tents tonight. Provaznik and I are pitched together. We have a lot of wood to build a bonfire and some straw to sleep on the night will be cold but we prefer that to rain.

NOVEMBER 14   "Where do we go from here" is the question of the hour. Every one has different opinions.[6] Will we be home Christmas will we go to the Rhine and so on.

My platoon rolls packs this afternoon and starts back to our camping place where [we] left yesterday. On the way back I get to see Bushman. His Battalion was returning they had been over supporting the marines. His company got about cut in two in a siege of fire they went up against. All along the road back we saw soldiers busy salvaging stuff or burying dead horses and men. We stopped at (Cesy) [Cesse] and took out a couple of mines some soldiers were guarding.

Only part of the kitchen had left for the other place. Enough cooks were left here to open up cans of corn willy and cut sour bread. Office is here so I was fortunate in getting letters one from Ma, one from Will he is in Wales, a reassuring one from Clara and a very good one from Laura Brooks Lund.[7] Learned that Hafen's oldest child was killed and that a letter of mine had been published in Wash. Co. News.[8]

Joe Jarvis wrote a note in Clara's letter and told how bad he felt that he did not get in.[9] I know he tried but his thumb is off. A good man too. I must write him.

We have been hearing a rumor for the last two days about the war possibly starting after 72 hours. The time is past and all is quiet. We heard an explosion today it made us nervous but proved to be blasting in the river.

NOVEMBER 15   Our platoon was patching roads up at Tailly. I am going to write down the names of places from now on. I have not spelt the name of this town right but it is where division Hdq is in that beautiful Chateau. They had some doughboys there working on the roads as well. The poor devils had come from Stenay about 8 miles and nothing to eat but a couple of sandwiches. They had not had to do such a task before and were cursing their luck. We have had to make such hikes often though we only went 4 miles today.

There is a rumor that all enlisted men are to be transferred to the regular army and draftees will return home first. I am neither one. I volunteered and came with the drafts.

Nights are getting very cold but things are drying up. I think it will be fair from now on.

We ate dinner with Reg. Hdq at Tailly. We didn't have mess kits but the fellows let us have theirs. War brings out the dividing up qualities in a man also other good qualities. If he has none it brings out and develops bad ones. The front will tell whether a man is a sheep or a goat. If he is a goat it won't improve him but if he is a sheep it may make a goat of him.

I must take some time to wash and shave. I have not washed my face or shaved for four days. During the last month the only time I have washed is when I shaved. I have thought of the times when I was a little boy and Ma had to dig my ears out. I would have looked upon such a condition as this as ideal. We have had no facilities for washing so we all go dirty by common consent. Here we are up in a loft without even a candle. We have a big pot in the middle of the room with a fire in and I am writing my notes by the light of the flame. After I shave I am going out to hunt up Bushman. His outfit is down the road in some barns.

We have fresh meat to eat tonight.

NOVEMBER 16, SATURDAY　　　Very cold last night. Prov & I nearly froze. We worked on same road job today. Nothing has happened except that we eat at Reg. Hdq. Again. They short changed us so some of us (Hill, Smoot, & I) got a couple of cans of beans and some hard tack from their kitchen when the chance presented and we fed.[10] I got the cramps from eating too many cold beans.

Last night I had a good visit with Bushman. We talked over the school proposition. We decided that the officers training would not teach us anything useful so we thought that if we got home in February or March we could go back to school at home and finish with a few hours to the good.

I have been in a negative state of mind the last day or two. I am a creature of moods and they come and go as the different winds. I must get into some good wholesome company when I get out and sort of tune up.

I got a letter today from Prescott. He looks for war to continue till Spring. Charley wrote so did Grandma Lytle and I got a long letter from Alberta.

Everyone is killing time now. No one is interested in work now that the war is over. We see string after string of horses going back they are being turned in. They are all poor and banged up and tired but I heard a fellow say he even envied them at that for they were going back.

Ten men from our company went to France today on pass for a week.

Bushman is coming over for the evening.

NOVEMBER 17, SUNDAY　　　Roll out 4 o'clock. Roll packs. Load outfit on trucks pack ourselves in a truck and proceed up to the river where we were the other day to join the company. On our way up we meet the 2nd Division doughboys, engineers, artillery and all. A string several miles long they were starting on their way to Germany.

We spent the forenoon getting located first we unload everything at a farm near here and up the river but they moved us to an old German barracks where we are. The town is Pailley [Pouilly] about 10 miles below Stenay and is on a highway the yanks are trying to construct. Some of the second division are passing this way and we have been out this afternoon helping them get their outfits up a hill between times we tamped rocks in the road.

Provaznik & I have spread ourselves out on the ground in an old mill building used by the Germans for a barracks. While I am in here writing this the fellows are lining up out side in the cold waiting for their supper of bacon and potatoes. They are yelling "Feed us and send us home" I don't feel good so am in no hurry to go out.

Before we went out to work this noon they inspected our gas masks and gave us a mask drill and gas lecture. What next?

Papers say that the Germans are starving. I hope the Kaiser and his armor bearers starve but I quite agree with the allied sentiment to feed the people. There is not much danger of the Kaiser starving. It seems that he is a back number nothing much is said of him. He was a temporary block in the march of progress but the world has gone on by him.

I must get out to get a breath of air. No stoves. Fellows have built fires in here anyway and the building is full of smoke.

NOVEMBER 18, MONDAY   We are up against the aftermath of war now. We are cleaning up and it is about as interesting as dishwashing. Slept well last night but got late to reveille this morning and our red hot captain gave us a bawling out. Not personally for there were others so he addressed the company.

All the officers are hardening from the general to the lowest loot. Major gave orders that we must not "go" to work any more we must "march" to work. And worst of all he caught a sergeant with his collar unbuttoned.

The company is divided some work, some clean up and some drill. It is my day to work. I shoveled gravel or we did we are putting it on the road.

Lt. Howbert was transferred today. I hate to see him go.

Time seems to drag. All we think about and talk about is going home. Perhaps we will get over it later.

I ate no supper tonight. I don't feel good. It seems that I have a rotten place in me for a stomach. Many others are sick. It's the bad chow. I hate to go on the sick book.

We sign the payroll so perhaps we will get money soon. No need for it here.

NOVEMBER 19, TUESDAY   How I wish for some material and the opportunity to write some letters.

We are getting military again. Here is our time table resembles a train schedule. Rise 5:45 Reveille 6:00, calesthetics 6:05 to 6:20, Breakfast 6:30. Police up and make beds 7:00, work 8:00 to 11:00 dinner(?) work 1:00 to 3:00, Retreat 4:30 supper (?) bed—we have no candles so that problem regulates itself.

I am lucky to manage for enough candle to write the notes of my diary.

My stomach feels like a swill barrel. I can't eat am to[o] weak to work so I just stall around or that is all I did today.

I think that we could well send our doctors home to fight the flu for all the good they do here. They could leave a buck behind to serve the pills. I know exactly what they would do if I went over they would give me physic.

We are all getting lousy everyone is scratching at least. It must be from the straw that we are sleeping on too late now and there is little chance to rid ourselves of them.

I neglected to mention that Rogers and I stole the officer's jam the other day.[11] I couldn't eat any on account of the cramps but we treated the platoon. I am a tiny bit conscience smitten for the captain has put a special guard over the rations so some has to suffer. It is not a good job watching these cold nights.

NOVEMBER 20, WEDNESDAY   I had to get on the sick lame and lazy list this morning. It is my first time to go to a doctor in the army. He gave me some O.D. pills the same kind a fellow gets for a broken leg, he also gave me some little white chalk like pills. I had to take the O.D.'s in his presence. It was my platoon's turn to bathe and clean up so I got in on that. We have a little bath house the dutch left. We pump the water into a tank on a wagon and a gravity system leads the water to the showers we build a fire under the tank to heat water. Plenty of wood here. Bill Braner and I were keeping fire going. I was pumping water Bill was cleaning his gun and the wheels got afire ruined the wagon nearly let the tank fall before we came to ourselves. So I got a change of clothes and cleaned up. This afternoon I didn't do anything.

The Germans left this town pretty dirty and it has fallen to the engineers here to clean it up. The place is not shot up much and there are many civilians left. Mostly old people and children. I wrote a letter for Michand last night and he told me some things he had learned from the people. (He speaks French). There are no less than 16 half Boche babies due here. It seems that some of the women for policies sake or other reasons lived with the German soldiers and officers. Also a pretty girl up here fared ill indeed if she did not submit herself to the invaders.

The latest dope we have is that we are going to Germany. I am glad too for I don't like the idea of staying back here to clean up the leavings. We are all getting insignia to sew on our arms the middle west division w in a circle. Pay day for September. I draw 163 francs.

NOVEMBER 21, THURSDAY   I am still under the weather. Went over to the doctor got some more pills and marked quarters. I have no hunger. I tried some mush for breakfast but it was too sweet and gagged me. I can't keep warm in bed and it is such a draughty building that one freezes near the stove.

Have a couple of envelopes so I write to Alberta Cram and mother also Charley sent the Stars and Stripes to Mother and Alberta. It will answer for a letter especially since my head won't work to think of things and my hand doesn't want to write them. I only want to remind them that I got through with all my buttons on.

Silcott's mother wrote to Ward Holt tonight or he got the letter tonight. She wanted him [to] ask Harry to write. Ward is worrying how he is going to tell her that Silcott got his head blowed off in the St. Mihiel drive.

The captain came in and tied into me for not making my bed. I had been lying in the bed till he came. I love that man.

NOVEMBER 22   Got a very nice bawling out from the major for not snapping up to attention when the captain spoke to me.

This afternoon the captain made me work. I didn't tell him I was marked quarters but he knew I was. There was another fellow as sick as I that he put to work as well.

I don't feel bad today only I can't eat. I have not eaten all day and very little for three days. I am weak and easily exhausted. I tried to write a letter to Nell but failed. I sent my father days card to Prescott.

Never was I so discouraged. I long for nothing as much as to get into my own overalls. Today's treatment fills me with bitterness.

NOVEMBER 23, SATURDAY   We had a regular field inspection today. Our new colonel came and looked us over. Asked the fellows a few questions how they liked their grub and so forth. Everyone liked everything it is the easiest way to get rid of the questions. Soldiers learn that it does not pay to kick about things they don't like because they have to complain to the fellows they sometimes wish to complain. None of us like our captain but what good does it do to say so. None of us like the major but what is the use he is over us.

We leave here in the morning for Germany. I am not ship shape and I dread the hike. I am dreadfully weak in the knees. I hope they take us there and on down the Rhine and home. I want to get out of this. I am wasting my time now that the war is over. This is the best part of my life and I ought to be out making a name and a home.

We have been reading in the Stars and Stripes about all the candy the boys have been getting up at the front. Tonight we got the first candy we have had since we left the St. Mihiel and there we only had candy a time or two. The candy probably comes over but it never comes up here. I got more than my share. I was with Michand tonight writing letters and he let me in on his it seems that he got two rations. Sgt Russell stole some and was around selling it at 10 francs a box ½ pound.

10

THROUGH BELGIUM AND LUXEMBOURG, NOVEMBER–DECEMBER 1918

THE MARCH FROM FRANCE TO GERMANY TOOK TEN DAYS. BURDENED BY their heavy packs, the soldiers moved at an easy pace, averaging between ten and twenty miles a day, although some days the men rested, making excursions to nearby localities or conversing with civilian residents. The Belgians related accounts of German atrocities carried out on Belgian civilians during the occupation. Anderson found the Belgians hospitable, friendly, thankful for their liberation, and his sympathy for them is very evident in his diary. In Luxembourg, where the majority of the population spoke German, residents were also friendly toward the American soldiers. "When we bid good by to the good people we make friends with they warned us against the German women." With warnings from the civilian populations of Belgium and Luxembourg against the Germans, Anderson and his comrades must have wondered about their reception as an occupation force by the defeated enemy.

NOVEMBER 24, SUNDAY   We start on Sunday to Germany. 5 months ago today we struck this country. We roll out at 4 o'clock start at 7:00. Provaznik stayed to come in the truck he has bad feet. I get him to bring my helmet (dutch) and a few other things so I have enough to carry.

We spent the day in good old I.D.R. fashion one hour hikes or rather 50 minute hikes and 10 minute rests always fall out on right of the road. I had terrible cramps all the morning otherwise I was making the hike all right. At noon I went to the doctor and asked for the most drastic remedy he had; he gave me some tiny white pills they did the work. I passed the afternoon very well. We are now 15 km within Belgium and we have come 30 km today. I made the hike better than I thought. The Belgians had erected a lot of welcome arches along the road. We saw the flags were different (black yellow red) though we did not know that was the Belgian flag till the natives told us. We are advised not to buy food from these people but we got the old lady in the house where we are staying to fry us some potatoes. We pay them well though [they] pretend to refuse money. He brings us in some beer. I drink bottle not strong. We ask him if he has pie and he brings in a big bundle of straw we found that paille (pie) is straw in French. Belgians speak French. I have 2 blisters on my feet but good sleep will put me in line for tomorrow.

NOVEMBER 25, MONDAY   We have been plugging along all day and it seems a long day too. We thought we were going to eat dinner at noon but they kept us on the road till 3 o'clock where we were supposed to stop we found we had to move on as the place was crowded so we ate a sandwich and proceeded. We stopped long enough to get a French, or Belgian lady to cook some spuds. They were good. I don't think plain boiled potatoes ever tasted better. I gave her five francs and felt it a bargain several other fellows did likewise so she got about $5.00 for a pot of potatoes besides selling a lot of apples.

The town we are in is Vance, Belg. And we have marched about 30 km today to make it. We are billeted in the front room of a Belgium home.

My head was bowed most of the day but I made some observations. We saw the shade trees cut down for miles by the Germans. The forests had been stripped of the best timber. The towns and people looked about the same as in France. The manure piles before the houses were just as large and the fields are intensely cultivated. The big thing that speaks Belgium is the attitude of the people they have every town we enter decorated with the allied flags and they all have erected arches of welcome and appreciation to their liberators. In a way this is a triumphal procession and we would enjoy it were it not for the burdens on our backs. I fared well today though all of us came in with aching muscles.

NOVEMBER 26   I am taken with Belgian hospitality. The mother here got up early and got some hot milk for us. I swiped a loaf of American bread and gave in return for some rye bread and butter and coffee the lady gave me before the other fellows got up. We are paying them for everything we get. A yank pays well as long as his money lasts. The people are so taken back with American methods. American officers ask them if they can billet any soldiers but the Germans brought the soldiers and told them to billet and feed them and they did not get paid for it. There is no question about the abuses these people endured. A young man with his family was shot in the face several times by a German machine gun. The soldiers set the gun up and turned it loose with no provocation.[1]

The people seem to have plenty of food and most of them have cows though there are few horses. I mean by plenty of food—bread and potatoes sugar and fat is scarce. There are many children and dogs. The dogs are utilized however to pull carts.

They say we have many kilomets (Kill-em-yets the yanks call them) I hope to make it as this days rest has helped me. We had general equipment inspection today.

Nearly all the U.S. flags in Belgium are home made some of them are very odd. I am getting the little girl here to make me one to take as a souvenir. I shall send her one from the states.

NOVEMBER 27, WEDNESDAY   Drill this forenoon go for a short hike to get limbered up. This afternoon we have pack inspection. These inspections are not all necessary but they keep us occupied.

These people treat us fine. Hot milk again this morning. They would give us anything but then we pay well for all we get. Our company bought a pig today for Thanksgiving dinner it weighs about 150 pounds and cost even 500 francs. Our squad bought 5# of beef today it cost 28 francs. We got the lady here to fry it and to boil some potatoes to go with and that added 7 francs or 5 francs each besides we gave some meat to the lady. I watched them kill the pig they burn the hair off.

I like these people but they live too close to nature to suit me. Their barns and stables, as in France, are in the same building. The only difference between the people and the cattle is a wall. These folks are seemingly well to do they have 2 big oxen and 3 milch cows to get to the stable one goes out of the side door of the kitchen in fact the smell we always have with us and all the dirt is dirt from the kitchen is swept into the next room, the stable.

Now a word about the story we hear at every hand. There is no doubt that these people suffered at the hands of the invaders who came in and took possession took what he wanted and did as he pleased.[2] The cases I cite are things that Michand tells me. He says these people can only think of one thing and that the wrongs the[y] suffered. I visited with the man of this house one of his neighbors where Michand stays. There was an old man who sat with bowed head behind the stove he had been suspended by the arms 48 hours. Another man who sat in the room had just escaped from a labor camp in Germany. His brother died there from hunger and ill treatment. A lady here is a widow because her husband refused to let the soldiers take his horses. In one house they beheaded a babe. They burned a young husband before his bride. They took all young women to Germany to work they are gone yet. They took all the brass and copper the people had and forced them to raise food for the Boche army. The atrocities in other towns were worse. In Arlon hundreds of people were slaughtered that fear might rule the rest.

Towards the last it seems that the Huns tried to be good fellows they bought things from the Belgians the result is there is much German money here. The German mark is worth about 25 cents.

I came home this evening with the man of this place we walked arm in arm because it was dark and muddy and he knew the way. My heart was full of hate for the Barbarian Boche and with sympathy for the man beside me and his people. I could not talk his tongue nor he mine but we understood each other.

NOVEMBER 28, THURSDAY   Thanksgiving day away from home and roast pig for dinner. For breakfast bread and milk. Now lets see what there is to be thankful for.

The war is over and I am all together yet. We are billeted in a nice comfortable room with a fire to sit by instead of a pup tent on a muddy hillside. We have stopped here long enough to get rested. On the other hand we are homesick. I am homesick to get back to work for myself next year this time I want to be in school.

We celebrated Thanksgiving by singing America. Bro Lipsann led the song from a prominent position on a manure pile.

I got Michand [to ask] if they were robbing themselves by cooking potatoes for us they were amused and said that all around here were plenty of potatoes. This man was to give the Boche 168 sacks but due to the short notice retreat they did not get them. The Boche would have taken grain but the people were too wise to thresh much ahead. But now they are all busy and all day one can hear the flails beating out the grain. They thresh on the stable floor and one would swear that he could not eat the bread but when he sees these nice big loaves he forgets his scruples. Write to Clara & Prescott.

NOVEMBER 29, FRIDAY   Morning. We pull out of here at 10:00. I hate to leave the place. The old lady bustles around like her family is leaving. She gives all the fellows coffee in their canteens but Owen & I got milk. I got her a lot of bacon rines and Owen got some soap for her so we had a warmer spot in her heart. She also gave Owen and I each a patty of butter.

Afternoon: We are near Arlon and are come 9 Km. We have 8 or 10 km to the Luxembourg border.[3] It is a cold damp day and we have a chilly billet. The people we are billeted with are very poor and very indifferent. They speak German or French most of the children in the street speak German. Our boys are more at home for many of them speak German.[4]

The rest of the squad are just having a big feed downstairs. It is costing 30 francs. I did not get in on it because I can't spare the money. I must send some of this money home for other purposes. There is some booze in the town (Stockem) and a lot of the boys are busy hunting it. It is because so many of them can't leave the booze alone that we are not permitted to stop in a big town like Arlon.

NOVEMBER 30   Some of the fellows slipped away and went to Arlon last night. They report it to be an up to date city. Cafes, pretty girls, shops and so on but in the hands of the M.P.s. I hope to get loose in some big town in Germany or Luxemburg long enough to buy some souvenirs. We tried a new scheme last night the whole squad made a sort of trundle bed and slept together. We fared fairly well. I have [a] finger that was very sore so it prevented my sleeping. This morning I went to see the doctor and he told me I was getting a felon.[5]

Pack inspection, rifle inspection, billet inspection and venereal and cootie inspection today. Nearly everyone has cooties even I. We were told that hereafter we would pay for all equipment we lost or threw away. I gave a pair of shoes to the Belgian we stayed with in the last place now they give me another pair to carry not that I need them but just to prove that life is one damn thing after another.

DECEMBER 1, SUNDAY   A month ago the drive started. We only made 17 KM today but we are in Luxemburg. I am feeling fine too. Country is rough and here is a great deal of forest of beech and oak it is well cared for, in fact it is a cultivated forest.

I hope the felon on my finger is short lived for it certainly gives me a lot of grief even when we are marching.

These people all speak German. We were told not to fraternize with them because they might put a spider in our coffee or soup. Well the first thing 4 of us bucks did was to rent a room for the night we bought some milk and stole some bread for which we traded for rye bread. As I write this the folks here in the house are eating their supper after they finish we will eat ours on their table. There are two fellows in the bunch who speak German so we are chumming right up to them. They say they don't like the Germans neither do we so we have common ground to start from. They are going to treat us to cider after while and after that I suppose they will tell us more about how boastfully the Germans started for Paris and how hurriedly they came back. These people were not imposed on during the war as were the Belgians but they none the less suffered as the prices of things will show. Shoes cost from 100 to 500 francs. Suits from 500 to 1000 francs. They probably would have suffered more had they entered [the] war on either side. They have no army the army of Luxemburg is a mere police force of 250 men.

DECEMBER 2, MONDAY   We hiked 20 km. Further toward the Rhine today. I made the hike well but for a toothache and my felon which keeps a bucking night and day.

This is a very romantic country. Woodlands all along the way, beautiful ledges and other scenery that the people sell to tourists.

Food is scarce, high prices. We paid a franc for a liter of milk. In this town we can't even buy milk and what other food bread and meat, that was for sale was soon bought at fancy prices. I did get some candy bought about 4 tablespoons full of small green hard drops that tasted like camphur for 2 marks. Meat sold at a small pound for 5 marks $1.25 "Red" Jones and I had access to some liver sausage so we managed for a small panful. It is to smear on bread.

One evidence that this place is neutral, the houses are not all numbered and checked outside saying how many men each place will hold. The people in fact are not neutral, most of them receive us warmly. We marched under an arch in one town today that was decorated with the red white and blue of the allies and Luxemburg and on the arch was written "Welcome to our Deliverers."

The name of this town is Fels it is built in a narrow canyon very scenic and beautiful.[6] There are high rock ledges on either side and on each ledge is the ruins of an ancient castle out of the piles of stones grow trees, symbolic of the new order of things.

DECEMBER 3, TUESDAY   Red, Bill, and I slept together in the same bed. There was not room to lie abreast so I got in at the foot and fared well. I had still with me my aching tooth and throbbing finger. Last evening Dorsch ("red") and I found a place where we could get milk not much however. We spent the evening with the family, there is a young married couple who are planning on going to America. Many are in that fix. This morning we went up after more milk and I took a can of corn beef up and gave to the lady. Last night, I neglected to say, they sang us the Hymn National of Luxemburg. It was good.

I have been a little sick today from eating too much of the liver sausage I swiped lst night. Red was in the same fix so we gave the stuff away. Moral ----------?

I get a chance this morning to climb up to the castle on the hill. It is an imposing position and in peace time is a lookout for tourists. As I wandered around the old ruins I wished that the rocks could talk. There were cells and towers and passages the very silence of which wrapped the place in an atmosphere of romance.

The story is told that the castle was destroyed by the tenants who toiled in the valley below.

When we bid good by to the good people we make friends with they warned us against the German women.

On our way to the place where we are now about 12 kilometers most of its up and down hills that would have been more pleasing were it not for the burdens on our backs. Because of the hills we were very tired when we got here. It is a picturesque town. It also has a castle or two. We are billeted in a big school house and the fellows are arguing whether we are in Germany or not. I think we are still in Luxemburg.

GERMANY, DECEMBER 1918—MARCH 1919

FOLLOWING THE ARMISTICE, ALLIED TROOPS OCCUPIED GERMAN TERRI-
tory west of the Rhine—a region that bordered Luxembourg, Belgium,
and France. The Allied occupation of Germany included soldiers from the
French, British, Belgian, and American armies. The British held the northern region, the Americans the middle section, and the French the southern area. Headquarters were established in three "bridgehead" cities on the
Rhine River—Cologne for the British, Koblenz for the Americans, and
Mainz for the French. It was generally held that those divisions that had
most distinguished themselves in battle were given the honor of serving
in the army of occupation.[1] The American forces were assigned the region
that stretched from Koblenz, an ancient Roman city established at the confluence of the Rhine and Moselle Rivers, to Trier, further up the Moselle
River and another Roman city where the Porta Nigra, the Black Gate, and
other ruins recall the Roman occupation nearly two thousand years earlier. During his three months in Germany, Nels Anderson visited both of
these important German cities. However, he spent most of his time in the
Waldeifel sector, of which the town of Kyllburg, located on the Kyll River
approximately twenty-five miles north of Trier and fifty miles southwest of
Koblenz, is the primary railroad stop on the track between Gerolstein and
Trier. At the beginning of the occupation the Battalion headquarters was
located in several towns—Gerolstein, Pelm, Lunebach, and Nattenheim
before landing in Oberkail, four miles southeast of Kyllburg, on January
4, 1919. In Oberkail, Anderson found lodgings with a seventy-five-year-
old widow, whose husband had died in 1871. For the two months that
Anderson lived in her house, he only referred to her as "mother," and a
mother-son relationship quickly developed.[2] Though Anderson spoke little
German, he did make a conscious effort to learn it from the local population, especially from mother and the "many rosy cheeked girls here which
is some inducement to learn the tongue."

Although the German villages had been spared the ravages of war that had visited so many of the villages of northern France and Belgium, Anderson noted evidence of the war in that "nearly all the children and men we meet have some of the army uniform on. The children nearly all have those round red band soldier caps." Further evidence was to be found in the lack of young men—many having been killed in the more than four years of fighting—and the dismal prospects for marriage for the many young women who remained in the towns and villages.

Shortly after arriving in Germany, Anderson was assigned to the battalion headquarters, first as a runner and helper in the office, then later as a teacher for "illiterate" soldiers. His assignments allowed him to travel between battalion, regimental, and brigade headquarters—usually onboard German passenger trains, but, at times, by motorcycle or on foot. With considerable free time, Anderson observed church services, weddings, funerals, dances, Christmas and New Year's celebrations, a German election, and made excursions to Trier and Koblenz. He records visits and friendships with several Germans—a soldier just returned from Serbia, a widow whose husband died in the war, the mother of a prisoner of war who had been captured during the St. Mihiel campaign, an old man and veteran of the 1870 Franco Prussian War who had lost his two sons in the recent war, an attractive young school teacher whose boy friend was in St. Paul, Minnesota, and a group of friendly young ladies from a remote village that Anderson visited on several occasions as "the first yank that ever hit that neck of the woods."

The light duty and assignments that excused him from drills and formation and the friendships among the German population did not suppress Anderson's desire to take advantage of an army program that allowed soldiers to attend colleges and universities in Europe. Shortly after his arrival in Germany, Anderson submitted his application for the program. In late February the battalion major called Anderson into his office "and told me that there was a chance to go to a French University if I knew French. I told him I knew French when as a matter of fact I can't count to five." A week later he set out for Montpellier in southern France.

DECEMBER 4   I can't say much for the place we were at last night except that everyone had a lean hungry look. They seem more interested in our marks and the food they could beg than in us. I got to speak to a lady who had been in New York. She was a poor person along with the rest of them. She said that feeling was bitter against the Germans but that the people had put up with so many hardships that they had little faith in anyone they looked upon everyone as an exploiter.

Last night I took my shirt off and found many cooties which accounts for the holes I have scratched in me.

We marched into Germany today.[3] It was a very matter of fact entry. No yelling or boasting. Not even a flag waving. No one to oppose us or welcome. The people we met looked stolid indifference. I can't name the town unless I go out and hunt it up.

Nearly all the children and men we meet have some of the army uniform on. The children nearly all have those round red band soldier caps. Some of the fellows cursed them for the caps sake because those things brought back memories.

We only came 15 km today so we got here in time to look the situation over. We are billeted in a barn the man here just returned from 4 years on the Eastern front glad to get back says war is "Nicht goot" trys to tell us the Kaiser is a scoundrel.[4] I hope he means it.

Owen and I found a place to get some potatoes cooked. The lady gave us some plums that she had preserved for 4 years wouldn't eat them themselves. She spared us some milk too and we bought some apples.

We were warned to beware of these women least we get poisoned but this woman (2 sons in war) has too much of the mother spirit.

DECEMBER 5, THURSDAY   Bill and I slept together in a hay mow last night. I used to dislike Bill, he is a poor illiterate fellow and a professional work dodger. I used to think that was a grievous offense when the guns were shooting. Bill used to drop out when we would go out to the front to work then he would "get lost." But he was always in bed when we got back. I have got to know him since and find he has a big heart. I wrote a letter to his mother for him today. I also start a letter to the Elk Rapids Progress.

Chickens sure catch it when the yanks come to town—so do the yanks 6 & 8 marks each. I watched this returned soldier kill a chicken today. He put it between his knees held its head with one hand and pulled the feathers off it's neck with the other then he cut its throat. His little children looked on with great interest. I couldn't kill a chicken with an axe but I suppose a German military training would make me otherwise.

Well Owen and I managed for some flour and coffee today which we gave to the German lady and she made us some waffles. She had one egg that she wanted to give us but we wouldn't take it but we did eat some fried potatoes and this evening she is going to cook some oatmeal we got hold of Oh yes yes we are going to feed.

I have got to go on guard tonight. I don't even know my general orders. I did once but have not had use for them so they left. I know the content however.

This town has about 400 people and 20 of its soldiers have been killed. France is not the only country bled white.

DECEMBER 6   I joined the church 10 years ago today. I thought of that last night as I walked my post. My church has been a great help to me. It has filled me with a desire to be a good citizen. I am not the man I ought to be or could be but I mean to make a new effort when I get back. In the army I shall merely try not to lose ground.

We marched 24 km over bad roads today mud ankle deep in places. It has been raining considerable of late but I have not mentioned it. The roads were so bad that when we came to a hill it was necessary to push the wagons up. That with the lack of sleep last night leaves me pretty tired this evening. My feet and clothes are wet from rain and sweat but in spite of that I expect to sleep for I broke the felon on my finger.

It was rather late when we got here but a bunch of us got the lady here to cook us up a feed of potatoes. The chow will be ready over at the kitchen in an hour or so. The mail caught up to us and I was lucky to draw a couple of letters.

I see many children and women and old men in these towns they are all strong and robust, apparently and great beggars too though not as bad as the children in France and England. I note also a scarcity of horses and nearly everyone works cows and oxen. They have a sort of go ahead fireproof harness. Chain tugs and a steel bar (padded) that fits across the forehead. These animals truly earn their bread by the sweat of the brow.

DECEMBER 7, SATURDAY   We keyed ourselves up today for 25 km but they only took us 17 so we have got something for nothing. I made friends with the people we stayed with last night. Through Owen, who speaks school German, we talked about different things, mostly America. I took the name and address of the boy there.

I am billeted in a barn again tonight. It is always my luck to draw a stable. If they have to turn a pig out I get a stable. Some of the others always get feather beds. Others get to sleep in living rooms on the floor where at least they can have a light.

I nearly forgot to mention that there was a young lady at the place I stopped last night. She was engaged to a fellow who was killed at Riga he left his children and she has taken them. Merely a heart affair. The name of the town is Fliessem. I should like to talk to these people to get their story at present all I can do is to wave my hands.

Owen and I got in a place this evening we got them to cook some spuds for us we paid for it with soap. The old man was very chilly and that didn't go well but later on he thawed out and was quite sociable.

These people are all Catholics it seems they belong to the same church as the people on the other side whom they oppressed but even they pray to the same god they do not do his works these people seem to be more religious for all along the road one sees crosses of stone and wood on which the savior hangs. They seem to make their religion a thing of show rather than of the heart.

Last night an issue of candy came there were eleven pounds for 250 men (Stars & Stripes says ½ lb per man per week) so the platoon leaders drew for it the 4th platoon got the candy. Our company led the march and the 4th platoon led the company. We called them the "little chocolate soldiers."

DECEMBER 8, SUNDAY   We got ready to pull out at 9 o'clock. Beauchamp the top cutter, hunted me up and wanted to know if I had good feet. I told him I had good feet and legs but my pack was a grief. He told me to report to Battalion hdq. as a runner. It is a little better job though there are a lot of extra steps to it. No barns to sleep in. Even have a chance to get a bed.

The town we were in last night is Densborn. It is on the Kyll river a branch of the Moselle and the Moselle is a branch of the Rhine. We are in Gerolstein now which is 15 km up the Kyll. R.R. runs along the river. My company is in a big barracks but we runners are in a hotel. I think I sleep in a bed tonight.

One of our lieutenants got his leg broke yesterday and had to return he is Lt. Bryber from Salt Lake. Lt. Neel is in charge of the Company. He is a fine fellow. We left Capt. Axon back in France he is on leave. I hope he gets lost or transferred. I prefer cooties.

I am not with the company now but with Batt. Hdq. I am one of the major's servants. I never cared much for this major either.[5]

We are following close on to the Rainbow (42) division. They are supposed to be a crack division. We fought to their right in both drives.

I drop Clara a few lines tell her about this land that has been closed to the world for four years.

I was about to buy a watch today. Swiss movement for $18.00. I need a watch and I could sell it in the states.

There are many rosy cheeked girls here which is some inducement to learn the tongue. One fellow I know is willing to try. Some yanks and Germans were talking about the German slogan "Got[t] mit uns"[God with Us]. This fellow said yes we've *got mittens* too.

DECEMBER 9   Well I had to sleep on the floor last night there wasn't beds enough to go around. We have breakfast without bread. Horses go hungry too because rations haven't caught up to us. Hansen and I must take some stuff to Regimental Hdq. at a place called Isensmidtln (that's the way it sounds.) [Eisenschmitt] The round trip is about 80 km. We have walked 35 of them today and have 25 of them to go on the train in the morning. We walked them because of ignorance. The way to get to Reg. Hdq is to ride the train down the river from Gerolstein to Kyllburg 25 km and then catch a truck inland. Well we rode part of the way from Gerolstein to Kyllburg and walked the rest then we walked in to Isensmidtln [Eisenschmitt] and catch [a] ride back here to Kyllburg.[6] We rode with some M.P.'s who were taking some red cross ambulances to Koblenz to be used as police patrols.

On this job one can make his observations and I made mine today. How enterprising these Huns are as compared with the French. We saw boys along the road skinning horses. Saw women every where working, carrying big burdens and wheeling barrows or carts. Hansen and I met three women who were pulling a two wheeled cart loaded with potatoes they were stuck and we helped them out of the rut. They don't wear the pants but they ought to.

We have rented a room with two beds in [it] for two francs each. We bumbed [bummed] our supper from the M.P.'s and I have spent the eve writing post cards. Our train leaves in the morning we have some stuff to take back but it is not important so we deemed it wiser to stay than walk the 25 k in the dark. It is a shame for us to get in these clean beds as dirty and lousy as we are.

DECEMBER 10, TUESDAY   I am pleased with my running job it is a little harder than being with the company but we enjoy more freedom. This old idea of lining up 3 or 4 times a day to have our noses counted is a bore. We have more opportunity here to view things. Oh we have to go in pairs and carry guns. It is not necessary but its war and "orders is orders."

We had no trouble getting on [the] train but we got carried by Pelm. When we left yesterday we were told the Batt would move to Pelm 3 km up the river. Instead of getting off at Gerolstein and walking out we thought the train would stop for us. We did not understand their German nor they our English so we got carried 8 km by. It was not a bad hike though it went hard on Hansen he was sick from drinking too much beer in Kyl[l]burg. We saw a great black bombing plane in one of the fields it had probably been used to drop eggs on Paris and other places.

At this job I can get a little more to eat. I had two dinners today. Runners can eat at any kitchen.

Everyone in my company is taking baths but I can't because of going to Densborn with a message. Sgt Major gave us the wrong dope on trains and we lose three hours because of missing a train. We are now in Densborn where we'll have to spend the night in the station. I am awful hungry. The lieutenant we brought a message to offered to get us something to eat but Agey the lad I am with tried to be heroic and said we were not hungry. I had to be heroic to and keep still.

German trains are manned (or womanned) with some charming little brakies. They wear regular uniforms. All train men here look like soldiers. On the train I met a soldier returned from the Serbian Front he showed me pictures in which one could see hunger and oppression written in the faces of the people. I only wished I could have talked his language or he mine so I could have expressed my feelings to him.

DECEMBER 11   It was unnecessary for us to have slept on the depot floor in Densborn last night. About 11:00 a freight stopped that was going our way. My buddy wouldn't ride it. This depot floor made me think too much of the good old days back home when I was on the bum. Anyhow we got back this morning in time for breakfast and the rest of the day I have been sitting around. The major is sick in bed so things are not rushing any. This afternoon I go to Kyllburg and back. Troutman and I went. We made good train connections. Reg. Hdq. are at Kyllburg now.

We have jolly ride to & back. Buy a lot of stuff at the Y in Kyllburg. See a lot of French prisoners coming from German camps.

Meet a Mexican today from Springerville he tells me that Johnny Slaughter had been killed. Good soldier was Johnnie.

Mail came in today. I get the long telescope Mother sent me. Problem is what will I do with it. Get a letter from Winnie Terry she tells me of my old pal Jake getting married.[7] Sister Gillespie (good old soul) sends me 3 copies of the White and Blue so I spend some time getting linked up with the old Alma Mater. I need clean clothes & bath.

DECEMBER 12, THURSDAY   Watched rations last night. We divided them between the companies this morning. It is hard to get rations up here. S.O.S. or someone steals all the good things such as milk, sugar, candy and flour before it reaches us. Jam always has been a bombproof food at the frontlines unless it is especially escorted up for the officer's mess. Jam and such food as the folks back home think we are getting is called *see food*. We never get it however.

My conscience is becoming so seared that all I need is an opportunity to steal anything I see that is good to eat.

I have found out that a fellow can get these German people to cook anything. I had them make some potato pancakes today. They will do anything for a fellow if he can get them fat, soap, or sugar.[8]

All I think about nowadays is to eat. It is about all I have to do. I am really doing no good for my country by merely staying here and eating up good food the folks back home have to save up and then buy liberty bonds to pay for.

The Major is still sick. The most of the fellows seem well pleased that he is. It seems that he had no sympathy for us when we were sick or tired.

Big guns pass here on their way to the Rhine. Rumor has it that Japan & America are going to war. Bosh. I hear that Wilson is coming over for the peace conference.

I write letter to Sis. Gillespie today. I don't get clothes to change but I go over to the roundhouse and get a bath. Fine bath tub and hot water. I wash out my clothes in hot water and put them on but I am sure I have many cooties left.

DECEMBER 13, FRIDAY   An unlucky day and I had a grievous the forenoon. I was supposed to run up stairs every 30 minutes to see if the major wanted anything. I wonder if he is sick, between times I stayed in the battalion office.

Every night now they sound riot alarm. It is always at an unexpected hour and means that all men must fall in under arms. It is a good way to keep the fellows from getting absorbed in letter writing, or reading, or gambling or drinking.

I go to Reg. Hdq. And back today. On way down see newly wed German soldier and wife very loving. Try to talk with them but we make poor headway. I get a lot of paper from the Chaplin desire to give it to "E" company but Sgt Major stops me says if I bring stuff up I must bring for all the companies or none. Hereafter it will be none or on the sly.

I saw a National Cash Register in a waiting room of dept at Gerolstein today. Here they have I & II class rooms and another waiting room for III &IV class passengers. In each is a bar where beer is sold to both women and men they eat black bread with it and seem to enjoy it.

DECEMBER 14, SATURDAY   Slept on floor in office to watch. This morning rise early and take train for Kyllburg get there 9:30 stay all day. Fellow by name of Dixon is with me. During day two other runners come down and say that outfit has moved and was going to Budesheim. I was sorry to hear that for Dixon and I bought 120 bars of chocolate each to take back and we had to hike 8 km to Bud. While I am in Kyllburg I see Chaplin about the University work the A.E.F. was to give.

We go back to Gerolstein & walk to Budesheim. Dixon's feet fail him. We stop at Boche home in Budesheim where we trade chocolate for supper. Learn that outfit has gone on because of no billets so they were making today's and tomorrow's hike in one 35 km (poor devils). We have good feed give a yank artillery man 2 bars of chocolate to steal us some bread.

We go to Prum about 12 or 15 km. We walked about 6 and catch a truck. When we get to Prum we found that the company had gone on to Pronsfeld, 8 km. We had got lost some how from the other two runners so we decided to hunt a billet. We hailed a yank and a German. It turned out to be an officer and later a red cross man. He seemed to have had too much nourishment and was leaning on the German for support. The German turned out to be Herr Hoffman a diamond and jewelry merchant he took us to his home and here we are the Red Cross man has given us chocolate not knowing of our supply. Both the German and his wife, a very attractive woman, who speaks French did all they could to make us comfortable. They would not let us sleep on the floor. They didn't know our reasons for not wanting to crawl into that nice clean feather bed.

Red cross men here are fine fellows who have been serving at the front. They are going on to Koblenz in the morning.

DECEMBER 15, SUNDAY   Sunshine today though roads are none the less sloppy. It is the first time the sun has been marked duty for many days.

Dixon didn't get up this morning. His feet or his back bone perhaps both have failed. I took the papers and orders and came on. The Red Cross man was on hand to take me to his hotel where I got a good feed of coffee jam & bread. It was stuff furnished by the Yanks and all it cost was a mark for service. Woman at the place speaks English—Marks going down fast.

Prum is a beautiful town with more than its share of crooked narrow streets. Great school here—church.[9]

The jewler [*sic*] would take nothing for the hospitality so I went around to his store and bought a souvenir ring to take back to the kids.

I had no trouble finding the outfit. It was an 8 km hike. I enjoyed it met all the Germans in their Sunday attire going to church. Meet and walked with a boy he talked a great deal. I judged from the tone of his voice when he asked me questions whether he wanted me to say "Yaw" or "Nein" and did accordingly.

Found men all along the road who were hobbling along after spending the night at different places on the road. Found those who did make the hike were all in. It is foolish to hike men 35 km after night with full packs. It is worse it is criminal especially when it is not necessary. "F" Company got in with 50 men it lost more men than "D" & "E" combined. The "F" Company captain rode a horse and on one occasion abused a man for falling out. Lt Neel and "Pap" Coy of the other companies hiked with the men and more men tried to stay. "Pap" Coy of "D" Co. always carries as big a pack as his men.

I had no trouble getting rid of the chocolate & tobacco I bought. Boys pleased to get it.

I find a good letter from Clara waiting for me she has the Flu. A letter from Alberta.

We move this afternoon go to a town 3 km from here where there is more room.

DECEMBER 16   Well we are in the little town of L----- [Lunebach] I didn't leave out name because of the censor but because I can't spell it. I would hate to be a little boy over here and study geography. Or in any of these country. In Belgium I saw the little fellows gathered together by the priest and taken to school on Saturday too. As yet I haven't seen a child play in Germany. They seem to occupy themselves by standing around and looking hungry. They all have old heads on their shoulders. It seems that the joys of childhood have been denied them.

Saw a very humorous funeral today it was none the less impressive. Everyone in attendance walked behind the casket chanting some song.

Major is up and around again though he says that he feels very "rocky." I learned incidently that he is a batch though he is getting gray. I like him but can't stand his sweet smile. When one permits himself to be guided by first impressions he would think that if the Major's wrath arose he might slap a person on the wrist. He and other officers are living in state now private cooks & all.

I spoke to Lt. Neel today about going to school. He promised to do what he could.

Some German refugees came in (women) They said they were so abused by French troops of occupation that they have come to yank territory. They know that yanks stand for a square deal and I have heard of cases where yanks fought French who tried to impose nastyiness on the Dutch. (In Bitburg where a French soldier pushed a woman over.)

DECEMBER 17, TUESDAY   The town we are in is Lunebach. This afternoon I bring message to headquarters. Lunebach is on railroad so I merely take train to Gerolstein then change to Kyllburg. I get train out of Kyl[l]burg back here to Gerolstein where I am stranded for the night. I should have said "We" for I am with Buzzard, a pretty good kid.

We had a hard time to find a bed but we finally butted into this private place where we have been well received. They are an old couple but very cordial. The old lady got us a feed of bread and fried spuds and coffee (barley). I spent some time with the old man looking over a bound magazine of 1912. The old fellow was greatly worked up over the sinking of the *Titanic* of which several articles were written. He showed us pictures and lamented that such a "gross shiff" [large ship] should meet such a fate. I wondered if he had ever heard of the *Lusitania*. I thought many things but didn't have the heart or the tongue to wave a bloody garment.

This old man had been a soldier in the war of 1870–71 and had spent 10 months in Paris.[10] He is the father of two sons and no girls his sons both got killed in this war one in '14 and the other in '16. All he has for one of them is a gold medal and the bullet that killed him and he has a big picture of the other. I could not understand very much he said but that he and his wife were just sitting around waiting for the reaper. They have no thought of malice of any thing but their sorrow. This is a scene I see on the other side of the curtain in my enemy's house. I can't hate this man or these children in the street but the thing that they did through 50 years of mis education. I have been fighting the ragged eagle and the spiked helmet rather than the German fireside. In a way these people are like our captive German cooties they are taking their captors captive.

DECEMBER 18, WEDNESDAY   We get good feed at the old German's this morn. He refused money but we left 4 marks a piece under the loaf of bread.

This afternoon I go to Reg. Hdq. In a side car. It was a good trip but a trifle cold. We go around by Waxweiler and Bitburg.

We pass through a little town near Bitburg where I learn that Bushman is. On the way back we stop at Bitburg where our quartermaster is located and I buy a lot of tobacco to take back to the boys. I get fellow to stop in town where Bush is. We get supper of beefsteak and bread sandwiches and I have long parley with Bushman. He was corp. of guard so we had to make it short. We are going to try to go to school.

We brought a lot of mail and there were two letters for me. One from Prescott written Nov. 8 when we were getting ready to make another strike. He said that they were celebrating victory but added a note saying that the bubble broke. The bank wrote and told me I had $37.00 to the good. Not much but better than a debt.

DECEMBER 19, THURSDAY   I spend most of the day in the office writing a letter to Prescott. I am not able to think of nothing to write about. I watch the weather it tried to snow, to rain and to shine.

I did not have any work so I spent my idle moments over the dutch ladies stove. We managed for a gallon of Karo syrup and I was trying to cook it down to candy. I have cooked all day but still it won't get hard when I drop it in water.

Dixon the fellow I left at the jewlers [sic] house in Prum a few days ago with bad feet, came back today. He has been all over the country. I saw him the other day in Gerolstein and he seemed to be enjoying a vacation. He came back today and put up [a] hard luck story about being in hospital and being lost. It didn't hold water. The major rode him down with a steam roller his captain did worse but he put on a penitent face and escaped.

I had a good talk with the major this evening. I find he has a good solid make up behind his smooth silky exterior. It is only camouflage. We talked about a lot of the problems of army life from the soldier's and the officers point of view. He told me that he would do what he could to get me a school appointment. Our talk drifted to religion and education and there we found common ground even though he is a straight backed Presbyterian and I a Mormon.

This bad weather makes me feel grateful that the war is over and we are housed.

DECEMBER 20 We bought some flour today and had a waffle fry. We are not supposed to but then it is to[o] late for the censor to get a hand in.

I went on the motorcycle to Brig. Hdq, at Prum today. It is 12 km. I bought a lot of post cards and tried to get a fountain pen but there was no such thing in town. The reason is that gold is so scarce one can get splendid souvenirs in silver but not in gold.

An Italian, who has been held here as an internee during the war, applied to the yanks for permission to be taken to the States or Italy. They all want to go to the States. I think he will be sent back through military channels and disposed of accordingly.

We move tomorrow. It promises to be a very strenuous day.

DECEMBER 21, SATURDAY Trudge through mud all day. Snow part of the way. Some one suggested that we were getting webfooted and a great deal of quacking ensued. Why are we wandering thus over the country and what profit is it to us or any one else? All these huskies could do a lot of useful work at home. I could do more good by merely going to school. The Germans are not going to come back on us. We are not watching as much as ourselves. The guards we post are to keep our own men in line. We guard our rations but to keep ourselves from stealing and trading to the natives. We have a big police system and Red Cross trucks for patrols but it is our own boys who are handled. Take us home Uncle where we can do some good.

I hear Pres. Wilson is going to visit Trier xmas. Trier is 40 km from here.

The town we are in is Nattenheim. We may not stay long. The major says he will move if he can find a better place if he can get permission. We are pretty comfortably located here but many other fellows are crowded.

The chaplin is coming to talk to us tomorrow. It will be the first service he has had since we left Humberville in July.

DECEMBER 22, SUNDAY   It looks like we will be here for Christmas. I hope so for this is a fine place where Hdq. is billeted. It is the typical German family. Mother is the Mrs. Katzenjammer type of woman fleshy and jolly. Last night she gave us a nice feed of coffee cake and another cake made of bread dough but covered with sliced apples. She says she could make good things to eat if she had the stuff that Americans have. She has two big red faced girls. They are regular white hopes with great powerful hands and feet not meant to grace dancing pumps. One of them could work a 40 acre farm. Give me the yank girl who can work or play as the time demands. There are some mischievous little kids here they are always dirty and hungry. One of them got in his mother's sugar today. It made me think of the good old days when jam was on the top shelf. (That is where it is in the army) The father is an old man who does not say much he just grins and smokes his pipe.

We went to Kyllburg today (9 km) passed through the place where we made our second stop in Germany. Flies[s]em stop to see the people we stopped with. There is some nice scenery between here and Kyllburg. We walked across lots and drank a lot of it in. I think that I soaked more of it into my feet for the ground was very sloppy.

Officers are planning their X-mas dinner they can't buy food from the natives and desire a duck. Solution—Send to Luxemburg. He gave us a good hint not to parade in front of him with food we buy. He did not say he would try to catch us. Our chow is not sufficient and this extra we get from the enemy sort of bridges the gap.

No chaplin————no meeting.

DECEMBER 23, MONDAY   Christmas must be a great religious feast for these people. They seem to believe that "man does not live by bread alone." They go to church every morning. I learned that they were going to have a baking of bread blessed for Christmas.

These people bake bread too, they have a big bin like a watering trough in which they mix. When they get the loaves made they have the tables and chairs all full. Big loaves too, 18 inches in diameter and 4 to 6 inches thick. When they cut it they hug the loaf to their bosom and saw it off in big irregular slices. They bake in a big oven of stone or brick after having first built a fire of faggots in the oven. A faggot is a bundle of brush.

Xmas packages are coming. I got a letter from Mrs. N. L. [Nelson] and mine is on the way. I hope C.[lara] tries to send one too.

Some outfit back home sent me a P.O. money order for a dollar. I can't get it cashed here so I will have to send it back to someone at home. I write this even to the P.O. box I got the buck from.

This evening I am helping the rosy cheeked girl peel apples for Christmas we have a half bushel already. The other girl is kneading dough and the rest of the fellows are waging a poker game for cigarettes.

Mr. Prescott wrote a very good letter in which he spoke of the great problems of peace. Those problems are what make the future attractive and make me happy that I am alive.

DECEMBER 24, TUESDAY   I made a trip to Kyllburg in the motorcycle today other than that I didn't do much but enjoy myself and cook my cooties. I parted with many a bosom companion today but I am satisfied it will take a long time to rid myself as my bed clothes are full so are my O.D.'s.

The major passed while I was boiling my clothes. I only have one change. I was wearing my jacket & pants. He told me a good way to finish the job was to press my suit. Very practical (?) He didn't tell me what to wear while my clothes were drying and I was pressing my suit.

A real German Xmas or as near as they could get it on account of the shortage of good things. We could guess what it would be in times of plenty. I have had all the jelly and coffee cake I could eat today. We hate to take it but they won't take money so we are going to give the old man our sox (wool is scarce) and perhaps later we can manage for some soap & sugar. Beer has been on the table too all day it is weak on the account of the war. I drank a glass but I never learned to like the stuff. They brought out a bottle of schnapps strong liquer and passed it around. I had to drink a thimble full. It left tracks all the way down.

The girls just got through playing a joke on us they brought in a bottle of clear liquid. I didn't take any because it looked like atho [ethyl] alcohol. It turned out to be salt water. I expect they will be giggling this time tomorrow.

They have a Christmas tree for the kids—no presents: we have none to put on it.

DECEMBER 25   First day since I have been in the service that I haven't heard a bugle call or roll call. The children routed us out early (we sleep in room where x mas tree is) I got up and lit the candles on tree lest they be disappointed then let them in. Outside was our first snow fall soft and beautiful just like poets picture it. It is always beautiful when one can look out on it. Those poets never carried a pack in it all day.

Got to the church here very crowded. I can't understand but it has to do with xmas. Drop a mark in the hat to make up for my ignorance.

Here it is Christmas and our boxes have not come. I shall drop a line to Mrs. N. L. to thank her for the box that is coming. Father time made us a present we have a right to wear our first gold service chevron this morning = 6 months in the A.E.F.

We were reading an old magazine and saw a piece of poetry written by some soldier in the states it was entitled "A Hitch in Hell." Some of the fellows are writing to him to tell him that his hell is a flower garden beside life on the front. That is the way we amuse ourselves.

DECEMBER 26   If I were a little boy I should like to spend Christmas in Germany. They have "Weihnachten" for two days. Two days rest for the soldiers. I get plenty of that on this job. I am getting fat and lazy. There isn't much variety in this life. One sees nothing to get interested in so time is a drag. Such time I like to dream away, anyway to get rid of it for it profits nothing.

We are beginning to hear one rumor after another about going home in a month or so. Perhaps it is so when there is so much smoke there ought to be a little fire. I might be studying German if I had some books, as it is I can only guess my way through. Back home we have an expression, "Christmas gift" to be sprung on the folks in the morning. I tried to say it to these folks. I said "Christag gift" but it didn't seem to take. I have found since that "Christag" is not a word and "gift" means poison.

DECEMBER 27, FRIDAY   Begging is an art in this country. Just now two begger children came to the door. They began by chanting a long prayer that was intended to loosen up the heart strings before the[y] appealed to the purse strings. That is making capital of prayer.

I have seen a lot of gypsies real story book gypsies from South East Europe. They are dirtier than soldiers on a drive. They were camped along the way. When folks pass by they hail them. I never stopped so I don't know what their game is. I am told that they read futures and pasts and some of them have girls who traffic. They trade and I suppose steal now and then. Outside of those I have seen no tramps of the American style. Weary willies would be quickly disposed of in Germany. We need some of that kind of Kulture in America.

Agee is sick. He is one of the runners. He and I went to Fliessem yesterday. I stopped to visit the German family I know there and he went down the street to Co. "D" office and promised to call me out when he returned. I went in ate apples and coffee cake and waited for him was going to have him come in and have some too. After an hour I decided he must have returned so I beat it for home. Sure enough he had slipped away from me but he only beat me in five minutes and had not yet reported. He was planning on making a good fellow of himself. He is about as popular with the other fellows as he is with me so he doesn't get much sympathy. The Major has recommended the hospital.

I cooked my cooties again today. They are the germs I hate worst in Germany. I hope to eliminate them before I leave Ger *Mania*.

DECEMBER 28, SATURDAY   I am glad we are not marching today, it is raining overhead and freezing under foot. One can scarce stand much less walk. Every time I go out in the cold wind my toothaches. I went to the doctor and he can do nothing. In spite of the weather however the battalion had inspection. "F" Company had to go according to I.D.R. they held forth in the field. I saw them standing out in the rain inspecting rifles as I was going over to tell Co. "D" at Fliessem not to hold inspection outside.

The official butcher has come to town. He is a short heavy set man with a wild red beard and blood all over his clothes. The kind of fellow I would run from when I was a boy. People must not kill hogs or cattle without permission then the butcher comes and weighs the meat and makes the allowances. 48 lb. Is permitted a person per year. The rest is sold at a price fixed by the authorities. I learned some other food dope today. ¼ liter of milk per day is allowed for children under 2 years. Butter 36 grams per person per week, sugar 1 lb per month, prices are fixed. It is plain to see why they crave them.

I wish I could get rid of these lice. I pick them off every night but still they linger.

Another fellow and I put 4 on a sheet of paper last night to see them fight. It is no joke. They do fight. It was no joke for them for we treated them in the end as the Romans did the gladiators in the arena.

DECEMBER 29, SUNDAY   Doesn't seem like Sunday. Nothing has happened to stir up anything to make the day different than yesterday or from what tomorrow promises to be.

I have done a big financial business. I collected 10 francs from Jew Stein. Loaned 10 to the Sergeant Major, 10 to Kaiser, 10 to Long Genteris, 5 to Sheets and 5 to Staff.

I have no objections against loaning money but it is not good in the army while there are so many chances of change and transfer.

The little girl in this family is very sick the mother was worried so I went up and told our doctor. He came down and later sent medicine. That surprised them very much and they blessed the doctor for his solicitude.

DECEMBER 30, MONDAY   The Sergeant Major & I cooked our clothes today. "Red muzzle," one of the other runners had so many that he threw his under clothes in the stove. He is sick today as a consequence.

I wish that the power [that] be don't seem to care or they would give us some clean clothes. For nearly two months I have had but one change of clothes in two months. I have to wash them and put them on again. Many others in the same fix, few others have the chance to clean up that I do they are busy learning close order drill and other stuff we have forgotten in the drive.

The powers talk to us through general orders. They live in state themselves and never come in personal contact with the soldier. He must take things as they come and say nothing. The mule is better off for he can kick.

Dr. James A. Francis from some where speaks to us tonight tomorrow I will tell what Dr. James A. Francis from California had to say.

DECEMBER 31   I had to go to Fliessem last night so only heard a part of the Doctors talk. As I was passing by I heard him say "Every American soldier in Germany should conduct himself as a gentleman." You are right doctor. Later I learned the general opinion was that he was sent out to boost up the morale of homesick soldiers. He talked about our splendid record and a lot of that stuff.

I am not interested in these G.H.Q. moralizers. I want to go home. I want to get out in civil life and take my chances with other men. I am content to be a private in the uniform but in civil life I expect to see if Lt. Fickle was right. I am going to be a "general of tomorrow." Even if I have to go to congress.

This evening winds up the year. The old calendar on the wall with Hindenberg's picture on has been relegated to the flames. "Mother" is putting on a big feed. Burley and some other "Schnapps hunds" are out trying to get something stronger than corn coffee.

JANUARY 1, WEDNESDAY   We make a new start today. We will leave the old behind. (or try to) The Kaiser and his group and all the destruction it caused to eliminate him, I hope we leave big armies and armaments. The future should hold nothing but peace and democracy and humanity with everyman and every nation enjoying it's chances without fear of "Big Brothers."

It is a nice sunshiny day and I am in good humor. I write a letter to Alberta Cram also get one from Bushman, he is taken up with the school idea but is of the same opinion as I that it is another A.E.F. joke.

One of the soldiers in "F" company got made an "example" of today for permitting some Germans to ride in his wagon. More strict orders are out not to fraternize. We must not even be in the same room with them. Merely move about them with an air of haughty indifference. I don't love them nor do I expect to take a German bride back with me but I do believe in being friendly as long as they are.

JANUARY 2   Col. [John C. H.] Lee, [Division] chief of staff, whatever that is, paid us a visit today and gave the major some dope to scatter. And dope sure scatters here. Every time soldiers meet they are asking about dope. And the stories are going the rounds what a Lieutenant or a Major or an M.P. or a "Y" man said. These rumors as they travel increase in size like snowballs but they are always one brand with the going home label on. Well the Colonel told the major and the major told me that we were the last division to go home of the national army units. That news doesn't take very well but it travels none the less. The most popular rumor now is that the postal authorities at New York are not receiving anymore mail for this division.

I have to sleep in the office to watch the phone. "Red muzzle" has been sleeping there but he slept too sound. The Major who sleeps upstairs heard the phone ring came down and answered it and Red never knew he was in the room. Red goes back to his company.

We are to move from here soon. I hate to leave these good feeds every evening.

JANUARY 3, FRIDAY   We leave this place tomorrow. If we don't get a better one I shall regret the move. "Mother" Neirerburg has been very good to us. Red took her foot measure and [is] going to send her a pair of shoes when he gets home. I took Marie's measure for the same purpose. She is a sweet girl if she has got big feet. If it were not for international complications I would take her but she is my enemy.

Some mail came today, many x-mas boxes but not mine some of the boxes were broke and the candy trickled to the bottom of the sack. I got a good big handful of chocolate drops. I believe I am getting dishonest. When I came to the army I could be trusted to guard a pile of chocolate a hundred feet high but not now.

Country life in this country is a bore. All these people do is tend cows, pile manure, sit by the fire and go to church.

JANUARY 4, SATURDAY   The powers had quite a parley today whether to move or not. Capt. Block of the supply office wanted to hold inspection. He forgot that the fellows have stood enough inspections the last month to last a year. Col. Leland wanted to move today and let the boys rest tomorrow (Sunday). The major didn't care to express himself on such a momentous question so the Colonel had his way and we hiked from Nattenheim to this place which is about 7 km on the opposite side of the river from Kyllburg. It is Oberkail, a bigger town too.[11]

Hdg. is in a fine place owned by a feeble old lady and her daughter. Judging from the looks of things she was rich once but has this home which is well furnished but not cheery. Most of the furniture is old the stove has the date 1700 on it. I imagine she had more before the war. On the [wall] is a fry pan that has written in it "Der deutch haus frau opfersin, Gab kupfer fur das eisen hin." Meaning she has given all her copper to the government. Am glad we don't have another 20 km.

Got a nice xmas card and some gum from Alberta today. She writes very sane letters and I like to hear from her. It sort of keeps me tuned up.

Well Hansen and Red are relieved and I am the only other runner. I sleep in the office tonight.

JANUARY 5, SUNDAY   People here are not willing to give room especially beds. They probably learned that we are lousy. Orders are that the natives can only retain beds for old men women and children. We get the rest. That is the Hell of war but it is better and more consideration than they showed the Belgians. I have made friends with mother here and the result is I sleep on a mattress tonight instead of on the bare floor.

This evening a lady came in to visit mother and we all drank some kind of red wine. I learned that the lady had a son who was a prisoner in France. He was taken by the yanks on the St. Mihiel Front. I told her that we were there together we drank to his early return. I drank to mine as well.

Some magazines came in today. I took them around to the company P.C.'s Later I went around and saw that not a one had left the officers but the clerks and officers were reading them. Next the sergeants will get them and in time they may get to the bucks. So fares the simple soldat at all times. Is it any wonder he is sour and curses the army.

JANUARY 6   I am setting up with "Mother." We are bibbing sour weak wine. She is very patient so I am picking up the flow [of] dutch fast. I have been getting her history and here it is. She is 75 years old her husband died in 1871 and she has been a widow till now. I am getting pretty solid with her swiped some coffee for her and that pleased her very much.[12]

Well the chaplin came up and gave us a good talk on faith. Faith in ourselves, in the other fellow, and in God. He also spoke of the effort to get school work started said that the illiterate would be obliged to take reading and writing.[13] Others could enroll if they wished. Major tells me this evening I am to be one of the battalion teachers.

I go up into the attic of this house today. It is a regular curiosity shop. I get [a] box there to ship my helmet home in. This home is full of antiques. Nearly every piece of furniture is old some pieces 200 or 400 years old.

JANUARY 7, TUESDAY   Made a bold start today at establishing a school for the illiterates note that word "Illiterates." It is the first time I have heard it since I have been in the army.[14] It passes around like a thing that doesn't taste good. There seems to be a general pity for the fellows class[ed] thus. There are three of us fellows supposed to teach the three R's in this battalion. The Chaplin is acting superintendent of education and maps out the work.

Oh it looks good on paper. We got all ready to go ahead notified the companies and got a place to hold forth when the major threw the monkey wrench in the machinery. He said that we couldn't act on the chaplin's authority but must wait till he got orders etc. as to prescribed course————?

So in the meanwhile while things develop I am just going to rest easy. I am custodian of the woodhouse key, and the official swiper of candy and soap when the rations come in. It does not pay to take interest in ones work in the army.

Some more Christmas boxes came but not mine.

JANUARY 8, WEDNESDAY   A note on happenings in the world. Got orders that all units of the A.E.F. would fly flag at half mast and have fitting ceremonies this afternoon to honor Theodore Roosevelt.[15]

Learned at this late date that W. G. McAdoo resigned a month ago because the earnings of his job were not sufficient.[16] Perhaps a good reason but not a wise one to mention.

Another great event, got a letter from Clara. She says no school so she is nursing flu cases. Having good luck though she says that there are many deaths around Garland where she is. Her folks are there and wish me well—Thanks.

Theressa wrote and told me about a new dress and a lot of parties and how she missed a train. Very interesting!(?)

A letter from Charley another from Mother. They say that Mrs. Pink is marrying Wm. Osborn. Mrs. Pink's husband drowned with father.

I learned too that Joseph H. Smith is dead.[17] A very loving and capable man.

The girl here is not mother's daughter but a "hired hand." I am trying to write to Clara and she is sitting beside me reading to "mother." She is handling this slobbery language at a very rapid rate and reading in such a high keyed voice that rasps my nerves. Mother is half asleep and playing solitary. Once in a while she looks up and makes comments that is evident she is more awake than it seems.

A fellow tried to tell me that it was unconstitutional for Wilson to come to the peace conference.[18] It makes me think of the claims some fellows used to make before we came over. They held that it was unconstitutional to take drafted men away from home to fight if they objected. How some heads do work!

I am reading a very revolutionary play by Bernard Shaw it is called "Getting Married."[19]

JANUARY 9, THURSDAY   The whole equilibrium of the battalion has been disturbed over a fiddle. Some of the boys were playing a violin they found in the guard house in Nattenheim when we left the fiddle was missing. The people sent word and all the men in "E" and "F" company have been questioned but to no avail. The thing will cost Uncle Sam 100 marks besides 25 gallons of gasoline used by Captain Albert in making two trips to Nattenheim to investigate.

I wonder if our army will have to be saved from that disease we fought so hard "Militarism" We are getting as foolish about forms as the German army. There is an order out now for all public servants to salute U.S. officers that includes village policemen, mail carriers and train men who wear any kind of uniform. I don't know whether that includes bellhops or not.[20]

Fulbright and Salter and I went to Kyllburg today to see the chaplin about details about ordering our school. We found that the chaplin didn't know any thing to tell us except do what we could he didn't even have a sheet of paper to give us to work with. While in Kyl[l]burg I bought a couple of German phrase books that I shall study in the meanwhile. There is an order against having classes to study German but nothing against studying it. It is a foolish order to my way of thinking for we need to know the language even to hate the Germans.[21]

Got paid today for two months. Paid in marks. Value of marks going down. I got 483 Marks.

JANUARY 10, FRIDAY Major caught one of the Co. "E" office force with his jerkin unbuttoned today and the whole company headquarters had to drill 15 minutes after supper. It was great to see those poor birds running up and down the street with their arms in the air. I thought How educative!

They have a new system. The general thought of it. They hang signs out every day to tell us what to wear and anyone caught wearing anything else will be punished. That is the advantage of a general.

Another buck & I went to Kyl[l]burg today. The order was jerkins here. When we got to Kyl[l]burg the M.P. made us wear the jerkins under the blouse for the orders was blouses. Baker is right he says that the army is surrounded by attractions but the attractions merely *surround* us.

It has been a very uneventful day. I have nothing to do that counts. Oh yes I wrote up a lot of lists of words for my school to use when we will get formal notice to begin. I wrote down a list of German words I knew and found I have over 250 to my credit.

Some "y" talent entertained here tonight the first we have had since we are in the A.E.F.

JANUARY 11, SATURDAY The whole darned outfit stood inspection. We even had our cooties inspected. I was busy preparing for it when the Major told me I didn't have to stand it being a teacher. Gee this teaching is a graft. It's a shame to take the money. They will be calling me a gold brick pretty soon. This is the first time since I have been in the army that I have got out of anything. I intend to occupy my time however wrestling with the German tongue. I have met a charming dutch schoolmeam who will make it more interesting.[22] She has spent the evening cutting little animals out of paper and telling their names and things about them.

Nothing of interest is happening except that everyone is getting more homesick.

JANUARY 12, SUNDAY   I spent a lazy day trying to study and write letters. Wrote a letter to Mrs. Nelson in which I did a lot of whining because my Christmas package had not come. About that time the mail came in and lo and behold my box and in good shape. One has no idea how small 3 x 4 x 9 is till he tries to remember all his friends. I had to remember the school meam too. I took her home last night but she wouldn't allow me to take her arm. I suppose she thought I was trying to take liberties so I borrowed her lexicon and framed up an apology. She is a pretty nice girl and I didn't want to offend her. Her brother and father were killed in the war.

The Y.M.C.A. brought in some motion pictures. First since we left Funston. Some of the S.O.S. must be going home that the "y" can give us more attention.

The Chaplin came up today and I sent $100 home I have been holding it thinking I might go to school but not now.

Mrs. Nelson sent a copy of the Provo Herald in which there was a write up about the wooden shoes I sent also an extract from my letter.

JANUARY 13   I note in the Provo paper that Heber Grant has been put at the head of the church. I am glad for he is a live wire and a good saint.[23] I feel that I have been away from the good influences of home and church that I need to get back to be tuned up.

The schoolmeam made a lot of curly waffle cakes and brought over. The Sergeant Major is getting interested in the schoolmeam So am I she is so American like in her looks and ways. When she speaks it is all spoiled. She is or was engaged to a fellow in America the war shattered things for the time being.

My school started this evening at 8 o'clock. I had 3 Italians and a Swede. Others would come but are not coming at night unless they are sent for. I think I will like the work but we will not get much support from the major. He insists that all military duties formations should be stood first and school after.[24] I have taken the liberty of disagreeing. A lot of this military training is just a means of killing time and if the men could go to school in the afternoon and learn to read and write it will go towards making him a better citizen whereas a lot this other stuff sours him. The fellows that do come have a good attitude but they don't like the idea of going to school at night when others are resting. It looks like a punishment to them and it should be held up as an opportunity.

JANUARY 14, TUESDAY   Some woman who "Mann had gafallen in der krieg war" [Husband who died in the war] came here today. She and mother must have had some difference for they shook their fists and screamed at each other a great deal after which the woman took our hired girl, Trout [Traut], away. Then I saw the brieftrager who is postman town crier and trouble shooter, in a quarrel with an old lady. The old lady was bringing some wood home that he seemed to think she should not have. Her children and she protested and yelled till they were red as beets but he unloaded the wood just the same. They all wanted to hit him but didn't dare for he was the law.

Major caught me today with one of my buttons unbuttoned. 15 minutes drill for the headquarters detachment, later he caught Burley, 15 minutes more. We have both been unpopular all day but I am more so now for this evening when the rest of them went out to drill I couldn't be present on account of my school. I passed the rest of them going through exercises in the street and heard them say "there goes the ___ ____ ____ _____ now." All will be well in the morning. They may laugh next.

JANUARY 15, WEDNESDAY   It has been a very nasty day with rain all the while. The battalion went for a practice hike. Rolling kitchens wagons full packs and all. This afternoon they came back wet to the hide and in a very bad humor. I didn't go so I missed that bit of development calculated to make better soldiers. The I.D.R. says these hikes should be taken and so they went. I got wet to[o] today. Another lad and I went to Reg. Hdq. Kyl[l]burg for the colors. I carried back two flags. I can say that I carried Old Glory on German soil. When I got back "mother" prepared me a nice dinner then I went over to visit the schoolmeam and got a few cakes so I fared very well.

A man in Co. "F" is being tried for falling out on the march from Pelen to Prousfelt when "F" Co. lost so many. The captain rode up to this fellow and told him to get up and go on, the fellow said he could not. The Captain grabbed him by the shoulder and the lad told him "hands off." The captain had him arrested for insubordination and the poor bird is going to serve time on that captain's testimony. I have always fared well but this is the way some fellows are treated and some don't have any more chance to present their case than poor Vivian had. So the justice we sometimes get is a poor substitute for the genuine.

Oh Justice! When through all the world
Is felt thy wonderous power.
The Army be thy resting place
We need thee every hour.

JANUARY 16   I found out that "Mother" uses snuff. I have heard of women using snuff but I thought they all lived in Arkansas. Then I suppose "mother" has as much right to use snuff as the French women have to smoke.

I kill most of the day reading a very silly novel "The Lighted Way" by Offfenheim.

A good letter from Prescott came today and best of all another Christmas box this one from Nell Lytle and Eva Overson at St. Johns. There was a nice cake in like the one Mrs. Nelson sent also their pictures.

I have been taking up my school problem with Beauchamp ("E" Co. Top) My students don't come they are willing to go to school but are either afraid to start or won't go at night. They will need to be urged. Not by me. I refuse to be truant officer.

Yesterday I hooked some oatmeal for the schoolmeam to make waffles of. This morning the Sgt. Major asked me about it. He kept referring to it in my presence then I found our sugar was gone. Later I learned that he took the sugar over to the schoolmeam for waffles. She let the cat out. He knows I gave her the oatmeal though there is a doubt in his mind that I know about the sugar. We are both guilty of the same thing and therefore we accuse each other not.

JANUARY 17, FRIDAY   Nothing to record except that my school is a shining failure. I should have 20 students but I have none. So I meet with the other teachers every evening and if soldiers come we teach them and if not we don't. I am satisfied the school would be a success if the men could come by day. A man who is duty ridden with formations and such that he has no interest in is not apt to take much interest in himself. I find the major is on my side.

I wrote to the schoolmeams beau who lives in St. Paul. She let me read some of his letters for a foundation. I merely told him in an indirect way that she was well and faithful. I hope the communication passes for her sake.

They have put me on a committee to provide entertainment for the battalion. That probably means I am on the program.

JANUARY 18   A "Y" man was issued to us today. A real "Y" man. We had one with the regiment all the while but he went home. I never knew we had one till he went home. He was a bombproof and a gold brick.

Another surprise was candy. It seems that the one pound a week the Stars and Stripes talked about is just catching up.

Surprise No 3—the Reg. Band newly formed is coming up to entertain this evening. I shall not go for music is not my forte. I shall visit the school meam and take a lesson in German for my school will not hold.

The company's had another inspection. The major went to Trier. He brought a dutch dictionary each for myself & the Sgt. Major.

JANUARY 19, SUNDAY   Last night was the first time I got in bed before eleven and this morning is the first time I got up after seven for a long time.

I still sleep in the office and build the fires every morning. It sort of gives me an excuse to stay here and soothes my conscience as well. I get by pretty easy anyway. I am only supposed to be on duty 10 hours a week but I would rather do 10 hours a day in civil life.

Mother wrote a good letter in which she tells of Billy returning and hearing of Belles death for the first time. Poor fellow, he waited 4 years for her. Mother said that she used to dream about Dad a great deal before Belle died and he always seemed lonely. Since then she has seen him but once in her dreams and he was with Belle and was happy. I am glad of that dream for it will end her grief she has had enough. Two deaths by violent means in one year.

A very humorously written letter from Charley in which he tells of Frank's efforts to conquer other worlds since he failed to get in the army. Many days ago I wrote to Theressa and told her I never would take the offensive in a love affair again. She wrote and asked me how I would act on the defensive. I shall tell her that there is no danger of that if the girl sees me first for I sound better than I look.

The Huns are having an election today women and all are voting. Some of these people never voted before so they all went for the Centrum Party by advice from the priest.[25]

JANUARY 20   I like the major but not as a soldier. He is cultured and sweet mannered and fair but he is utterly void of initiative. He is conscientious and servile to a fault. As a soldier he is as a beautiful mountain stream, tasteless, colorless and clear as a crystal. It is conscious of one thing only and that strict exact obedience to the one law that orders it. The major obeys his orders to a letter he never over obeys nor under obeys one of them. He never starts anything or threatens to nor permit others to without orders. All of this works hardships on the men.

The food we get now is nearly always short weight so the soldiers are getting short changed there is a great deal of kicking but the major kicks not. The hay was so wet and rotten today that it wasn't fit for bedding. Very often the potatoes are rotten and froze and today another quarter of meat was bad.

Today we tried to form some kind of a class to study war and problems growing out of it but the major discouraged the idea. I try to get my students excused from riot [roll] call every evening but to no avail. Orders say the whole outfit must stand. That includes every man. Other outfits in the division don't even have riot call.

I had no school tonight my illiterates were all at a crap game. The "bones" seem to have a greater attraction than the 3 R's.

I am teaching with two good fellows Fulbright was "F" Co.'s old mess sergeant but he got busted. He is a capable instructor. Salter is a good teacher too but not very masculine. He has a girl back home and he quotes poetry when he writes to her if he can't find verse that suits he makes it. When he talks to me all I have to do is close my eyes to see visions of powder puffs and tea gowns decorated with morning glories.

I sent the $100.00 money order home that I got the other day. I also sent a check to the bank to have $50.00 of it sent to mother.

JANUARY 21   Our new "Y" is coming out in great shape the man in charge is alive he has a lot of reading matter. Old of course but reading matter he has a small library and a supply of tobacco and eats in so we are coming back to ourselves. I got a book from him to use in my school. The soldiers are helping to put up a stage in the hall. Soon we will have foot lights. Orders are for all outfits who can must have a stage.

I note that the peace conference is in full swing. I wish they would cut the army down to 500,000 men as proposed so we can go home.

Spent the evening with here in "mothers" room with a dutch man and a fraulein who is visiting "Mother" The dutch man Kriengs is an ex soldier. We played "Schwartz Peter" a card game in which the looser gets a black spot on his face. I have received my share.

JANUARY 22, WEDNESDAY   The battalion went on another hike today that they might be kept in physical shape. The major did not go he went somewhere in the side car. It was not a bad hike they say the roads being froze and in good shape.

I don't have to go on hikes for exercise. I keep in pretty good shape carrying wood.

Some of "mother's" relatives wrote to her today about her furniture and antiques. They must think she is due to get bumped off soon and they want to buy her furniture so it will be theirs when she passes away.

One of the German women came in today with a complaint against Dillinder, he has been breaking up her furniture and robbing her of her light. The major promised to attend to the matter. So the enemy gets treated by the yanks.

JANUARY 23   Very uneventful. Rations came in and I got my bit of sugar.

I turned down a pass (day light pass) to Trier. I didn't have time and one day is not enough to go 40 km to visit a city and return that eve.

Perhaps I will get another chance to go to Trier.

JANUARY 24, FRIDAY   I went to a little town off in the woods today to get some apples.[26] I went with a girl who lives there but stayed here with mother last night. I was royally received at her home. She had 3 pretty sisters of 18 to along in the 20's. My only regret was that I could not speak to them. I was the first yank that ever hit that neck of the woods so many of the neighboring women and children found excuses to run in a few moments. All types and ages came in some with and some without teeth. I was very patient and looked the other way while they looked me over as the Indians must have viewed Columbus.

They had a good dinner and served me as if I were a prodical [prodigal] to apple flapjacks, fried potatoes, bread and milk. I ate till I had to hold my plate to keep them from refilling it.

Later on it occurred to me that I made a fierce blunder. By force of habit I ate with my spoon all the while.

These people pray in concert before and after eating they have a tailor made prayer that they chant in a monotone. They say it parrot like their minds and hands occupied with other things the while.

I got 25# of apples for the major at a mark a pound good apples.

It is about 4 km over there. I shall return the first opportunity for they are good cooks. Place is called Holz Houch [Hof Hau]

It has been cold of late.

JANUARY 25, SATURDAY   We had a little programme in the hall tonight. I was on it. That program has been worrying me for a week. I have not been able to think of anything till today. I wrote up a little parable as a basis for a sermon on the text "Bear it all with patience." To finish off the "sermon" I wrote some jingles in which I made reference to a few griefs of the soldiers. I took advantage of the situation and went what I thought afterward was too far. To my surprise it took like wildfire and even the Major ok'ed it. A lot of the fellows afterwards asked for copies of the verses.

There were some things on the bill that were tainted with the nasty and it made me think how far men will go when there are no women to keep them thinking better things.

I am glad we are in Germany instead of France. If we were in France we would be out building roads and cleaning up towns or perhaps cleaning up the battlefields. Here the people clean the streets and the natives are hired to work on the roads under yank direction.

The dutch school teacher's had a convention here today. I don't know whether it was educational or political but they held forth at the school-meams and had coffee and cigarettes and all (some of the women smoked.)

JANUARY 26, SUNTAG [SONNTAG—SUNDAY]   I am starting on another note-book or tagebuch. I started the other before we saw active service in the hope that it would see me through the war. It did more it saw me into the Rhineland. I hope this will last till I get back into civilian clothes. I was wise in getting a good sized book.

Writing a diary requires a lot of work and it requires a lot of scheming to find the time to write. Often I could get no candles to write by so had to get by a fire. Mine is the only diary I know of in the Battalion and naturally I attracted a lot of notice. I was accused once of being a spy but I played safe and never put anything into this that I could not put in a letter. My diary is quite popular now for fellows who want dates and little bits of information.

A German was arrested tonight for selling schnapps. It may go hard. The other day a man was fined 3000 marks for the same offense.

A "Y" man preached to us this afternoon he had a text that was issued by G.H.Q. He talked to the question, "What are you going to say when you get back." They seem to be afraid up there that we might "love our enemies" so they send preachers around to minister the gospel of hate. He told us it was our duty to love France and England. I felt like asking if it was not our duty to love all peoples. Write to Prescott.

JANUARY 27   The old stove (built in 1700) that we heat this office with is a nuisance. The smoke sneaks out the back way through a four inch pipe about 20 feet long and it has several curves. Much of the heat goes with the smoke. It takes about 400 pounds of wood a day to keep it going sometimes it is too hot and then it is too cold. The stove is in the office but we have to fire it from the hall. The wood is wet and the steam from it goes part way up the chimney and condenses then drips nasty black stuff all over the hall floor. Some of those drops fell on the major's suit and the stains won't come out. I can only say, too bad.

We had court today to try the Dutchman [German] who sold schnapps. They marched all of "F" Co through the office trying to find the fellows he said threatened him if he didn't sell liquor to them. They couldn't find the men or he was afraid to identify them so the[y] fined him 300 marks and let him go being a man with large family. I got mother to send to Frankfurt for some of those war frying pans that the people got for giving up their copper. An excellent souvenir.

A fellow from the 341 M.G. gave us a little musical tonight he sang some good and bad songs and played his accordion. So we didn't have school this evening.

I have a new job on my list. I have to put out the signs that tell the men every day what they are supposed to wear. So we don't even have to think what clothes we have to wear we are like the lilies of the field.[27]

JANUARY 28, TUESDAY   I got a Washington County news today and from it I learned of the death of my old school pal, Sterling Russell.[28] He was killed in the Argonne it seems. I learned that he was married to L____[iza] Farn_____ [sworth] They both graduated in my class. It's a shame that good men like Sterling [die] and no accounts like me get through without a scratch.[29]

A good letter came from Mr. Prescott. He envied me my trip to the Rhine. He hoped I could get to stay over here and soak up the scenery and go to school if I liked for he had read in the papers of the educational opportunities we were going to have. Some of those home folks must think we go to Paris every Saturday night and live in the Y.M.C.A.'s or in front of a Salvation Army doughnut stand the rest of the time. That is not their fault for only such stuff has been allowed to get into the papers.

The Major is going to gin up the school. Tomorrow night every man who can't sign his name, write his letters or read his letters from home will be at school if he has to be put under arrest.

I don't know what I would do if a dozen men will come to school. I haven't a pencil a piece of paper or a piece of chalk. I have one little book and no prospect of more.

I got after the major again tonight about my school appointment. He says try again.

JANUARY 29, WEDNESDAY   I read a letter in the Dixie paper that gave me Roy Cox's address so I sat me down and poured out my heart to him while the battalion went on a hike. When I saw my old squad go by with their "gross" [big] packs on I told them they were a fine body of men and they asked me how it seemed to be a gold brick. It doesn't hurt my conscience to gold brick now that the war is over.

There is a little one horse saw mill down here. I had to go down there today to check up the work. Some of our men are making feed boxes. They have to make one for each horse in the division. A thousand feet a day is all the mill can cut so the fellows have a snap using up the lumber. They are also making a lot of tampers for the jerrys to use on the roads.

The captain marched 8 men down to school tonight. I had my hands full. Nothing to teach with and some of them don't know their A.B.C.'s. They, most of them, can't read. I wonder what joy they get out of life.

There is a wedding in town tonight. If I knew more dutch I would go.

The Major has been gone all day. I don't know why, he said "on business." It may be a feminine attraction and it may have been to avoid the hike.

We got the dope that 32 divisions sail ahead of us. Mother gave me a piece of honey cake tonight 5 years old but still good & moist.

JANUARY 30, THURSDAY   I have been reading a piece in the Saturday Evening Post of Dec. 15, 1918 by Isaac F. Marcosson. He tells of how well the boys up at the front are provided with chocolate and other sweets. He gets all these good things because it kills his desire for liquor. He says that besides the issued food the soldier can buy "*Extra* jam, candy, and plenty of canned fruit" at the commissarys and welfare societies.

We haven't been getting it and there are a million soldiers who have been on the front who are itching to give the lie to such statements the people have been reading. The fact that we didn't get it doesn't hurt as much as to read such write ups that are printed in the home papers with no other purpose than to tickle the ear.

The yank has been a good sport in this war he took his lot and said very little. He didn't desire to write home his grievances. He growled about things he had to endure but he never sent his complaints home. He couldn't had he desired for it was forbidden but the forbidding didn't bother him. He wanted folks to think all was well. He didn't kick because it wouldn't be fair play.

Now that the things are over and we have a chance to look around we get a magazine or so from the states and all the story's are full of distorted ideas of the front. The writeups are full of exaggerations but not a word of the other side. Not a man writing from the soldier's side of things. These writers come over and sip tea with the generals take a few notes snap a few pictures and hurry back with their "scoop." From now on the people will begin to find out what was hid behind the silence. Scandals and scandals will be uncovered.

JANUARY 31, FRIDAY   Out goes January and still we stay.

My friend Cohn is suffering from a relapse of the mumps. Sheets & I made a trip to the little town in the woods where the 4 dutch girls are for some more apples for the major. We had a good feed and one of the girls Gretchen, gave me some coffee cake to bring back. I feel sorry for those poor girls. All the young men are gone to war the best ones killed. They haven't a chance to get a beau much less a husband.

I have 12 students in my school now. So I am pretty well occupied. They have lot of fun about the little one man school I have been conducting for two weeks. Even the major is enjoying the joke they think it is on me. It is now. Fulbright and I are alone. Salter is in the hospital we have about 30 students. We will get along better now for a lot of books came today. Our "Y" man rustled them from some place. We have a very good "Y" man.

Another issue of candy came today. Uncle is beginning to find us.

FEBRUARY 1, SATURDAY   I had my first leave of absence today and went to Trier. The sergeant major and "Jew" Stein and I went together.

I must tell of the details in order.

Rose 5:00. Mother (who never goes to bed till 1 o'clock) left a breakfast in [the] oven that was still warm. We reported to the major in his room he was in bed but he looked us over to see that we had our fingernails clean and shoes polished. He told us how to behave, not to put beans in our nose and so forth. Truck takes us to Kyl[l]burg and we take train to Trier 40 km. On the way to Trier Stein made friends with a German girl and deported himself in a very unprintable manner in our presence and in the next compartment. But She did not object.

Trier is an old Roman city it has a few ruins that bear witness so that we visited them all. We visited the Ampitheatre with its modern improvements. Stein called it the M.P. theatre. There was the old baths the Kaisers (Caesars) palace and the old church. The church was very beautiful within. The most interesting thing was 2 wee girls in the church. They were making the rounds from one statue to another crossing themselves and praying before each. They were not conscious of our presence.

We went out to the museum where we saw many things of more or less interest. Weapons and tools and jewelry of other days. Saw a piece of bone with a hand made spike nailed in it. A ghastly mummy and such stuff but most interesting was a big hole in the rear of the building made by an allied air bomb.

In a hundred stores they were selling souvenirs. They have made the town a souvenir market for the yanks. I didn't buy any iron crosses but instead got some books in English. I got "Ships That Pass in the Night." Oscar Wilde's "Ideal husband" and a book "The Future of America" by Wells and I also got a pretty little table cover to take home. It cost about $2.50.

We eat dinner and supper at the Red cross served by real yank women. They only serve yanks visiting Trier. About 300 men were there each meal. Price 2 marks.

The Y.M.C.A. had nothing to give us. I am told there was more at the Officer's "Y." The K.C. also had nothing but paper. Oh the Y had plenty of reading matter and a nice hall. I left for home too soon to see the show put on at the Y by the 353 inf.

We had to walk from Kyl[l]burg out 6 ½ km but even at that we got here at 9:30.

I showed mother the table cover I got I did not tell her I was going to take it home. She thought it was beautiful and she thanked me she thanked me so fervently I just let her keep it.

The girl friend is out of luck.

FEBRUARY 2, SUNDAY   I went to church this morning and listened to the chaplin give a long dry sermon. The talk didn't interest me but I got to thinking about myself and I realized that I have been living a very dry unprayerful life. I am losing sight of the great spiritual side of life that should be developed. It is necessary to pray from the heart if one would fill from the heart.

The army drys a man up his thinking and spiritual sides are not toughened except in a negative manner.

"F" Company moved away today, they went up to Prem.

I notice that there is a move back home to give discharged soldiers a bonus.[30] One fellow was extremely liberal and suggested $300.00.

The three girls from the place where I get apples came in today. They came to have the yank dentist. They invite me to come over. Perhaps.

The school meam came over this evening we had a little visit. She told me that the 89th div had the German colors in their insignia. She is right here is the insignia [sketch of insignia with Black, Red, White] The insignia is suppose to be the letter "W" in a circle standing for "middle Western" division. The different branches of the service have their colors in the center of the W, we being engineer have red and white and the letter is black. W is the initial of our three generals at Funston Wright, Wood and Winn (Right would win) Fellows say that it stands for Work Walk and wait at present.

FEBRUARY 3   I must say a few words about my students. I have ten and they are a hard boiled lot. I have 3 Italians and they "killa da Anglish" something awful. I have a Swede who is a good student but is too far advanced for what I can give him so I tender him special treatment on the side. The others are indifferent and semi indifferent yanks hailing from the river bottoms and the Ozarks.

The other day I asked one of them to spell two he did. I asked him to spell another word pronounced the same but with a different meaning his reply—"Ah hell! If you want it spelled spell it yourself." One of them—Jones puzzles most of the time over his name. He says if he can write his name he has education enough. Lutz is of the same opinion.

A sniper was shooting at Jones and another fellow in a shell hole on the St. Mihiel Front. Jones peeked over then he got his rifle and took long careful aim. Some one shot at him and the fellows yelled at him to get down or they would get him. Jones fired, "By gawd, that one won't."

A lot of these fellows are good plain go ahead soldiers without fear but they seriously object to being forced to go to school at night while the other fellows are resting. I don't blame them. Over in the states they pay men $30 a month to wear the uniform and go to school, why are not men who have seen service entitled to the same consideration?

FEBRUARY 4, TUESDAY   It is "Stunt night" so we have no school. They are putting on some kind of an impromptu programme in the hall. I shall not go. Stay home and read.

They had inspection and I had to loan all my stuff to fellows here who were short so they could pass for the chief of staff, our colonel and some other celebrities came up to look us over. We have a new colonel now, he is from Alaska. Got his D.S.C. in the tank corps and just transferred to us.[31]

I had a worse job than standing inspection. I had to thaw out the toilet. It is a beastly job but I ought to be willing to do a bad job once in a while. If the proverb is true I will soon have my peck of dirt eaten.

I hurt a fellows feelings today. I told him that the catholic church was the Kaisers best friend. He is a catholic and a fine chap.—Antillia. Regardless of what the church did to preserve civilization in the past it is or was being used by the powers in Germany to teach the people unquestioned obedience to authority. The Catholic church never has put a premium on new ideas but allows the people to run along in the rut. It teaches them good things now but it doesn't say to its members "Stand on your own feet think for yourself. You have your own souls to save."

FEBRUARY 5, WEDNESDAY   The school meam has a sister who is visiting with her. They came over this evening to drink coffee with "Mother" and me. They brought some cake over that we couldn't turn down even if it is forbidden to eat their food. Cake here doesn't mean the same thing as cake in the states. This cake does not make a fellows mouth water for they do not have the sugar or butter or flour and least of all the eggs.

I am having my troubles with fires we have nothing but green wood so I spend most of my time blowing the fire with a long pipe, and getting smoke in my eyes.

I went to the dentist today and had my tooth drilled out. My! How it hurt. It hurt worse because I am such a coward. I always go to the dentist's chair like it were the gallows. I am to go back in a week. I expect the tooth will ache on by leaps and bounds till then. He put some cotton in it but it does not help.

Pay day. I got 163 francs. They are giving us a lot of new money to be used especially in the army of occupation. I don't care much for this soap wrapper money they put it on such poor paper that it wears out if a soldier carries it in his pocket a month. Then it is thrown away.

I shall try to get a pass to England. I can't go to school so that will be a
good substitute.

FEBRUARY 6, THURSDAY   We held school from 2 till 4 today and hereafter it
will be held in the afternoon. That pleases me and will make the men come
with a better spirit. It is good to have ones evenings off. This evening Krings
and I slipped away and went to the place where I have been getting apples.
We spent a very pleasant evening. A lot of the young people came in to give
me the look over. They were all big awkward boys and some returned soldiers. I thought what they could do to me if they desired for I was alone in
the midst of "mine enemies." They regarded me with a sort of awe as though
I were the "Super man" that they have been reading about. I ate my fill of
fried potatoes but that is not the only value of such a visit. I like to get a
chance to study these simple country folk.

I missed a good entertainment here today. Some Y.M.C.A. girls accompanied by a mere man entertained. There was a singer a reader and a fiddler.

I write a letter to Mr. Prescott yesterday. I sent one to Charley. That evens
up my correspondence for a long time to come. I shall not throw out any
more letters as bait for no one bites.

FEBRUARY 7   The "Y" man who slept in, slept in the major's room (the
one who helped entertain) came down this morning and told me to have
"that old lady build a fire" in his room. I didn't like the idea of a young
blood like him asking an old woman 75 years old to make a fire for him why
the major wouldn't ask it. I told him that she didn't make fires he asked who
did. I said whoever needed fire made it around here. He went away wiser I
hope if it were possible. It bores me to have some of these bombproofs come
around after the guns are shooting and demand service that a front line man
won't ask. Captain Albert told me after he went out that he deserved the
rebuke.

Later the "Y" man in charge here came in with a complaint that the
German children were attending our entertainments. The captain called me
into the office and asked my opinion (He knew what it would be) I told the
"Y" man that as long as the Germans didn't crowd the yanks out they should
be permitted to attend but yanks first. I told him the argument he put up to
punish every German by being personally mean to him whenever the occasion offered was not right. I believe Germany should pay all she can pay that
is justice and Christian but for a "Y" man to drive children out of an

entertainment because they are "Hunlets" is revenge and antichrist. America and the Y.M.C.A. stands for bigger things than that. I put in another application to go to school.

FEBRUARY 8, SATURDAY   The A.E.F. seems to be show mad of late. Company "D" put on a show tonight and after it was over Lt. Neel called a couple of us aside and asked if Co. "E" couldn't put on a better one. So we may be putting on something in the future. The Battalion is going to fix the stage up with electric lights painted scenes and all. We have a couple of artists. One of them painted a background it looks like Arizona hills but he has it adorned with oriental or tropic verdure. We have an orchestra of a violin a drum a bell and a piano. The fiddle usually ran madly ahead and the other parts had to use the pauses to keep up. Or at least it seemed so to me, being no judge.

Our basketball team consisting of one man assisted by 4 others went to Bitburg to play some artillery regiment and came home with the bacon.

It is a bitter cold day but the companies had inspection any way. The major and Cap. Albert went to Prum and while the boys were out on the hill being inspected by Cap (Pop) Coy I was thawing out the toilet pipes again or blowing the fire to coax the green wood along. Snow on road has become glassy and we can scarce stand with our slick hob nails. Autos cannot run unless they have chains and we can scarce walk up a slope but the sledding is fine. I have been out sliding down hill with the little Huns.

FEBRUARY 9, SUNDAY   I wish I had a good pen. I tried to buy one in Trier but could not. I saw three pens in the whole town and they were bad before the war. Two of them were Watermans and cost 21 marks. There is no gold or rubber for pens.

We were to have formed a bible class today but I got up late and had so much trouble with the fire that I never thought of it till noon. Then I learned that the chaplin had come held service and was ready to go back so I hunted him up and apologized.

I never saw such slippery streets "Aviator" Hill fell and cut a big gash in his head today cause [sketch of wine bottle and glass]

We are to give a programme in a few nights. I am to give a reading. I can't find anything so I have to make something. I am doing that today.

Mother gave me some lemonade this evening. It tastes like it was made of tea and raspberries. It was a gloomy color and I feel like a miser for drinking it. Mother has been very good to me. Yesterday she gave me some rare antiques. A couple of pewter soup plates and a pewter oil lamp. The major tried to buy them but he could not get her in a selling mood.

Some of the boys have been to Koblenz. I will try to go next week. Letter from Mother.

FEBRUARY 10, MONDAY   I was over in one of the hotels today and by mistake bolted into Capt. Cassity's room, he is our dentist. It was 4 o'clock and he was still laying in the feathers. I went down to the infirmary and found a buck doing the dentist work. He was doing the captain's work for a buck pay $33.00 and the captain was "laying the body." So even Uncle Sam gets cheated at times.

Today I cleaned the stove pipes and had them all on my neck for having the house full of smoke. One elbow of pipe was so rusty I had to get a dutch man to make a new one. I made a paper elbow but it caught fire and caused a panic and more smoke though it held for two hours till the other was being made. I had to pay for the new pipe. The gov owes me about 15 marks for things I have paid for at school and here chalk, lights, and so on but it is such a hopeless job to get money from Uncle that I am content to get my pay.

A company of 90th div players got stalled here on their way to Prum so they are going to entertain tonight.

Major is all wrought up tonight a sergeant and Buring were trying to take the car to go riding. Hubbard, the driver objected and the sergeant hit Hubbard. They are out now after the sergeant it was in the morning papers.

FEBRUARY 11, TUESDAY   There is no sting that hurts like that which comes with the knowledge of having failed. I failed tonight. Another fellow and I were to put on a dialogue and it went flat. It was a dirge. A soldier audience is the most heartless. If you don't get them they get you. There is joy in having your audience and humiliation in losing. Some people don't care but it hurts me to have my audience slip away from me. Though I feel beaten tonight, I expect to come back again.

I gave a little lecture on the beginnings of America. It went off well. We ran over time and still had interest.

Mail today but all I got was a paper that Eva sent from St. Johns.

I am lonesome. I wish I were a kid so I could cry. I never have felt as blue since I have been over here. I wish I could meet some real cheery friend to drive this bitterness out of me if it be bitterness.

FEBRUARY 12   The Sergeant Major is "Krank," that means sick. He lost 160 f. in a crap game yesterday and then he paid me 12 f. that has been due many days.

He is a pretty good fellow and we have had some differences of opinion still we are like brothers. We argue like brothers we have to for we need each other at times when we stand in need of a little soap or sugar or milk, etc. We have charge of dividing the Battalion rations. Rations have been terrible short of late so we have not dared to take out for our (officers) mess. Last issue was 200 rations short besides short weight and bad food a ration is 3 meals for a soldier.

The 353 inf. Entertained tonight. They had a Hawaiian who sang native songs and played. He charmed us and was encored several times.

I had the nerve taken out of my tooth today. It has not ached for several days.

My school is going fine. I had to have one man arrested and brought in. A great joke for all concerned. None of them hold hard feelings towards me they look upon me as a fellow victim. I have one fellow who is sulking just sulking and smiling about it. I can always get them interested in my history talk and they have requested that we have a little discussion of problems current. Especially labor problems.

This evening I rub mother's hands. They get stiff and swollen from the cold.

FEBRUARY 13, THURSDAY   I hung around here all day but the rest of the boys went out for a practice march it was a hard trip the roads being so slippery.

Mother is baking a cake tonight for herself and me. It is eggless, butterless, sugarless, and few extracts. It isn't quite that bad but as near it as possible.

Mother is as jealous of me as an ardent young lover. I gave her the electric bulb I bought for the school but do not need now. I took her hand and touched the current. It was the first time she ever felt electricity.

I write out a petition tonight to the general. I didn't send the other in. I wrote this out on the typewriter. Lt. Neel told me to write my own recommendation and he would sign it. I am also going to have room for a recommendation from the Major. I know I have sufficient credit to make it but it is a question of rank and influence. Some Capt. or Loot is apt to draw the lucky cards. I have one chance in about fifty.

My girl from Holz Houch came over to see me again today and she brought me some nice apples.

There is a lot of talk about going home next month but I think there is a very poor chance too many men want this to continue.

FEBRUARY 14   Major gave me a splendid recommendation for a furlough and my petition goes in to the general today.

The priest died today and all the town is sad. I have seen him often. A very large man with long white hair. They are grieving more for him than for all the children that have died. I have not spoken of that in my diary but several children have died. School is closed so we can use the schoolroom. Probably the flu.[32] Bad weather and crowded rooms. The yanks have crowded in and the family have had to move into the kitchen or worse stay in the room with the yanks. They don't ventilate their houses so they have to suffer they don't only breathe the bad air but in many cases the children have to breathe so much smoke.

Well I got a letter from Alberta. She gave me the address of my old side kick Fred Pearce and I wrote to him tonight. Alberta tells of terrible ravages of the flu till I am glad I came to the war for safety. Her mother died with it. Got a good letter from Roy Cox. He is up near Koblenz.

This evening we went to a very absurd picture show. We had lots of fun but not from the pictures.

All our horses have lice or something so they took them to Bitburg today to be dipped. I roamed through the woods today for exercise saw many deer tracks.

FEBRUARY 15, SATURDAY   I wrote three letters today Charley, Mrs. Nelson and I have forgotten who the other letter was to but no matter they won't answer. I have sworn off from writing to people who write to me because they think it is their duty to keep up the spirits of the soldiers. When the guns stopped shooting they stop writing. They stop with a sigh of relief pleased with a memory of sacrifice they have made to win the war.

The 356 inf. put on a show here tonight. It was very good, some good original stunts and music. Some of these show men surely take their cracks at things they don't like. They do it to get the crowd.

They are having us all send cards home. Every soldier and officer in the A.E.F. must send a card home to tell his nearest of kin he is alive. I sent one to mother. And that reminds me the other letter went to Grandma Lytle.

I washed and boiled my clothes again today. I think I have got the last of the cooties. They are hanging out on the line and "mother" is trying to get me to bring them in and hang them behind the stove lest some spitzboob [rascal] gets them tonight. A great deal of stealing since the war.

There is a movement back home to forbid the service stripe. There will be a great howl from here if it is true.

FEBRUARY 16, SUNTAG   Laundry soap is a treasure up here. A yank can get more from these Germans with soap than money as money is of little value here.

The army of occupation has developed a lot of laundry soap diplomats. I am afraid that a lot of unholy alliances have ensued and I shouldn't be surprised if after the yanks left there wouldn't be many German Americans left to bear witness that we were here.

I got an invitation to go to H----[Hoch Hau] this evening so Provaznik and I slipped away and spent the evening there. We danced or rather they did and we had a good feed much was of most interest. We both got wet going over for it has rained all the day and I had a hard time explaining to mother when I got back how I got wet without telling her the truth. She is more of a disciplinarian than the major.

FEBRUARY 17, MONTAG   The people continue to die here. It must be a sort of flu. Death seems to have no terror for these folks. They seem to move about at their usual pace in their usual mood. Most of the victims are children.

One of our soldiers also died. I hear that there are many deaths in the division.

The latest news is that we are the 32nd division to sail. So if they move troops as fast as they have been perhaps we start about Sept. perhaps not.

I note by the paper that the Dutch are getting bullheaded again. It may be necessary to march on to Berlin yet. I hope that they have sense enough to take things as they come and be satisfied that [they] are being treated a darn sight better than we would have been had they won.

Some of the boys who went out about two weeks ago to pick up trucks abandoned by the dutch between here and Koblenz just returned. They have had a lot of grief because the trucks were in bad shape. They brought back several however.

They issued candy today. Each man got two bars. I managed for two more and left them in my over coat. Some kid or some yank beat me to the 4 of them and now I am as poor as ever.

FEBRUARY 18　　The reaper got another child today. They buried the priest. It was a solemn affair and more long faces and tears than for the dozen babes that were taken.[33]

Doctors are beginning to take anti Flu precautions they spray every twice a day.

I note by the paper that the college courses to be offered are mostly for "officers desiring to finish their college work." That puts the crimp on my chances to go to school. If I go it will be in spite of things.

Yanks are going souvenir mad. One of our fellows went to Koblenz and got a nickel plated helmet he paid 500 marks for it. It is classy but I wouldn't pay that for a dozen.

A couple of "y" girls and a man came up this afternoon and gave us a programme. It was good.

General Winn came up this afternoon to inspect. Major was gone and Capt Albert hid. We told him that Capt A. was out inspecting billets. He looked around a while and left.

FEBRUARY 19, WEDNESDAY　　Last night one of the neighbors took me home with her to see her child. A flu victim. I don't know whether I was sorry for the child or not. I don't know that the mother was. A child in this country looks into a gloomy future. Of course the mother will put on the weeds. They wear mourning here different periods for different members of the family according to the degree of consanguinity. The school meam has 11 months more to wear black for her brother.

Company "E" is putting out a little history and I have been writing some verses to go with it. I finished them today. I named them "Jingles to Ourselves."[34]

I note by the division intelligence report that we are to be the 18th division so that means at least 3 months yet. It may change again soon. It is a great sacrifice for the average man to sit around over here and twiddle his thumbs now that the war is over. I wouldn't mind the stay if I could go to school but it seems that the school like all other good things over here is "For officers Only." One fellow who got a furlough told of how often he saw that sign in Paris. It was even on the nurses. He suggested that we have one more war "For officers only."

The major is all smiles tonight. He got news that he was going to get a furlough to England the land of his fathers. A lot of these Greeks and Italians who have been looking forward for months for leaves to visit their homes are being disappointed.

Sgt Major was away today so Harris and I had all the work to do. Besides I have both "D" & "E" students in school.

FEBRUARY 20   Everyone in camp is raging tonight over a write up in the New York by some Captain Harris some of the stuff Headlines—"Yanks not yearning to discard Khaki"—Some phrases from the interview—"Why should they be? Take the case of the average private. He is clothed. He is fed. He is elaborately and well cared for. In addition he has - - - his $30.00 per month plus his extra 10% overseas pay." Again "Most American lads in the army never enjoyed such incomes that could be freely spent and none nearly so well as themselves appreciate that fact." Those are the sentiments of a Sam Brown boy. I read in the paper that Clemenceau has been shot and think it's a shame that such a grand man should be assaulted and the Captain run loose.[35]

I wrote a long letter to Alberta and started to figure out a letter to Senator King in which I will put that paper clipping wherein the captain says the boys don't want to go home. I shall tell things from the soldier's point of view.

We are short on books in school so I have to write out tasks on the typewriter for the beginners.

Band came up and entertained this evening but I did not go.

FEBRUARY 21, FRIDAY   We had to arrest some dutch today for breaking quarantine. It seems that they did not know what quarantine was. They have Dyptheria [diphtheria]. Fined them.

Arrested three young chaps for going around the country without a pass and sentenced them to 5 days on the road.

These people have a terrible fear of officers. They come into the office all atremble. Men sometimes are so frightened they can scarce speak. They judge our army by their own and are surprised too.

I write a letter to the Nelson girl today.

I sent that letter to Senator King. I told him that we common soldiers were in the army for a bigger thing than a job and it was an insult to red blooded men to tell the word behind their back that they were satisfied with a $30.00 job with no responsibility. I told him that we had served willingly and would serve again but when the job was done we wanted to get out and anything he could do would be appreciated.

The Q.M. telephoned tonight that they had a quantity of good eats on hand if we would send over which is evidence that the S.O.S. is either going home or catching up.

FEBRUARY 22, SATURDAY   I told mother that today was a holiday for Americans but she couldn't understand how we could have a "Fest" without a great feast. There are many things these dutch can't understand about us. They can't see how it is possible for a yank to be a man without raising a beard or mustache to prove it. Some of them seem to fall for us bald faced boys.

I got a letter from Mr. Prescott. It came in 19 days. It seems that many Americans now that the war is over have nothing to do but hate and thinking of new ways to hate. They are worse than these soldiers who faced the huns. I'll have to tell him that over in France the M.P.'s had to keep the French and yanks from fighting whereas over here the big job is to keep the German and yanks apart.

My letter to Senator K. got by the censor OK and will be sailing the seas soon.

A "Y" show came here today just before the "Y" man here got in a supply of hard candy and we had a lot of fun throwing it around the hall between acts. The "Y" man came out to make an announcement and they threw a lot at him.

FEBRUARY 23, SUNDAY   Yesterday and today rest. I must write down the names of Mrs. Nelson's girls before I forget. They are Cally and Dorothy and the little ones are Muriel and Barbera.

Lt. Steel and I went into the "welt" wood today with some German girls. Krings was along and took some pictures. Lt S. would not get on the picture because it is "verboten." The girls sang some songs. One war song that was intended to cheer their soldiers against us not many months back. The song stirred me up and made me think of them as my enemy again. So we had a very dry time.

Feed is getting better of late for some reason. We even had apple pie today.

This forenoon I went to Reg. Hdq in the side car with the payrolls. This afternoon the major went down and this evening he called me up and told me that there was a chance to go to a French University if I knew French. I told him I knew French when as a matter of fact I can't count to five.[36] Chaplin came up to preach tonight and he congratulated me on my chances.

The chaplin made a good talk tonight in defense of the Bible. It is not necessary to defend the bible it defends itself.

I shall try to go to Koblenz in a day or so. Beauchamp took my name tonight.

FEBRUARY 24, MONDAY   Got a letter from Charley he is out of spirits and I don't wonder. He is home alone and there is little to encourage him.

"D" Company moved to Nattenheim today. That is where we spent Xmas. Capt Albert is going over to take command while "Pop" Coy goes on pass. New Order out now that every yank must have a bed. All male Germans between 10 & 55 must sleep on floors if there are not beds enough. If we were in France we would be sleeping in barns not only that but we would be moving their manure piles and making their roads.

I am in the toils. I must learn the French language "while you wait," as it were. All day I have been as tangled up with French verbs as the War Department is with red tape.

I am the butt of every joke in the office. The Sergeant Major suggests that I give up the idea. He says that I am shutting some other fellow out but all I can say is that if the other fellow goes he will be shutting me out. He has a friend in mind. I am going to hang till they cut me loose.

FEBRUARY 25   I am still tangled up in the French verb. There are as many parts to a French verb as to a Ford automobile. I believe that with a verb book in a French family for a few days I could learn much faster. There is a fellow here in the office who speaks French but he is too willing to teach I can't absorb it as fast as he gives it.

I got a nice letter from Winnie Terry. She tells of the great many boys who are returning home and a lot of local gossip.

There is a big cock and bull story in the paper about 30,000 soldiers in the Army of Occupation taking advantage of educational opportunities. I am having quite a job teaching my school. I have to keep two classes going at once and not half enough books to go around.

I hoped to go to Koblenz tomorrow but we got cut down on the number of passes so I shall go another day.

FEBRUARY 26   Major left today and we had a great time. Among other things we got out his extra clothes and had a "staff" picture taken. It will shock him very much if he sees it. I wore his fur collar for a Russian cap.

Then we stopped a dutch wagon pulled by two yellow cows and got snapped again.

A wedding in town. Big celebration tonight. I would like to go for they may have good eats.

The 355th Inf. are going to put on a show here tonight. The Colonial Minstrels.

Mother has hired one of the German girls from Hoch Hau to help her a few days. I spend so much time trying to talk German to her that my French suffers.

Tomorrow I am going to Koblenz to look at the "Watch on the Rhine."[37] I must get ready and spend the rest of the night worrying about getting up at 4:30. Mother is busy too she is making a pie for me to take tomorrow. An apple pie made with bread dough.

FEBRUARY 27, THURSDAY   I am back from Koblenz. I got in this morning at 3:45, too late for bed so I am writing up the trip. I enjoyed every minute of the trip though I didn't see the football game that I went to see. The game was between the 89th and the 4th divisions for the Army of Occ. Series. Our division won.[38] I felt that I would see other football games so spend my time seeing the town.

Ten of us from "E" Co. walked to Kyl[l]burg this morning got there 6:00 took train for a little town this side of Trier where a special train of yank Box cars took us to Koblenz. There was more than a trainload of our division fellows. There were 3 car loads of buglers alone. They had all been to a buglers school at Trier and were going up to root for the 89th. We could scarce hear each other talk at times on account of the blare of buglers.[39]

I met Leo Mortensen an Arizona boy that used to be in my class he is with the artillery and is playing in the 164 brigade band. I carried his trombone and passed into the car with the band as a full fledged member. It gave us an excellent opportunity to visit. I had a box of lunch and he had a canteen of cider so we fed as well.

The railroad ran down the Moselle to Koblenz. It was a very scenic trip. Many tunnels on the way. We passed through the longest tunnel in Germany so I am told, 3½ km. The Moselle is hedged in clear to the Rhine by high rock ledges. Every foot of land is utilized for vine for this is the home of the famous Moselle wine. The hillsides are so steep that they have to be terraced off like stair steps in order to afford place for grapes to grow. Everyone was busy getting ready for spring. We saw women and old men along the foothills gathering up the rich soil that had washed down and carrying it in baskets to the top of the hills.

I found Koblenz a very busy place. It seems like I saw more officers and red cross and "Y" workers there than in the whole A.E.F. Koblenz is a new attraction so the social whirl has moved from Paris to the Rhine. I will say however that I was pleased with the "Y" service the men were getting there. It is just like the papers back home describe it to be every where.

My poor soldier purse didn't permit me to buy many souvenirs but I visited some of the stores. I did get Mother a little butter bowl for an "an danken."

We left about 6:00 o'clock for home. I was fortunate to get in a III class where I could sit down. Most of the fellows had to ride in those box cars so generously provided by Uncle Sam. For them it must have been a cold miserable ride. We passed many idle passenger coaches on the side tracks. The train traveled very slow making many long stops so we didn't get to Trier, about 75 KM till about 2:30. Beauchamp and Stein, who went down Wednesday went down Wednesday [repeated], came back with us they say they had a good time, put on civilian clothes to avoid M.P.'s and went out with the girls.

FEBRUARY 28   The major made us fellows all get out this morning for exercise so we went out in the woods and played games. We played back out and then we had a fight with pine cones.

These woods are beautiful in winter and must be more so in summer.

Mother made the major a present today of a very rare stone oil lamp. I did a lot of scheming to get her to. He wants the lamp she gave me. Then he gave me such a good boost to go to school that I felt he ought to have something in return. Probably will regret I got it for him if I don't get to go. Tomorrow is the first and no signs of an order yet.

I turned in some of my old clothes today for new. Our kitchen moved up to where "D" kitchen was so all we have to do is to cross the street for chow.

MARCH 1, SATURDAY   It looks very much like I am not going to go to school. I hadn't ought to go since I know so little French. On the other hand I feel that if I did go I could meet my class requirements. It is merely another disappointment to swallow. I must not kick because that would brand me as a sore head which would be the case.

I got a good letter from Nell. She tells of a Mexican family that got wiped out by the flu. 12 members gone. The 13th is John Salazar a soldier in the 353rd. He has been over the top three times and still alive.

I got a Dixie paper today that had a pleasant atmosphere about it. Also the Grand Rapids paper with a piece by Frank H. Simonds in which he supports all of the French greed. I feel that France ought to be paid and Germany ought to suffer but Mr. Simonds in this article doesn't reflect the American idea of justice he is pleading for revenge.

I took the dutch girl home today. The one who has been working here. On my way back I was practicing French in a loud voice and started a deer. A beautiful little animal about ½ the size of our yank deer. Major was out hunting wild boars today. He saw a boar but missed him. Says he saw a deer too but we are not allowed to shoot them being out of season. The Allies do not desire to slaughter off the game for these people. That is more consideration than their armies would show us.

MARCH 2, SUNDAY   Every cloud has a silvery lining yesterday I only saw the dark of the cloud today. Capt. Bird telephoned and said that I had better come down for my money if I desired to get paid before going to school.[40] That changed the color of everything and I have been walking on air ever since. I hiked into Kyl[l]burg with fear lest some one ask me some thing about my French but was some what relieved when I learned that Cap. Bird had his wires crossed and thought I was going to an English University. Perhaps I am.

I had to make several trips to the office before I got my money (160f) but I didn't mind that. I had to walk around the streets in the rain for half an hour with my overcoat under my arm. I couldn't wear it because the order of the day was blouses. The weather changed but the orders didn't. I didn't mind that either for I hunted up a "Y." It was run by a yank woman who must have come from Boston judging from the way she rolled her R's. She had been in "Frawnce" a "yeah."

This evening I have been getting ready. I collected some autographs from the fellows and disposed of some of the stuff I didn't want to carry. Clocks set ahead.

12

BACK TO FRANCE, MARCH 1919

THE TRIP FROM OBERKAIL, GERMANY, TO MONTPELLIER TOOK FOUR
days, including nearly twenty-four hours in Paris. Anderson was driven
in the battalion Ford to Kyllburg where he boarded the train. He transferred in Trier, where he caught the first train for Metz and then continued
on through the St. Mihiel sector to Toul. From there he jumped aboard a
French troop train for Favresse where, with the help of a Frenchman who
could understand his German, Anderson and several other Yanks located a
train bound for Paris. Anderson found "that Paris is 'no place for a preachers
son' and I decided to that 24 hours is enough for me in this place without a chaperone because he has to dodge the Vampire here at every turn."
With so much to see and so little time to do it, Anderson contented himself with observing the people—the Parisians and other visitors—and not
trying to take in all the landmarks. His observations of a market place and
from a sidewalk café offer an interesting glimpse of postwar Paris. Walking the wrong way and trying to find the Lyons Station while loaded down
with his pack and a sack full of reserve rations, Anderson was rescued by
"some Yanks in a Ford" who took him to the station where he boarded a
French train that took him through Dijon and Lyons to Avignon. There he
transferred for Montpellier, a city of about 75,000 people, where the many
flowers and blossoming fruit trees offered an appealing welcome after the
three months of winter in Germany.

As he mingled with other American soldiers in Montpellier, he wrote
that "my greatest worry is over. I thought I was to be the only black sheep in
the flock but lo and behold I find very few of the fellows have much French."

MARCH 3   Some of the neighbors came in to bid me good by last night. A
girl from over the way came in and baked me some waffles. This morning
mother fixed me up a box of lunch. She had two eggs that she has been saving a long time for me but I didn't have the nerve to take them so we divided

them. She gave me some apples and filled my canteen with red wine from
raspberries. Mother really hated to see me go poor old soul. I hated to go. I
found I had made attachments in the outfit that were hard to break. I parted
with my helmet and gas mask and guns as though they were living friends. All
the fellows wished me good luck and the major had the Ford bring me to
Kyl[l]burg. Capt. Bird told me that if I had everything to hit out for Montpellier France wherever that is.

I went to Trier or to the first station before I got to Trier where Bushman's outfit is. Bush was not there but in Trier to a horse show. So I carry my
pack to Trier and the M.P.'s won't let me go up town to find the horse show
so take the first train to Metz. That is where I am now.

Metz is a beautiful city but forbidden for yanks. It is a French leave area
and if yanks went in they would run the prices up for the "frog's" who have
only 15 or 20 francs to see the whole world on.

When we were on the St. Mihiel front we were opposite Metz and the
big guns near Novient shelled the city every day. I take a train out of here to
Toul and will cross the Hindenburg line near where we were stationed.

I am learning a few things about European R.R. systems. Officers ride lst
class non coms 2nd class and bucks 3rd class. In the states we all road [rode]
like we were American citizens. I hope this class distinction don't follow us
home.

MARCH 4, TUESDAY   Morning—I am in a little place called Favresse. Where
it is I can't say. I got a train for Toul last night and then my problem was to get
out of Toul. A French troop train came through and I got on. It was crowded
but it was moving and that is better than standing around the depot. We got
to this place about 4:00 this morning. It is a sort of railroad station in a desert
where many trains are lined up and as trainloads of soldiers come in they
unload and get on the train going their way. There were several of us yanks
who could not find our train but finally I found a Frenchman who could
understand my German and he put us on the Paris train. I don't know if I
must go to Paris to get to Montpellier or not but I shall go to Paris unless I
am stopped. I am curious to see the place.

Evening—I am in Paris and will be here till 2:30 tomorrow. It is not
enough time to look the city over so I shall content myself with walking the
streets and making observations. That is what I did this afternoon.

I don't see many Americans as I expected, but there are many other soldiers from the allied armies. More French officers than anything else and

every one with a beautiful or an artificial girl attached to him.Then there are the side walk restaurants or cafes where the people sit and sip beer and wine.

This afternoon I have seen more loving on the streets than during all my life on American streets. Couples go with their arms around each other in the streets even if crowded places and in the cafes it is ordinary to see couples locked in each others arms as unconscious of the passersby as the passers are of them. Loving seems to be a very popular outdoor sport here. I spent most of the afternoon looking for a Y.M.C.A. In doing so I got lost and wandered down near the river. There I saw the Americans and their French girls. It is more secluded there. I decided that Paris is "no place for a preachers son" and I decided too that 24 hours is enough for me in this place without a chaperone because he has to dodge the Vampire here at every turn. If a fellow can live in Paris and keep the green monster from rising within him he has stood a great test.

A Frenchman begged me for tobacco. I had none but told him that I could get him some if he showed me a Y.M.C.A. On arriving at the place it turned out to be a Red Cross joint where I could get supper so I made a date with my Frenchman to meet him on a certain corner at 7:00 when the commissary opened and I would have cigarettes for him. I ate my supper and went the other way. I couldn't face him again. He walked too close to me. He hovered over like a mother hen. He fairly smothered me with affection.

I went to a picture show this afternoon and while I was sitting there two girls came in and sit by me. They wanted to talk but we couldn't. I knew what their business was so I told them I had no money which directed their attention away. They were only a pair of the many that hail a fellow on the street. I have had to remind myself again and again this afternoon of my duty to myself and the girl I may get sometime. I will expect her to be clean and it is her right to demand as much.

Today must be some kind of a holiday judging from the crowds on the streets and the decorations in the windows.[1] I see many children going around with masks and false faces on. I even saw young men carrying little balloons around and young ladies wearing false noses. As I was trying to find my way back to my room I met some girls with men's clothes on. One of them said "Hello Kid" so I judge she has met yanks before.

People hold their hands out here for money as if they thought we were banks.They won't take the French Army of Occupation money, but they sure love the other. I am paying 6 franks for a bed that I could get any where in the states for 50 cents.

I am going to bed early. Tomorrow I shall spend the forenoon looking the town over as a silent spectator. That is more interesting and instructive than to view landmarks. I won't have time to hunt up the Y.M.C.A. and take the sightseeing tour so I will stand around and watch the people who pass. They are always a study.

MARCH 5, WEDNESDAY   I came very near getting my Croix de Guerre last evening. I stopped a team. I don't think they had any intention of running till some people along the sidewalk began yelling at them. They were not hard to stop so I didn't wait for the honors.

This morning I drifted around till I came to the market place and I spent an hour or two looking things over.

I saw everything there good to eat and some things I didn't think were good. The venders were lined up with their wares on either side of the street. The little stores had their goods displayed in front till there was scarce room to get along the sidewalk. Every seller was a specialist in one article. One man sold nothing but corks. There were snails (So it's true they eat snails) and a hundred different kinds of fish. All kinds of meat even to ghastly looking calf heads cut in two. There were all kinds of smells each place had its own odor. Most prominent was the cheese monger where was much limberger.

All classes of people seemed to be there. Thin faced hungry looking women squatty old bags, well dressed beauties, soldiers, and all buying their goods in little dabs. I watched a very attractive woman buying oysters from a dirty potman and she was arguing about the price (I suppose). I noticed her because she wore a costly fur coat.

I sat for a while in one of those sidewalk cafes. I didn't know what those side walk restaurants [were like]. I didn't know what to order so when the waiter asked me a question I said "oui" (yes) and the result was a glass of some stuff I could scarce drink. I sat there an hour or so and watched the people pass. Many soldiers with many garbs mostly officers. I didn't know there were so many different kinds of allied uniforms.

I did not get to visit a "Y." The truth is I was lost all the while. I had the addresses but I could not even pronounce the names much less find the places. The "Y" is there and no doubt doing a good work.

At 12:30 I started with my pack and reserve rations (a sackful) for the Lyons station. Some yank soldiers in a Ford picked me up and took me there. I found I was going the wrong way.

Montpellier, I found was down in the southern part of France and I had to buy a ticket 15F. They crowded us "simple soldats" in like sardines and started south with us. There was no seat for me so I stood till an M.P. told me if I wished I could ride in the corridor of the car ahead. It was a lst class carrying officers "Y" girls and nurses. There was a seat at the end of the corridor and I sat on that till we passed Dijon and Lyons when there was room for me in my own car.

About 9:30 an old lady nurse with two service stripes came out of one of the apartments and complained that she would not stay in there longer for the officers and nurses were behaving so badly that she was ashamed to be in with them. She may have had reason and she may have been a crank. This much is true. Nurses are not permitted to mix with the enlisted men so the officers have the monopoly. It does not concern the fellows at the front for they never see a nurse (female) and these are the first I have seen.

MARCH 6 This morning about 4 o'clock we got to Avignon. Avignon is a city of importance in papal history.[2] I was delighted with the place. The town was asleep when we arrived and we wandered for two hours through the narrow crooked streets before the people began to stir. It is a walled city but much of the town is with out the walls. When daylight came we found it to be a hotel town though I didn't see anything unless it was the general quantity of things that would draw a traveler. There is the old church where the popes held forth and that is about all. Things I wish to mention about Avignon I said it was quiet. Well, it was after day light but before I heard many cats howling at different parts of the town. The other thing is the place was fairly clean as we were leaving I noticed nearly everyone out cleaning the streets in front of their homes.

From Avignon to Montpellier I noted that we were getting into a country that was rocky and barren in places but in all other places was olive tree and grapevines. I never saw so many vineyards. In Germany the vines climb little poles but there they are trimmed down to a little stump about two feet high.

We were supposed to ride 3rd class and the woman conductor tried to get us to get out of the lst class compartment and go back but we shook our heads and said "no compree" and she left us sitting on the couchins. There were three of us in the same compartment and all coming to school. One of the other fellows was a Negro. A couple of ladies came in and one of them had to sit by the colored lad. She was a little timid but soon was at ease.

The French have a lot of African troops serving in their army but they never ride the couchins.

Now I am in Montpellier.[3] It is a town of about 75,000 perhaps larger now since all these towns have grown so fast.

The climate is fine. A lot of flours [flowers] are out and some fruit trees are blooming.

My greatest worry is over. I thought I was to be the only black sheep in the flock but lo and behold I find very few of the fellows have much French.[4]

Some of the fellow were put in hotels others in private homes but most of them at a place called the Petit Lycee an old school building. A bed there costs 25 f a month rooms cost from 50 to 75 f. Uncle pays the room rent up to 150f. I wanted a room but was modest to start and said I was willing to go to the Petit Lycee. Tomorrow I am to report to my professor and get lined up with work.

One great grief in this town is to find ones way so many narrow crooked streets so the Y.M.C.A. has furnished each of us with a map of the town. Uncle Sam pays us $2.00 a day to eat on. I was referred to a restaurant where the charge is 6 franc a day. They serve the meals in courses with long rests between. I don't know whether I like the system or not but I am told it is French.

They say this school has a great medical faculty and there are a couple of big hospitals here including the military hospital. For that reason there are many crippled soldiers. Already I have seen a hundred or more French soldiers with legs or arms missing.

I think I will be well pleased here. I am told we are the first yanks in the place.

13

SCHOOL IN MONTPELLIER,
MARCH–APRIL 1919

THE SIXTEEN WEEKS NELS ANDERSON SPENT ATTENDING CLASSES IN Montpellier offer a stark contrast to the weeks of war in France and the occupation in Germany. To be sure, the five hundred American students in Montpellier were still soldiers and subject to the drudgeries of inspections, guard duty, a two-class system of officers and enlisted men, army regulations, censorship, and bureaucracy. Anderson struggled to learn French, as did most Americans, and, though a careful manager of his finances, money was a constant worry. Yet the classes he attended, the cultural events that Montpellier afforded, the warm welcome given the Americans by the French, and the civilian friends he made, offered Anderson a unique opportunity to immerse himself in the waters of a European intellectual community and social life that only a few American soldiers received.

MARCH 7, FRIDAY   Imagine a yank soldier eating at table with a napkin under his chin, a maid bringing his chow in courses and plenty of clean dishes each time. If I could send a picture of myself to the boys back in the outfit and let them see me while they were standing in the mess line waiting for slew they would all faint.

The Y.M.C.A. has set up a little cafeteria out at the Petit Lycee where they serve a roll and cocoa for half a franc. The French eat no breakfast just have a roll and coffee. So the Y serves us birds who roost at the Lycee. I can see that my francs are not going to last long. I paid for a week's board 2 meals a day/42 francs 20 francs for 40 breakfasts at the "Y" and 25 francs for room or bed rather at the Lycee.

After breakfast they lined us up and gave us a lot of orders read some menu about our glorious record and how we should conduct ourselves told us that we must not forget that we are still in the army.

This afternoon I went out and hunted up the place to register it was [at] the university and the prof I was to see was a "Y" man. He lined me up for my classes I am to take special French and Political Economy as a side line for appearance's sake.

I visited one of my classes it is by a French man who taught French in England. He is a "bear cat" and knows more about our english grammer [sic] than we do.

This is a co-educational institution and many of the young ladies speak English so that will help the yanks to have a good opinion of the place. They are very willing to go out of their way to help us—and visa versa.

We are going to have a great deal of liberty here of course there will be a lot of army regulations that will bore us at times but on the whole we are going to enjoy many privileges which I hope won't be abused.[1] One man an officer has already been sent home. He had a room with a good family and brought a woman in from the streets. He was on his way "toot sweet."

We are to have a big reception down at the theatre tonight. I shall go if I can find my way. These streets are more than I can figure out. They are all crooked and many of them are too narrow for a wagon to go down. Some of them have sidewalks but in the narrowest the side walks are reduced to mere curbs. The narrow streets are called "Rues" and the wide ones with trees on are "boulevards."

MARCH 8, SATURDAY   We had a fine time last night at the reception in the theatre. It started at 9:00 and lasted till 12 bells. I came home earlier than that however. I was not drinking and after the programme that was the only thing that took place. All kinds of choice drinks were passed around freely and as freely drank. Before I left many of the fellows and some of the new students were feeling good.

All the notables of town were there including many French officers. I talked to several French civilians and officers who spoke English. One French lad introduced me to his sister and Aunt and I am to call tomorrow. There were some speeches made though I did not get close enough to hear. No one seemed interested in the speeches. Capt. Morgan our Commandant made a talk. Of course everyone applauded for all the speeches whether they heard or not. Some Jugo-Slav [Yugoslavian] students sang some songs (quartet) it was as good as I have heard though I knew not a word. The French Students all came out with different colored tam-o-shanter hats on. Each nationality here has its own class and colors. This morning some of our boys found they came home with Jugo-Slave [*sic*] student caps on. Band played American music.

This morning I went to my Political Economy class. It is a mixed class yanks and French. When the Professor came in with his robe of many colors all the students rose till he was seated.[2] They stood again when he rose to leave the room. Most of his lecture went over my head but I think in time I will understand him for he speaks slowly and thoughtfully. After class I talked with an Australian who understands French and he says that the professor is considered one of the best in France. The Australian was an Oxford student down here for his health he still wore the uniform and the government was sending him to school. I think his days are numbered he had his chest caved in in action and his 4 wound stripes told of other engagements.

I visited two French classes today and neither of the teachers speak English. One is a very quiet patient lady and the other an infectious gesticulating little fat man. He speaks in a high keyed voice and acts out all his words. His patience is very limited.[3]

MARCH 9, SUNDAY   This forenoon I studied French very patiently but can't see that I am gaining any ground.

This afternoon I went out to visit the people I met the other night. I found them to be a well to do family living in a beautiful chateau. They had many servants and even a watch man at the gate who hailed me and rang a bell to let the people at the house know some one was coming. A servant met me at the door and took me in to the presence of the family just like in the stories. I found the family to be the leavings of some old family that looked far into the past. I saw a lot of pictures on the walls of soldiers (officers) of long ago also priests and gallant ladies and gentlemen which I was told were members of the family so I concluded that the family boasts blue blood. The present head of the family is a major in the regular army. They also had a fine collection of antiques and a good library.

I started out to the officers tennis court with the girl and her brother. The court was being used so we came back. I was glad for I don't play the game. They said that they would have their own court but "Papa couldn't afford it." I asked the boy (a husky chap of 18) why he didn't do it. He said he would but "papa couldn't afford it." I saw that he couldn't think of doing work only in terms of servants so I gave up.

They were sure good to me and I enjoyed myself because they spoke English. Many French study English since the war. It is popular they study

German too. It is necessary. There are several members in the family. The aunt I spoke of is a widow. Her husband was killed in the war. He was a captain.

I must mention something the girl said that shows how void they are of puritanic modesty. I asked her how large the family was and this the reply. "We are five now but we will soon be six." Her mother was present too and never raised an eyebrow.

There is a custom in this country I must mention. Respectable girls do not go out with men without a chaperone.

MARCH 10   Last eve I went to a picture show. I enjoyed everything but the pictures I could not read the writing in French so it was hard to follow the plot. Though I didn't think there was much plot. It was the same old eternal triangle—two men and a woman. They serve their pictures here like they do the meals. Between reels they have rests and the people go out and smoke or promenade.

At 5:00 this evening the faculty of the University entertained us to a very interesting program consisting of speeches in French and one in English. The "Y" man, Prof. Plaisance, who is Dean for the Yanks responded in French.

They have a cozy little hall with three great paintings that interested me. The Pro[fessor] who spoke English told us what they meant. Each painting was about 40 ft long and 10 ft high. The two historic ones was the Pope giving the Bull that established the University and the other was of its 600 anniversary in 1909 when Prof Adams of Cornell and 2 other American Professors visited.[4] In it are shown students from all countries. For all nations come here.

Now a word about the faculty. They came out in all their glory even Solomon would have been out shone and the coat of many colors that used to be the boast of Joseph would have been surpassed by the splendor of the gowns the professors wore.

The Rector wore purple trimmed with white and black. Others wore black trimmed with red and white ermine and yellow with white. Each type of gown for different professions and different degrees of scholarship. They told us that the different details of the gowns stood for events in history. The doctors here wear a gown unlike any other place as a reward for some great service. Most of them were old and bearded. One had to be led in. Most of them had medals. One had a great star hung around his neck it was inlaid with diamonds.

They organized all the students in companies. They can handle them better that way. They divided us into squads with an officer at the head of each squad. Chaplin Moore is my squad leader.

MARCH 11, MARDI [TUESDAY]   I only had one class today and I got little out of it because the teacher speaks only French. It is the lady. She is a good teacher however.

This afternoon I went down to the Alicot Villa where I was Sunday. We had tea and buttered toast. It is easier to drink tea and wine in this country than to explain why one does not drink it. I spent a very pleasant afternoon out there. The young widow insisted on giving me "ze lezzone" so I spent an hour or more trying to pronounce the French u. It is very difficult for yanks to get we speak with a different twist of the tongue. The widow says we eat our words.

I feel good tonight. I got a bath and a hair cut. Hair cut only costs a dime here, it is the only cheap thing I've found.

The men have been greatly wrought up of late over an order that is out. We are not allowed to be seen on the streets with girls out of the regular French customs. That means a chaperone. Well on the strength of those orders the M.P.s have separated several couples and some of the girls were of prominent families and naturally took offence. The order is of course to prevent the fellows from promenading with vampires for such would make us lose out with the best people we get a chance to meet.

A bunch of fellows went to the Captain and the result is we can walk with a girl provided we conduct ourselves properly. Everyone feels better already.

I have been writing some letters today to sort of catch up.

It seems that the peace conference is at a standstill. Nothing in the papers of interest not even anything about shipping the troops home.

MARCH 12   These people seem to live a great deal in the past. They all boast of their past all the towns and institutions if they have a past point to it with pride. They measure the value of things by the years it can boast. This University has 600 years of past and that to my mind is a terrible thing. They spend too much thought on the past and too little on the future. Everything one comes in contact with here the statues the bearded professors with their robes and the handwriting on the wall throws around one an atmosphere of long ago. Probably they think that the future will come along anyway so they

concern themselves with the yesterdays of things. That is one of the funda-
mental causes for so much international hatred and jealousy over here. I am
glad I came from a country with only a future.

It has been rather cold today. I have no place to go study so I have been
rather uncomfortable.

I write to the bank for $50.00 to pay my tuition and then I dropped a
few lines to the White & Blue at the B.Y.U.

The Y.M.C.A. hostess gave a tea for the yanks and their French friends.
Many French people were there. Some of the French girls sang (in English)
some of our popular Yank songs as "Be-e-eautiful Katy" and "I want to go
Back."

I see that the war council has decided to cut the German army down to
100,000 men with 12 years voluntary enlistment and no forts on the Rhine.
The rest ought to follow suit.

MARCH 13, THURSDAY   My tuition at the University is costing me 250
francs. I paid 25 f down today. It would only cost me 30 francs if I knew
French. So much for ignorance.

I wrote to Mr. Prescott and suggested that Frank H. Simon[d]s was a pes-
simist and that if he and other writers who are writing hateful things and
turn their attention to reconstruction it would help get our minds off the
horrors of war. We can get the lessons of the war without studying out new
means of hating the enemy. We ought to go the limit in justice but lets not
dabble with revenge.

I promenaded today. Promenading is a favorite sport here. It means to get
out and walk the streets and parks. Everyone promenades. There is scarcely a
horse or automobile in sight when the people promenade. In this country
the people seem to have two holidays Sunday and Thursday that is the reason
there is no school today. So I picked up a little French boy and together we
walked about all the afternoon and "parley vooed."

Much wind but the sun is shining. We are in sight of the sea hence the
wind.

MARCH 14   I met a couple of Utah fellows today who are here to school.
One is Jesse Weight from Spring[ville], the other Hal Hales from Spanish
Fork.[5] Both old B.Y. students. They were in the radio service with the 82nd
div. Also met a fellow from Lt Bushman's company. He says that Bush did not
have a chance to put in his application.

I visited the University library today and met a lot of surprises. Evidently a library is not much of a drawing card in these schools. They don't have over 10,000 volumes and they [are] big dust covered books. Some old men in charge and only six people using the library. 2 yanks, a chinaman 2 women (French) and a man (French). The only books that looked like they had seen service were the French-Latin, French-English, French-German and French-Spanish dictionaries. It was a cold cheerless place and I am told it is only open 2 hours a day 4 days a week.

MARCH 15   They put me on a detail this morning to clean up around the Petit Lycee. The principal reason I am on it is because I am a private. The privates are doing all the work nearly about the place and they are being out numbered by non coms who get out of everything. It is my first time to serve. Some poor fellows have had to work everyday. The work is of little consequence but it is not fair to put it all on one group of men and they the minority. It forces them to miss more than their share of classes and they have to pay as much as the fellow who does not work. We are not soldiering now we are students and it is not American to pick on any one group of men when we ought to be on the same level. We can have discipline and justice but let us do away with disrespect for lower ranks. Because certain men hold better positions in the army than others is no argument that some of the lower dogs have not got capacity. They tell us that we came over to make the world safe for democracy yet we tolerate such undemocratic practices to exist in our army.

I am just about discouraged with the French language. The more I study the more hopeless it seems. I am with the Americans too much. I shall try to get in touch with some French people more. I will get a room if I can and am permitted to move.

MARCH 16, SUNDAY   I am over the grouch I had on yesterday. Things have changed a little since then. One of the companies tried to fill out the guard roster and could not for there was not privates enough in the company, so the powers that be decided to put all enlisted on the list so sergeants are walking guard today. And Non coms will walk with the Bucks tomorrow. I am on guard today. It is not much of a task. Just saunter around the streets with a band U.P. on the arm and see that yanks deport themselves properly. We have no guard house and no orders as to what to do so we are to use our own judgment or keep out of sight.

I was guarding the restricted district. That is where the fast ladies range. All the fast ladies are not there but it is necessary to have a restricted district. It is an army tradition so we have our restricted district. I toured about the district this morning. It covers about 10 blocks or 4 yank blocks and I must confess I did not see anything there to interest anyone. The women were all old stars that were far on the down hill move. They stood around in the streets soliciting and begging cigarettes or trying to look pretty. I didn't see one that had a charm. The real dangerous are those over in the best part of town. They have many charms or wiles, which ever is right and they are they who get the money from our boys.

It was a terribly windy day the dust was so thick at times that I had to get under shelter. The result is my eyes are about to fail me.

MARCH 17   I had to meet this morning and march with yesterdays guard down to the Peyron [meaning unclear; perhaps Montpellier's Place Royale du Peyrou] where they lined us up facing the new guard. Our officer saluted the officer of the new guard and they dismissed us. It took nearly an hour. I missed my breakfast and was late to class. We were all pretty sour about it and one of the fellows said that that was the best way to find out how the soldiers stood if they run an army man for president. After every war we have had the people have elected an army man for president. I hope it is not repeated.

All my spare time I wandered around town trying to find a place to get a room. I didn't find a room but I did find a place where I took tea with a lady and her daughter. The girl spoke English. There is a boy there who also speaks some. Another fellow spoke a little German as I did so we passed the time very pleasantly. I am to return for tea Thursday when the English speaking lad will go with me to help me find a room. There are many rooms in town but the best places are not advertised. The others have signs out.

MARCH 18, TUESDAY   I am dropping into a rut of sameness about the same things happen every day in about the same way and at the same time. I did however miss a class today. That will not happen everyday if it does out I go.

Hales and I had a talk today about common interests and friends known to us both. He has had a lot of sorrow since he came over. His wife died his brother (Josh) killed.

I put in an hour or two today translating French and I believe my batting average is going up. I am not as hopeless as I used to think.

They issued bread cards to us today. One can't get any kind of food here without cards which must be gotten from the authorities every month. It was that way in Germany. Although yanks were forbidden to buy any kind of food in Germany due to shortage. Some people think there is much food in Germany because the prices are low they should remember that the price is not governed by supply and demand but by the civil law and that were it not for that the prices would run wild and the poor would suffer more than they do. The price of soap is evidence of that.

My prof asked me a question in French today. I answered "Pomme de terre" potato and every one laughed. I saw the point when they told me he asked me to name a kind of fish. That was beat by a major last week. He was asked how old he was and he replied "Indiana." Many such happen every day.

MARCH 19, WEDNESDAY   I handled my French well enough today to rent a room. I also told the lady that I would not be able to move till I could have the place inspected. Not that it is necessary but it is military and its orders.

I listened to a very interesting little discourse by a lieutenant on wine and its uses. He was a second loot in G.H.Q. or something in Paris. He is known as "Jones'ey and edits our school paper. He told of how different wines was drank at different times of the day and at different courses of the meal or on different occasions. Then he told of the different wine making processes. The French are adept at making fancy wines most of which they export. The rich in America were good customers hence France is opposed to America going dry.

The how when and where of wine drinking is as complicated as the eating over here. I must confess that if I had to eat a meal from a bill of fare I would be lost. I take comfort in the thought that I am a star boarder and they bring the courses as they are planned by the master mind in the kitchen. She is a lady, and a clever cook. Everything always tastes just right.

Some of the fellows are spoiling a good thing down here they are sluffing class after class and getting others to answer the roll for them. The powers will shut down on us soon.

MARCH 20   We have venereal inspection. First since the armistice for many of us but it will [be] quite regular from now on. Men who become affected are not only court martialed and sent away but stand good chance of remaining till all the rest are gone home as they are put in labor battalions.

I was terribly wrought up this morning over this French money and banking system. It is common knowledge there that if a soldier gets ten miles away his money is apt to be no good. I had some French money paid to me in the army of occupation. I took it to the bank but they referred me to the Treasury General which I found tucked away in an upstairs of an out of the way street. It made me think of the bank Dickens describes in the "Tale of Two Cities." Well they told me I would have to go to Coblenz to cash the money. That was too much. I told them in good English that they were more tricky than the Germans and a lot of other unpalatable things that I am glad now they didn't understand. My present sentiments are that I will be glad to get to a country where a dollar is worth 100 cents from coast to coast. The "Y" cashed the money for me.

I got my squad leader the Chaplin to inspect the room he passed on it and I shall move headquarters there Saturday or Sunday. I paid 20 francs down it will cost 70 francs a month. I paid 20 F. on my board and now 10 F. is all there is between me and poverty.

Being a holiday today I went visiting. At 2 o'clock I called on the young lady and her mother for tea. We ate figs and chocolate and bread and jelly. Besides that we passed to and fro a lot of compliments that came from the lips and stopped at the ears. It's foolish but its French and I am afraid its getting to be American too.

At 4:00 I proceeded to the Major's where I had another invitation. It was a nice social tea and I should have enjoyed it were we not in such an elaborate dining room. Like an art gallery.

After tea the widow (the aunt I spoke of) entertained me with her war pictures. It seems that she was pretty intimate with aviators. Two of her brothers were aviators in the famous "Stork Squadron." They were killed. Her husband an infantry captain was also killed in action. All she has to show is their medals a watch, rings, coins, pen, etc. that kind friends sent her. Yes she has a heart full of bitterness.

She had some autographs from the King of French Aces whose name I can neither spell or pronounce now but he was a consumptive who had pushed his way into the air service. He knew he had not long to live so he planned to sell out dear which he did. She told me they led very gay lives.[6]

MARCH 21, FRIDAY   My name is on the guard list again for the 24th just 8 days since I was on guard. This is coming around too soon. I hadn't ought to be due for guard for 2 weeks yet as there are over 500 men here.

That is an ideal example on how a fellow fares and there is no come back. We can't even write home because if we register a kick through the mail the censor will head it off. The censorship at this stage of the game is all rot. It only will make the growling harder when the fellows do get out.

I don't mind belonging to the army. I content myself with the thought that the chains that bind the soldier are self elected. Later the army will belong to the soldier. I am curious then to know what he will do with it. Some of the soldiers over here have suffered a lot of injustice due to red tape and misappropriated authority. I expect to see many of those fellows when once more they enjoy the privilege of standing on their hind legs and speaking their sentiments, who will say hard things many of them probably over drawn.

I met a mighty fine lieutenant today. He was in the air service. Many of these officers are princes the snobs are in the minority. A snob has a splendid chance over here to develop and it is the few snobs (many of them men who never saw hard work or hardship before) who get men down on officers in general.

MARCH 22, SATURDAY   I was put on a detail to work this forenoon to work around the Lycee. I hung around a while and couldn't find anyone to take charge of me so I beat it. I learned later that we were to stick around so we would be there if something "turned up." All the Micarobers are not dead yet.

I moved into my new room today so am more comfortable and contented, for the present at least. I have a real bed that I have to climb into and 4 chairs to sit on. I have two man size mirrors and a few other articles. A beautiful view of the street. Street is 20 feet wide closed on one end and open on the other. I am on the 2nd floor there are two floors above me. All the other buildings are as high so sunshine is at a premium.

I regret very much that I do not understand my Economics prof. His lectures they say are good. Prof Gillie said he was here for his health else he would be in Paris. All the bright lights go to Paris.

Gillie spent the hour talking on things of interest.

He spoke of the great antagonism between Catholics and Protestants here. Even the children won't lend each other books.

I learned from him that all teachers here are employees of France, the state. The University is a great system scattered over the whole nation and this and other universities are members of one great faculty. The system he said was cumbersome and bound with red tape. He said that professors are listed in classes that ranged as ranks in the army. Professors of the same grade get the same salary no matter where located. He said that catholic teachers have been discriminated against by this administration, which is Protestant. It is not the custom in France to leave or will money to universities so they do not fare as well here as in America.

He talked about French morals and said that France wasn't as bad as painted. He said that we judge France by Paris and Paris is a city prepared for the stranger. In Paris they make capital of what the stranger comes to the place to find. He claimed that the resorts of ill fame were more frequented by the foreigners than the French.

MARCH 23, SUNDAY   Over here Sunday is Dimanche. It is a day of prome-nading. Promenading is a bore to me. But with these people it is a favorite sport. The great promenade is the Esplanade. It is a straight away park lined with four or five rows of great trees. It is about 400 feet wide and a quarter mile long. Imagine after the leaves are out it is a favorite retreat.

I have some bed. It is a little too warm and cozy for an old stick like me. There is a feather mattress below and another on top that serves as a sort of bombproof or lighting protector.

I went to a ball game today but it was a bore. No one seemed much con-cerned about it. There is none of the old college life here. It will not linger under the auspices of military management. Any system that puts officers in one class, non-coms in another and bucks in another will not suffer the good old democratic college life to express itself.

At 2 o'clock I went to the art museum. It is a beautiful collection of paintings and some sculpture and metal work. Of course I am no judge of that stuff so my observations are limited. There are several hundred paintings there and I liked to look at them but I saw many others that seemed to be absorbed in them far beyond my humble power to appreciate.

MARCH 24   I got up rather early this morning. I have no watch so I have to play safe and meet all my appointments an hour early.

I went down to the Petit Lycee to try to get the money refunded on my ticket from Paris—15 Francs and one weeks rent at the Petit Lycee that I did not live there but paid for. I got the Petit Lycee money but not on the tickets.

I like my work here in school. I am not picking up the French as fast as I would like however. A lot of good stuff is being shot by me because my ears are not yet in tune. I can't follow the lecture very well so my mind naturally wanders. I watch the students (French). Some of them have beards, most of them have mustaches and a few are clean shaved.

This afternoon I was sitting on the Esplande when a fellow passed and handed me a ticket to the picture show. I saw the St. Mihiel battle staged in California. The captain was wearing his Sam Brown belt "over the top." Neither he or his men had gas masks. Naturally the captain got wounded unto death (as it were) and the girl in the case happened to be johnny on the spot and under shell fire, carries him to shelter. They didn't seem to know that women are lucky to get 5 km from the front lines.

I read stories in the magazines as absurd. One author forgot that lights were not allowed at the front. Not even as far back as London but he had his hero, a captain (always a captain) reading a message by the "flare of the lights of his automobile while the enemy's three-inchers were tearing the ground around him." I wish Roosevelt were living so he could denounce such as nature fakers.

I had a French barber nibble my hair off today. It was so long that I was afraid to be seen in public.

MARCH 25, MARDI   I have a great time today trying to get a receipt from my land lady. I paid her 20 F on the 20th and moved in on the 22nd. So to prevent red tape I had to get a receipt from the 22nd. I had a hard time making her understand that I wanted a receipt. I couldn't pronounce the words so she could understand and she couldn't read the word in the dictionary. She wouldn't know her name if it were printed in box car letters. I drawed pictures and made motion and fumed and before I got it into their heads I was sweating and exhausted. Finally they said they understood and the old man went over to get a neighbor to make the receipt. When he gave it to me it was exactly like I didn't want it so I sat me down and changed the figures. I turn all my receipts in and in a week or so, perhaps, we get our money.

Got a very valuable tip today on deportment in French society. Never introduce one French friend to another. For there are people here who do not want to meet each other for religious or traditional reasons.

Lost my pocket book today. A fellow told me about it even before I missed it. I didn't have much in but a few francs and the R. Road ticket I hope to redeem. I got it all in good order.

One of the fellows at my boarding house has received his discharge and started for the port today. Lucky dog and unlucky too for this stay here is not without its returns. It is a good investment.

I visited a French history class today. It was taught by an old man, very bald and very gray. He was a little old bookworm type of man, as yellow as the old books in the library. He had no teeth so that altered his speech and then he talked very fast so I did not get very much out of it. I did catch the general drift of his lecture. It was about Louis XIV but it seemed that he rung in too much German history. He got very agitated at times referring to the Germans so I came away with the impression that his course was more anti-German propaganda than history.

MARCH 26, MERCREDI [WEDNESDAY]   I sluffed a class today in order to attend a "tea" given at the Petit Lycee by the student body for their French friends but especially the faculty.

I invited the lady and daughter I visited the other day. There was also a pretty young madam there visiting. She is the wife of a French officer who is in Germany at present so I brought the three of them. After the tea we sat around and listened to good old American ragtime music, there was dancing but because of my hob nail shoes I did not participate.

We got a good shower of rain today just enough to flush out the streets so the town smells better tonight. When the showers come the urchins seem to be too busy to beg. They like to play in the mud here also. Other times all one hears when he meets them is "goodbye—cigarette?" or "good bye—sing sing goom?" (chewing gum).

I am afraid I will have to cut out the polite society till I can get some shoes. They told all of us who had hobnails that if we desired others to turn in our name and size and they would get an issue. No telling when it will come so many of the fellows are buying shoes. I don't need shoes bad enough to pay from 50 f to 70 f for a pair.

MARCH 27, THURSDAY   The schools in France have their holidays on Thursdays and Sundays. This forenoon I studied but this afternoon the majors son and I went to a banquett given by the L'éclair in honor of the Americans. The L'éclair is one of the local dailies. It is a catholic news paper, not only that but it is the organ of the rich people and royalists here.

That is probably the reason for the many bottles of champaine that were served. A band of children dressed in white suits and tamoshanters furnished the music, or I should say the schoolboys band from one of the catholic schools. They had several drums of different sizes and different sizes of brass bugles or trumpets. The music was bombastic but it was pleasing to watch the youngsters try. But on with the banquette.

There were several speeches given in French and responses in French by our dean and commandant. All of which we applauded vigorously. Then came the champaine. Later the press turned out a souvenir sheet with all the speeches on and then we started for the ball game. I found that the major's son had taken too much of the bubbling liquid and we couldn't stay long at the game. He was very lovable and jovial but not noisy like a drunk yank. He is the first Frenchman I have seen drunk. They all drink that red wine with water. But it is not strong and drinking has become such a habit that they don't go to excess. Most of the strong high class wines they export.

On our way home we met some boys with a bicycle. I borrowed the bicycle and started coasting down a grade. Everything went lovely till I went to work the brake and discovered there was none. So I had to jump before it got to going too fast and doing so I broke one of the hand grips. After I got of, I noted that there was a brake on the handle bars. But what I wanted to mention was that I offered to pay but the lad would take no money. The major's son told me that the little fellow was of good family. We hear that term over here a great deal but "good family" does not mean the same as back home. They measure a "good family" by its traditions, or wealth or position. One can't argue that he came from a "good family" over here if he was born a plebe. We may get that way in the States but at present a fellow can get on no matter what his origin if he has push. I have seen some fellows live on the glory of their fathers but the cases are rare.

I took my French friend to the gate and left him. I promised to call again for I like his personality. He tells me that he is going in for agriculture. I don't imagine he will succeed for he never has worked. He never has had to for he is of good family.

MARCH 28   I had a talk with a French man today about prohibition. He explained that it would injure France if the States went dry. I told him that the United States were going dry because the people have learned that liquor is not a good thing. He couldn't talk my tongue or I his but he referred me to an article in the local paper written on prohibition. I couldn't read the piece but another fellow told me that among other things the piece said that the prohibitionist as a teetotaler might be classed with the anarchist Cotten [Cottin] who shot Clemancèau. Cotten claimed to be an abstainer.

I learned today that all meat shops with a horse head over the doors sold meat that did not "cleave the hoof." They have different butchers here for horses for cattle and for hogs. I am told that horse meat is not only good but popular. I have heard soldiers accuse Uncle Sam of feeding horse meat but I don't think it is the case.

I am thankful that I do not live out to the Petit Lycee. Those fellows out there catch the worst of it at every turn. I saw them get rounded up today for a detail. They get more work because they are nearer to it whereas we who live in rooms are hard to find.

MARCH 29   I am on guard today. Not much of a task now as we do not have to be on the job all day as last time when we stayed in reserve 4 hours and on post 4 hours. They have decided that the town would run along pretty well if we did not stand to but 4 hours. I am to walk post this evening from 8 to 12.

Mr. Gillie gave us a talk today on French morals. He said that France was more moral than people gave her credit for. He said France was not so puritanic as England but every bit as clean. He said London was more corrupt than Paris only London puts out her best side. He has lived in England 30 years and claims he knows them. He said one element that seemed to make morals seem lax in France was the rigid marriage law. There is so much cost and red tape to getting married officially that many couples just didn't get married. When the war broke out there was a great rush for marriage licenses. Many did not have a chance to get married and the consequence is many widows with families who can't get help from the government.

We talked about German in the schools. He told us that the war did not stop the teaching of German.[7] They figure it is necessary to know the language of the enemy as a means of self defence. I like that stand for this war is not killing German. It will still be one of the 4 great commercial languages and it is fanaticism to put a ban on it. Of course the Germans went too far in the states in using the text book for propaganda. But we could have the language with other texts. I don't care to study it but many others do.

If we are going to keep in the trading circle we must know the language of the people we deal with.

I went out today for tea with the people I visited the other day. The young lady from Tunis was there and she and the daughter played and sang. I tried out a few French words on them and they worked so well that I came away feeling well.

MARCH 30, SUNDAY   I stood guard last night from 8 till 12 down in the red light district: not the only red light district in town but the worse one. Yanks are not supposed to be down there and the University Police must keep them out. I had guarded down there before but it was daylight. It is different at night. They all come out like bats or night hawks. And the crowds of French soldiers and French colonial troops—Chinese and Algerians flock down there. Most of the girls down there have lost their charms long ago and now they are just about at the end of the rope though I did see three or four real pretty girls that I pitied. They were all out in the streets and they all begged cigarettes like the little children we meet on the street every day. It was not worse than some wide open towns I have seen in the states but it seems that the people over here take a more tolerant attitude towards the social vices. We are fighting those evils harder in America. We figure that our woman power is worth something and we are trying to eliminate those forces that pull manhood and womanhood down to the bottom in a few short years. To us social purity is a great national asset and should be guarded as sacredly among the poor as the rich. I went to bed last night proud of my Americanism.

This morning I went to church. It is a Protestant church and the yanks have permission to use it after the French have finished. Then many of the French stayed to our service. They seem to enjoy hearing so many men's voices singing. It is not a common thing over here.

Chaplin Moor gave a very good talk on the place of religion in future world relations. He talked around a very good thought. He said that if we would make the world safe for Democracy we must make a Democracy that is safe for the world.

This afternoon another fellow and I were walking in the park when we met an English lady who was a governess. She was quite talkative and it was very refreshing to listen to her.

After that I visited the art galleries and looked the paintings over again.

MARCH 31, MONDAY   A committee was formed at the Petit Lycee for the purpose of doing and proposing things for the comfort and convenience of the men. The committee is headed by a captain assisted by a sergeant, a corporal and a buck. That's good.

I note by the paper that my division (89th) has won the A.E.F. football championship for which I am grateful. It will please Gen Leonard Wood too (our old General).

I wrote a letter back to the outfit to have my mail forwarded. I have been here more than three weeks without a letter that is too long.

A fellow gave me a ticket to the concert tomorrow night. It is a 5.75 francs seat. I don't know whether I have a 5 franc 75 centime appreciation for music or not but I am going to give the hall a "once over."

Went down to the city officials for my month bread card. All ranks and classes of people were down there getting books to buy coal and food. I am not going to give all my tickets out at once because I might take a notion to change boarding places and might go without bread.

I have started on a big job, I am rewriting this diary. I wanted to send it home because I might lose it so after a lot of figuring I decided to write it on fool's cap paper and send it to Mrs. Nelson about 10 days to the time It will be a sort of disinteresting serial story for them.[8]

APRIL L, TUESDAY   I didn't stand formation this morning because I had a class but I learned later that the company was reorganized in squads and platoons. So we are getting back to the old form again. Some more strict orders about calling roll in every class. Some fellows are cutting classes again or rather—yet.

There is a new order out that every student must put in at least eight hours a day, so they are going to have each student hand in a statement each week showing the average and total number of hours he has served his "Parlous Francais" Imagine a soldier *on his honor* turning in less than the required number of hours. One fellow very aptly suggested that we are well named SOLDIER students with double emphasis on the first word. I don't intend to let these new rulings bother me very much. I'll put all my time in and keep out of sight so they won't get me for details.

I am more than busy copying my diary. Copied 21 sheets today. I find it is too bulky.

I went to the concert this eve. It was a sort of benefit. The Soprano pleased me if she did sing in French. She had wonderful control of her voice. The violinist played in French too. All I can say is that he had a delicate touch.

The Pianist was great. One of those long haired pale faced kind. He fairly put over a barrage a time or two. A couple of his selections though I really enjoyed. On the whole I was bored.

APRIL 2, MERCREDI   I am getting down to the practical way of learning French. I am seizing every opportunity I get of conversing with the folks downstairs.

We had a chocolate drinking today out to the "mad house," nearly every soldier brought some French friend and they had a very jolly time. It would have been better for me if I knew more French. I could not speak with any of my teachers who were there so I merely had to shake hands. I brought the major's family of course they speak English so I am all right. We didn't dance today because one of the catholic sisters died. There were three of them who used to be at the Petit Lycee when it was a school. After the students left they continued to remain. There are only two of them now. So I had to take the Major's wife and sister (the widow) and daughter home. I had to promise to call Sunday for supper and I am to teach the girl to one step and waltz. I never knew how myself. They are royalists of the old brand that have no interest in anyone but their own. They thought it odd that I patted some dirty street gammons on the head who begged gum from me as we were walking home. All these children beg.

I got a good letter from Major Black today he is acting commander of the regiment tells me that Captain has returned and is in charge of my company.[9] I am going to tell him when I write that I am glad I am away from the company. Captain Axon made me work one time against doctors orders and I was sick too. Went to a picture show this evening saw two French plays. In one it ended by one of the principals dying in the other a triangle love affair, all three of them got killed.

APRIL 3, JENDI [JEUDI—THURSDAY]   Had quite a talk with one of the Y.M.C.A. ladies stationed here. I told her of the general prejudice against the Y at the front. All she could say was that she was sorry but that we expected too much of the Y.M.C.A. I still think that the Y.M.C.A did much more for the S.O.S. Not only that but the S.O.S. had freer access to the good things in Uncle Sam's larder too. The Y is treating us fine here in fact just like the papers say it was serving all the yanks over here. I hope that the feeling against the Y among the combat divisions dies down.

We had some closer order drill this forenoon. Later I found I was on guard and didn't need to drill. Some officer is going to get the D.S.C. and they are drilling us for the occasion. It seems that he was brave in action and the powers are just finding it out. Now they are going to have 700 of us drill and train up so we can parade while they decorate him.

This afternoon they called all the soldiers out to the ball ground when they got there they made them stand around and watch a ball game that they had no interest in then they made them drill so for most of the boys the day was spoiled for study or anything else.

I was fortunate in being unlucky enough to be on guard again. They had me acting corporal of the guard. I didn't have to walk post but had to stay in the orderly room which is as bad. I ought to be out there now but am going to bed instead. It is 11:30. I am supposed to be up till 12:30 all nonsense.

APRIL 4, VENDREDI [FRIDAY]   This day hasn't been a very bright star in my crown. I don't think I learned anything and I know I haven't done anything either good or bad. I spent the forenoon looking for a fellow who would show me where there was someone who would tell me where to get my eyes tested. He told me that the French hospital did that work free for allied soldiers.

This afternoon Hales & I went around to find a place where we could get room and board. We found a place but they wanted 200 francs a month or between $55.00 and $60.00 That's a sample of French hospitality. They treat us fine but we pay for all we get. America is getting no charity from France or anyone else for that matter. We don't need it it is true we are a young rich nation, but we should not forget that we have bought with blood and money every bit of good will that ever has been showed us. France during the last 4 years while she fought for her life was fighting our fight and for that reason I don't begrudge what we have done.

I was passing a park with Hales today. In the park is a great statue of Louis XIV on a fine horse. It is the best bronze statue I ever saw. Horse and rider about 20 feet high. Hales drew my attention to the fact that the saddle had no stirrups then told the story of the statue. It was made by a famous artist just before the war. He was in a hurry to finish it and in his hurry forgot to put stirrups on the saddle. It wasn't noticed till after the monument was unveiled. Well it hurt his pride so he committed suicide. All the people are proud of the statue and all know the story. It looks very much like Japan will not join the League of Nations.

APRIL 5   We are to have a dance next Wednesday. It will be for soldiers only. No officers will come. It seems that they will walk different ways from now on. I don't know why but have been told that the last dance at which all ranks were present some officers complained that they were not having as many dances as some of the men and some other things added brought about the separation. The dance is to be down town and any soldiers wishing to go must hand in his name and the name of the lady he wishes to bring. A committee of French women will pass on the names. "Inspect them" as the fellows call it. The dance does not promise to be popular, for different reasons, some have no money others have no shoes and others don't like the idea of having to have the girls passed on when officers can go "uncensored."

My land lady handed me a dunner today. I can't pay though I owe for 5 days. The money has been at the office for 3 days to pay us but due to red tape it will be late. I imagine these people are afraid I'm a cheat. They couldn't write the notice so got a friend to do so and sign their name. I was trying to talk to the old man the other day. He is a shoe maker, a fine old fellow, but he asked me if they spoke English in the United States. I said yes.

I went out to tea today and bargained with the lady for board for 180 francs she told me of a room nearby. I went and saw it it is a fine place and if I can get permission I will move. This street is very dirty.

APRIL 6, SUNDAY   A big day. 2 years ago we entered the war. It is the day the church was founded and some people think they can prove that Christ was born on April 6th.

This morning I sent another section of my diary away. I also wrote to Alberta Crane.

Hales and Weight and I held a sacrament service in Weight's room. We had a good talk afterward and all resolved to live as well as we knew how. All of which did me good.

After dinner we were to have inspection but no one came to inspect me so I went out and hunted a lieutenant to give me the once over (or my quarters) I told him I wanted to move so he volunteered to look at the room I wanted to take. On the way to where my room was to be inspected he told me that he had taken a room on that part. He said it was on Cannan street No 10. It turned out to be my room. He came after I did and paid down. It was a strange coincidence but it was his by right. He was a good fellow and said he would OK any room I picked as I am looking for another chambre.

I got a good letter from Silas Bushman today. I feel sorry for Bush. He by right should be here in school. He is still trying.

Well we decorated the Hero today. I didn't see the ceremony. We were standing at attention. All I saw was the crowd at the other side of the Esplanade. The man decorated was a Lieutenant. It seems that he was wounded in action and refused to go back. He stayed wounded and in action for 10 days then went back. That is all there is to it. A yank band came down from Nimes and we did a lot of marching and parading to please the town folk.

After the decorating (I might add that everyone in town was out) we marched through the crowd to the Cathedral where the Cardinal was to hold a service. It was catholic and attendance was optional, nearly everyone went in for the novelty if nothing else as this is said to be the first time in history that a Catholic Cardinal ever came out and addressed foreign Protestant soldiers. I just got to see the old fellow. He is so old his voice won't carry very far. He was dressed in long red and white robes. Our glee club furnished the singing.

I had a very interesting evening at the Major's. I got to see most of their house. It is a regular dream palace. Imagine me walking with my hob nail shoes on rugs an inch thick. The supper was great even to the finger bowls. I know I would have felt more at home eating with the servants but I put on a bold front and floundered through. I was very cautious to make no blunders.

The principle topic was the League of Nations international hate and divorce. These people hate the Germans they have reason now but this hate is old it is taught to the children and passed on. This widow hates the League of Nations because it would in time admit Germany. They hate so intensely now that they can't look forward to a time when there might be good feelings between all nations. Hate hurts the hater most by casing his heart in a shell no love can pierce.

APRIL 7, LUNDI [MONDAY]   I tried to find a room today but there seems to be none vacant around where I want to be; near my boarding place. I found a very nice three room apartment for less than I pay here but I didn't have the nerve to take it. I had a good chance to air what little French I had conversing with the mes dames.

This afternoon I tried to get into the commissary but was not permitted because the afternoon was turned over to Medical officers. There isn't 10 medical officers here that I know of yet a whole company of men have to be put out because of Medical officers. When I was there there wasn't a medical officer in sight or any other kind for that matter but I couldn't buy anything.

Pay day today. I was one of the unlucky fellows who did not get ration money. I just got my wages, 170 francs, they made me pay a 50 f university fee so I didn't have enough to pay what I owe on room and board. One of the boys loaned me 100 f so I can get by till Monday when we will get the rest—perhaps. Some of the money they gave me is no good in this town. The

Y.M.C.A. or the commissary may take them but it's worth as much as they are worth to get good money for them. I had to smile at the officers who paid us. They had six shooters lying close at hand. That stuff bores a fellow. Also they had guards with drawn revolvers at the doors. We never saw that on the front lines or even in Germany. Captain Morgan tried to tell us today the he was standing good for bills in case we beat them. Imagine a soldier beating a bill.

APRIL 8, MARDI   This morning I went in again to see if I could get money refunded on my ticket from Paris to here. Nothing doing they told me I did not need to go by way of Paris. I didn't like that because I went over the route given me by the M.P.s. What I should have done was to get transportation from the R.T.Q. whatever that is. I never heard of an R.T.Q. till I got down here so I wasn't treated fair. I saw Paris and that little experience was worth the loss on the ticket.

I wanted to get some stuff at the commissary. It wasn't my day. Yesterday was my day but we were cheated by the medical officers. I went in and got the stuff and signed up as belonging to the company buying today. I have just about decided that as long [as] I play fair I am going to be out. I thought I was smart but since I have learned that half the men in the outfit are signing up with the buying company.

I was invited to dine at my prospective boarding house. There are six French students there they are a wild bunch. I am the only yank. I am going to learn French fast.

After supper I took the madam and her daughter to the "Cinema"—picture show. It was not good. A French humorous reel was not bad though it was a little to[o] amorous. I note that Charley Chaplin is very popular over here. In fact most American players are.

I spent the afternoon writing on my diary. I am making progress slowly.

APRIL 9, MERCREDI   I can't get eyes tested here by American doctors so I go to the French hospital where I got fitted up with a prescription. It was difficult since I knew so little French and the doctor so little English. I could not explain to him that I didn't use my left eye but wanted a glass that would help my right eye which was normal but weak. My left eye has always been the silent partner.

While I waited on the doctor some French Moroccan soldiers (Negroes) came in for treatment. The doctors spoke very harsh to them later a

chinaman came in he also abused him. The French seem to herd these colonial troops they have here.

It took most of the forenoon to get my eyes tested so I had to miss the
morning formation and two classes. Now I am going to send the prescription
in to Uncle Sam for a pair of glasses. They may not get here for a month so I
went to an optician here and ordered a pair of clamp glasses which only cost
19 francs. They will be ready tomorrow.

The hospital seems to be a catholic institution (There are many catholic
institutions here) at least there are a lot of sisters out there. I wonder what joy
those women get out of life even the young ones go hobbling around like
they were aged, and all the cares of the world seem to be on their backs. They
are bundled up in so much clothes, robes and one thing another I wonder
they don't roast. They wear big hats that look like aeroplane wings. That
reminds me I saw a great aeroplane go over today. It was a peculiar model.
Mother hates to see me leave here. They have cut down the hours we have to
study from 8 to 6 and from 4 to 3 on Saturdays.

APRIL 10, JURDI [JEUDI] THURSDAY   A soldier from the 6th Div by the name
of Shorts slept with me last night. He eats where I do and we have run
around a bit. He wanted to go on an excursion this morning and I got him
to sleep with me so he could get up early. This morning my land lady brought
up a note written for her by some friend, which she said that I must not
bring friends to sleep with me but if I wished two of us could rent the room
for 100 francs a month. I am going to move. She's a bore.

Yesterday a yank camera man came into a class room and took our picture. This afternoon we all met on the steps of the Parow, a park, and the same
cameraman took a flock shot of us.

I write cards today to Aunt Roxa, Bishop McArthur, Lottie Blazzard. I
get a letter from Sergeant Major Wissman who spoke of his gay trip to Paris
and the division making preparations for an early trip home. "Mother"
dropped a few lines written in German which I can't get now that my German is receding before the French. Harris wrote about Hd.q. being a Gold
Brick Squad. And Antillia wanted to learn about music lessons and living
here he would go to school.

I got my glasses today they cost 19 francs. I don't know how they are
going to fit for a while.

Boys take excursion to a nearby mountain different excursions will be
offered to students during the Easter vacation. I may go.

I talked to a man who wants to go back to his regiment. His division is leaving. He sluffed classes and formations for a week but no one would report him so he has started to study.

I write all day copying my diary.

APRIL 11, VENDREDI   I am eating at my new boarding place and I think I shall like it. I think it will be good for my French. There is an old man there (ex officer) very learned, speaks several languages and is studying English. I find my French is best understood by him. He has a son a tall thin white boy as active as he is skinney and very bright. He is always cutting some capers and amusing the table. He seldom smiles himself. The other boys call him Charley Chaplin. The first impression I had of him was that he was a single, innocent, spoiled child. Later (after dinner) he showed me some of his work and I decided he was merely spoiled or rather took liberties with his father. He is a budding artist.

I hate to leave my old boarding place, it was quite home like but there were too many Americans. Where I am it is easier to speak French than to try to make them understand English.

I am beginning to get ahold of the French a little. It is beginning to lose a lot of its old mysticism. I have some good teachers. I get a lot of good out of visiting classes. Was in one this forenoon when the camera man came in and snapped us. He darkened the room and then made a flare. It was quite an explosion and gave the professor quite a shock. He looked foolish when we all laughed. These pictures are for advertising of some kind and in both where I was they had us pose as being very attentive and the teacher was very eloquently "lecturing" picture show stuff.

APRIL 12, SAMEDI [SATURDAY]   This has been my red letter day. I have done nothing but think of the letters I have received that is all I can write about.

1. I got a letter from Clara. My hopes are high again I am batting .300. It may be the last I get till I get home. She can do as she pleases with me. I have spent three hours this evening answering it. It was 2 months coming and was mailed a week after it was written.

2. I got a letter from mother she seems to be getting along O.K. Says she is going to get married. I don't know who to but I think I can guess probably she is better married if she has some one who will be good to her and care for her since she is to proud to live with any of us. She advised me to get married and make me a home.

3. Charley wrote poor kid he is sick again grip [grippe] this time he has [bad] luck but is very patient.

4. Alberta Cram wrote. She is in the midst of her grief due to her mother's death. A fine girl, Alberta told me to be sure to come to see her when I return.

5 & 6. A letter from Minnie Whiting & Pancy McCray. Minnie said she was too lazy to get out of bed to write and Pancy said she was just as mean as ever. They were both my students. Pancy used to hate me.

7. Eva Q. wrote a very sweet note said that she feared the yanks would all bring French girls back and the girls at home would be left out. I wish I could help her.

8. I got a cheery letter from Roy Cox he is still near Coblenz and homesick.

9. Miss Theressa from Nebraska wrote. She has been my "marasme de guerre."[10] I think she is tired of writing and so will have to please her by quitting.

10. Mr. Prescott wrote a long interesting letter which I appreciated, he is strong for the League of Nations and Wilson. He thinks Taft may run again. I would vote for Taft against a military man. I have a sneaking idea that Pershing will run.

11. Where I was in Germany I wrote to a fellow in St. Paul for a German girl. Today I got a letter from him with his compliments to the girl. They were to be married before the war but have not written since. I wish I could get the letter to her.

12. From the bank they sent mother the $50.00 and returned the receipted check and a note that I had $61.38 left in the bank. Bro. Miles sent a few words of greetings.

APRIL 13, DEMANCHE [*SIC*] SUNDAY   I sat here in the room writing so much today that I got a grouch on. I finished up my first 100 pages today. Then I went out on the Esplanade to watch the people promenade. It was not interesting so I returned and went up to the place where I board. I met the old man who eats there. He took me up to his apartments. He has a regular curiosity shop. Everything is dusty and unsystematic. It looks like he hasn't cleaned it up since his wife died, if she is dead. I found out that he is a collector of old curios and antiques. He showed me some of them and tried to explain their significance. He has a miniature painting of "Mary Queen of the Scots" that he says is worth six cent Frances, 600 F He may be right. I know I'd sell it for that very quickly if I had it.

The girl at my boarding place I tried to spell her name but failed, but she made a cake or thought she did. She was very much elated and brought out the cake. It was a custard pudding covered with a coat of chocolat. I praised it because I know there are two things that must be praised a mother's first babe and a girl's first cake.

After supper I sat around and talked about the trip across the ocean and the conditions then I talked about rooms. I want to get another room where I can get my petit de joure included that is the custom in this country to include the breakfast with the room and dinner and supper are the real meals and are labeled the Pension.

Well we had to have formation this morning. I don't see any reason for it unless it is to show us that they can get us out on Sunday if they feel like it. They made arrangements for the excursion to nearby points of interest. Cost 30 or 40 francs. I am broke.

While I was loafing around this afternoon I heard some music near the Esplanade. It turned out to be the boy scouts. They had been out on a hike and were just returning. They marched like soldiers with a trumpet band at their head. People here have high regard for the Boy Scout idea.

APRIL 14, MONDAY   I have been in my shell most of the day. I didn't even know I had classes. I sort of got the idea that because the French were having vacation that I was also having it. I found out this evening I was a truant.

This morning I got to talk to the Y. Lady, Miss Lingle. She is a daughter of one S. B. Lingle who owns a resort in Michigan where we used to live. It is a strange coincidence we had quite a talk.

I turned in the name of the major's daughter to go to the dance on the 23rd. This afternoon I went out to the Major's and fixed it up with the old folks. It is not definitely decided yet who will escort us if we go but at present it looks that it will be the major. It is quite a complicated proceeding to get a girl out in this country. I hand the girls name in to the man in charge of the dance he passes it to the committee of French women who pass on it or reject it. They send the girl (and her chaperone) an invitation by mail. Then I take the girl if she gets the invitation.

This is fest week for the Jews and Jews in the outfit can get passes. Jews can get more passes than any breed of soldiers.

An excursion of regular students started for Carcason [Carcassonne] today to visit ruins. Come back tomorrow. I may go to some of those nearby towns to see roman ruins. I am not particularly interested however.

Well I think I have a place spotted where I have a room. The house is being repaired. I will call in a few days. bien—(well)

APRIL 15, TUESDAY   My boarding mistress and the girl went away for a visit so that they might get the train, we ate dinner early. The old man, the commandant didn't come later and I ate another dinner with him for the sake of company. It seems to be hard for a Frenchman to eat alone. When the madam left for her 6 hour trip she bid me a fond goodby. More so than usual. Sometimes I wonder if these people don't get tired of shaking hands. I have to shake hands every time I meet them or leave. I even shake hands with the servant though it is not customary here to recognize them. I usually shake hands with her on the side so she won't feel slighted. I guess it's the plebian in me.

I took a bath today but couldn't change clothes because I didn't have money to pay my washing lady. I have been asking for credit till I haven't got the nerve to ask more. Its very humiliating the way Uncle treats us.

While at the Y today I ran across a book by a Frenchman on America & her problems. I looked through it and saw something about "Utah-Mormons" and the author went on to talk about the Mormon problem. His solution was that since so many of the children cling to the faith of their fathers that time alone would eradicate the evil. Being such an expensive religion the people would in time regard it as a luxury and drop it. So I know how I shall cease to be a problem in time.

Mother wrote says she is not going to be married that Will is in England Charley left home and John still in the army.

APRIL 16, WEDNESDAY   First day of vacation. I must pay landlady or move today. Looked for Hales or Weight to borrow money can't find so come up to room to decide. While I am hesitating the landlady comes and duns me for a Franc. I didn't have it and wouldn't have paid it if I had. She wanted it to pay for the oil I burned in [the] lamp. I am paying her 80 F for the room which is more than it is worth. I decided to move. I have no place to go so I am staying tonight at the house of my boarding mistress. She takes a sort of mother's interest in me. I took my pack up to the room of a friend (a simple soldat) for I didn't have the nerve to bring it here. It has been through the war and looks it.

I came to supper a little early tonight and found I was a little late for tea though not too late for the company. The company was the lady from Tunis who I took to the dance a long time back also her sister. A very charming but none the less, substantial girl who is studying science here. I only know her as the "doctor." We had a short semi French visit.

They issued Francs tonight. I was about despaired but for my patience I got 400 f even to hold me till the ghost walks again. I can look the world in the face now.

This forenoon while I was out to the Y. I picked up a copy of the Atlantic Monthly. I saw a selection in it entitled "The Sage Brush Farmer's Wife." Or the "Farmer's sagebrush wife." I glanced through it and noted that the author was Annie Pike Greenwood and I remembered that she is the author of our college song.[11] I read the selection. It was good, a series of letters by a farmer's wife telling in a clever way the wartime problems of the average farmer. It was if anything a little artificial and she daubed too much of the patriotism stuff on. There is too much of that.

APRIL 17, THURSDAY   I spent the day writing out at the Petit Lycee though my eyes bothered me a little and I could not work well.

The lady I spoke to about rooms sent me a blacked cased envelope (she must be a widow) and told me I could have the room without petit dynse for 70 F a month which is high without my "little breakfast" but she has the room and I haven't any so it's a bargain. My next trouble was to get the place approved so I hunted up a Lieut from one of my classes he took my word on it being a good room and wrote out an approval of the place that he had inspected and found O.K (absent minded wrote too far.) I went and saw the captain of the company he told me we couldn't rent rooms for over 50 F and sent me to the adjuent [adjutant]. I knew what I would get from the adjuent. "Bro. Theodore" I went into the office but he wasn't there so a happy idea struck me. All his consent amounted to was a bawling out and instructions to the clerk to change the address on my card in the directly [directory]. I went over to the clerk and had him change the address. So there is the lecture I missed. Half of soldiering is avoiding the bumps.

I came early to supper and the daughter had company. It was her friend the "doctor." I like the "doctor." She is quite a substantial girl. Her charms are not beauty but a very attractive personality. We had a good visit and spent the time watching them look at Kodak pictures of each other. The doctor is from

Tunis and showed me pictures of her home there. One thing spoiled it all. She showed pictures in which she smokes cigarettes.

We went to the picture show tonight. One of the best shows I ever saw. Called "Kristus" and corresponds to our play known as the "Holy City." The story of Christ's life. Some of the best scenery I've seen. There was very good music. Two ladies sang solos at different parts of the play that were very beautiful. Crowded house even aisles were full. I couldn't help but keep my mind on a couple of wounded soldiers who sat behind. One had arms off the other no legs. I sat between my boarding mistress and her daughter and they read some of the screens as my eyes were pretty bad. This evening when we got back my boarding mistress, I call her mother, bathed my eyes in some solution. I stay at her place again tonight and sleep in daughters room.

APRIL 18, FRIDAY   I was on guard again today. Guard here has dwindled down to less than a joke. No one comes on time not even the Lieutenants. No one cares whether the ball rolls after he gets there. I spent the forenoon writing and reading at the Petit Lycee till my eyes gave out then I came down to pay for my room. The other day the lady offered me my choice of two rooms for 70 francs a month today she wanted 80 F for one and 90 for another. A case of French foresight. No French man would pay that. He would do well to earn it. Well I got her down to 70 F on one room and I am in it tonight.

This afternoon I stood guard 4 hours. I walked around town some time bought some trinkets and spent 20 francs for a watch. I have been traveling by guess long enough. A fellow wastes too much time if he does not carry a regulator with him. When I got tired of walking around I went out on the Esplanade and sat on a bench. A middle aged lady sat on the same bench and we started chatting. She gave me her address and I shall call on her later.

Come to supper early tonight "doctor" is there. She helps me sew a chevron on my new coat. She shows me some pictures I [t]ook one of her in some African costume. She learns of it and is angry with me. It won't last long. I think she wants me to ask her again for the picture.

The Commandant's son, the long skinny lad I spoke of came back yesterday from a long ride. It was a joyful reunion. I like the boy he is so witty and original and he is affectionate too. Every time he comes home he kisses the commandant in the center of a bald spot just above the forehead. I have thought the bald spot is very convenient to be kissed since the boy is so much the taller. The father never responds not even by looking up; he even seems unawares.

APRIL 19, SATURDAY   Slept in my new room last night. Had the house all to my lonesome. The landlady will not move in till Monday. She warned me against bringing any "femmes" in to spoil things. I hadn't thought of it till she spoke. The forenoon I spent here in my room writing during the while two doctors came in and took the two 90 Franc rooms across the hall. One of them did not want the front room because the light was too bright for study. He wanted to trade with me but we couldn't make the lady understand so we let it go. So after all I will have a major for a Bunkie if sleeping in the next room makes him one. The other doctor is a captain both students.

This afternoon the girl at my boarding place the skinny kid the married lady from Tunis and her sister, the doctor, got on the street car and went about 4 miles out in the country. We had a good time and besides stealing all the flowers we could bring home, I made a lot of observations. I noted that this is a very dry ungrateful soil. In summer I imagine everything drys up. The grass is green now and everything is in bloom. The ground is very rocky and it is only here and there that one sees patches of mellow soil. Most of the land is into vineyards and is made tillable by having laboriously gathered all the rocks and built walls with them. The walls are built up with mortar and are about 18 inches thick. They are about 5 feet high and stuck in the mortar is usually a lot of broken pieces of glass. The fields are not large, from ½ to 2 acres being average, so one sees more walls than anything else. I noted that many of the houses on the little farms were closed so I suppose the people only live there a season.

The girls got pretty tired walking over the rocky places with those abominably high French heels. I wish that girls would some day learn that high heels are foolish.

This evening the skinny lad and I went down to the Café Du France. It is a long café (a café here serves only drinks) with all kinds of rooms and can serve a thousand people. It is a place where the gay women come to meet their prey it is also where the men go to be met. I saw all kinds of birds there from hens to gay old roosters. Many Americans were there. I then went in the billiard room where I saw a very clever billiard player perform.

APRIL 20, SUNDAY   This morning I went over to Weight's room. Hales came over later we had a little reunion and talked religion a while. Had sacrament.

At morning formation 10:00 they called for the money on the dance. It nearly took my breath. I got my ticket and paid 25 francs. Just think of it I wish now that I was not honor bound to go but the invitation has been sent to the major's daughter and her mother. I'll know more about the dance later it is sufficient that the hotel keeper knows he has us in a pinch and so he pinches he raised the price. Hospitality from the other side. I will have to deny myself some excursions I had hoped for.

I spent two hours before dinner and three after writing on my diary and still it is not half finished. Am sending seventh letter today.

This afternoon I spent a while up town visiting the lady I met by the Esplanade the other day. She has a perfect palace of a home. I shall know more of her later. She seems to be a widow. It was a good French discussion for she knows no English. These people are peculiar they never ask about ones affairs and don't tell of theirs. The people I board with I don't know anything about them they don't know anything about me. It seems that everyone lets everyone alone by common consent.

I got a letter from mother today it has been lost. Today is Easter Sunday or "paque" [Pâques] as it is here known the Y served us with an egg each. Y is good to us here. I enjoyed hearing the church bells ring today. They are chimes and seem to play sacred music that pleases.

APRIL 21, MONDAY   Our boarding mistress is gone for a vacation and there are left only the old man his son (the skinny kid) and myself. We talk French only.

Letters today good one full of news from Mrs. Nelson. She has a new girl. Another from Alberta that was a good sisterly spirit one from Fred Pearce who is in Canada farming. I took time to write to Fred and Alberta.

This afternoon I went to the Café Du France and watched the people come and go while there Susanne, the girl who used to visit some where I used to eat, came in. I was glad to see her. She was well dressed and had on a fine ring. I don't know when I have ever had a warmer more sympathetic feeling for a girl. She is soliciting for a living she looks upon it as a legitimate and more paying business than work in a restaurant.

Went to a picture show tonight on way home saw a fight. French officer and a civilian young fellow. Not much of a fight they just pushed and pushed each other around.

On the whole this has been a very dull ordinary day nothing about it to distinguish it from other days except that it was an Easter holiday and we could not get into the stores. It took me an hour to find a place to get some ink. In France they have more kinds of stores than I knew it was possible to have. There are three kinds of butchers, horse pig and cow, bread baker pastry baker Book stores and stationary. They carry their own line and no other. All the perfumes and toilet articles are sold by the barber.

APRIL 22, TUESDAY   We learned this morning that our student dance was indefinitely postponed. I am glad for two reasons. I can't afford it and on the other hand I would have had to go without a partner as tomorrow the day of the dance is the anniversary of the death of some member in the Major's Family. They told me when I went up to tell them of the dance being postponed.

Two more letters today. One from Grandma Lytle full of tenderness and a prayer for all her boys over here. There is room in her heart for an army. I must write to her tomorrow. The other letter from Prescott.

The principal thought [what] he had was the league of nations. He is in favor, so am I. He says it is an untried theory but yet it may be desirable. We are in the puddle now with the rest of them and we have to govern ourselves accordingly. Every time the world moves we move with it. We are bound together by many bonds that we like to deny the existence of but they are there none the less and it's time we were supplanting them with tangible ones. He lamented that certain Americans with provincial conceptions were trying to make the league of nations a political football. I hope they or the most of them give it more serious consideration for humanity's sake.

I wrote a letter to Mr. Prescott this afternoon.

This evening I went out with two French friends for the sake of my French. We went to the picture show and looked at French write ups and American pictures. It was another triangle a double triangle. A man and wife, a single girl go between, and a villain. The usual end, the girl spends the rest of her days with the love for the married man buried in her heart. The villain turns black and vanishes.

APRIL 23, WEDNESDAY   School started today. I half regretted for I think I was learning as much French by my conversation.

We signed the pay rolls today for rations for room and wages. I ought to get better than 575 francs pay day.

It seems that the peace conference had to bring Germany to time again. She tried to get to discuss the peace terms over at Weimar but the allies told her to send men with authority to sign up for the country.

I am sorry that there are some petty interests trying to assert themselves at the conference also some big country's that are too anxious to get away with the lions share. I wonder if harmony will ever come out of this chaos.

APRIL 24   No school today so I write, study, and kill time. This afternoon the skinny lad from my boarding place came up and we sang songs out of a Y songbook.

The boarding mistress & her daughter returned today. The girl was as happy as if she had been gone many days. These French are great home people. They don't see far from their doorstep much less France.

I thought I got a bargain today. I bought a razor strap. When I got up to the house and put the razor on I found that it was coated over with a kind of gum that rolled off with rubbing while under was very rough leather. If a fellow wants something substantial he must go elsewhere all these people deal in is trinkets and souvenirs.

Judging from the papers there is a great deal of unrest in the A.E.F. They are not getting the boys home fast enough. There is too much red tape. I am afraid there are a lot of men who have good jobs who are against seeing the army disbanded too soon so they are holding a lot of bugaboos up as excuses for a large army over here such as return of the Germans or Bolshevism and stuff like that. We can be a potential force without from 500,000 to 1,000,000 men over here so why not get them home. We hear a little of discontent but how much more would we hear with a censorship lifted. There is no reason why the censorship should not be lifted now that there are no military secrets to give away. We are all Americans and if we have not sense enough to write our own letters how will we know to vote afterwards. Write to Cox.

APRIL 25, FRIDAY   I am starting to drop in the circle. I study and plug and plug and study. Write a letter to Bushman, send off another section (10th) of my diary. This afternoon after class I dropped into my boarding place. My boarding mistress had company and among them my charming friend, the doctor. She told my fortune with the cards and sent me away feeling good, two ladies are smitten on me and I am to jilt the third so the world looks bright. I am to get some money and a young lady is to give me a surprise.

Well the peace situation is grave. The Italians are coming in for the lions share they want to close the Jugo-Slavs out of the Adriatic.[12] Wilson shut down on them he said that it was just that the Slavs should have a port of outlet. Orlando said Wilson's stand is contrary to European methods which is probably true. I can't see that it will weaken the allies any to have Italy out of it. Italy entered the war on a selfish motive. After she won her point she found that she had not wanted enough so now she wants more. The French people I have talked to seem to think that Wilson did wrong but I think he is OK. If the Poles are going to have Danzig then the Jugo-Slavs are entitled to a port. They fought as well as Italy and they suffered more. I note that Baker & Pershing are in Germany and reviewing the 23rd and 89th Divs. I suppose the fellows will be going home soon.[13]

APRIL 26   I find I am not bold enough [to] be a good French student. I shall ride my modesty and self consciousness down hereafter. I have been afraid to be laughed at. I have been afraid of the words in some cases. I can't call a young man a son a "fils" (fees) a manly young man doesn't appeal to me as being a "fees" and a mother is a "me're" (mare) it is easier for me to call a mother in law a "belle mere" for there are certain qualities of leadership about her. An eye is an "oeil" and an egg is an "oeuf". I can't pronounce them yet. "Pluie (plueee) is rain and "prouce" is thumb and so it goes. I can't conceive of the word standing for the thing. The French word oft presents a picture of something opposite. I find one must not try to reason out why things are called what they are. But things must be taken as they are.

The French are siding in with the Italians in their hoggishness if that is a just classification for the Italian land hunger. These people don't seem to think of the Jugo-Slavs. In their arguments they refer to treaties and ancient boundaries but not a word will they say about justice to a new people who fought and who need a door to the world. They like Wilson as long as he does not stand between them and their grabbing. Why they didn't know what they were fighting for over here till Wilson stated his 14 points. Now they want to twist those issues into all kinds of shapes or abandon them at their convenience and they want to have Wilson stick to them according to their own interpretation of their significance.

My boarding mistress told me tonight she had in mind a rich young lady who wanted to marry if I knew some yank so inclined. I told her that there were many here who would consider it but most of them were not interested in an unsight unseen proposition but if the average yank was attracted by a girl and it was agreeable to her he would take her without regard for her money.

I turn down a proposition to go to the country with the doctor and my boarding missus.

Some college has challenged us for a debate. I put my name in for try out.[14]

APRIL 27, SUNDAY   I have been in the army a year today. I have kept this diary faithfully all the while but I have decided to quit. The events from now on are ordinary every day events and I can keep them in notes which I will write each week. This has been the biggest year of my life. I am glad I have gone through it. My future will be richer by the experience I have had and the observations I have made only a part of them are written in this book.

    This afternoon I borrowed a pair of shoes and went to a party at the majors there were many young folks there and we danced and had a big time.

NOTES, APRIL–AUGUST 1919

AFTER NELS ANDERSON ENDED THE DAILY ENTRIES IN HIS DIARY ON April 27, 1919, he remained in Montpellier nearly ten more weeks socializing, making several excursions, completing classes, taking exams, and receiving a diploma, before leaving on July 1 for the port of Saint-Nazaire and the return to the United States. Under the heading "General Summary of important and lesser events," Anderson provides a brief one line—sometimes one word—summary for each day from April 27 until his discharge on August 2, 1919.[1] Anderson's comrades in the 89th Division remained in Europe until May 12, returning to the United States two months before Anderson.

Upon his return, Nels Anderson enrolled in the fall semester at Brigham Young Academy. Efforts by fellow students and others to get Nels to talk about his wartime experience and to view his experience in heroic terms were unsuccessful. He "offended a patriotic friend once when I...said that when I was at the front I did not feel in greater danger than when I worked in a Bingham Canyon mine."[2] On the first anniversary of the Armistice, November 11, 1919, while Anderson was a student at Brigham Young Academy he writes, "there was a program for the soldier-students. Some avoided the meeting. We were asked to don our uniforms. Each who came to the meeting had to tell of his experiences, some hardship. I had to say I could recall no hardship worth mentioning. Someone said to me later, 'I understand; it must have been too horrible to think about.'"[3]

GENERAL SUMMARY OF IMPORTANT AND LESSER EVENTS

April 27—quit diary—call on major's family.

28—quarrel with French about Fiume.

29—Take French girl & mother to show.

30—Read League of Nations.

May 1— "Reds" threaten to parade. Riot in Paris.

2—Weight & I giggle at French tragedy.

3—2 men shipped to labor battalion.

4—go to Agues Mortes [Aigues-Mortes]. City of Crusades.

5—Visit zoology museum. Dine out.

6—Visit old rich lady by theatre.

7—Pay Day 607 F take mistress to show.

8—Lie to majors daughter to avoid party.

9—Prof. dies is interred all profs appear at funerals with coats of many colors.

10—wrought up over insolence of German delegates.

11—Mother's day. Y.M.C.A. give flowers French mothers invite yanks out lady who invited me got sick.

12—My division sails. I note many women in sleeves.

13—Have been put on the yearbook staff.

14—Wonders & I are tead. Letters from & to friends.

15—All go to Cette [Sète?] 15 miles are wined and dined. I got seasick. Dance meet swell girls get souvenirs from French man see yank ship.

16—get book from Company "E." $50.00 from bank.

17—Sluff classes for year book's sake.

18—On guard, sit in office Write letters. Study.

19—Finish & send last of diary.

20—Chicago man talks on future.

21—Work on year book—Tea out with P. & S.

22—Study French go to Bible class.

23—Take French girls to Y show they can't get our jokes. French is getting clearer.

May 24—Get letter from a French lady (old).

25—Busy day go to Narbonne see its relics & antiques cheap trip.

26—buy yank music for girl at boarding house.

27—Write pieces for yearbook get letters Clara to teach at St. Johns.

28—T[ea] & dance many chaperones. French friends wish Germany wouldn't sign treaty. They would blow up Berlin.

29—go to Arles on Rhone River. Noted for beautiful many Roman ruins.

May 30—On guard. Take "Doctor" & pink girl to show. Sluff landlady and daughter.

31—Spend ½ day writing French letter.

June 1—Sunday charming girl lives across way we flirted some today. Promenade Instead of going to church.

June 2—Peace is slow in coming.

3—Meet girl across way.

4—Go to "Y" T[ea] Big crowd good time flirt with girl across way we both have field glasses.

5—Study hard, flirt a little, pay board, send souvenirs home Argue with Rich French on labor.

6—My pass to Nice cancelled.

7—[My pass to] Marseilles [cancelled].

8 and 9—Sunday Rise early take tram to and f Narbonne Perpign[a]n Ca[r]cassone Spanish Border & such.[4] See Bull fight at Nimes. Meet fine French family visit old Roman structures.

June 10—Change boarding places. It cost too much to keep my boarding mistress in society. Visit girl across way promise to take her to show but whole family tagged so I didn't.

11—Days hot Eves cool. Student counsel bucks yearbook staff.

12—Dull day Lecture on venereal diseases.

13—get last issue of Stars & Stripes, waste time on detective story.

14—Spend good day near the Spanish border.

15—Wrong girl back home gets serious.

16—V. inspection. Mope by reviewing stand.

17—10 day leaves cancelled. 3 day leaves substituted. I ask to go to Nice and Italy. Take French friends to show. After show ladies smoke. I shall go home single.

18—Forenoon visit Jardine de Plants. Afternoon partee on trip visit Avignon City of Popes go on to Marseilles.

19—Go to Nice City of dreams to Monte Carlo a fairyland, see many things am in 7th heaven of touristery.

20—Special Auto sightseeing all day too grand to tell can only be felt like a great painting. People here sell pleasure.

21—Back to Marsielles [sic] a fine city. I see most of it take ride around Isle of Monte Cristo see long straight street.

22—Back to school pretty sleepy. 3 day trip cost but 85 francs. Afternoon I visit great medical museum of the univ.

23—Only exams held today. We buy Mille. Charbonelle a Kodak.

June 24—More exams I get by Ok. Go out in country to gather flowers.

25—Big dance. Everyone happy.

26—We are hearing French lectures on French problems (????) [in text].

27—Officers and soldiers give scholarship tablet to U. of M. [University of Montpellier] Yank show evening, success.

28—Receive diplomas—Peace signed. Visit lady near theater.

29—Go to Palavas and swim take bundle to train. Dine out on chicken.

30—Last formation last orders, last farewells, pay, wine, tears. A sad dance and then that leaving with whole town out. We were well liked.

July 1—Travel.

2—Travel.

3—St. Nazaire uncertainties.

4—deloused get clothes.

5—Loaf. Read see show.

6—Wait buy lace write letters.

7–8–9—Wait loaf read inspection.

10–23—On ship good trip.

24–27—Waiting & cussing.

28–31—Westward Ho.

Aug 1—Cheyenne—red tape.

Aug 2—Discharged.

NOTES

FOREWORD

1. Nels Anderson, "Doughboy Diary 1918–1919." MSS 1299, L. Tom Perry Special Collections, Harold B. Lee Library, Brigham Young University, and an electronic copy in my possession.

2. Arthur Guy Empey, *"Over the Top": By An American Soldier* (New York & London: G. P. Putnam and Sons, 1918), 60.

3. Although he became a proud citizen, illiteracy slowed Nels Sr.'s adaptation to modern values. Throughout life he believed elves went about by night sizing up how one treated his animals and blessing or cursing farm operation as a result. See "On Workers and Their Culture," 1/24/80 Anderson Collection, at the University of Utah. The Armand Mauss Collection at Utah State Historical Society also has considerable Anderson correspondence and manuscript papers.

    In this respect Nels Sr. reminds one of "Bret," the haunted wife in O. E. Rolvaag's classic Norwegian novel, *Giants in the Earth* (New York: Harper & Brothers Publishers, 1927).

4. Nels Anderson, *The Hobo: The Sociology of the Homeless Man* (Chicago: University of Chicago Press, 1923).

5. On hobo work force as a second phase of the opening frontier see "On Workers and Their Culture," among other papers at the University of Utah Special Collections.

6. See Nels Anderson, "The Education of a Sociologist: the Autobiography of Nels Anderson," unpublished manuscript, Nels Anderson Papers, MSS 0122, Box 10, Folder 4, Marriott Library, University of Utah (hereafter cited as "Education of a Sociologist"). As far as I know, this exists only in a manuscript of some 350 pages apparently written in 1977.

7. See Charles Peterson, "One Man's West: The Mormon Village," *The Journal of Mormon History* 3 (1976): 3–13; and Klaus J. Hansen, "The Long Honey Moon, Jan Shipps Among the Mormons," *Dialogue: A Journal of Mormon Thought* 37 (Fall 2004): 3, 12–13. Among the best accounts of Anderson's arrival in Mormon Country was one made available to me recently by my good friend Douglas Alder, the "Joseph Alma Terry," Voices of Remembrance Oral History Foundation account of his arrival in Clover Valley (23–24) in the Dixie College Library.

8. Nels Anderson, "On My Being a Mormon," Paper delivered in the 1970s, Armond Mauss Papers Utah State Historical Library.

9. Anderson, "Education of a Sociologist."

10. Ibid.

11. Ibid.
12. *The Banyon* in 1920 shows thirteen graduating, six from Provo, seven scattered from Arizona to Idaho and no one graduating who gave a Salt Lake City address. In one place Editor Anderson says there were sixteen seniors, and in another twenty. Interestingly seven of the graduates were women.
13. Cited in James B. Allen, "Reed Smoot and the League of Nations," *Brigham Young University Studies* 14 (1973): 72–78. Also see "Education of a Sociologist," 179.
14. "Education of a Sociologist," 183.
15. For an example see Jerry W. Willis, *Foundations of Qualitative Research for Education* (Thousand Oaks, CA: Sage Publications, Inc., 2007), 5–9, which consists of a section on "Chicago Sociology, a label applied to a group of sociological researchers teaching and learning at the Sociology Department of the University of Chicago in the 1920s and 1930s.... " Chicago sociologists shared certain common theoretical and methodological assumptions. "They all saw symbols and personalities emerging from social interaction (Faris, 1967). Methodologically, they depended on the study of the single case, whether it was a person, a group, a neighborhood, or a community (Wiley, 1979)."

    They also relied on firsthand data gathering for their research.... Robert Park," one of Anderson's foremost mentors "came to the University after careers as a reporter, and a public relations representative focusing on issues of race for Booker T. Washington.... Whatever they studied, they did so against the backdrop of the community as a whole, what Becker has called the scientific." Anderson arrived just as this Chicago School was cranking up and was under heavy fire from more theoretical schools of thought and without too much in the way of published data to carry their case. In this situation *The Hobo* was among the very first things published and was seized upon eagerly by defenders and attacked vigorously by all others. As a new graduate student with almost no background in the formal aspects of the system he was at the head of the attack and faced major professional difficulties as a result. See "Education of a Sociologist."
16. There is likely a large amount of public data that documents Anderson's Chicago, New York, and Washington DC experiences. However, in interest of time and distance, I have depended entirely upon several of his own works including *Desert Saints* and his unpublished "Education of a Sociologist," and a dozen or so papers he read that summarize his career. On the Records Project related information may be found in Jerre Mangione, *The Dream and the Deal: the Federal Writer's Project 1935–1943* (New York: Little Brown and Company, 1972).
17. Education of a Sociologist," 198–205.
18. Ibid, 223–26.
19. See Nels Anderson Collection, Marriott Library, University of Utah.
20. Nels Anderson, *Desert Saints: The Mormon Frontier in Utah* (Chicago: University of Chicago Press, 1942), xxi–xxiii.

21. Gary Topping, *Utah Historians and the Reconstruction of Western History* (Norman: University of Oklahoma Press, 2003).

22. Anderson, *Desert Saints*, especially Thomas O'Dea's "Foreword, and "Preface to the 1966 Printing" by Anderson and fn 31 (192) on Lee's relative prosperity. The most prominent studies of the Mountain Meadows Massacre are: Juanita Brooks, *The Mountain Meadows Massacre* (Stanford: Stanford University Press, 1950); Will Bagley, *Blood of the Prophets: Brigham Young and the Massacre at Mountain Meadows* (Norman: University of Oklahoma Press, 2002); and Ronald W. Walker, Richard E. Turley Jr., and Glen M. Leonard, *Massacre at Mountain Meadows* (New York: Oxford University Press, 2008). The most recent study, by Walker, Turley, and Leonard, follows Anderson's lead reporting that "John D. Lee's total property value increased from $2,500 in 1850 to $49,500 in 1860, in part because of his industry but also because of the emigrants' property" (*Massacre at Mountain Meadows*, 254).

23. Anderson, *Desert Saints*, 440–46.

PREFACE

1. Edward M. Coffman, *The War to End All Wars: The American Military Experience in World War I* (Lexington: The University Press of Kentucky, 1998), 59; John S. D. Eisenhower, *Yanks: The Epic Story of the American Army in World War I* (New York: Touchstone, 2001), 25.

2. See C. J. Masseck, *Official Brief History of the 89th Division, U.S.A., 1917–1918–1919* (1919), 9; and George H. English Jr., *History of the 89th Division, U.S.A.* (Denver: Smith-Brooks Printing Company, 1920) (copies of these publications are available at the United States Army Military History Institute, Carlisle Barracks, PA). At full strength, the 89th Division numbered 28,105 men. Included in the 89th Division were two infantry brigades with 8,475 men in each. The 177th Infantry Brigade included the 353rd Infantry, 354th Infantry, and 341st Machine Gun Battalion. The 178th Infantry Brigade included the 355th Infantry, 356th Infantry, and 342nd Machine Gun Battalion. The 164th Field Artillery Brigade with 5,069 men included the 340th, 351st, and 342 Field Artillery, and the 314th Trench Mortar Battery. The 340th Machine Gun Battalion included two machine gun companies of 178 men each. The 314th Engineers included a headquarters company with medical and ordnance detachments with 172 men, plus six companies of 256 men each designated as Company A, B, C, D, E, and F. Other units in the 89th Division included the 314th Field Signal Battalion, 488 men; the 314th Train headquarters, 68 men; the 314th Motor Supply Train, 501 men; the 314th Engineer Train, 84 men; the 314th Ammunition Train, 1,341 men; the 314th Sanitary Train, 951 men; the 89th Military Police Company, 205 men; and a Division Headquarters with 304 men.

3. Anderson, "Doughboy Diary."

INTRODUCTION

1. Nels Anderson, "On My Being a Mormon." Address delivered at a meeting of the Society for the Study of Mormon Life at the Annual Conference of the American Sociological Association, New York City, August 28, 1980. Copy of address in the Nels Anderson Papers, MSS 0122, Box 10, Folder 16, Marriott Library, Special Collections, University of Utah, and Armand Mauss Papers, MSS B 1015, Box 60, Folder 6 at the Utah State Historical Society Library.

2. Nels Anderson, *The American Hobo: An Autobiography* (Leiden, The Netherlands: E. J. Brill, 1977), 2.

3. Anderson, "Education of a Sociologist," 160. Nels writes of learning about "the skeleton in our closet": "At the end of my brief home visit during the 1915–1916 winter holiday Father took me to the railroad station. During that ride, Father talked, the effort was very difficult. Finally he put it this way; "I want to tell you about Willie. I am not his father....I saw Mama crying when I went in a park. She told me she was going to have a baby....I told you because you should know."

4. Anderson, "Education of a Sociologist," xi.

5. Anderson, *The American Hobo*, 5.

6. In April 1919, Nels Anderson met the daughter of S. B. Lingle who owned the resort. The lady was working with the YMCA in Montpellier, France. See the diary entry for April 14, 1919.

7. Anderson, *The American Hobo*, 34.

8. Ibid., 41.

9. Nels Anderson, *The Hobo: The Sociology of the Homeless Man* (Chicago: The University of Chicago Press, 1923), 41.

10. Anderson, *The Hobo*, 61.

11. Anderson, *The American Hobo*, 99.

12. Ibid., 106.

13. Ibid., 112.

14. Ibid.

15. Ibid., 110. When Anderson wrote his recollection of the event in his diary for July 24, 1918, he recalled, "I found myself in love with the old man and in sympathy with the people who suffered such hardships that they might build homes out there in the desert where the howling mobs would not molest them."

16. Anderson, *The American* Hobo, 114.

17. Ibid., 125. Anderson recounts the conflict is his autobiography: "There were four children in the family, from Clarence, soon to graduate from the Brigham Young Academy to a girl about twelve. Between these two were a son and daughter. The house was crowded for sleeping space....Jimmy approved my idea that the unused chicken coup could be made into a perfect bedroom. It was a place where he stored things, including my tool chest and bed roll. Together, we estimated what needed to be done. I would first whitewash the walls, in the unlikely event that chicken lice were around. I would put in a

floor and a window, lead a wire in for an electric light and I would heat the
room with an oil stove. I would pay the cost, which would be minor, and do
the work myself. When the idea was told to Aunt Clara, Jimmy present, she
"bucked stiff-legged." Jimmy told me to go ahead that she would accept it
later. I did the work. With the extra boards I made a chair, a bunk and a table.
For me it was ideal but Aunt Clara could not shake the idea that I was bringing
chicken lice into her house. She suggested that I leave. I had no trouble finding
a boarding house very near the academy."

18. Ibid., 128.
19. "The Dixie." Published by the Student Body of 1916, 25. Copy available at the
    Dixie State College Library Archives, St. George, Utah.
20. Ibid., 58.
21. Anderson, "Education of a Sociologist," 134–35. In later years Nels learned
    that his brother Lester and Ione had a romantic relationship that was broken
    off by her parents because Lester was not a Mormon. Both Lester and Ione
    married separate partners but exchanged letters from time to time. In a letter
    to Frank Anderson, dated March 28, 1977, Nels writes that Irene's father
    would not let his daughter marry a non-Mormon. Nels Anderson Papers, Box
    2, Folder 2, Marriott Library, Special Collections, University of Utah.
22. Anderson, *The American Hobo*, 142.
23. Ibid., 143.
24. Ibid., 143.
25. Ibid., 146.
26. Ibid., 147.
27. Noel Iverson, "Nels Anderson: A Profile," *Labour/Le Travail*, March 22,
    2009. Noel Iverson was a colleague of Nels Anderson's in the Department of
    Sociology at the University of Brunswick. He served as Anderson's editor-
    typist and took notes of the many conversations with Anderson. This paper
    was originally presented as the banquet address at the twenty-fifth Qualitative
    Analysis Conference, "The Chicago School & Beyond," held at the University
    of New Brunswick May 21 to 24, 2008. Harvard S. Heath, ed., *In the World:
    The Diaries of Reed Smoot* (Salt Lake City: Signature Books, 1997), 424, 431.
    Smoot did not resign from the Brigham Young University Board of Trustees,
    but offered to do so. His diary for November 13, 1919, notes "I wrote Pres.
    Geo H. Brimhall of the BYU University suggesting I[t] might be wise for me
    to resign as Director of the B.Y.U. as my position on the League of Nations
    was not in accord with the President of the Board, a large percentage of
    teachers and their wives and the Student Body. I would do so if my position
    brought embarrassment to Pres Brimhall. . . ." Smoot's diary entry for
    February 25, 1920, notes that George Brimhall was in his Washington DC
    office for a conference. "He felt sorry for the action on the League of Nations
    by the BYU Faculty, Student Body and Wives of the Faculty. He promised me
    he would do everything in his power for my re-election."
28. Iverson, "Nels Anderson: A Profile," 14n11.

29. Anderson, *The American Hobo*, 157–58.
30. Ibid., 158. The term "file leaders," seems strange in this context, but McKay most likely was emphasizing that Anderson should demonstrate obedience to both church and school leaders.
31. Ibid., 158.
32. Nels Anderson to Patricia Madoe Lengermann, 26 May 1977, in Nels Anderson Papers, Box 1 Folder 2, Marriott Library, Special Collections, University of Utah.
33. Anderson, *The Hobo*, 171, 177. Reitman had spent time "roaming casually over the United States," and earning the title, "King of the Hobos" and identifying himself as "a tramp by twenty years' experience," who "still intercedes for hobos and guarantees their bills in case they do not make good. He is still a refuge for the sick and afflicted and not a day passes that he does not treat some down-and-outer free." He was also the founder of the "Hobo College," which operated in rented space in Chicago and was a place for lectures and discussion "at which hobos of serious bent would gather."
34. Anderson, *The American Hobo*, 164–65.
35. Ibid., 163.
36. Ibid., 170; Iverson, "Nels Anderson." In a more explicit statement to his friend and colleague, Noel Iverson, Anderson stated, "They thought that a man who knows hobos must know whores.... That was why I never got a job in [a] university."
37. Anderson, *The American Hobo*, 182.
38. Iverson, "Nels Anderson." Iverson goes on to note that Anderson also found certain intellectuals in the Work Projects Administration (WPA) condescending in their relations.
39. Ibid.
40. Anderson, *Desert Saints*, xxii.
41. Anderson, *The American Hobo*, 182; Iverson, "Nels Anderson." Anderson told Noel Iverson that he was guilty of writing and circulating a sarcastic jingle about the treatment of a secretary by his boss, Jim Grady, Assistant to the Director of the War Shipping Administration. Grady could not prove that Anderson was the culprit, but he "gave Anderson a poor rating, labeling him 'uncooperative' and 'arrogant.'" Iverson explains that "Anderson knew Grady was a card-carrying Communist (as were several officials of the WSA), who saw to it that his wife was hired by the agency. So when Anderson came to interview a banker from Colorado for a job with the WSA he warned the man that he would be wise to "watch out what you say around here, there are communists in the organization." Word of this reached Grady's ears, who called Anderson into his office and declared, "You aren't in tune with this organization. I suggest you resign." Knowing that if he were fired there would be a hearing that would expose Grady's communist sympathies, Anderson refused. Grady then offered Anderson a posting to Durban, an Allied shipping port on the southeast coast of Africa. But Anderson rejected the posting,

knowing, as did Grady, that Durban was about to be closed down, once the Allies had cleared the Mediterranean and opened the Suez Canal. Grady then asked, "Where would you like to go?" Anderson suggested the Persian Gulf, which he knew no one wanted—they "were afraid of disease and felt that the Arabs would stab you in the back. But I knew that wasn't likely to be true." It is ironic that Anderson, who found the communist presence in the government bureaucracy and in labor unions annoying, if not contemptible, would, during the McCarthy Era of the early 1950s, be investigated several times for disloyalty. Anderson mentions these investigations in his correspondence. See Nels Anderson to Alice H. Cook, 1 August 1972 and 15 November 1976, Box 3 Fld. 27; Nels Anderson to Everett Cooley, 12 June 1977, Box 3 Fld. 28; Nels Anderson to Robert Hinckley, 17 April 1967, Box 4 Fld. 5; and Nels Anderson to Editor, Greenwood Press, 16 June 1977, Box 4 Fld. 33, in Nels Anderson Papers, Special Collections, Marriott Library, University of Utah.

42. Anderson, "Education of a Sociologist," 273–74. Years later he recalled his first impressions upon arrival in the German capitol. "In some streets near the heart of the city almost every building was down, brick and mortar knee deep. Men and women were throwing the bricks to one side or the other. I knew that bricks have a way of wearing the skin off the finger tips. Many of those workers wore makeshift mittens of rags, their work was only to make a path through the street.... One impressive first member [memory] of Berlin was that of the drawn and empty faces of men and women picking up bricks. When winter came we saw hundreds of men wearing parts of their military uniforms, especially overcoats, permitted if dyed another color."

43. For a report on the general objectives, program operation, major activities, and projects undertaken by the Labor Relations Section, see "Labor Phase of the Cultural Affairs Program for Germany," August 20, 1952, in Anderson Papers, Box 1, Fld.3, Marriott Library, Special Collections, University of Utah.

44. Anderson, "Education of a Sociologist," 289.

CHAPTER 1

1. Jennifer D. Keene, *Doughboys, the Great War, and the Remaking of America* (Baltimore: The Johns Hopkins University Press, 2001), 9; Anderson, *The American Hobo*, 151; Anderson, "Education of a Sociologist," 163. Nels Anderson had requested permission from the draft board to continue to work as a teacher during the school year in order to pay off a two hundred dollar debt. It was understood that he would enlist as soon as the school year was over. Anderson preferred to enter the army as an enlistee rather than a draftee, but does not explain why he decided to enlist in the army. Later, in his diary, he implies that in order to have any future in politics after the war it would be essential to have served in the conflict. He does not offer patriotic duty or hate for the Germans as reasons for enlisting, though there is a sense that he did not want to miss out on what many considered the adventure of a

lifetime. See entries for June 17th and 29th. As an enlistee Nels Anderson was in the minority as, according to Keene, the nearly 3.9 million man army by November 11, 1918, consisted of 72 percent conscripts.

Many years after his World War I experience, in *The American Hobo*, Nels Anderson added the following details about his enlistment and leaving St. Johns. "The local physician, a Dr. Bowden, was himself planning to enlist. We were on friendly terms. I made it a point to visit him a number of times, using each visit to fix in memory the eye-test chart on his wall. With the left eye I could read easily the top three or four lines. When the time came to take my physical examination I got a perfect score for the right eye. With the left eye I was able to recite from memory the smaller letters on the lower lines. To me the end was worth even a sneaky trick." In the later "Education of a Sociologist," Anderson added the following detail: "When I walked to the bus station in St. John, Grandma Lytle holding my arm, my little bundle of necessities under the other arm, I was hoping for few to be getting on the same. What I had not expected, there were eleven other recruits waiting, each hovered around by two or more kin. A pair of handsome Mexicans were there. Other kin were trying to solace their mother. A high judge of that area made a little good bye speech and there had to be a response from the 'boys.' The chairman, perhaps of the draft board asked one and another to answer. All backed away. I, being the high school teacher, had to do it, saying what had to be said."

2.   Anderson, "Education of a Sociologist," 163; Anderson, *The American Hobo*, 151; Merrel E. Hixson, *"E" Company, 314th Engineers, American Expeditionary Forces* ([Germany: s.n., 1919?], copy available at the United States Army Military History Institute, Ridgeway Hall, Carlisle Barracks, Pennsylvania). Camp Funston, now included within Fort Riley near Manhattan, Kansas, was one of sixteen Divisional Cantonment Training Camps established during World War I. Construction of the two thousand acre camp began in the summer of 1917 and nearly fifty thousand recruits, mostly from the Great Plains and most of whom were assigned to the 89th Division, were trained at Camp Funston before their deployment to France in May 1918. Regarding his experience at Camp Funston and assignment to the engineers, Anderson wrote: "We were sent to Camp Funston in Kansas where the 89th Division was being trained. We were given about two weeks of token training. On the rifle range I learned the proper way to hold the rifle and to shoot from different positions, very necessary for one who never touched a rifle. We learned something about throwing grenades and each threw three grenades. We learned the elements of drill, very necessary if great numbers have to be moved; squads, platoons, companies and regiments can be moved about like blocks. Otherwise they are a crowd. I did not care for it but took it all in the stride. Before a week passed, while taking "boot camp" training the white-collar soldiers, looking at our papers were assigning us to different branches of the Army. To my great satisfaction, I was assigned to the engineers. As I came to recognize on the basis of later experience with the military, that

was a sensible decision, not often achieved in the army." Nels Anderson was assigned to Company E of the 314th Engineers Regiment which was part of the 89th Division. Just why or how Anderson applied for the Engineers is not explained. He did maintain a life-long interest in engineering and at the University of New Brunswick his favorite class was a course he offered for engineering students. Anderson was pleased with his assignment because, "The engineers were the least burdened with the nonsense requirements of the military."

At Camp Funston, according to Merrel, E Company "...received its preliminary training and was filled up to its full authorized strength with carefully picked men skilled in civil life pursuits which would enable them to grasp the duties of military Engineers within a limited time.... Instructions in modern warfare methods, Infantry drills, Military engineering and formalities was the program of 'E' Company during the few months of training preparatory for overseas duty. During the months of training, drills were so impressed on the minds of every man that they will be remembered long after the horrors of the war are forgotten."

3. Camp Mills, located on Long Island, New York, about ten miles east of New York City. Named for Major General Albert L. Mills, the camp operated until March 31, 1920, as a temporary camp for soldiers leaving for and returning from Europe.

4. English, *History of the 89th Division*, 39; Masseck, *Official Brief History of the 89th Division*, 4; Hixson, *"E" Company*, 6. English notes, "On the very day of the embarkation the story of German submarine activities along the coast of the United States was made known. In the few days preceding, some twenty or thirty small craft had been sunk by submarine raiders, some within forty miles of the harbor of New York. This was a piece of German terrorism, intended to delay and hinder the transportation of troops, as is now manifest from the fact that the cowardly pirates of the sea confined their attacks to small and defenseless vessels."

Masseck adds, "At the time of the sailing, German submarines had just appeared off the eastern coast and excitement was rife as to the possibility of an attack. The Division, therefore, got its first direct contact with the grim reality of war as soon as it had left the lower bay of New York; surrounded by torpedo boats and submarine chasers, and convoyed by dirigibles and aeroplanes, not to mention a staunch British cruiser, the principle convoy, some fifteen ships in number, bent its course for some unknown port in Europe. No attack was made either off the American coast or off the British Isles, the fleet reaching Liverpool safely on June 15, 1918".

Hixson avers that the concern about German submarines was warranted. On the return voyage from England the *Carpathia* "was sunk by a German submarine off the cost of Ireland."

5. Nels Anderson indicates that he wrote this introduction to the diary after he returned and that prior to his departure he had sent the first part of the diary,

that covering his first days on active duty, his training at Camp Funston, Kansas, and the journey to Camp Mills, to friends. This part of the diary has not been located, and it may not have survived. After his return and up to the time that he penned this introduction, Anderson had made no effort to retrieve the diary and it seemed that he concluded the diary had little value.

6.   *Their Yesterdays* was a novel written by Harold Bell Wright (1872–1944) and was first published in 1912. A popular writer in the first quarter of the twentieth century, Wright produced novels that outsold those of every other American writer. According to critics, his popularity was due to his publisher targeting rural and largely uneducated people and Wright's own skills of description and storytelling through which he took readers to unknown places where they learned about other ways of life. *Their Yesterdays* chronicles the development of an unnamed man and woman who were childhood friends, but had not seen each other since youth. Later they return to their hometown, meet, fall in love, and marry. However, during the course of the novel Wright describes the passage of each through the thirteen great facets in life: dreams, occupation, knowledge, ignorance, religion, tradition, temptation, life, death, failure, success, love, and memories.

7.   Edward M. Coffman, *The War to End All Wars: The American Military Experience in World War I* (Lexington: The University of Kentucky Press, 1998), 78. The Young Men's Christian Association (YMCA) was organized as a nonsectarian and nonpolitical organization in London, England, in 1844 to help young men find God through prayer and Bible study and to develop high standards of Christian character. Within a decade other YMCA's were organized in Europe, Australia, and North America, leading to the formation of the World Alliance of Young Men's Christian Associations in 1855. During World War I, the YMCA continued its mission by providing meeting places and personnel at home and near the battlefields to offer soldiers opportunities for spiritual renewal, counseling, and diversion from the demands of war. Of the YMCA and World War I, Coffman writes: "At the Y hut with its Red Triangle insignia, the soldier could find stationery and stamps or he might use the long-distance telephone service. At night he could forget army routine by attending a movie or watching the antics of his buddies at the weekly stunt night. Or he might just want to get away from the barracks, sit in a comfortable chair, and read a magazine or a book. There were also educational classes with emphasis on reading and writing for illiterates, naturally, conversational French for others. One private expressed a view many shared when he wrote, 'Here is light, warmth, decency, civilization.'" A less effective role for the YMCA was, at the insistence of General Pershing, the operation of post exchanges in France. This dual role for YMCA field secretaries as both businessman and social worker confused and frustrated soldiers, especially when the YMCA was responsible for the dissemination of scarce commodities through the post exchanges. This led to considerable criticism of the YMCA by the soldiers. (See entry for April 3, 1919). The YMCA also established the

War Prisoners Aid to promote the welfare of prisoners of war. Officials visited prisoner of war camps to determine the educational, recreational, moral, and religious needs of prisoners.

8. Keene, *Doughboys, the Great War*, 25, 70; and Coffman, *The War to End All Wars*, 80, 133. General John J. Pershing insisted on frequent inspections for venereal disease and did not permit infected soldiers to serve overseas because he did not want to have to care for potentially infirm troops in France. When some troops with venereal disease arrived in France, Pershing insisted that stateside security be improved. Consequently, once troops passed their final venereal inspection, officials refused to allow them to leave embarkation camps. Officials also closed down 116 red light districts and attempted to eliminate streetwalkers from towns near camps in a concerted effort to reduce the spread of venereal disease among soldiers. Once in France, General Pershing issued three general orders on the subject of venereal disease. Through publications, lectures, regular inspections, instructions to unit commanders that they were accountable to keep venereal rates at a minimum, orders to individual soldiers that if the contracted a venereal disease they should expect a court-martial and punishment, and, as a measure of last resort, providing soldiers with prophylaxis, the venereal rate was as low as less than one case among each 1000 soldiers.

9. Hoboken, New Jersey, is located on the west bank of the Hudson River across from Manhattan. Initially settled by colonists from Holland and the Netherlands in the 1630s, in the late 1800s Hoboken became an important shipping port and industrial center. Shipping lines used Hoboken as a terminal port and during World War I more than three million soldiers passed through the port en route to the battlefields of Europe. The soldier's hope that the war would be of short duration gave rise to the slogan, "Heaven, Hell or Hoboken...by Christmas."

10. "Feeding the fishes," was a polite but graphic way of talking about seasickness and its common manifestation of vomiting that was prevalent among ocean-traveling soldiers. See the remaining entries for the voyage—notably June 12 and 13.

CHAPTER 2

1. For a discussion of the role of the US Navy in the war see "The Navy Does Its Share," chapter four in Coffman's *The War to End All Wars*.
2. Coffman, *The War to End All Wars*, 229.
3. "Carpathia" www.encyclopedia-titanica.org accessed on March 1, 2010.
4. Hixson, *"E" Company*, 6. In addition to the 314th Engineers were soldiers of a Battalion and Regimental Headquarters of the 330th Infantry. The historian for E Company described the Carpathia as "a large camouflaged steel liner, one of the fourteen ships of the convoy, had braved the waves for 18 years and showed marks of service. During the thirteen days aboard the *Carpathia*, packed to its fullest capacity with three thousand soldiers, there were many

occurrences that will bring laughter in years to come to all those who shared the sea sickness, anxieties and hardships endured aboard a transport."

5. The *Titanic* sank on April 15, 1912.

6. *Lions of the Lord: A Tale of the Old West* was written by Harry Leon Wilson (1867–1939) and published by Lothrop, Lee & Shepard Co., of Boston, Massachusetts in 1904. Several of his novels were adopted for Hollywood films including the Lucille Ball–Bob Hope 1950 movie *Fancy Pants*.

7. Anderson uses the then-common meal designation of breakfast, dinner, and supper which today would be designated as breakfast, lunch, and dinner.

8. While declaring his intent "never to leave the U.S. again for either pleasure or profit," Nels Anderson did spend most of his life after 1942 outside of the United States, first in the Middle East during World War II, then in post-war Germany from 1947 to 1965, and then in Canada from 1965 until his passing in 1987.

9. In mentioning the folks at home going without sugar and white flour, Anderson suggests the meatless, sugarless, days civilians were encouraged to observe by the Committee on Public Information as a means to free up more food for the war effort.

10. The city of St. George and surrounding area in extreme southwestern Utah is known as "Dixie"—so named in the early 1860s when Brigham Young sent settlers to the region to grow cotton.

11. The modern naval semaphore system dates from the early 1800s and was first used during the Battle of Trafalgar on October 21, 1805.

12. The initials S.O.L. are used as an abbreviation for "Sorry out of luck," or, more likely in the army vernacular, "Shit out of luck."

13. Anderson, *The American Hobo*, 151. Anderson recalled with great disgust the food situation on board the *Carpathia* and in England. "The food was never palatable and never enough. One meal we had sour beans which caused running to the toilets and there were too few toilets. One meal was a stew of Australian jackrabbits which was negatively received. The British had no friends in our regiment. Our two days in England on a bread and jam diet left us hungrier still."

14. Nell Lytle was the daughter of Grandmother Lytle, with whom Nels Anderson had lived in St. John's before entering the army. In his autobiography, *The American Hobo*, Anderson wrote (150–51) that Nell lived with her mother in a big house. "Nell, about twenty-five who held, uncommon for a woman, the position of County Clerk, record keeper for Apache County, as big as the state of Connecticut.... At parties, dances or brown beans and chile cookups in the desert by moonlight, Nell was my partner."

15. English, *History of the 89th Division*, 40. George English described the need for soldier stokers as follows, "There was a shortage of crew in some of the vessels and volunteers from among the troops were called for to serve as stokers. The response was instant. More men applied than were needed. Although their commanding officers explained to them that the service would be entirely

voluntary and pointed out the danger attending their position in case of submarine attack, they gladly served throughout the voyage, receiving the compensation from the ship captain ordinarily paid for such service.

16. Nels Anderson was not wrong to expect that America's future political leaders would need a solid record of service during the Great War. This had been true following the Civil War as the era had been dominated by political leaders who had served. Two of the most popular twentieth-century American presidents—Harry S. Truman and Dwight Eisenhower—were officers during World War I, and their predecessors—Franklin D. Roosevelt and Herbert Hoover—held key administrative positions during the war. While Anderson indicates a desire to serve as a congressman, he did not pursue a career in elective politics though his time as an administrator during and after the New Deal undoubtedly benefited from his military service.

17. The keeping of diaries was, in fact, against army and navy regulations. However, it was a regulation ignored by enlisted men and officers alike. While some diaries were kept by soldiers in France, it is easy to understand why, under battlefield conditions, it was such a difficult endeavor and why so few diaries were kept.

18. Nels maintains a regular correspondence with Mr. Prescott. He does not identify him by first name, but subsequent entries indicate he was from Nels's home area of Elk Rapids, Michigan.

19. The unnamed girl is identified as Theresa Mack in Anderson's October 18, 1918, entry. However, there is no additional information or indication of how she came to correspond with Nels Anderson.

20. "Throw Out the Life Line" was written in 1888 by Edwin S. Ufford, a Baptist minister in Maine and later Massachusetts. The second hymn that Anderson mentions, "Let the Lower Lights Be Burning" was written by Philip P. Bliss in 1871. The inspiration came from a lighthouse on the shore of Lake Erie near Cleveland, Ohio. With God providing the upper light to guide souls back to Him, His followers were responsible to keep the "lower lights" burning to assist others to come home safely. The first two stanzas of both songs are given to provide some flavor.

> Throw out the life line across the dark wave;
> There is a brother whom someone should save;
> Somebody's brother! O who then will dare
> To throw out the life line, his peril to share?
>
> Refrain
>
> Throw out the life line! Throw out the life line!
> Someone is drifting away;
> Throw out the life line! Throw out the life line!
> Someone is sinking today.

"Let the Lower Lights Be Burning"
Brightly beams our Father's mercy from His lighthouse evermore,
But to us He gives the keeping of the lights along the shore.
Let the lower lights be burning! Send a gleam across the wave!
For to us He gives the keeping of the lights along the shore.
[or Some poor struggling, sinking sailor you may rescue, you may save.]

Dark the night of sin has settled, loud the angry billows roar;
Eager eyes are watching, longing, for the lights, along the shore.
Let the lower lights be burning! Send a gleam across the wave!
Eager eyes are watching, longing, for the lights, along the shore.

21. Eva Overson was one of the young ladies from St. Johns, Arizona, that Nels Anderson knew. She was born August 14, 1897, in St. Johns to Henry Christian Overson and Margaret Godfrey Jarvis. She married Leroy Parkinson Tanner on August 26, 1923, in St. Johns, Arizona. Tanner was a World War I veteran. Eva died on December 30, 1932, in St. Johns.
22. Sam Brooks, a native of Saint George, had been a student with Nels Anderson at Dixie College.

CHAPTER 3
1. Winchester was an important location in the Roman road system in southern England. Its best known landmark, Winchester Cathedral, was begun in 1070 and is the longest cathedral in England.
2. Anderson, "Education of a Sociologist," 274. In later years Nels did smoke cigarettes, but switched to a pipe in postwar Germany when cigarettes were a much-valued commodity. He wrote: "It bothered me much when walking through a street knowing that someone would be following at a distance waiting for me to throw the cigarette butt away. I turned to smoking a pipe. Pipe tobacco was not rationed. I would distribute my ration of cigarettes to German friends."
3. Hixson, *"E" Company*, 7. Regarding the food in England for Company E, "All those who had longed for a footing on land, so that their appetites would return were favored but greatly disappointed in satisfying those appetites, as the limited rations issued to the American soldiers were insufficient, and the facts that OUT OF BOUNDS signs greeted the Yanks at all sales canteens added to the displeasure."
4. Charles F. Dienst, *History of the 353rd Infantry Regiment 89th Division National Army* (n.p.: Published by The 353 Infantry Society, n.d.), 25 (copy available at the United States Army Military History Institute, Ridgeway Hall, Carlisle Barracks, Pennsylvania). The severe restrictions were the result of misconduct by American soldiers in Winchester before the arrival of the 89th Division. According to Dienst, a soldier with the 353rd Infantry Regiment, "Some Yanks immediately preceding the arrival of the 353rd Infantry had torn up

the town in Winchester. Staid Englishmen told how these uncouth men threw a lariat around the neck of the Statue of King Arthur.... As a result of their hilarity, passes to Winchester could be had for groups only and an officer must be in charge of each group." The statue was most likely that of Alfred the Great, described by Nels Anderson in his entry for June 27, 1918. That statue was rendered by Hans Thornycroft and unveiled in 1889 as part of the millennial celebration of the death of Alfred the Great who was the first king of England who united the Anglo-Saxon peoples under one ruler. He fostered religious scholarship and education and was credited with inventing the civil structure and judicial system for England. He ruled from Winchester and is buried in the city.

5. The handwritten letter, signed by King George and dated April 1918, read "Soldiers of the United States, the people of the British Isles welcome you on your way to take your stand beside the Armies of many Nations now fighting in the Old World the great battle for human freedom. The Allies will gain new heart and spirit in your company. I wish that I could shake the hand of each one of you and bid you God speed on your mission." Copy obtained from Carlisle Army Barracks Library.

6. Richard von Kuhlmann was the German Foreign Secretary and Chairman of the Brest-Litovsk Conference.

7. The Armistice would come in four and a half months, on November 11, 1918, approximately half the time predicted by Anderson.

8. The Battle of the Piave River was fought between June 15 and 22, 1918, when Austrian forces attempted to cross the Piave River in northern Italy southeast of the city of Trento and north of Verona along the southern foothills of the Italian Alps. This last major offensive by the Austrian forces was pushed by their German allies and resulted in approximately 200,000 Austrian casualties as Italian forces counterattacked forcing the Austrians back across the river. The defeat was a major factor in the disintegration of the Austrian army.

9. The connection of Winchester, England, and the towns of Winchester in the New England states of Massachusetts, Connecticut, and New Hampshire, does not indicate a direct link with the early pilgrim settlers at Plymouth, Massachusetts. The earliest, Winchester, Connecticut, was settled in 1732 and incorporated in 1771. Winchester, New Hampshire, was settled in 1733 as Arlington and incorporated twenty years later in 1753 as Winchester by Governor Benning Wentworth who reportedly named the town for Charles Paulet, 3rd Duke of Bolton, 8th Marques of Winchester, and constable of the Tower of London. Winchester, Massachusetts, in the greater Boston area, was incorporated in 1850 and named for William D. Winchester, a wealthy businessman who was expected to endow the town with part of his wealth. He did donate three thousand dollars to the city, but died within a few months of the town's incorporation without having ever set foot in the town. The Pilgrims, those who established the Plymouth colony in 1620, came from different locations throughout England, with the town of Scrooby, in the

county of Nottingham, northeast of London, as the home of pilgrim leader William Brewster and other Separatists who went first to Leyden, Holland, in 1608. Winchester, located southwest of London, is not listed as the home town for any of the original Pilgrims who sailed on the *Mayflower.*

10. Isaac Walton (1593–1683) is considered the father of angling and is best known as the author of *The Compleat Angler* (1653). As a youth, he was apprenticed to an ironmonger. He became a member of the Ironmongers' Company. Later he became a successful writer and biographer known for his passion for fishing.

11. Sergeant Edwin M. Heinricke, was a lithographer who lived at 6606 Vermont Ave., St. Louis, Missouri.

12. Henry Lauder (1870–1950) is considered the greatest music hall comic/singer of the early twentieth century. He was one of eight children born to John and Isabella McLennan Lauder. His father died when Henry was twelve. At age thirteen, Henry went to work in a flax mill and later became a coal miner. He won amateur singing contests and, wearing a kilt and outfitted with a crooked walking stick, began to sing in small music halls. His popularity soared. He married Annie Valance, and their only child—John Lauder, a captain in the Argyll and Sutherland Highlanders—was killed in action on the Western Front in France on December 28, 1916. In September 1917 he established the Harry Lauder Million Pound Fund for Scottish soldiers and sailors wounded in the war. He became the first British entertainer to visit both British and American troops on the battlefield, and for his war work was made a knight of the British Empire in 1919.

CHAPTER 4

1. The Belgian town of Lens is in the province of Hainaut, with a population of 3,900 in 2000.

2. In reflecting on his situation a year before, Anderson hints at an explanation of why his enlistment was delayed until a year after the United States had declared war on Germany. He was working to save money for school, he believed that the war would be over in a short time, and then the death of his father brought unforeseen difficulties for the family. Anderson's father had drowned in a fishing accident during the summer of 1917. After receiving news of his father's death, Nels returned to Michigan from Utah by "riding the rails."

3. Hixson, *"E" Company*, 7–8. The French boxcars were known as "8 Chevaux–40 Hommes," and were designed to carry eight horses or forty men and were approximately half as large as American boxcars.

CHAPTER 5

1. Although Anderson's company was not sent to Italy, a detachment of American troops did go and participated in a July 4th celebration in Rome. See *New York Times*, June 29, 1918, 10; July 2, 1918, 13; and July 5, 1918, 1.

2. Dienst, *History of the 353rd Infantry Regiment*, 27. A fellow soldier in the 89th Division described the French village to which he was assigned, "the village

itself, with its dirty streets through which cattle roamed at will. The rows of
stone buildings seemed to represent the architectural skill and labor of the
dark ages; at any rate, it represented nothing modern. Living rooms and cow
stables were all one building. Wooden ladders led from the street below up to a
second story hole-in-the-wall, and piles of manure made up the front yards."

3. Ibid., 41. An example of the process Anderson describes comes from the
353rd Infantry Regiment encamped in the town of Rimaucourt not far from
Anderson's Company in Humberville. "During the stay in Rimaucourt there
was more or less cognac and French wine available for those who thirsted.
In the beginning no rules or restrictions were laid down locally. The first
two days three members of the battalion partook too freely of these new
drinks. Prompt was the punishment, prompt also was the action of the men
of the battalion to prevent similar misconduct. In each company a small self-
appointed detail saw to it that any member of their company, who showed
signs of going too far in the consumption of these beverages, was quietly
conducted to the little stream behind the town and thoroughly drenched. The
result was that no rules were necessary to govern the men in this respect."

4. The *Stars and Stripes* was published weekly from February 8, 1918, to June
13, 1919, under orders of General John J. Pershing. At its peak, the newspaper
had a circulation of 526,000 readers. The newspaper's mission was to provide
American troops in France with a sense of unity and an understanding of their
part in the war effort. The eight-page paper also featured news from home,
sports news, poetry, and cartoons.

5. Gene Smith, *Until the Last Trumpet Sounds: The Life of General of the Armies John
J. Pershing* (New York: Wiley, 1998). The captain was reflecting the views
of both Woodrow Wilson and General John J. Pershing. After attempting to
negotiate a peace with the combatants—"Peace without Victory," as Wilson
called it—and being unsuccessful, Wilson finally agreed to enter the war in
order to secure a stronger position from which to direct the peace process
which he fervently hoped would bring an end to war. With Wilson's backing,
Pershing insisted that the American forces fight as a distinct army, rather than
allowing American soldiers to be used as replacements for the devastated
British and French units.

6. English, *History of the 89th Division*; William M. Wright, *Meuse-Argonne
Diary: A Division Commander in World War I*, Robert H. Ferrell, ed.
(Columbia: University of Missouri Press, 2004), 10–11. Nels Anderson
clearly had no interest in the command structure of the 89th Division. This
entry is mistaken in identifying William H. Wright as commander of the
89th Division at this time, although Wright did become commander on
September 6, 1918. It is interesting that Nels does not provide any detail
on what seems to be an interesting administrative/command history of the
89th Division. The 89th Division was organized by General Leonard Wood
in August 1917. He commanded the Division until November 1917 when
he and an aide went to France to observe the situation there. In his absence,

Frank L. Winn commanded the Division. Wood returned from France in April 1918 and resumed command of the 89th Division and was expected to lead it to France. However, on the eve of the Division's departure for France, in a controversial move by General John Pershing, Wood was relieved and command assigned to Frank L. Winn. The rivalry between Leonard Wood and John Pershing was well known and it is assumed that Pershing wanted to keep Wood far away from France and the opportunity to further his reputation, perhaps at the expense of Pershing himself. Wood was given duties in the United States. Frank Winn commanded the 89th Division during the voyage to France and until the eve of the St. Mihiel offensive, when, in another controversial move by Pershing, William Wright was given command of the 89th Division and Winn returned to command of the 177th Brigade under Wright. In his diary entry for September 6, 1918, Wright describes the awkward transfer of command: "Proceeded to Lucey, head quarters of the Eighty-ninth Division, and found Brigadier General Winn in command. He had not been notified that I was coming and was considerably upset. Did not understand why he had been relieved, etc. I did not understand this as I had asked Colonel Heintzelman if General Winn had been notified I was coming and he told me he had been." At the conclusion of the war, Wright was promoted to command the 1st Army Corps and Winn resumed command of the 89th Division which he held until the return to the United States in May 1919.

7.   Gerald Williams Berry was born in St. Johns, Arizona, on July 20, 1890, to William Wiley Berry and Rachel Emma Allen. Apparently Berry and Anderson had been students at the Brigham Young Academy in Provo and although they had not much association there, because of their tie to St. Johns had much in common in far away France. Berry died on May 4, 1955.

8.   Agnes Brown was born in St. Johns, Arizona, on March 18, 1900, to John William Brown and Cynthia Louisa Berry. As Nels Anderson notes, she was one of his students in St. Johns. Her marriage to William Stanton Hamblin took place in Salt Lake City on June 7, 1918. She lived in St. Johns until her death on June 25, 1981. Edna Butler was born on June 3, 1896, in St. Johns, Arizona, to Henry Butler and Harriet Belinda Russell. She married Joshua Smith Gibbons on June 7, 1918, in Salt Lake City. It is likely that Edna Butler and Joshua Gibbons accompanied Agnes Brown and William Hamblin to Salt Lake City where they were married on the same day in the Salt Lake Temple. Edna lived in St. Johns until her death on December 4, 1978. It was a common practice for Mormon couples from Arizona to travel to either the Salt Lake Temple or the St. George Temple for their church-sanctioned marriage. Later, when the Mesa Temple in Arizona was completed in 1927, most Mormon couples from Arizona were married at that location.

9.   The term shave tail, especially when used disparagingly to describe a second lieutenant, originated during the Mexican War from the practice of shaving the tails of newly broken mules to distinguish them from seasoned ones.

10. Bastille Day, July 14th, is a national holiday in France that commemorates the first victory of the people of Paris in the French Revolution. After the Estates-General refused to dissolve in defiance of King Louis XVI and transformed itself into a constituent National Assembly, the King called out troops. The morning of July 14, 1789, civilians seized weapons from the armory at the Invalides, marched to the Bastille, and stormed the fortress releasing the prisoners held there. The insurrection was commemorated the following year, 1790, and in 1880 the French Parliament passed an act making July 14 the national holiday of the Republic. Many localities in France celebrates the day with a torchlight parade on the evening of the 13th, followed the next morning by the ringing of church bells, another parade, games and other events, and concluding with dancing and fireworks at the end of the day.

11. Guy Rencher and Johnny Slaughter were the sons of non-Mormon Texas cattlemen who had moved to Arizona in the 1880s. Benjamin Guy Rencher was born in Blanco, Texas, on January 24, 1889, to Peter Preston Rencher and Betha Stubbs. He married Ramona Eigholz on June 2, 1920, in Los Angeles, California, and died on December 30, 1972, in Redmond, Deschutes County, Oregon. John Hamilton Slaughter was born on April 2, 1889, in Apache County, Arizona, to Peter Eldridge Slaughter and Mary M. Chick. He died on October 27, 1918. There is no record of Slaughter's burial in France during World War I, however a list of those from Arizona killed in action during World War I and compiled by the Veterans of Foreign Wars, Department of Arizona, does list John H. Slaughter from Springerville (http://www.azvfw. org/KilledWWI.htm; accessed February 9, 2010). Nels Anderson records a report of his death in his entry for December 11, 1918.

12. Lehi L. Smith was born in Snowflake, Arizona, on March 19, 1891, to Jesse N. Smith and Emma Larson. He joined Company F of the Arizona National Guard in Snowflake on March 21, 1913, and, according to the *Holbrook News*, May 19, 1916, served on the Arizona/Mexico border with other National Guard members. In June 1917 he left on a mission for the Church of Jesus Christ of Latter-day Saints and returned in March 1918. He married Drucilla McKay on March 20, 1918, shortly before he left for military service. His bride returned to Idaho to live with her parents. Lehi Smith was killed on October 28, 1918, (see the Nels Anderson entry for November 11, 1918). He is buried in the Meuse-Argonne military cemetery near the village of Romagne, twenty-six miles northwest of Verdun in France. A memorial service was held for him in Snowflake, which his widow attended. Drucilla returned to Idaho where she married Charles Christian Johnson in Malad, Idaho, on June 20, 1921. They had three children. In 1930, Emma L. Smith visited her son's grave in France under a program sponsored by the United States War Department for mothers and widows of American soldiers killed during the war.

13. Military Discharges, Apache Co., Film 57.14.13, Arizona History and Archives Division, Phoenix, Arizona. Records indicate that Jose B. Salazar, born in Springerville, Arizona, was a farmer by occupation and joined the army

shortly before his twenty-fifth birthday. The 6'1" Salazar is credited with service during four campaigns in France—Lucey 8/8 to 9/11/1918; St. Mihiel 9/12 to 9/16/1918; Euvezin 9/17 to 10/7, 1918, and Meuse-Argonne 10/19 to 11/11/1918. He was discharged at El Paso, Texas, on June 6, 1919, received $104.63 including a $60.00 bonus plus travel pay to St. Johns, Arizona. Salazar's companion was most likely Tranquilino Padilla who joined the army at St. Johns, Arizona, on October 4, 1917, and saw action in France during the Fismes Offensive in the Vesle Sector; St. Mihiel; and the Meuse-Argonne offensive. He remained in Europe as part of the army of occupation until August 6, 1919, and returned to the United States where he was discharged in September 1919 with $115.51 in pay that included a $59.90 bonus and travel pay to St. John's, Arizona.

14. Nels Anderson was likely referring to the practice of hobos jumping freight trains for needed transportation and not paying for a ticket to ride a passenger train.
15. Nels Anderson is most likely referring to the beginning of the German offensive known as the Second Battle of the Marne which began on July 15th.
16. Regular pay for soldiers was $30.00 a month, so Anderson's pay raise of $3.00 amounted to a 10 percent increase.
17. C. R. is most likely Clara Rogers, who was born in 1894. If Nels hoped that Clara would be the young lady he married, he was disappointed. She married Lawrence Sherwood in St. Johns in 1920 and lived there the rest of her life. Nels did marry twice. On January 7, 1924, he married Hilda Benowits in Chicago. She had immigrated from Russia and was about ten years younger than Nels. One son, Martin, was born to them in 1925. After Nels left for the Persian Gulf during World War II they no longer lived together. In 1947 Nels met Helen Merchel in Berlin. By at least 1953 Nels requested a divorce from Hilda. The divorce was granted in 1970. Shortly thereafter Nels and Helen were married in Fredericton, Canada. Helen died in 1977, Hilda in 1972.
18. The original diary includes a small sketch showing the trench to be eight feet wide and about five feet deep with a two foot wide walk way in the bottom of the trench, below a one and a half foot firing base. Dump from the trench is thrown in front.
19. English, *History of the 89th Division*, 46. The reason for the chlorination was explained as follows: "Due to the presence of quantities of manure and other filth in the streets these towns were extremely unsanitary. All the water was contaminated, and had to be chlorinated before being used for drinking purposes. Primitive is a mild word to describe the living conditions of the men."
20. See entry for August 2 for a description of the rations.
21. Belle was Nels's sister who he had encouraged to leave Michigan to attend Brigham Young Academy. Nels had borrowed money to help pay for Belle's tuition. See entry for August 8, 1918.
22. Russ Banham, *The Ford Century: Ford Motor Company and the Innovation that Shaped the World* (New York: Artisan, 2002), 44. Although Nels Anderson

does not record the reason he supported Henry Ford for the United States Senate, one might speculate that it was because Ford favored the establishment of a League of Nations, an institution that Anderson fought for after the war. President Woodrow Wilson urged Ford to run for the Senate believing that Ford might convince other senators to support United States participation in the League of Nations. It may also have been that Anderson admired Ford for his engineering and technological prowess. Ford lost the controversial election to Republican Truman H. Newberry by 4,500 votes out of more than 400,000 votes cast.

CHAPTER 6

1. Hixson, *"E" Company*, 9–10. E Company traveled in a convoy of sixty trucks and arrived in the village of Minorville about six kilometers from the German front lines in what was known as the Lucey subsector of the Toul sector. The Lucey subsector extended from west of the village of Flirey eastward to the vicinity of Limey, approximately four kilometers, and southeast of that line approximately eight kilometers.

2. For an interesting discussion of the term *Domus Dei* as the Latin name used throughout the ages for Christian churches, see Duncan G. Stroik, "Domus Dei et Porta Coeli," in *The Institute for Sacred Architecture* 3 (Winter 2000): [2].

3. Orilla Woods Hafen, Mary R. Edwards, and Elbert B. Edwards, *The Woods Family of Clover Valley, Nevada 1869–1979* (Boulder City, Nevada: Woods Family Geneaological Committee, 1979), 54–56. Luther Murkins Terry was born April 18, 1873, in Hebron, near or at the Terry ranch. He married Charlotte Melinda Woods, daughter of Lyman and Maribah Ann Woods, on July 17, 1900. The Terry brothers, Luther and Thomas, married the Woods daughters, Roxa and Melinda. Both couples lived at the Terry ranch during the first ten years of their marriage before moving to Enterprise. Luther, who was sixteen years older than Nels, had served an LDS mission to the southern states and both he and his wife were known for their hospitality and generosity. Luther and Nels established a friendship that continued after Nels left the Terry ranch/Enterprise area.

4. Toul is located between Commercy and Nancy and is situated between the Moselle River and the Canal de la Marne au Rhin. Toul was known to the Romans as Tullum Leucorum and later was the seat of the bishops of Toul from about 410 until 1807. Its present population is approximately 20,000.

5. Masseck, *Official Brief History of the 89th Division*, 7. Masseck records that "the first baptism of fire for the Division came on the night of August 7–8, when the front line battalions of the 354th and 355th Infantry were subjected to a continuous gas bombardment during the process of relief, [of the 82nd Division] from 10 p.m. until 4 a.m. The casualties were large, totaling between the two organizations about 700 men and officers."

6. The last time that Nels Anderson saw his sister Belle was their dinner in Salt Lake City after receiving news of the death of their father. Nels left for

Michigan. Belle stayed in Salt Lake City where she worked for a doctor. While in Utah, she suffered a severe case of food poisoning that her mother believed was intentional. Belle began her journey back to Michigan while Nels was en route from Michigan to Utah. Belle's accident occurred after her return to Michigan.

Later, in recounting the accident and his response to it, Nels wrote in *The American Hobo* (152): "Our first mail brought a letter from Mother reporting that Belle had died in an accident. She was helping move a heating stove which fell from the wagon on her. [The accident was sometime in June 1918.] I had to keep my depression to myself, being still a stranger in the company. The savings I accumulated in St. Johns I had sent to her, believing that would meet her personal needs until the war was over. At that time I assumed I would not be in the army even a year. She was the exceptional member of the family. Her dream was to become a writer, foolishness to all in the family except me."

7. Calley N. Thomas, "Life History of Nels Lars Nelson 1862–1946," Brigham Young University Library, Special Collections, BX 8670.1 .N3344t. Nels Anderson lived with the Nelsons while attending Brigham Young Academy. N. L. (Nels Lars) Nelson was born of Danish immigrant parents in Goshen, Utah, on April 25, 1862. He graduated from Brigham Young Academy in 1882 and taught at Brigham Young Academy. He authored *Scientific Aspects of Mormonism*. He married Maud Noble on May 25, 1904, and in 1916 he built a home at 663 North University Avenue in Provo, which included apartments in the basement that were rented to students attending the academy located across the street and south of the house. Nels and his sister Belle had lived with the Nelsons while students at Brigham Young Academy in 1916. The Nelsons had kept Anderson's items from St. Johns, work clothes, his tool chest, as well as items he sent from Camp Funston. It was to their home in Provo that Nels returned following his military service. N. L. died in 1946, Maud in 1954. They had moved to Downey, Idaho, in 1920. See March 31, 1919, entry and accompanying note.

8. Coffman, *The War To End All Wars*, 66–67, 275. The division relieved was the 82nd Division, which was known as the All-American Division because it was made up of southern mountaineers and farmers as well as a large number of foreign-born soldiers drafted from northern cities. Alvin York, the most famous enlisted hero of the war, was a member of the 82nd Division.

9. Dutch was a nickname for the Germans along with Fritz, Boche, Hun, and Jerry. Dutch was a corrupted Americanism of *Deutsch*, the German-language word for "German." Fritz was a common first name among German men. Boche is an alteration of "Alboche," a French slang word for German— combining "Allemand" (German) with "caboche" (cabbage) for the derogatory term "German cabbage or blockhead." Hun, or the Huns, referred to the warlike medieval Hunnic Empire formed under Attila the Hun, while Jerry is of indeterminate origin. Inconsistent use of capital letters and spelling

for these slightly derogatory terms in the diary reflect something of Anderson's informal approach to his writing.

10. This difficult letter to his mother was apparently regarding Belle's death, for which Nels felt responsible.

11. Corn Willie was the soldier's name for corned beef hash. Although Nels Anderson does not use the term, "monkey meat" was used by some soldiers for corned beef.

12. The soldiers were from the Alsace region—located west of the Rhine River and east of the Vosges Mountains on the border of France and Germany. It had long been contested by the two countries. Following the Franco-Prussian War in 1871, Alsace was annexed by Germany. After World War I it returned to France only to be annexed by Germany once again in 1940. Since the end of World War II Alsace has been part of France although the villages, towns, and largest cities—Strasbourg and Colmar—still retain strong German influences.

13. While Anderson spells the town as "Flieury", it is actually Flirey, and can be confused with Fleury, which was a town near Verdun destroyed during the fighting there.

14. Although Nels does not mention "trench foot" by name, he implies the need for proper care of the feet. The word trench foot was coined during World War I to describe the damage to feet caused by prolonged exposure (usually twelve hours or longer) of the skin to moisture and cold which softens skin, causing tissue loss and usually infection. Extreme cases may require amputation. The first signs of trench foot are itching, numbness, or a tingling pain. Later, the feet may swell and the skin change colors, becoming red, blue, or black. After feet are dried and warmed, the discomfort may continue for hours or days.

15. Cascarets were laxative tablets produced by Sterling Products, Windsor, Ontario, Canada.

16. The letter that Nels Anderson wrote to the *Washington County News* dated August 27, 1918, was published in the October 3, 1918, issue. It reads:

> Dear Mr. Wallis:
>
> I often think of my Dixie friends and as I look back from here I feel that the few years I spent in southern Utah are the most pleasant I have to think about.
>
> Probably a great many of the Dixie boys are over here. Perhaps some of them are near here but it is as hard to communicate with friends in the army over here as it is to locate them and it is just about as difficult to do either as it is to get mail to or from the States, so a few of us who are so unfortunate as to be isolated with a regiment of strangers get a little lonely at times. One thing I am thankful for is that we are kept busy most of the time, but during spare hours I wonder how people are here and there at home and I crave any kind of letter or paper bearing news about friends and things I am interested in.

I have been in the service four months today and have been on this side more than two months. I am a long ways from a finished product but I feel that when we get up here that some of the oldest men are as green as the greenest. The parade ground helps to make a good soldier for dress parade, but dress parade is a small part of life in the trenches. I heard a great many objections to bringing untrained soldiers over, but I don't feel as bad about it as I did. The fellows are learning faster here. It seems that one can get the spirit of things better when the air is full of it. Life in the training camp at home is too much of a picnic and about all one learns of war is inspection, heavy packs and marches. It all helps to discipline a fellow and that is very necessary, but I learned more the ten days I spent at the front than I could ever get at a camp at home.

Things are a lot different over here than I thought for. I have had to change a lot of my mistaken ideas. The newspapers give one a very distorted idea of things. I expected to find death staring me in the face everywhere, but I saw very little. I saw none of the enemy unless one might class trench rats as such. I am still rookey enough to cover my head at night lest they chew my ears. Then a word about shell fire. I used to worry more about it than I do now since I have been under it. I was about 20 feet under it down in a dugout. Fritz sent over about 500 big shells in about 30 minutes, we could hear them whistling and bursting all around, but when we came out we learned that the closest shell missed us by 100 yards and even though there were many men on duty who never took to shelter not a man was hurt. That was the Kaiser's hard luck.

Folks at home needn't worry about the boys over here. Uncle Sam is taking good care of them. He is more concerned over their welfare than they are about themselves at home. That is where the Liberty Bonds go and where Uncle stops, the Y.M.C.A., K. of C. and the Red Cross take up the job. That is what they want donations for. Those are our friends and they are stretching every dollar they get for our welfare and comfort. The soldiers enjoy them. God will bless them, and the least the home folks can do is support them.

France is not yet bled white, but she has given freely. The people make us welcome and the Yanks get along with them, but the "Sammies" and "Tommies" don't agree. Both like to talk and both recommend themselves highly. Then the Yank very foolishly tells the Englishman that we are here to fight his fight. Those differences are of little consequence since we are all pulling the same load.

Best wishes, your friend
Pvt. Nels Anderson.
Co E. 314 Engrs.,
Am. Ex. Forces.

17. The Company E Roster lists Private Horace W. Aven as a farmer whose address is 418 South 1300 East, Salt Lake City, Utah.

18. Anderson's reference to Henry Wadsworth Longfellow's epic 1847 poem "Evangeline" recalls the story of Evangeline Bellefontaine and her lover Gabriel Lajeunesse in the context of the 1755 expulsion of the French Acadians from Nova Scotia, their relocation to Louisiana, and the destruction of the village of Grand-Pre. The poem was read by generations of American school children and Nels Anderson had perhaps taught it to his students in St. Johns, Arizona. Oliver Goldsmith's poem "The Deserted Village," written in 1770, describes the abandoned English village of Auburn. Both poems describe a rich and contented village life that, like in the destroyed French villages that Anderson passed through, was lost to war and greed.

19. Keene, *Doughboys, the Great War,* chapter six, "The Politics of Race: Racial Violence and Harmony in the Wartime Army," 82–104. Conflicts over white and black use of YMCA facilities were not uncommon as race issues followed American soldiers from the United States to Europe.

20. Ruby Potter was born September 23, 1892, in Richfield, Utah, to Wallace Edwin Potter and Olive Andelin. She married Vernon Wilson Valentine on June 20, 1920, in Richfield. They moved to California where she died in Huntington Beach on March 10, 1978. Ruby's sister, Olive Pearl Potter, married Spencer Davis Rogers from Snowflake, Arizona, and lived there the rest of her life.

21. This is the only time that Anderson mentions the derogatory term "Frog" for the French and even in this context it is in explanation of the reaction of most American soldiers to what they perceived as an unsanitary and lazy lifestyle of the rural French.

22. Anderson, "Education of a Sociologist," 152, 166. Nels Anderson identified Sergeant Russell as a miner from the Ozarks and explained further the activities of the squad. Elaborating on his work with the demolition squad, Anderson wrote:

> One day Captain Freeman announced to the company that he wanted a special detail. He warned that the job would be highly risky. Stepping forward was slow. I did not want to be first. Among the thirteen who volunteered was a Sergeant Russell, a hardfaced miner from Joplin [Missouri] I was soon to learn that he had done some wandering about, working on construction, had been a harvest hand, in sum, a seasoned hobo. He was also a brager and a liar but still a man I liked....
>
> I had never worked with explosives, which was the specialty of our so-called "demolition" detail. Russell knew about explosives but not the kind we would handle or be on guard against, and our engineer captain knew only what he read or had been told after reaching the front. The responsibility was with Russell to find ways to get the jobs done and, of

course, to "mother" us. We had no accidents. He managed to see that his group could go in front when the company lined up for chow. Only sargeants were ahead of us.

Our first lessons had to do with special explosion to blast a pathway through barbed wire entanglements. The torpedo used was a long three-inch pipe of stove pipe materials and like stovepipe, was assembled by joining end to end 30-inch sections to form a tube fifteen to twenty feet long. The squad presumably would creep up in the night, blow the gap through the entanglements, then fall back to let the infantry pass through. We became efficient setting up barbed wire entanglements and blasting passages through them.

All that preparation to achieve what seemed a sure thing came to naught. After an hour or two of bombing never known before, all along miles of trenches. Then thousands on thousands of infantry crossed no-man's land to find the German trenches empty. The barbed wire had settled down so much in the weeds and grass they could tramp it underfoot or beat it down with the butts of their rifles. We did during our training put up a stretch of barbed wire entanglement in the dark of a dark night, probably twenty yards, to see if it could be done. We completed the "mission" and got back into our trenches without being discovered by the Germans.

CHAPTER 7

1. Coffman, *The War to End All Wars*, 280. Indicative of the lack of German resistance and the low German morale is the account of Sergeant Harry J. Adams of the 89th Division. "When Adams saw an enemy soldier run into a dugout at Bouillonville, he ran after him. He had two rounds left in his pistol, so he fired both of them through the door and called on the German to surrender. As the sergeant stood dumfounded, over 300 German officers and men filed out of the dugout. Adams was equal to the occasion; he brandished his empty pistol and marched the prisoners toward his platoon. His startled platoon leader thought the gray column was a counterattack force."

2. Hixson, *"E" Company*, 11.

3. Wright, *Meuse-Argonne Diary*, 17. Wright, commanding general of the 89th Division, recorded the artillery barrage: "Got up about 12:30 a.m. and the artillery preparation opened at 1:00 a.m. It was very heavy. Went up on the hill outside of the railroad cut and saw the sight. It was most impressive. The Boche flares were going up all along the line and the surrounding country and horizon was fairly lit up with explosions of heavy guns of all kinds.

4. Hixson, *"E" Company*, 12–13. Hixson reports that "At 5:20 a.m. on the morning of September 12th, 1918, on receiving orders to take their position at the enemy's first wire entanglement, the Engineers started to cut the way thru immediately. At 5:25 the signal was given for the advance of the Infantry and before the complete break of day the supposedly impregnable positions of the enemy had been completely taken and held at every point.

Their first, second and third lines of defense had been taken on the run. The advance of the 89th Division was so swift that casualties occurred by over anxious men running into their own barrage.

Before darkness came, Thiaucourt, Xammes and Benney, the objectives 12 kilometers from the old front line were taken and the front established 8 kilometers beyond. During the day's drive 3500 prisoners and quantities of supplies, ammunition and artillery were in their possession. Five towns and twenty-five square miles of French Territory was liberated by the 89th Division."

5. Hixson, *"E" Company*, 1, 28–29. On September 12, 1918, E Company suffered its first casualties of the war. Private Harry M. Silcott was killed in action. See Anderson's entry for September 14, 1918. Six men were wounded: Sergeant Edward Sirclum, Corporal Boyd Stapp, Private Gus Johnson, Corporal Guadalupe J. Guttierez, Private Roy M. Chapman, Private Charles P. Breitbarth, and Private Albert H. Gomph. E Company lost seven men killed in action and a total of 42 men wounded or gassed. Of the nine companies in the 314th Engineers, only F Company had more casualties with ten men killed and fifty-seven wounded or gassed. The nine companies of the 314th Engineers, including Anderson's E Company lost thirty-six men killed in action and 184 wounded and gassed. Of the 27,000 men in the 89th Division, 1129 men were killed in action, 5,761 were wounded or gassed, 58 missing in action, and 5 were taken prisoner by the Germans.

6. The 314th regiment commander was Robert P. Johnson.

7. Wright, *Meuse-Argonne Diary*, 18. The deplorable condition of the roads was of much concern to Division Commander Wright who wrote in his diary, "The road from Flirey to the north as far as the top of the hill is in a deplorable condition; although they have been working on it since morning they have done nothing but throw dirt in it, and the heavy traffic for the past two or three days had made the road worse. If we do not get the guns up and the Boche makes a counter attack I am afraid we will lose what we have gained."

8. Hixson, *"E" Company*, 28. Although September 13 was a quiet day for Nels Anderson, two E Company soldiers were killed in action: Private Walter Hall and Private Adam Spyrczak.

9. The division headquarters was located in the town of Flirey, which was located on the crossroads between Commercy to the southwest, Pont-a-Mousson to the east and Toul to the south, and St. Mihiel to the west. The Battle front was to the north. On the morning of September 14th, the Division headquarters was moved north to Euvezin.

10. Hixson, *"E" Company*, 13. The *E Company History* relates, "In Bouillonville, fortunately situated behind an abrupt hill which afforded partial protection from the German artillery, 'E' Company worked during the day preparing for their night's work in 'No-Man's-Land' which was under direct fire of the Germans. In the early hours of darkness there were details of Engineers loaded with supplies and equipment to construct barb-wire entanglements or to establish trench systems from the fox-holes occupied by the Infantry

which had given them partial protection from the Boche snipers and machine-gunners.

"Nearing the completion of the defense lines 'E' Company's energies were centered on constructing advanced P.C.'s and dressing stations within the ruins of Xammes, Thiaucourt, and Benney which had been under continuous shell fire from the opening of the St. Mihiel Drive, and were still being subjected to a great amount of gas and shrapnel shelling."

11. Wright, *Meuse-Argonne Diary*, 36. It is clear from Division General Wright's diary entry for September 19, 1918, that he expected to spend the winter of 1918–1919 at this location, hence the need the trenches.

12. Alberta Cram was born November 28, 1894, in Huntington, Utah. She married Joseph Egbert Davis on June 3, 1921, in Salt Lake City and died there on December 24, 1973. Her relationship to Nels Anderson and the unidentified Fred Pearce is not known, though it may be that they were students together.

13. Hixson, *"E" Company*, 29. On September 17, two E Company men were wounded, Private Louie Stock, and Private Leo Andezejewski. Seven were reported gassed, Sergeant lst Class James F. Gray, Private Arthur Behling, Private Robert C. Hinton, Private Frank Penman, Private Carroll Spitler, Private Elias O. Stephens, and Private Albert Erickson.

14. Hixson, *"E" Company*, 29. In addition to Private Jake Pollack, Private Floyd H. Weigner was wounded on September 18, 1918.

15. Andrew "H" Gibbons was born in February 1898 in St. Johns, Arizona, to Joshua Smith Gibbons and Nancy Louisa Noble. Eleven years younger than Nels Anderson and perhaps one of his students, it is understandable why Gibbon's mother asked Anderson to look out for her son. Gibbons returned from military service and married Lola Heaton on November 22, 1925, in Safford, Arizona. He died in Salt Lake City on March 3, 1963.

16. Grover Brown was another native of St. Johns, born there on October 17, 1892, to John William Brown and Cynthia Louisa Berry. He married Jeffie May Duke on May 15, 1918, in St. Johns—apparently just before he left for France. He died on March 19, 1973, and is buried in St. Johns.

17. Hixson, *"E" Company*, 29. Two E Company soldiers, Sergeant Orval R. Wasburn and Corporal Eugene P. Morehead, were gas victims on September 26.

18. Hixson, *"E" Company*, 29. The threat of gas continued on September 27th as Private Hallie B. Cooper was a gas victim.

19. For a discussion of the American soldier as souvenir hunter see Keene, *Doughboys, the Great War*, 59–60. Most of Nels Anderson's comrades and other American soldiers would probably not have seen much value in the wooden shoe, since the souvenir collectors were much more interested in tangible evidence—such as bayonets, helmets, uniform parts, and other items—that proved they had come in direct contact with the German enemy.

20. Bulgaria had entered the war as an ally of Germany and Austria on October 11, 1915, hoping to annex the Serbian province of Macedonia. Initially successful in Macedonia and in capturing a forty-mile strip of Greece, the Bulgarian army was eventually pushed out of the conquered territory by the British army, which entered Bulgaria on September 25, 1918. Armistice talks began on September 28 and hostilities along the Bulgarian front ended at noon on September 30. During the three years of war, the Bulgarian army lost 90,000 soldiers.

21. S. William Halperin, *Germany Tried Democracy: A Political History of the Reich from 1918 to 1933* (New York: W. W. Norton and Company, 1946), 52–60; and Holger H. Herwig, *Hammer or Anvil? Modern Germany 1648–Present* (Lexington, MA: D. C. Heath and Company, 1994), 214–15. The resignations came from Paul von Hintze, foreign minister, and Chancellor George Count von Hertling. By September 28, 1918, German military leaders General Paul von Hindenburg and General Erich Ludendorff concluded the war was lost and exerted pressure on Kaiser Wilhelm II to force the resignation of von Hertling and to appoint Prince Max von Baden as Chancellor. He immediately appealed to President Woodrow Wilson for an end to the war based on Wilson's Fourteen Points that included open diplomacy, freedom of the seas, removal of trade barriers, reduction in armaments, and the impartial settlement of colonial claims.

22. Eisenhower, *Yanks*, 24, 62. The Regular Army consisted of twenty regular divisions and eighteen National Guard divisions. The additional divisions that were created were organized into a separate category called the National Army. The first men assigned to the National Army came from those selected for duty on July 20, 1917, as part of the first nationwide draft lottery. Individual service numbers reflected a soldiers' assignment to the National Guard, Regular, or National Army. The Regular Army soldiers considered themselves superior to the National Army soldiers by virtue of their tradition, training, and assignments. However all divisions were organized similarly and all were under the command of General John Pershing.

23. Nels Anderson was most likely referring to Clara Rogers in indicating that he was partial to the name Rogers.

CHAPTER 8

1. Masseck, *Official Brief History of the 89th Division*, 23. Some anticipated a respite after the St. Mihiel Offensive. "It had been the original intention of the Allied Commander in Chief and General Pershing, after reducing the St. Mihiel Salient, and then threatening Metz, to pause at this point and to continue, during the following winter, the further consolidation and training of the American troops in preparation for the great smash in the spring in the Argonne."

2. Coffman, *The War to End All Wars*, 299.

3. Hixson, *"E" Company*, 17. After two continuous months at the front, E Company left Euvezin about 5:30 p.m. on the evening of October 7 with the understanding that they were "to be relieved and was to go back for a short and deserved rest. That evening about 5:30 'E' Company moved out of Euvezin and in a driving rain marched thru mud and water; giving the road-way to truck trains and ration wagons which were passing every few minutes, across the old No-man's land, thru Essey, Maizerais, Lahayville, Richecourt and Bouconville to Euville, a distance of 37 kilometers." This was the longest march made by Company E while in France, though they would march twenty-eight miles between Pelm and Pronsfeld, Germany, in December shortly after their arrival as part of the occupation force.

4. The town they reached after the fifty-kilometer truck ride was most likely Récicourt. The map accompanying the 314th Engineers, Company E history indicates that the Company was camped the night of October 9–10 at Camp DeMegon, located near the villages of Récicourt and Parois about eight kilometers east of the Argonne Forest and approximately twenty kilometers west of Verdun.

5. Frank J. Provaznik was a tailor from St. Louis, Missouri. See entry for October 22, 1918.

6. The small hamlet of Ivoiry is located about three kilometers west of Montfaucon and seven kilometers south of Romagne.

7. Hixson, *"E" Company*. Private William E. Conway was the soldier killed on October 27, 1918. In addition, Sergeant Elmer E. Denniss, Private King L. Hunting, Sergeant Vincent K. Kemp, and Corporal Joe B. O'Brien were wounded. Six soldiers were gassed that day—Corporal William A. Williams, Corporal William B. Monahan, Corporal Roy Hardesty, Private Mike Coligan, Private Ray V. Miller, and Private Harry A. Bock. Of the ten who were wounded and gassed, only Corporal Monahan returned to E Company while the others were sent back to the United States or assigned to duty behind the lines.

8. The defensive trenches were apparently located to the west of Romagne about five kilometers and a few kilometers east of the village of Sommerance.

9. Hixson, *"E" Company*, 29. Although none of those killed were from E Company, two men were wounded on October 29th, Corporal Ralph E. Hilterbrand and Private Tony Voilpe.

10. Hixson, *"E" Company*, 29. Nevertheless E Company suffered two casualties on October 30 as Private Bert J. McMahon was wounded and Private Robert P. Pinder was gassed.

11. Hixson, *"E" Company*, 28–29. The two other E Company soldiers killed on November 1, 1918, were Private Stanley J. Pilarski and Private John Yerko. The three men killed November 1 were the last of the seven E Company men killed in action. In addition, three men were wounded on November 1—Private Charles Dopman, Private Lewis J. Roff, and Private Frederick S. Rodgers. In both of his autobiographies, Nels Anderson recounted the death

of Philips. In "Education of a Sociologist" (164) he wrote, "I was at the front, first at St. Mihiel and then Stenay not more than three months when the war was over. We were exposed to enemy fire most of that time. Some of our company, around twenty-five, were killed. I was near and saw my friend, Philips killed by a bursting shell. . . . To me Philips was a hero. From Kansas, only child of a widowed mother, he had a girl but he deferred marriage because if [he] fell in the war she would be a widow. "It's hard," he said, "for widows to get good husbands." He had his mother adopt the girl. If he died, "she would inherit the farm." See *The American Hobo* (153) for essentially the same account but where Anderson quotes Philips on the reason for his not marrying, "If he left her a widow it would be hard for a 'used woman' to marry again."

12. Hixson, *"E" Company*, 29. E Company suffered one casualty on November 4, Private Hiram Fields.

13. Anderson, "Education of a Sociologist," 166–67. Later Anderson would write, "When the Americans moved forward it was for us to [search] each road for booby traps. My team mate was another Anderson, only tall and handsome. We very soon learned that the Germans in planting bombs rarely varied from three standard tricks. On the dirt roads over which most of our travel was done. The standard trick was to scrape a hole in one of the ruts where the wheels rolled. Over this the shell, detonator attached would be laid on a flat stone or two would be placed over the shell in such a way that the pressure of a loaded wheel on these stones would activate the detonator, exploding the shell. Obviously most of the road bombs were planted in a way that the location of the bomb was proclaimed by the tell-tale fact that the earth had been fresh disturbed. I never heard what the record of other army units was; there were no explosions on the roads inspected by the other Anderson and me. . . . On our side of the river was a village of perhaps two hundred houses and other buildings. Booby traps were planted in most of those buildings. Some were planted in the fire places. Some of the traps in buildings would be made of German 'potato masher grenades.' A German grenade was a tin can full of explosives. A fuse extended from the can through a hole to the other end of the wooden handle where it was fixed to a button. Pull the button, throw the grenade and in three or four seconds it would explode. Outdoors a cluster of two or more would be tied to a tree, a fine wire hardly visible would be across a path or road. In a house the wire would be tied to the window or door one might open."

14. Ibid., 167. Later, Nels elaborated on the abandoned village and the goat milking experience. "It gave one an uncanny feeling going about that village empty of people, furniture in the house, pictures on walls, clean things in the closets. The people had gone in a hurry a day or two before our arrival. I took from one place a handkerchief, a souvenir. The other Anderson also took some small item. We did meet with a mama goat. Her udder was full to bursting and she must have been in pain. Neither of us had ever milked a goat. It was my

colleague knew a goat is milked from the rear. We persuaded this one to stand on a table. One milks from behind. We both knew about milking cows, which helped little. Our fingers would get tired. We were rewarded with a little less than two quarts. Neither had ever tasted goat milk, a rich smooth pleasing taste compared with nothing I knew. In the course of the day we drank all but a cupful which we gave to a cat that followed us about."

15. Hixson, *"E" Company*. E Company suffered one casualty on November 7, when 2nd Lieutenant Everett R. Wilkinson was wounded.

16. The two soldiers killed were not members of E Company, as they were not named in the E Company history.

17. Coffman, *The War to End All War*, 129. Services of Supply was the army organization responsible for logistical support for the combatant forces. The nearly 670,000 men who were a part of the Services of Supply were "involved in the many tasks necessary to maintain a large army n the field. These men handled construction projects, managed railroads and hospitals, operated communications systems, and kept supplies moving toward the front."

18. Hixson, *"E" Company*. The company roster does not list anyone whose name was spelled Tithers, but it does list Wagoner Rufus Y. Teter, a farmer from College Mound, Missouri, who according to the E Company history was wounded on November 8. The only E Company casualty on November 9 was Sergeant Charles H. Bradfield, who was wounded.

19. Hixson, *"E" Company*, 18. Sergeant Herbert F. Goff was a Sta. Engineer from Advance, Missouri. Merrell Hixson provides the following account of E Company's work on the last night of the war. "Before nightfall of November 10th, orders were received to cross the Meuse at all cost; and before the fog lifted in the early hours of the following morning, the bridge sections and material were brought up, placed, spliced and put to use, enabling a sufficient number of infantry units to cross over to take the towns of Stenay and Pouilly and carry their front line beyond, enabling the construction of larger bridges to cross over the artillery."

20. Anderson, "Education of a Sociologist," 167–68; Hixson, *"E" Company*, 29. Later, Nels reflected on the feelings of anxiety during the Meuse-Argonne offensive on the eve of the Armistice. "Only a few days later the final drive against the Germans began. While it was on we heard that at eleven hours next morning the guns would stop shooting. I thought then and have not found the answer yet, why go on shooting and killing another twelve hours. I had been under fire before but it was only during that night that I was uneasy, counting the hours, saying to myself often, 'It would be just my luck to *get it* the last hour.' That happened to some." One E Company soldier, Private Robert McManenmin, was wounded on November 10, 1918.

CHAPTER 9

1. Benjamin Edgar Cruzan, "A Soldiers Diary: The Diary of Bugler Benjamin Edgar Cruzan, Battery F, 341st Field Artillery, 89th Division, 3rd Army

American Expeditionary Forces 1917–1919," Kansas Collection Articles, www.kancoll.org (accessed March 2, 2010); Masseck, *Official Brief History of the 89th Division*, 39. Cruzan, like Anderson, was with the 89th Division— Battery F, 341st Field Artillery, and recorded the last minutes of the war in his diary entry for November 11, 1918, as follows: "Officially Reported that it is over Batry F. Fireing her Last Shots. The Barrage Started at 8:42 a.m. and Lasted 15 min. then the Front was quite [quiet] only a small artillery duel. Then at 10:45 the artillery all around us Lights and Heavies struck up a terrific Barrage which Lasted 5 min. then one shot per gun per min which Lasted till 10:58 then the Last 2 min was spent the gunners feeding the guns as fast as could." According to Masseck, the Division headquarters received word that the armistice would go into effect at 11:00 hours. "Word was immediately sent out by all available means of liaison, including officer couriers, to the front line battalions. Artillery was directed to cease firing at 10:45, in order to avoid mistakes and violations of the armistice."

2. See footnote for July 14, 1918, entry.
3. Wright, *Meuse-Argonne Diary*, 165. General William Wright had issued orders against "hilarity or demonstration" by the American soldiers. After receiving word at 8:45 a.m. on the morning of November 11, "that an armistice had been signed and would take effect at eleven o'clock...I [General William Wright] directed Colonel Lee to keep up the fighting until that time and that it would stop exactly at eleven o'clock and the men would dig in on the ground they occupied and that absolutely no communication with the Boche under any circumstances or any subject would be permitted, nor would there be any hilarity or demonstration on the part of my troops."
4. "Minnie Wurfers" refers to the German artillery "minenwerfers" whose literal translation is mine throwers.
5. The town was most likely Martincourt or Inor.
6. Cruzan, "A Soldier's Diary." Benjamin Cruzan wrote of the rumors in his diary entry for November 16, 1918, "Rumor is we go to Germany and Rumor is we go to the Rear Rumor is the 4 best divisions are going home soon and we are included in the 4 I don't know which is Right but I would Like to do something. OH Joy Oh boy where do we go from here. 'That's the question.'"
7. Laura Brooks Lund was born January 19, 1895, in St. George to George Brooks and Emily Cornelia Branch. She married Miles Romney Lund on October 5, 1916, and died on February 16, 1925.
8. For the text of the letter published in *Washington County News* on October 3, 1918, see notes for August 27, 1918.
9. Joseph Smith Jarvis was born on March 6, 1894, in Eagar, Arizona, to Heber Jarvis and Susan Janet Smith. He married Mildred Boyer on June 1, 1922, in Salt Lake City. He died on June 12, 1989, in Mesa, Arizona.
10. Private Ralph Hill was a farmer from Eads, Colorado, and Corporal Elmer Smoot was a farmer from Elmer, Missouri.

11. Corporal Wayne Rogers, a railroad engineer, whose home address was 607 W. 6th St., Pittsburg, Kansas.

CHAPTER 10

1. Anderson, "Education of a Sociologist," 168. Anderson recalled that "we listened to the Belgian peasants tell of German atrocities. We believed. They were sure that when we reached Germany they would shoot at us from ambush. That didn't happen but I think many, including myself who were nervous just the same."

2. For the most comprehensive study of the question of German atrocities see John Horne and Alan Kramer, *German Atrocities, 1914: A History of Denial* (New Haven: Yale University Press, 2001). The authors list 129 incidents from August through October 1914 in which ten or more civilians were killed by German soldiers in Belgium, Luxembourg, and France. Among the most extreme actions were the destruction of the Belgian city of Louvain, with its university library of early books and medieval manuscripts, where 248 civilians were killed and 2,000 buildings destroyed, and Dinant where 674 civilians were killed and 100 buildings destroyed.

3. Here Anderson uses the French spelling for Luxembourg. Hereafter he uses the German spelling Luxemburg.

4. Many members of Anderson's 314th Regiment and the 89th Division were from St. Louis, Missouri, and the surrounding area where many German immigrants lived. Undoubtedly the soldiers to whom Anderson is referring were sons of those German immigrants who still spoke German in their homes.

5. A felon is an infection on the tip of the finger.

6. The name of the town is most likely Hollenfels, as present maps do not indicate a town called Fels in the line of march. However the town of Hollenfels does lie approximately forty kilometers east of Vance in the direction of Germany.

CHAPTER 11

1. Henry T. Allen, *The Rhineland Occupation* (Indianapolis: The Bobbs-Merrill Company, 1927), 13.

2. Keene, *Doughboys, the Great War*, 120–21. Historian Jennifer D. Keene offers the following description of the American soldiers' experience with German civilians during the occupation. "In the Rhineland, American soldiers discovered a popular summer resort area filled with picturesque castles and tourist spas, all untouched by the ravages of war. After months in the wasted regions of France, these appealing surroundings, coupled with the residents' hospitality, provided a much desired respite from the war's devastation. The Germans, many soldiers attested, ungrudgingly offered them good meals and comfortable beds, charged reasonable prices for wine, and treated them like colleagues rather than unwelcome visitors. . . . Some American soldiers spoke German, but ignorance of the language created few barriers for the rest

when their hosts conveyed their goodwill through actions rather than words. 'Shortly after they reach a town it is common enough to find that some old woman is baking cakes for them and giving them rooms in her house instead of the stable in which they are billeted,' one officer complained."

3. English, *History of the 89th Division*, 263. While Anderson indicates that they entered Germany on December 4, George H. English identifies the day as December 5. He writes, "On the morning of December 5th the Division began crossing the bridge at Echternach and entering the territory of Germany. Striking changes of environment at once were noted. The sign posts, which in Belgium were in French and in Luxembourg were both in French and German, now became all German. Many sign posts indicating roads had been taken down or destroyed, evidently in a spirit of petty malice by the retreating German Army. The roads became worse and were speedily ruined by the passage of our heavy trucks. German roads are not so well constructed as French roads, having lighter foundations and a narrower roadway. The stately, spire-like poplars which line the French roads and give a characteristic tone to the landscape, were now supplanted by smaller, wide branching trees, whose gnarled and twisted limbs gave, in the winter season, a melancholy impression of suffering. Should we mention our feelings on seeing green fields well kept—roofs and chimneys whole on the houses—fat cattle and well fed people in unharmed Germany—all after devastated France? Other emotions were sometimes excited. It is related that a disgusted K.P., engaged in digging a kitchen sink, was overheard to make the following complaint, 'This is a h--l of a country; not even a shell hole to throw things in!'"

4. Ibid., 286–87. While Anderson and his comrades considered a barn and hay loft much preferable to the dugouts, shell holes, and two-man tents that had been the rule during the fighting in France, a policy was soon enforced "that whatever accommodations were available, the best or the equivalent of the best, was to be allotted to the American military personnel." However, citizens were to be compensated for housing the American soldiers and regular inspections were made to insure that suitable conditions were maintained. Often these inspections revealed that regulations were not being followed as the soldiers preferred to allow their hosts to occupy the best rooms and spaces. When asked "why they permitted themselves to be so slighted, the answer in hundreds of cases was that they did not wish to discommode the people and were entirely satisfied with things as they were."

5. Anderson articulated the reason for his dislike of Major Gordon Black and his change of heart toward the major in two subsequent writings. In *The American Hobo* (154), Anderson writes, "For Black I had had an instinctive dislike. At inspection he would look at our fingernails, an invasion of privacy, look for spots on our brass buttons. His talk was soft, his sentences precisely uttered, he was himself always a little too spic and span, a full-time job for his orderly, and it seemed he made an effort to stand a little too straight. Within weeks my attitude totally reversed....Black was an unusual engineer. He had studied

the history of engineering and he was a reader of good novels and biography. He liked Rudyard Kipling's stories and poems. One evening he recited to me Kipling's long poem, "Sons of Martha." My interest in the sociology of engineering began with Black. Our acquaintance continued." Later, in his autobiographical manuscript "Education of a Sociologist" (164, 168, 170), Nels explains that "I was made messenger to the battalion headquarters under Major Gordon Black; for whom I had a dislike. I thought him too spic and span, too soft spoken and when he inspected the battalion he would make the men hold out their hands to see their finger nails. In his army one with dirty fingernails could not be a good soldier. I think all were offended by this invasion of privacy.

"After all that, there I was, now with clean fingernails and all, on the office staff of the major. Before many days I was eating out of his hand and proud to be with his staff. . . .

"Major Black was unusual, both as an officer and as an engineer. He was a reader of much more than the sport page. I had a marginal interest in good literature. In his presence I did well to remain silent. The first time I heard of Rudyard Kipling's long poem, 'The Sons of Martha,' was when he recited it whole. I was to learn in time that that poem of protest relating the eternal judgement [*sic*] insuring that the sons of Mary will ever be served by the sons of Martha. Many engineers I knew may not have read anything else by Kipling but they know about the 'Sons of Martha.' Until I spent those few months under the same roof with Black, I knew little about the engineering profession, the most important creator of our industrial urbanism. . . . We remained correspondence friends after the war."

6. "Historical Sketch of German Area Occupied by 89th Division," 7. http://www.usgennet.org/usa/mo/county/stlouis/89thdivision/89thoccupation.html; Joseph Roedder, "Report of the Enemy Occupation of the Kyllburg," *Chronik der Stadt Kyllburg: 800–2000 (*Kyllburg: M. Hoffmann Printer, 2000), 193. Kyllburg, where the 89th Division Headquarters was located, was founded in 1229 by Archbishop Dietrich of Trier who erected a convent there. The castle built on the cliffs above the Kyll River to protect the convent and the force of soldiers assigned to occupy it were one of the principal points of defense against the Counts of Marlburg and Luxemburg who made some claim to the area. The church was built in 1256. The population of Kyllburg in 1919 was estimated at 1,100.

    Roedder, a Kyllburg pastor, wrote the following account of the American occupation of his city: "The last German troops had barely marched through the town when the enemy armed forces followed in their footsteps. On December 2, 1918, the American soldiers occupied Kyllburg. Who had ever thought that the American flag would wave from the castle tower above Kyllburg. As we saw the first enemy troops on our roads and in our streets it penetrated to the marrow of our bones. At first they were very careful, timid, and reserved, but as soon as they realized that they had nothing to fear from our people they quickly became trustful and free. Afterward they were manifestly very arrogant, insolent, and shameless. Within a short time the entire area was full of troops passing through and the same spectacle was repeated with the enemy troops now in December of overcrowded quartering that we experienced in November with the German soldiers. For one week I had thirty men here in the rectory and it was similar in all the other houses, even the smallest houses were occupied by five or six men creating such a confusion that we hardly knew what to do. The passing of soldiers through our town lasted the entire month of December but by the middle of January the permanent occupation began. Kyllburg was the headquarters for an entire Division and we heavily occupied until the middle of May. The beautiful area, the good railway connections, and the pleasant accommodations for the officers in the large hotels seemed to please the Americans very much and Kyllburg remained full of occupation troops."

7.   Winnie Terry was the wife of Thomas Terry, the returned missionary who baptized Nels Anderson into the Mormon Church in 1910, and with whose family Nels had lived in St. George during the two years he attended Dixie Academy. Nels became acquainted with Jake Buchar soon after he arrived in Clover Valley. Buchar was an immigrant from Austria who had worked in the coal mines of Pennsylvania until he was laid off during the Panic of 1907. He wandered west looking for work. One of the Terry family met Jake in Modena and brought him to the Terry ranch and helped pave the way for the Terrys to accept Nels when he arrived some months later. According to Anderson in *The American Hobo* (108, 111), "From him they had already heard much about ways of the road all of which made me less a stranger to them. Being a foreigner, speaking very little English, he had had a harder time of it than I. . . . Jake and I were the ranch keepers. We occupied one of the houses, did our own cooking and washing, did the daily chores respecting the animals, and put in five or six hours a day on long-neglected work. Jake's background was village and farm life in Austria. Work was as much a way of life with him as for me. Above all, he was not lazy. If the Terry brothers came, they had no need to inspect what had been done or to 'lay out' what they wanted done." Nels and Jake rode into Enterprise from the Terry ranch to attend the July 24 celebration at which Grandfather Lyman Woods gave a talk that Nels remembered the rest of his life and played a role in his decision to join the Mormon Church. (See diary entry for July 24, 1918.)

8.   "Historical Sketch of German Area Occupied by 89th Division," 8. According to one account of the 89th Division occupation of Germany, "Probably the one thing that surprised the Americans more than any thing else was the plentiful condition of the food in the area when they took it over. The men of the Division, having just come from a protected tour in the lines, followed by a long arduous march through some of the worst devastated portions of France, were forcibly struck by the peaceful aspect of the country. The signs of full and plenty that abounded everywhere and the entire absence of suffering due

to the four years of war. They expected to see a land devoid of all prosperity—they found the opposite. They had heard of the food shortage in Germany, but as they passed through the villages they saw foodstuffs that were unheard of in most parts of France. There were eggs in abundance, fine creamy butter, meat and any quantity of potatoes and other vegetables. In the small shops along the roads they saw cigars and cigarettes in the show windows—wares that no French town could boast of. In short there was a general feeling of bewilderment until it became known that these conditions did not apply anywhere else in Germany."

9. "Historical Sketch of German Area Occupied by 89th Division," 7. Prum was founded in 720 as an abbey and became a wealthy city during the middle ages. When the French occupied the city in 1794, the abbey and church were confiscated. When the French left in 1814, the abbey and church buildings were given to the city and some of the principal abbey buildings remodeled for schools. In 1919 in the city of less than three thousand, there were six hundred students enrolled in the Prum schools.

10. The Franco-Prussian War of 1870–71 began after Leopold, a Prussian prince of Hohenzollern-Sigmaringen, accepted the candidacy to become king of Spain. The French objected strenuously to the prospect of a Spanish-German alliance through Leopold and insisted that he remove himself as a candidate. The controversy resulted in a French declaration of war on Prussia on July 19, 1870. German forces defeated the French at Sedan on September 1 and captured Napoleon III. The French armies at Metz surrendered on October 27 and Paris capitulated on January 19, 1871, the day after the unification of Germany with the crowning of William I, the Prussian king, as emperor of Germany in the Hall of Mirrors at Versailles outside of Paris. The Treaty of Frankfurt, signed on May 10, 1871, ended the war, provided that the French province of Alsace and most of Lorraine be ceded to the recently united German Empire, required France to pay a war indemnity of 5 billion gold francs (one billion dollars), and provided for the German occupation of Paris until the indemnity was paid. The final payment was made in 1873 after three years of occupation by the German troops.

11. Erich Gerten, Jörg Kreutz, and Claus Rech, *Oberkail: Geschichte eines Dorfes in der Suedlichen Eifel* (Oberkail: Ortsgemeinde Oberkail, 2001), 136. In 2001 a history of Oberkail recorded the arrival of the American soldiers and their stay in the village. "A part of the American soldiers secured quarters in Oberkail and in the next months determined the history. The American flag continued to be honored, however no longer on the schoolhouse, but on the Eifeler Hof Inn. Even civilians were required to respect the flag. After the peace treaty at Versailles through which the Rheinland was declared a demilitarized zone, France became the occupying force of the Allies."

12. Anderson, "Education of a Sociologist," 169–70. Nels enjoyed his relationship with Mother Bauer and that friendship led to other interaction with German civilians. One story not found in his diary but recorded later involves the

disposition of a horse. "Sitting with Frau Bauer evening after evening and sometimes during an afternoon permitted me to be present when she received visitors. Some of her neighbors seemed to think that, since the major was billeted in her house she would be in a position to wheedle favors from him. On such an afternoon she was visited by an elderly pair from a forest village. They related how when the German army retreated they left a bone poor horse. The horse was grazing on the land owned by the old couple, apparently not noticed by neighbors. They took the animal into their kitchen. The horse did well on the grass and other food they brought him. Lodging more than two months in her kitchen, he was beginning to be a problem as well as an inconvenience. The problem, to be expected, was why had the old couple been so uneasy when visitors came. If the wife went into the kitchen when visitors were present she would close the door in a manner that people began to notice. They were in a state of panic. Somebody, they thought, might tell the neighbors, so they came to explain it all to the major. If he received the couple officially he might conclude that the horse problem should be taken to a German public official. It occurred to me that an informal solution would be sufficient. I said I would see the Major, which seemed to me not necessary. I returned to the kitchen and wrote something like this on a piece of paper, 'You may keep the horse.' I had to use a German-English dictionary to get the idea over. That piece of paper they accepted as final."

13. Keene, *Doughboys, the Great War*, 28. The problem of illiteracy in the United States Army during World War I was serious as the illiteracy rate for white troops was 21.5 percent and 50.6 percent for black troops.

14. Masseck, *Official Brief History of the 89th Division*, 44; English, *History of the 89th Division*, 276. The education effort came as a requirement from General Headquarters under which, Masseck wrote, "post schools were instituted at which illiterates were taught and an opportunity offered for other men to obtain the rudiments of grammar school education." According to English, illiterates were defined as those "who could not read intelligently ordinary printed matter, such as the daily newspapers, and who could not write an intelligible letter."

15. H. W. Brands, *T. R.: The Last Romantic* (New York: Basic Books, 1997), 807–11. Theodore Roosevelt died in the early hours of January 6, 1919, at the age of sixty of a coronary embolism. The death was a surprise to the nation. Roosevelt had criticized Woodrow Wilson for failing to enter the war soon enough; Wilson had also rejected Roosevelt's offer to help lead the American forces in Europe. Roosevelt was outspoken in his support during the 1918 election for the Republicans winning a majority in the Senate and for his own ideas for the postwar peace. The former president had not discouraged suggestions that he run for the presidency in 1920.

16. William G. McAdoo, *Crowded Years: The Reminiscences of William G. McAdoo* (Cambridge, MA, The Riverside Press, 1931), 460–61, 498–505. William G. McAdoo, secretary of treasury during the Woodrow Wilson presidency from

1913 to 1918, had married Wilson's youngest daughter Eleanor Randolph
Wilson on May 7, 1914. McAdoo was also appointed director-general of
railroads on December 26, 1917. The Army Appropriation Act granted the
president authority to take possession of the railroads on behalf of the United
States as an emergency war measure. McAdoo resigned both positions on
November 14, 1918, three days after the Armistice was signed. In his letter
of resignation McAdoo claimed the inadequate compensation paid cabinet
officers, the lack of any compensation as director-general of railroads, and
the burdensome cost of living in Washington had depleted his personal
resources to the point that he needed to resign to give sufficient attention to
his personal affairs. Wilson held McAdoo's letter for ten days before accepting
the resignation. With McAdoo's recommendation, Carter Glass was appointed
secretary of treasury and McAdoo returned to New York City to practice law.

17. Bruce A. Van Orden, "Joseph Fielding Smith." *Encyclopedia of Mormonism* Vol.
4 (New York: Macmillian, 1992), 1349–52. While Nels Anderson lists the
name of the dead president of the Church of Jesus Christ of Latter-day Saints
as Joseph H. Smith, the name was Joseph F. Smith. Smith was born in 1838 to
Hyrum and Mary Fielding Smith. He was a nephew of church founder Joseph
Smith; both his father and uncle were killed in 1844 while incarcerated in
a Carthage, Illinois, jail. Joseph F. Smith became a member of the Quorum
of Twelve Apostles in 1866 at the age of twenty-seven. He became the sixth
president of the church on October 17, 1901, at the age of sixty-two and
served as president until his death on November 19, 1918.

18. Woodrow Wilson was the first United States president to travel outside the
country in an official capacity. Because no president had done so before some
considered it to be unconstitutional, arguing that the president could only
function on United States soil.

19. Maurice Valency, *The Cart and the Trumpet: The Plays of George Bernard Shaw*
(New York: Oxford University Press, 1973), 279–81. George Bernard Shaw's
play "Getting Married" was written in 1908 and is described by one writer as
"a curious experiment in plotless comedy...neither the bride nor the groom
now wishes to enter into matrimony, and their doubts precipitate a long and
frequently interrupted discussion of the disadvantages of marriage."

20. English, *History of the 89th Division*, 269. German citizens were subject to a
number of restrictions imposed by the American occupation forces. They were
not allowed to pass into Luxembourg or leave the American zone without
special permission. Furthermore, "regulations also required that all dramshops
be closed except during a few hours of the afternoon and early evening.
The sale of any intoxicant except beer and light wines was prohibited.
All weapons of every sort were required to be turned over to the military
authorities who collected them in depots and guarded them. Assembling of
the people was forbidden without permission, which however, was always
granted on request for a meeting for any lawful purpose, especially for political
meetings of all parties during the period before the election of delegates to

the National Assembly and the Prussian Diet. Returning German soldiers were required to remove their uniform within four days of their return. All persons in uniform were required to salute American officers and all persons were required to uncover and stand at attention when Army bands played the National anthem. Any interference with the troops or having in possession American Army stores or property was, of course, the occasion for sharp punishment.... Manure piles, those obtrusive features of every village in Continental Europe, were required to be neatly kept and covered with pine boughs. General cleanliness and the abatement of nuisances were required. All reported prostitutes were examined and women found with venereal diseases were arrested and sent to Trier for treatment in German hospitals.

21. Although the issue of teaching German in American schools was forbidden in a misguided attempt to foster American patriotism and dampen German morale, (see note for March 29, 1919,) it is most likely that the German language classes were prohibited among American soldiers as a means to help lessen the fraternization among soldiers and German civilians. This same thinking seems apparent in the army order for public servants to salute soldiers—to reduce fraternization, promote separation and respect.

22. Nels Anderson consistently refers to the unnamed teacher as the "schoolmeam." Just why he chose this idiom instead of the usual "schoolmarm" is not clear.

23. Ronald W. Walker, "Heber J. Grant." *Encyclopedia of Mormonism* Vol. 2 (New York: Macmillian, 1992), 564–68. Heber J. Grant was sustained as the seventh president of the Church of Jesus Christ of Latter-day Saints on November 23, 1918, the day after his sixty-second birthday. Born in 1856, Grant was called to the Quorum of Twelve Apostles in 1882 at the age of twenty-five. He served as president until his death on Mary 14, 1945.

24. English, *History of the 89th Division*, 276. Perhaps Anderson had good reason to protest the treatment of his students. The *History of the 89th Division* records that while the men were required to attend school they were to be "relieved from military duties which would interfere with their attendance."

25. Halperin, *Germany Tried Democracy*, 15, 129–31; Roedder, "Report of the Enemy Occupation of the Kyllburg," 194, 201. The Central (Centrum) Party was the political party of the Catholic Church in Germany and included a wide range of members "great landowners to lowly peasants, industrial magnates and factory workers, bankers and shopkeepers, professional men and artisans."

It is no surprise that in the heavily Catholic Eifel region of Germany that the majority voted for the Central Party. On January 19, 1919, national elections were held in Germany and more than thirty million Germans went to the polls to vote for 421 seats in the German Assembly. The results were:

Social Democrats 11.5 million votes 163 seats
Center (Centrum) Party 6.0 million votes 89 seats

    Democrats 5.5 million votes 74 seats
    Nationalists 2.9 million votes 42 seats
    People's Party 1.6 million votes 22 seats.

    The city of Weimar was chosen as the meeting place for the national assembly because of the excessive disorder and tumult in Berlin. The Assembly opened on February 6, 1919.

    Pastor Joseph Roedder of Kyllburg reported on the January 1919 national election noting that "the Social Democrats worked with great intensity here in the Eifel region. The general discontentment, the bitter experiences of the soldiers and all the terrible things that they had seen and heard and repeated at home was plentiful grist for the red mill. Because of the extensive use of all the rooms and buildings by the enemy occupation, I could not obtain a suitable location for a meeting to explain the coming election. Therefore it was necessary for me to hold the meetings in the church, So we held two meetings in the Maximin Church at six p.m. the evenings of January 6 and 7 to offer instruction about the seriousness and importance of the election and the responsibility to vote. The first meeting was for women and young ladies, the second for men and boys. Both were well attended and we were successful in the Reds [Social Democrats] even with all their effort were only able to win twenty votes. Even in light of this failure, the Social Democrats were able to establish an organization that in the beginning had about twenty-five members that, with three exceptions, was made up of inexperienced stupid young men between the ages of eighteen and twenty-two years. But the organization collapsed during the course of the year so that the Reds did not even hold a meeting here in advance of the 1920 election for delegates to the National Assembly." While the number of votes for the Catholic sponsored Centrum Party is not recorded for the 1919 election, the Kyllburg region remained a stronghold for the Centrum Party. In the 1932 provincial elections the Centrum Party received the most votes in Kyllburg—293 or 40 percent of the 731 votes cast. The other parties included Hitler's National Socialist German Workers Party, which received 155 votes, the German National Peoples Party received 106 votes, the Social Democrats received 26 votes, and the Communist Party 5 votes.

26. Anderson apparently visited the village of Hof Hau, which is located approximately four kilometers southeast of Oberkail. There remains an abundance of apple trees in the village.

27. In this sarcastic but humorous comment Anderson was apparently referring to the Sermon on the Mount in which Christ teaches "And why take ye thought for raiment? Consider the lilies of the field, how they grow; they toil not, neither do they spin." Matthew 6:28.

28. The announcement of the death of Sterling Russell was published in the December 5, 1918, issue of the *Washington County News*. The telegram, from the adjutant general in Washington DC and dated the previous day—

December 4—was sent to Mrs. Eliza F. Russell. It read "Deeply regret to inform you that Private Sterling Russell, infantry, is officially reported as killed in action November 7." The newspaper article went on to report that the young widow was a daughter of Mr. And Mrs. Joseph Farnsworth of St. George and that three weeks earlier she had given birth to a baby girl. Russell was the son of Mr. and Mrs. Alonzo Russell of Grafton. The December 26, 1918, issue of the *Washington County News* published excerpts from the last letter that Sterling Russell wrote to his wife on October 28, 1918. It reads:

> At the top of my letters you will notice I put "in France," but if we keep on going we will have to put "somewhere in Germany." We rise at six a.m. and stand retreat at 4:45 p.m. as it gets dark about 5 p.m.
>
> I must tell you something of our barracks. Imagine a city on the hillside where the houses are dugouts roofed over and placed in rows. These are our billets at present and there are about 150 men in one hut. For music we have the rumble of the big guns on the front lines, yet we are miles behind the first line. But I might tell you here the timidity of the front has long ago left me, for I know and have seen the horrible scenes of the battle fields where men's arms, legs, heads and even the whole body was blown to pieces by shrapnel. I would like to picture a few scenes I have seen and been in but must wait until I get home.
>
> If you will remember when I made the speech of acceptance of the flag, I said we would go over the top in France for our dear ones at home and that statement has been fulfilled as it was just three months from the date we left St. George until we did it, and all the boys who left that morning came out safe and sound but much the wiser. Now we are far behind the exciting places.
>
> I saw Willard Andrus and Willard Alger day before yesterday. Vivian Milne is here and I see him every day. We are all well and happy and are of the opinion we will be home within one year.
>
> We have been out rifle practicing and had a German helmet for a target. German equipment is very plentiful through this field.

29. Although Nels Anderson does not mention it in his diary, he did write a letter to the *Washington County News* editor Mr. Wallis, dated January 30, 1919. It was published under the headline "Nels Anderson Writes From Germany." The letter reads as follows:

> I wish to thank you for the copy of The News you sent me. It brought with it an atmosphere of Dixie that is dear to me. It brought the sad news of Sterling Russell's death. Sterling and I graduated in the same class. He was a good student and a clean conscientious fellow. I can imagine the kind of soldier he was, sensitive as he was in favor of right.

Judging from the date of his death, I take it he was killed in the
Argonne Meuse drive. We took part in that drive too. Our division
crossed the Meuse to the right and left of Stenay. Our doughboys were
driving up to the last "eleventh" hour. That was the second front for our
division. We had taken part in the St. Mihiel drive of Sept. 12, 13, and 14,
in which dates I note in The News you sent, other Dixie boys fell.

I note that most of the Dixie casualties were in the infantry. That
may mean one or both of two things. The Infantry is more dangerous
or most of the fellows were in the infantry. There is no doubt that the
doughboys have a great deal of danger. They hold the lines and not only
have artillery to contend with but machine gun fire as well. Very often
the artillery fire is directly at roads, road crossings, ammunition dumps
and gun positions, then the artillery, the traffic and the engineers catch it.
Everyone who comes within gun shot of the lines takes his chances, but
the dough boy, in my opinion, took more chances than any of us. We all
played our part but the infantry "drove them out" and "gathered them
in." They bore the brunt of the loss too. I am with the engineers; we are
to follow the dough boys while they are advancing. We are to bridge the
streams and keep up the communications as well as to keep up the barb
wire and look after fortifications. In the St. Mihiel drive we lost as heavy
as the infantry, but we fared better in the next drive.

We are faring better of late. The Y.M.C.A. has caught up to us at
last and it looks very much like the other welfare agencies might find us.
While the guns were shooting we didn't see much of them. In fact we saw
them so little that most of the men are bitter towards all of them. We have
no doubt that the stuff came over but the fellows back in S O S got all the
benefits. Since we have come to Germany I have managed to get hold of
a paper or two and I have read a couple of articles telling how the soldiers
up front were being provided for with more than they wanted. It may be
we are getting all we need, but we never got the jam and cheese and fruit
they say we do. A lot of that stuff is camouflage to tickle the ears of the
home folks.

Home folks read of vacations and leave of absence every four months
to visit London or Paris, and some soldiers do get to see those places.
Folks back home read of university courses being offer[e]d to all who
wish to take them. But that is more camouflage for I have been trying for
two months to get to go to school, but without success.

All of us realize that in such an immense organization it is hard to
keep every thing going as it should. We all expect hardships and many
inconveniences but misrepresentations in the press are inexcusable.

That's not fair and the Yank is going to say so when once he gets
into tweeds. He was a good sport and played the game fair while it lasted.
He didn't try to kick over the traces and hold back when he was asked
to work long days in the mud and water or to watch long nights in the

cold. I've seen fellows sick and discouraged and fever ridden so they could not eat army stew for days, but they went out on the sloppy roads because they were too proud to go on the sick book. They were in the game to win and team work counted. There was a lot of grief and worry and swearing on every hand but never was there a lack of team work and cooperation.

Those were days when we didn't get much consideration. For weeks we couldn't get paper to write home on, yet the papers brag how the welfare agencies provided for us.

We are not all pessimists, we can [line is illegible]. Some of us are home sick and that may be what tends to make us sour when we read such articles about the fellows at the front.

We are spending our time drilling while we are waiting for the powers that be to decide what they are going to do with us. There are all kinds of rumors afloat about going home but there is nothing that really says we are going for some time yet. In the meanwhile we are relearning a lot of the stuff they taught us before we went into the trenches. We had no use for the training they gave us so it slipped in the rush of things. They are teaching us the use and care of the rifle also how to put up barb wire entanglements and to march in parade. We are learning how to fix bayonets and how to stand like a soldier.

I am learning to misuse a few German words during my leisure. I have learned to ask for most of the good things these German mothers can make to eat. They don't have much on hand, but a good soldier can manage for things now and then, providing he is a friend of the mess sergeant.

We have been treated very well by the Germans and they tell us again and again they would rather have the Yanks than the French come to their towns. They are very thrifty and enterprising. We found that true of the Belgians and Luxemburgers but the French seem to take things a little easier.

Any time you can spare a copy of The News it will be welcome. Very respectfully, Nels Anderson, Co E, 314 Engrs, American Ex Forces.

The letter is in the Dixie State College Library Archives, but the date of publication in the *Washington County News* is not provided.

30. Keene, *Doughboys, the Great War*, 170–203. The bonus, popular with veterans who effectively lobbied their congressional representatives, was not supported by Presidents Wilson, Harding, or Coolidge, who believed the soldiers were not entitled to a bonus for simply fulfilling their duty as citizens. The American Legion was a primary force in pushing for the veteran's bonus, which was passed into law over Calvin Coolidge's veto in 1924. Veteran leaders agreed to accept bond certificates that would mature in 1945 rather than a lower but immediate cash settlement in 1924. However, after the onset

of the Great Depression, World War I veterans began to push for immediate payment of the bonus as one way to spur the lagging consumer spending. The effort to convince President Herbert Hoover and congress to agree to the early payment led to the establishment of the Bonus Expeditionary Force which undertook the Bonus March on Washington DC. The struggle lasted four years until 1936, when congress overrode a Franklin D. Roosevelt veto and veterans received full payment on their certificates.

31. DSC refers to the Distinguished Service Cross which was established by President Woodrow Wilson on January 2, 1918, at the recommendation of General John Pershing, for recognition other than the Medal of Honor for service rendered to the United States. The Distinguished Service Cross was intended to be similar to the citations awarded by the European countries such as the Military Cross and the Military Medal by Great Britain, Croix de Guerre by France, and the Iron Cross by Germany.

32. For histories of the epidemic see John M. Barry, *The Great Influenza: The Epic Story of the Greatest Plague in History* (New York: Viking Penguin, 2004); and Alfred W. Crosby, *America's Forgotten Pandemic: The Influenza of 1918* (Cambridge: Cambridge University Press, 2003.) The influenza epidemic, also referred to as the Spanish flu, touched every part of the world, with approximately 20 percent of the earth's population (25 percent in the United States) attacked by the virus, which left an estimated fifty million dead. World War I claimed an estimated sixteen million dead.

33. Gerten, Kreutz, and Rech, *Oberkail*, 137. A history of Oberkail records, "The year 1919 was…a very hard year for Oberkail. In addition to the cloudy political and economic conditions there was another great concern one that was a matter of life and death for the people. In February and March 1919 the flu epidemic spread and had deadly consequences for Oberkail. In three weeks seven children, three women and several men, including the pastor Johann Keils, died."

34. "Jingles to Ourselves" was very popular with the soldiers and was published in the announcement of the 10th Reunion of the 314th Engineers held in St. Louis, Missouri, on March 6, 1929.

> JINGLES TO OURSELVES
> We sing a song, a little song,
> Merely to remind us
> Of a journey fine to the German Rhine
> And all we left behind us;
> Of the leaving and the grieving,
> Of the pledges to be true;
> Pledges broken ere Hoboken
> Lost itself beyond the blue;
> The bill-of-fare, the filthy air,
> The surly crew and all,

The cheese and tea, till, holy gee!
We cursed the English gall.
The jams and jars in French box-cars,
The Frenchman's chilly welcome,
'Twas thus we came to play the game;
A hellish game and fearsome
Waiting, walking, working engineers,
Tricky, talking, shirking pioneers.
Over the brine to the firing line.
Over the ocean, on to the Rhine,
From old Camp Funston . . .

We got our fill at HUMBERVILLE
Of I.D.R. reviewing.
We held a trench to help the French:
The French went PARLEY VOOING.
We strung barb wire, we waded mire,
We went and took the chance.
We showed the Hun the way to run
When Yankee lads advance.
With shovel and pick we did the trick.
We dug the doughboys in.
We searched the ground where mines were found;
Nor thought we of our skin.
At Bouillonville, at Bantheville
We toiled from dark till day;
And you can bet we'll not forget
The bridge below Stenay.

We're growling hard-boiled engineers,
The packing, plodding pioneers;
Ever going, never knowing
Where the hell or why we're going,
Just going on like Soldiers.

And now at last the thing is past,
Our comrades are returning;
Yet here we stand on German land,
Our hearts within us yearning;
We've borne our ills, we've taken pills,
We've eaten all they've fed us.
We did our part with patient heart.
We've gone where'er they led us.
Mankind is free: Democracy

Now rules from shore to shore
We would from here to the homeland dear,
To tread home ways once more.

Our hearts are reaching over the waves.
Over and over the spoils and the graves.
Beyond the battle-land over the foam:
Take us back, Uncle, back to our home.
Back to the Statue of Liberty.
Written in Germany, 1919, by Private Nels Anderson, Company E, 314th
  Engineers

35. Edgar Holt, *The Tiger: The Life of Georges Clemenceau 1841–1929* (London: Hamish Hamilton, 1976), 227–28; David S. Newhall, *Clemenceau: A Life at War* (Lewiston, NY: Edwin Mellon Press, 1991), 439; and Margaret MacMillan, *Paris 1919: Six Months That Changed The World* (New York: Random House, 2002), 150–51. Georges Clemenceau was shot the morning of February 19, 1919, at 8:40 a.m. by a young anarchist, Emile Cottin. Clemenceau was in the rear seat of his car when Cottin fired between eight and ten shots into the automobile. Two bullets left superficial wounds, but a third struck the French premier in the right shoulder blade and lodged in his chest cavity, where it remained the rest of Clemenceau's life. The would-be assassin was captured, tried, and sentenced to death, but when Clemenceau interceded the sentence was reduced to ten years in prison. Cottin was released in 1924 after serving five years of the sentence. The shooting was motivated by sanctions Clemenceau had taken against anarchists, who were forbidden to hold meetings and who had been attacked by city police during a strike. Though Clemenceau soon returned to the Peace Conference deliberations, many felt that he no longer had the same energy and vigor as before the shooting.
36. Anderson, "Education of a Sociologist," 168–69. Nels was more interested in learning German than French, but knowledge of the French language was necessary to be permitted to study at a French university. In later years, Anderson recounted, "I asked the major if there would be objection to my learning French. An order had been issued that we were not to study the German language; that would lead to fraternizing with the enemy. I told him that our landlady, widow of a German officer who fell in 1870 in the Franco-German war. She had been raised a lady and knew French well. The major thought it a good idea. What I didn't tell him was that she knew no English and would have to teach French through German. In the course of study I learned more German than French."
37. Nels Anderson's visit to Koblenz was his first opportunity to see the legendary Rhine River. Koblenz is located at the junction of the Rhine and Moselle Rivers. The confluence of the two rivers has been known as "Deutsches Eck,"

the German Corner, since 1216 and is marked with monuments. Across on the east side of the Rhine River above Koblenz and the German Corner stands the mighty fortress of Ehrenbreitstein. Anderson's reference to the "Watch on the Rhine" was likely in reference to the strategic importance of Koblenz. The term was introduced to American soldiers as the title of a German patriotic anthem first written in 1840. It was especially popular during World War I with its memorable refrain "Lieb' Vaterland, magst ruhig sein, Fest steht und treu die Wacht am Rhein" (Dear Fatherland, you can be at rest, the Watch on the Rhine stands faithful and strong).

38. English, *History of the 89th Division*, 270; Masseck, *Official Brief History of the 89th Division*, 44. The 89th Division team won 14 to 0. The football team was assembled in early February and training headquarters established at Malberg near Kyllburg under the direction of Captain Paul Withington. "Men of known ability were called on to report for practice, and the Division was combed for men who had shown skill at the game in the organization teams. Although equipment had not arrived, the men began practice in their O.D. trousers and hob-nailed shoes…in the snow and slush." In the three games played in Germany, the 89th Division team defeated the 90th Division team at Wittlich on February 13 by a score of 6 to 0; the 3rd Army team at Koblenz 30 to 0 on February 20; and the favored 4th Division before an immense crowd at Koblenz on February 27 by the score of 14 to 0.

39. Cruzan, "A Soldier's Diary." Benjamin Cruzan was one of the buglers in the 89th Division. He had been ordered to Trier on February 24 and recorded in his diary entry for February 25 to 28, 1919: "We practiced on the Bugles all morning & p.m. up town every night. I eat at the red cross every chance I get. Thursday we Left our packs and marched to the station Left Trier 8:00 a.m. rode box cars up and back it was sure cold the game was fine the score 14 to 0 in our favor that make the 89th Div the Champion of the 3rd Army some football game."

40. Masseck, *Official Brief History of the 89th Division*, 44; English, *History of the 89th Division*, 276–280. Nels Anderson was one of 313 soldiers selected from the 89th Division. The division historians notes "in March, some 313 students, including officers and men, were sent to the French and English universities to pursue their interrupted studies or to indulge in the luxury of European post graduate work." Later in the month, when an A.E.F. University was opened at Beaune, France, out of the 6,000 who attended, 250 students and instructors were from the 89th Division. Other education programs were established to provide courses equivalent to those taken by freshman and sophomore students at universities and colleges in the states. In addition, a technical school and agriculture school were operated within the 89th Division occupation area.

CHAPTER 12

1. Nels was witnessing the Mardi Gras festivities, the culmination of the pre-Lent activities that ended the following day, Ash Wednesday.

2. Edwin Mullins, *The Popes of Avignon: A Century in Exile* (New York: Bluebridge, 2008). In 1309 the seat of the pope moved from Rome to Avignon where seven popes, all French, resided until the seat returned to Rome.

3. Montpellier is located seven miles from the Mediterranean coast in southern France. It is the chief administrative and commercial center for the Languedoc-Roussillon region. The city began as a trading station for spice imports in the tenth century.

4. Anderson, "Education of a Sociologist," 169–70. Later, Anderson provided a more detailed account of his arrival in Montpellier and his difficulty with French: "With full pack minus rifle and gas mask I arrived at Montpellier in southern France, a small city in a grape growing area and also the seat of an old university. I was made aware by circumstances how helpless one can be in a strange land when he knows not a word of the native language. A dozen well chosen words would have guided me from the railroad station to the Petit Lysee, a school which had been made available to the American soldier students. I had a map but the names of places on the map were not in the same script as the lettering on the street signs. I knew no French, and worse, words I could master in terms of meaning I could not speak to the understanding of a Frenchman. I could not say sister, brother, at my house, yesterday, and be understood without repeating words a number of times, each time with a different twist of the tongue. . . . I had the same problem following World War II when I had to speak German to the natives in Germany. I don't have a talent for learning languages."

CHAPTER 13

1. Anderson, "Education of a Sociologist," 171. In later years, Anderson offered the following assessment and description of his experience in Montpellier. "The student aid program which placed a few hundred students in each French university was sainely [*sic*] managed. One is tempted to be cynical about the awkwardness of the army in getting things. Some would be alarmed to learn the freedom we enjoyed. In the morning we had to report at headquarters, but that was not required every day. We were given a ration of money weekly with [which] to pay personal expenses. We lived in French homes where breakfast was included in room cost. Most of us ate our midday meals in some restaurant where we paid by the week. I ate my evening meal at the apartment of a widow who had three other evening boarders, a retired army officer, a young student and a photographer. . . . I went to classes five days a week, two for French lessons and one class in political science.

2. Ibid., 171–72. Anderson recalled that "being a French professor is somewhat of a ceremonial activity. In that class the professor came on the dot when the class would begin. He was preceded by one minute by an attendant who came on a trot. He would grab an eraser and clean the blackboard. When the professor wearing his black robe came sedately in the students jumped to their feet. The remained standing until the professor reached his desk and greeted them with a nod.

The professor spoke in a quiet even manner. Each student brought paper, a pen and a small bottle of ink. The only sounds for the hour were the low, even voice of the professor and the scratching of the steel pens, to me an irritating sound. The lecture ended, the professor made another bow and walked out. The students rose again and remained standing until he was out of the room.

That man whose name I never heard, did not engage in discussion with his students. The learning process seemed to be mainly in the hands of the students. It appeared to me that the students were expected to use whatever skills they had to master the contents of the course."

3. Anderson, *The American Hobo*, 155. Anderson later offered a more sympathetic statement about his French teachers and explains what activity was most effective for him to learn French. "During the first two months of our four or five months at Montpellier I was overly bewildered by that language. The two classes were helpful, one taught by a Mademoiselle Charbonelle who knew little English and was the more effective because of the lack, and the other by a man, Monsieur Gillee who talked much in English and was knowledgable in French culture. Some years later he was at the University of Chicago as an exchange professor and recognized me. He was good enough to give me my required French examination and lenient enough to pass me. Most of my learning was done on the street where I tried conversing with people, or in the parks where I tried talking to those sitting near me."

4. Although Nels Anderson offers the year 1309 for the establishment of the University of Montpellier, it was actually founded in 1220 and confirmed by a bull of Pope Nicholas IV in 1289. As early as 1160 Placentius, a noted medieval jurist, founded a school that became Montpellier's law school. The university was suppressed by the Revolution of 1789, but reestablished in 1896. Since 1970 three academically autonomous state-financed universities constitute the Universities of Montpellier.

5. "Brief Biography of Jesse Johnson Weight, Harold B. Lee Library, Special Collections, Provo Utah. Jesse Johnson Weight was born April 25, 1892, in Springville, Utah. After graduating from Springville High School in 1911, he completed a degree in agriculture at BYU in 1916. During the 1916–1917 school year, he taught at Wayne County High School in Bicknell, and at Moab for the 1917–1918 school year. He joined the Army on May 15, 1918. After returning from France he taught two years at North Emery High School in Huntington, then at Provo High School before going to the University of Chicago where he earned a master's degree in bacteriology in 1924. He returned to Utah to teach bacteriology at the University of Utah. While teaching at the university he completed premedical studies, then completed an M.D. degree in 1931 from Rush Medical College in Chicago. He returned to Provo where he had a long and distinguished career as a physician. He died May 19, 1970.

    The April 30, 1919, edition of *White & Blue* published a letter from Jesse Weight written in Montpellier and dated March 18, 1919. It reads:

Dear Editor:

It may be interesting to some of the students and faculty of the University to know that the Brigham Young University is represented in one of the noted Universities of France. Mr. H. Milton Hales, Class of 1916; Mr. Nels Anderson, who represented the B. in debate against the U. of Nevada in 1915; and myself, Class of 1916, were selected to attend this school from our various units of the A.E.F. in France.

The University of Montpellier, Montpellier, France, was founded about three hundred years before Columbus discovered America. It has played its part in educating some of the leading men of Europe for centuries.

The University faculty is a very competent group of men. They appear before their classes of interested French and American students in their scholastic gowns of many colors. The students sense of gravity of their work and strive to make their own every word that comes from the lips of the learned professor.

The work here is interesting, instructive and pleasant.

We send our kindest regards to the students of our dear old school, and to the faculty that has done so much for us.

Sincerely,
Jesse J. Weight

6. Jon Guttman, "Georges Guynemer: French World War I Ace Pilot," *Aviation History*, September 2006. The pilot was most likely Georges Guynemer, who became a French national hero as the first French ace with more than fifty victories. He was killed in action on September 11, 1917.

7. Frederick C. Luebke, *Bonds of Loyalty: German Americans and World War I* (DeKalb: Northern Illinois University Press, 1974), 216–17; *Salt Lake Tribune*, April 14, 1918; and *Deseret News*, April 18, 1918. It is interesting that both France and Great Britain continued to teach German during the war, recognizing that knowledge of the language would be helpful both during and after the war. Many Americans, however, saw the teaching of German as anathema to the American war effort. Luebke discusses the teaching of German in American schools during the war.

In Utah, the State Textbook Commission and the State Council of Defense passed resolutions calling for an end to teaching German in all schools and colleges because "the teaching of the language would be an aid to German propaganda in America, and the presentation of...everything unfavorable to the German nation...would tend to weaken the morale of the German Army." Principals in the LDS Church school system voted unanimously to eliminate the teaching of German for the duration of the war even though some educators "declared that they saw not the slightest relation between the teaching of the Teutonic language in the classroom and the successful waging of the big war."

8. It is likely that this copy of the diary was sent to the Nelsons and then Anderson retrieved it when he returned in 1919 and kept it with him, until leaving during World War II, after which it remained in possession of his first wife, Hilda, and was located by Martin Anderson after his mother's passing. We are fortunate that this copy survived. See August 9, 1918 entry and accompanying note.

9. See diary entry for December 8, 1918 and accompanying note.

10. "Marasme de guerre." It is not clear how Nels Anderson intended this French phrase, which usually means the doldrums, tedium, or boredom, of war.

11. Annie Pike Greenwood went on to write more about her experiences as an Idaho farmer's wife, which were published as *We Sagebrush Folks* (New York: D. Appleton-Century Co., 1934) and reprinted in 1988 by the University of Idaho Press.

12. Macmillan, *Paris 1919* (New York: Random House, 2001), 292–305. Nels is referring to the demands by the Italians for the port city of Fiume, which reached a climax in April 1919 when the Italian military occupied Fiume as part of the armistice agreements. Italians were a slight majority among the 50,000 residents of the city, but Croats outnumbered Italians in the suburbs. Woodrow Wilson refused to grant the Italian demand that the Italian-Yugoslav border be drawn so as to include Fiume in Italy. Italian Prime Minster Vittorio Orlando threatened to leave the Peace Conference and shortly thereafter the Orlando government fell—in large part because of the Fiume controversy. Finally, in 1920, Yugoslavia and Italy reached an agreement that provided for Fiume to become a free state. Twenty years later, in 1940, Mussolini annexed Fiume to Italy. After World War II Fiume became part of Yugoslavia and was renamed Rijeka.

13. Cruzan, "A Soldier's Diary." Benjamin Cruzan recorded General Pershing's review of the 89th Division in his diary entry for April 23, 1919: "We are in Trier today the whole 89th is to be reviewed by General Pershing it was a nice day we went to the aviation field close to Trier Pershing decorated those to be decorated and the Red flags, then the Div passed in Review then we all assembled in the Zeppelin shed Secartary [*sic*] of war Baker & C&C Gave us a talk and the next day I took a ride in a airplane up 15 min and a 1000 feet high some trip I have had enough of it now one trip was good."

14. Nels had participated on debate teams at Dixie Academy in St. George, and at Brigham Young University in Provo.

CHAPTER 14

1. Anderson, *The American Hobo*, 156. After his discharge at Fort Russell in Cheyenne, Wyoming, Anderson returned by train to Provo. He writes, "Walking from the station to the Nelsons with my bag of personal possessions over my shoulder, I was stopped several times by persons who recognized me. I was not sure that all the kind words were well meant, especially when asked why I returned so late. I felt that some suspected I had been detained in France because of some delinquency, that I carried something less than an honorable discharge."

2. Anderson, "Education of a Sociologist," 164.
3. Anderson, *The American Hobo*, 156.
4. Anderson, "Education of a Sociologist," 172. Nels Anderson reports that "I was among the soldier students who would ride the trains in one direction or another. We never paid although the railroad companies expected conductors to collect the fares. We would act friendly but were unable to understand what the conductors would have. At that time there were many small towns in southern France where American soldiers were seldom seen. Few were seen riding the trains. The French passengers on the train yelling at the conductor. They might have resisted had the train crews tried to put us off. We free riders visited most of the cities of south France; Marseilles, Nice, Carcassonne, Narbonne, Nimes, Avignon, Arles, main towns of the Midi, which is south France."